Volvo XC60 and XC90
Owners Workshop Manual

M R Storey

Models covered

(5630 - 272)

XC60 (two- and four-wheel-drive) & XC90 with 2.0 litre (1984cc) &
2.4 litre (2400/2401cc) turbo-diesel engines

Does NOT cover petrol models

© Haynes Group Limited 2013

ABCDE
FGHIJ
KL

A book in the **Haynes Owners Workshop Manual Series**

ISBN **978 1 78521 307 6**

British Library Cataloguing in Publication Data
A catalogue record for this book is available from the British Library.

Printed in India

Haynes Group Limited
Sparkford, Yeovil, Somerset BA22 7JJ, England

Haynes North America, Inc
2801 Townsgate Road, Suite 340, Thousand Oaks, CA 91361, USA

Disclaimer

There are risks associated with automotive repairs. The ability to make repairs depends on the individual's skill, experience and proper tools. Individuals should act with due care and acknowledge and assume the risk of performing automotive repairs.

The purpose of this manual is to provide comprehensive, useful and accessible automotive repair information, to help you get the best value from your vehicle. However, this manual is not a substitute for a professional certified technician or mechanic.

This repair manual is produced by a third party and is not associated with an individual vehicle manufacturer. If there is any doubt or discrepancy between this manual and the owner's manual or the factory service manual, please refer to the factory service manual or seek assistance from a professional certified technician or mechanic.

Even though we have prepared this manual with extreme care and every attempt is made to ensure that the information in this manual is correct, neither the publisher nor the author can accept responsibility for loss, damage or injury caused by any errors in, or omissions from, the information given.

Contents

Contents

REPAIRS AND OVERHAUL

The XC90 was first introduced in June 2002, although sales only started in 2003. The XC60 was launched in May 2008, with sales starting later in the year. Described by Volvo as luxury SUVs (Sports Utility Vehicles) but more often referred to as 'soft roaders' both models have some off-road capability, but neither can be described as true off road vehicles. All XC90 models are four wheel drive (designated AWD – All Wheel Drive by Volvo). XC60 models are either AWD or front wheel drive (FWD).

All engines are 5-cylinder common rail diesel engines, previously used in other Volvo vehicles. A 2.0 litre version of the engine was introduced in 2010 for XC60 models. The 2.0 litre engine is not fitted to XC90 models.

Transmissions are either 5 or 6 speed manual, or 5 or 6 speed 'Geartronic' automatics with computer control. The automatic transmission features mode control selection, allowing the driver to alter the transmission characteristics to suit normal or winter driving requirements.

AWD models feature a transfer box, propeller shaft, an 'active on demand coupling' (AOC) a rear differential and two rear wheel driveshafts. The AOC controls the amount of power delivered to the rear wheels.

Braking is by discs all round with anti-lock braking (ABS) and Electronic Brake force Distribution (EBD) fitted as standard. Many models also feature traction and stability control. Volvo call this DSTC (Dynamic Stability and Traction Control).

Power-assisted steering is standard on all models. An engine driven pump provides the power for the steering on all models except newer XC60 models. These models feature Electro-Hydraulic Power Steering pump (EHPS).

A wide range of standard and optional equipment is available within the range to suit virtually all tastes. As with all Volvo models, safety features are of paramount importance, and the comprehensive airbag system and Side Impact Protection System (SIPS) offer an exceptional level of driver and passenger protection throughout the vehicle.

Provided that regular servicing is carried out in accordance with the manufacturer's recommendations, the Volvo V70 should provide many years of reliable service. Despite the engine's complexity, the engine compartment is relatively spacious, and most of the items requiring frequent attention are easily accessible.

Your Volvo manual

The aim of this manual is to help you get the best value from your vehicle. It can do so in several ways. It can help you decide what work must be done (even should you choose to get it done by a garage). It will also provide information on routine maintenance and servicing, and give a logical course of action and diagnosis when random faults occur. However, it is hoped that you will use the manual by tackling the work yourself. On simpler jobs it may even be quicker than booking the car into a garage and going there twice, to leave and collect it. Perhaps most important, a lot of money can be saved by avoiding the costs a garage must charge to cover its labour and overheads.

The manual has drawings and descriptions to show the function of the various components so that their layout can be understood. Tasks are described and photographed in a clear step-by-step sequence. The illustrations are numbered by the Section number and paragraph number to which they relate – if there is more than one illustration per paragraph, the sequence is denoted alphabetically.

References to the 'left' or 'right' of the vehicle are in the sense of a person in the driver's seat, facing forwards.

Acknowledgements

Certain illustrations are the copyright of Volvo Car Corporation, and are used with their permission. Thanks are due to Draper Tools Limited, who provided some of the workshop tools, and to all those people at Sparkford who helped in the production of this manual.

Working on your car can be dangerous. This page shows just some of the potential risks and hazards, with the aim of creating a safety-conscious attitude.

General hazards

Scalding

• Don't remove the radiator or expansion tank cap while the engine is hot.
• Engine oil, transmission fluid or power steering fluid may also be dangerously hot if the engine has recently been running.

Burning

• Beware of burns from the exhaust system and from any part of the engine. Brake discs and drums can also be extremely hot immediately after use.

Crushing

• When working under or near a raised vehicle, always supplement the jack with axle stands, or use drive-on ramps.
Never venture under a car which is only supported by a jack.
• Take care if loosening or tightening high-torque nuts when the vehicle is on stands. Initial loosening and final tightening should be done with the wheels on the ground.

Fire

• Fuel is highly flammable; fuel vapour is explosive.
• Don't let fuel spill onto a hot engine.
• Do not smoke or allow naked lights (including pilot lights) anywhere near a vehicle being worked on. Also beware of creating sparks (electrically or by use of tools).
• Fuel vapour is heavier than air, so don't work on the fuel system with the vehicle over an inspection pit.
• Another cause of fire is an electrical overload or short-circuit. Take care when repairing or modifying the vehicle wiring.
• Keep a fire extinguisher handy, of a type suitable for use on fuel and electrical fires.

Electric shock

• Ignition HT and Xenon headlight voltages can be dangerous, especially to people with heart problems or a pacemaker. Don't work on or near these systems with the engine running or the ignition switched on.

• Mains voltage is also dangerous. Make sure that any mains-operated equipment is correctly earthed. Mains power points should be protected by a residual current device (RCD) circuit breaker.

Fume or gas intoxication

• Exhaust fumes are poisonous; they can contain carbon monoxide, which is rapidly fatal if inhaled. Never run the engine in a confined space such as a garage with the doors shut.
• Fuel vapour is also poisonous, as are the vapours from some cleaning solvents and paint thinners.

Poisonous or irritant substances

• Avoid skin contact with battery acid and with any fuel, fluid or lubricant, especially antifreeze, brake hydraulic fluid and Diesel fuel. Don't syphon them by mouth. If such a substance is swallowed or gets into the eyes, seek medical advice.
• Prolonged contact with used engine oil can cause skin cancer. Wear gloves or use a barrier cream if necessary. Change out of oil-soaked clothes and do not keep oily rags in your pocket.
• Air conditioning refrigerant forms a poisonous gas if exposed to a naked flame (including a cigarette). It can also cause skin burns on contact.

Asbestos

• Asbestos dust can cause cancer if inhaled or swallowed. Asbestos may be found in gaskets and in brake and clutch linings. When dealing with such components it is safest to assume that they contain asbestos.

Special hazards

Hydrofluoric acid

• This extremely corrosive acid is formed when certain types of synthetic rubber, found in some O-rings, oil seals, fuel hoses etc, are exposed to temperatures above 400ºC. The rubber changes into a charred or sticky substance containing the acid. *Once formed, the acid remains dangerous for years. If it gets onto the skin, it may be necessary to amputate the limb concerned.*
• When dealing with a vehicle which has suffered a fire, or with components salvaged from such a vehicle, wear protective gloves and discard them after use.

The battery

• Batteries contain sulphuric acid, which attacks clothing, eyes and skin. Take care when topping-up or carrying the battery.
• The hydrogen gas given off by the battery is highly explosive. Never cause a spark or allow a naked light nearby. Be careful when connecting and disconnecting battery chargers or jump leads.

Air bags

• Air bags can cause injury if they go off accidentally. Take care when removing the steering wheel and trim panels. Special storage instructions may apply.

Diesel injection equipment

• Diesel injection pumps supply fuel at very high pressure. Take care when working on the fuel injectors and fuel pipes.

⚠️ *Warning: Never expose the hands, face or any other part of the body to injector spray; the fuel can penetrate the skin with potentially fatal results.*

Remember...

DO

• Do use eye protection when using power tools, and when working under the vehicle.

• Do wear gloves or use barrier cream to protect your hands when necessary.

• Do get someone to check periodically that all is well when working alone on the vehicle.

• Do keep loose clothing and long hair well out of the way of moving mechanical parts.

• Do remove rings, wristwatch etc, before working on the vehicle – especially the electrical system.

• Do ensure that any lifting or jacking equipment has a safe working load rating adequate for the job.

DON'T

• Don't attempt to lift a heavy component which may be beyond your capability – get assistance.

• Don't rush to finish a job, or take unverified short cuts.

• Don't use ill-fitting tools which may slip and cause injury.

• Don't leave tools or parts lying around where someone can trip over them. Mop up oil and fuel spills at once.

• Don't allow children or pets to play in or near a vehicle being worked on.

The following pages are intended to help in dealing with common roadside emergencies and breakdowns. You will find more detailed fault finding information at the back of the manual, and repair information in the main chapters.

If your car won't start and the starter motor doesn't turn

☐ If it's a model with automatic transmission, make sure the selector is in P or N.
☐ Open the bonnet and make sure that the battery terminals are clean and tight.
☐ Switch on the headlights and try to start the engine. If the headlights go very dim when you're trying to start, the battery is probably flat. Get out of trouble by jump starting (see next page) using a friend's car.

If your car won't start even though the starter motor turns as normal

☐ Is there fuel in the tank?
☐ Is there any moisture on electrical components under the bonnet? Switch off the ignition, then wipe off any obvious dampness with a dry cloth. Spray a water-repellent aerosol product (WD-40 or equivalent) on ignition and fuel system electrical connectors.

1 Remove the battery cover, and check that the battery cables are securely connected.

2 Check that the mass airflow meter wiring is securely connected.

XC60 model shown, but XC90 models are similar, except that the battery is located beneath the load area at the rear of the vehicle. Check that electrical connections are secure (with the ignition switched off) and spray them with a water-dispersant spray like WD-40 if you suspect a problem due to damp

3 Remove the engine cover and check the fuel rail and injectors for security.

4 Check that none of the engine compartment fuses have blown.

Jump starting will get you out of trouble, but you must correct whatever made the battery go flat in the first place. There are three possibilities:

1 *The battery has been drained by repeated attempts to start, or by leaving the lights on.*

2 *The charging system is not working properly (alternator drivebelt slack or broken, alternator wiring fault or alternator itself faulty).*

3 *The battery itself is at fault (electrolyte low, or battery worn out).*

When jump-starting a car, observe the following precautions:

✓ Before connecting the booster battery, make sure that the ignition is switched off.

Caution: Remove the key in case the central locking engages when the jump leads are connected

✓ Ensure that all electrical equipment (lights, heater, wipers, etc) is switched off.
✓ Take note of any special precautions printed on the battery case.
✓ Make sure that the booster battery is the same voltage as the discharged one in the vehicle.

Jump starting

✓ If the battery is being jump-started from the battery in another vehicle, the two vehicles MUST NOT TOUCH each other.

✓ Make sure that the transmission is in neutral (or P, in the case of automatic transmission).

 Budget jump leads can be a false economy, as they often do not pass enough current to start large capacity or diesel engines. They can also get hot.

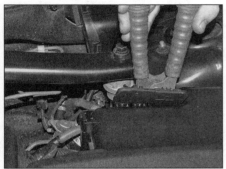

1 Connect one end of the red jump lead to the positive (+) terminal of the flat battery

2 Connect the other end of the red lead to the positive (+) terminal of the booster battery.

3 Connect one end of the black jump lead to the negative (-) terminal of the booster battery

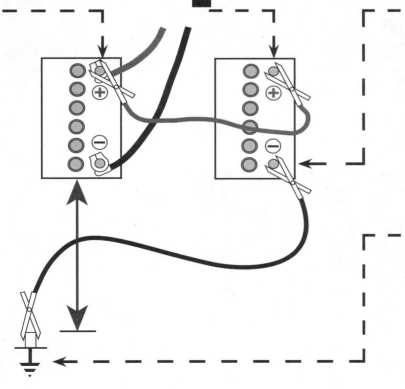

4 Connect the other end of the black jump lead to a bolt or bracket on the engine block, well away from the battery, on the vehicle to be started.

5 Make sure that the jump leads will not come into contact with the fan, drive-belts or other moving parts of the engine.

6 Start the engine using the booster battery and run it at idle speed. Switch on the lights, rear window demister and heater blower motor, then disconnect the jump leads in the reverse order of connection. Turn off the lights etc.

Wheel changing

⚠ *Warning: Do not change a wheel in a situation where you risk being hit by other traffic. On busy roads, try to stop in a lay-by or a gateway. Be wary of passing traffic while changing the wheel – it is easy to become distracted by the job in hand.*

Preparation

☐ When a puncture occurs, stop as soon as it is safe to do so.

☐ Park on firm level ground, if possible, and well out of the way of other traffic.

☐ Use hazard warning lights if necessary.

☐ If you have one, use a warning triangle to alert other drivers of your presence.

☐ Apply the handbrake and engage first or reverse gear (or Park on models with automatic transmission).

☐ Chock the wheel diagonally opposite the one being removed – a couple of large stones will do for this.

☐ If the ground is soft, use a flat piece of wood to spread the load under the jack.

Changing the wheel

1 On XC60 models the spare (if fitted) is located beneath the luggage area floor cover Lift out the spare wheel and remove the tool tray. Place the wheel under the sill as a precaution against the jack failing. Note that the spare may be of the 'space saver' type.

2 On XC90 models the spare wheel is located beneath the vehicle. Lift up the luggage area cover, remove the jack and use the jack winding handle to lower the spare wheel.

3 Where fitted, pull the wheel trim from the wheel. Before you raise the car, loosen each wheel bolt by half a turn only. On models with alloy wheels, use the special adapter.

4 Locate the jack head in the reinforced jacking point, nearest the wheel to be changed (XC90 shown). Turn the handle until the base of the jack touches the ground then make sure that the base is located directly below the sill. Raise the vehicle until the wheel is clear of the ground.

5 If the tyre is flat make sure that the vehicle is raised sufficiently to allow the spare wheel to be fitted. Remove the bolts and lift the wheel from the vehicle. Place it beneath the sill in place of the spare as a precaution against the jack failing.

6 Fit the spare wheel, then insert each of the wheel bolts and tighten them moderately using the wheelbrace.

7 Lower the vehicle to the ground, then finally tighten the wheel bolts in a diagonal sequence. Note that the wheel bolts should be tightened to the specified torque at the earliest opportunity.

8 Some models do not have a spare wheel fitted. On these models a small compressor and bottle of sealant are provided. Full instructions are provide on the lid of the compressor. Note that sealant will not repair large cuts or damage to the sidewall of the tyre.

Finally . . .

☐ Stow the jack and tools in the correct locations in the car.

☐ Check the tyre pressure on the wheel just fitted. If it is low, or if you don't have a pressure gauge with you, drive slowly to the nearest garage and inflate the tyre to the right pressure.

☐ Have the damaged tyre or wheel repaired as soon as possible.

⚠ *Warning: You should not exceed 50 mph when driving the vehicle with a space saver spare wheel fitted – consult your vehicle handbook for further information.*

Identifying leaks

Puddles on the garage floor or drive, or obvious wetness under the bonnet or underneath the car, suggest a leak that needs investigating. It can sometimes be difficult to decide where the leak is coming from, especially if an engine undershield is fitted. Leaking oil or fluid can also be blown rearwards by the passage of air under the car, giving a false impression of where the problem lies.

Warning: Most automotive oils and fluids are poisonous. Wash them off skin, and change out of contaminated clothing, without delay.

HAYNES HiNT *The smell of a fluid leaking from the car may provide a clue to what's leaking. Some fluids are distinctively coloured. It may help to remove the engine undershield, clean the car carefully and to park it over some clean paper overnight as an aid to locating the source of the leak. Remember that some leaks may only occur while the engine is running.*

Sump oil

Engine oil may leak from the drain plug...

Oil from filter

...or from the base of the oil filter.

Gearbox oil

Gearbox oil can leak from the seals at the inboard ends of the driveshafts.

Antifreeze

Leaking antifreeze often leaves a crystalline deposit like this.

Brake fluid

A leak occurring at a wheel is almost certainly brake fluid.

Power steering fluid

Power steering fluid may leak from the pipe connectors on the steering rack.

Towing

When all else fails, you may find yourself having to get a tow home – or of course you may be helping somebody else. Long-distance recovery should only be done by a garage or breakdown service. For shorter distances, DIY towing using another car is easy enough, but observe the following points:

☐ The front towing eye is located alongside the spare wheel. Prise out the cover and screw-in the towing eye **(see illustration)**. Use the wheel brace to fully tighten the eye.

☐ The rear towing eye is provided beneath the rear of the vehicle.

☐ Use a proper tow-rope – they are not expensive. The vehicle being towed must display an ON TOW sign in its rear window. Only attach the tow-rope to the towing eyes provided.

☐ Always turn the ignition key to the 'on' position when the vehicle is being towed, so that the steering lock is released, and that the direction indicator and brake lights will work.

☐ Before being towed, release the handbrake and select neutral on the transmission. On models with automatic transmission, special precautions apply, as follows (if in doubt, do not tow, or transmission damage may result):

a) The car may only be towed in the forward direction.

b) The gear selector lever must be in the N position.

c) The vehicle must not be towed at a speed exceeding 30 mph, nor for a distance of more than 30 miles.

☐ Note that greater-than-usual pedal pressure will be required to operate the brakes, since the vacuum servo unit is only operational with the engine running.

☐ Since the power steering will not be functional, greater-than-usual steering effort will also be required.

☐ The driver of the car being towed must keep the tow-rope taut at all times to avoid snatching.

☐ Make sure that both drivers know the route before setting off.

☐ Only drive at moderate speeds and keep the distance towed to a minimum. Drive smoothly and allow plenty of time for slowing down at junctions.

☐ The driver of the towing vehicle must accelerate very gently from a standstill and must bear in mind the aditional length of the vehicle being towed when pulling out at junctions, roundabouts, etc.

Introduction

There are some very simple checks which need only take a few minutes to carry out, but which could save you a lot of inconvenience and expense.

These checks require no great skill or special tools, and the small amount of time they take to perform could prove to be very well spent, for example:

☐ Keeping an eye on tyre condition and pressures, will not only help to stop them wearing out prematurely, but could also save your life.

☐ Many breakdowns are caused by electrical problems. Battery-related faults are particularly common, and a quick check on a regular basis will often prevent the majority of these.

☐ If your car develops a brake fluid leak, the first time you might know about it is when your brakes don't work properly. Checking the level regularly will give advance warning of this kind of problem.

☐ If the oil or coolant levels run low, the cost of repairing any engine damage will be far greater than fixing the leak, for example.

Underbonnet check points

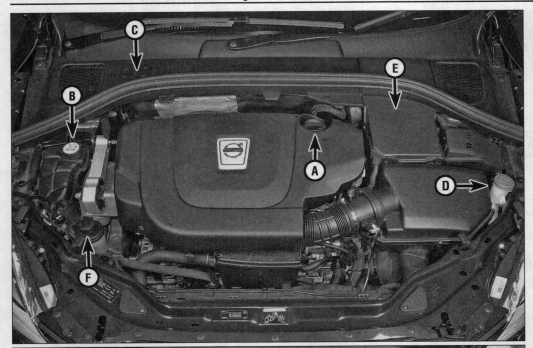

◀ XC60 models

A *Engine oil filler cap*
B *Coolant reservoir (expansion tank)*
C *Brake (and clutch) fluid reservoir (under cover)*
D *Washer fluid reservoir*
E *Battery*
F *Power steering fluid reservoir*

◀ XC90 models

A *Engine oil filler cap*
B *Engine oil level dipstick*
C *Coolant reservoir (expansion tank)*
D *Brake (and clutch) fluid reservoir*
E *Washer fluid reservoir*

Engine oil level

Before you start

✔ Make sure that the car is on level ground.
✔ Check the oil level with the engine at operating temperature, and between 2 and 5 minutes after the engine has been switched off.

 HAYNES HiNT *If the oil is checked immediately after driving the vehicle, some of the oil will remain in the upper engine components, resulting in an inaccurate reading on the dipstick.*

The correct oil

Modern engines place great demands on their oil. It is very important that the correct oil for your car is used (see *Lubricants and fluids*).

Car care

● If you have to add oil frequently, you should check whether you have any oil leaks. Place some clean paper under the car overnight, and check for stains in the morning. If there are no leaks, then the engine may be burning oil.
● Always maintain the level between the upper and lower dipstick marks (see photo 3). If the level is too low, severe engine damage may occur. Oil seal failure may result if the engine is overfilled by adding too much oil.

1 On most models, the dipstick is located on the front of the engine (see *Underbonnet check points* for exact location). On models with no dipstick the oil level can be checked by turning the ignition on and scrolling through the information display until the oil level is shown. Full details are in the Chapter 1 of this manual. Withdraw the dipstick.

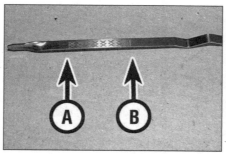

3 Note the oil level on the end of the dipstick (XC60 model shown) which should be between the upper mark (B) and lower mark (A). Approximately 1.0 litre of oil will raise the level from the lower mark to the upper mark.

2 Using a clean rag or paper towel remove all oil from the dipstick. Insert the clean dipstick into the tube and then withdraw it again.

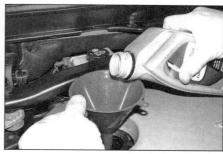

4 Oil is added through the filler cap hole. Unscrew the cap and withdraw it. Top-up the level. A funnel may help to reduce spillage. Add the oil slowly, checking the level on the dipstick often. Do not overfill. Refit the cap on completion.

Coolant level

 Warning: Do not attempt to remove the expansion tank pressure cap when the engine is hot, as there is a very great risk of scalding. Do not leave open containers of coolant about, as it is poisonous.

Car care

● With a sealed-type cooling system, adding coolant should not be necessary on a regular basis. If frequent topping-up is required, it is likely there is a leak. Check the radiator, all hoses and joint faces for signs of staining or wetness, and rectify as necessary.

● It is important that antifreeze is used in the cooling system all year round, not just during the winter months. Don't top up with water alone, as the antifreeze will become diluted.

1 The coolant level varies with the temperature of the engine. When the engine is cold, the coolant level should be between the MIN/MAX marks on the side of the tank (XC90 shown). When the engine is hot, the level will rise.

2 If topping-up is necessary, wait until the engine is cold. Slowly unscrew the expansion tank cap, to release any pressure present in the cooling system, and remove it.

3 Top-up the level by adding a mixture of water and antifreeze to the expansion tank. A funnel may help to reduce spillage. Refit the cap and tighten it securely.

Brake (and clutch) fluid level

Note: *On manual transmission models, the fluid reservoir also supplies the clutch master cylinder with fluid.*

Before you start

✔ Make sure that your car is on level ground.
✔ Cleanliness is of great importance when dealing with the braking system, so take care to clean around the reservoir cap before topping-up. Use only clean brake fluid.

Safety first!

● If the reservoir requires repeated topping-up, this is an indication of a fluid leak somewhere in the system, which should be investigated immediately. Note that the level will drop naturally as the brake pad linings wear, but must never be allowed to fall below the MIN mark.

● If a leak is suspected, the car should not be driven until the braking system has been checked. Never take any risks where brakes are concerned.

⚠ *Warning: Brake fluid can harm your eyes and damage painted surfaces, so use extreme caution when handling and pouring it. Do not use fluid which has been standing open for some time, as it absorbs moisture from the air, which can cause a dangerous loss of braking effectiveness.*

1 The MIN and MAX marks are indicated on the front of the reservoir located in the right-hand rear corner of the engine compartment. The fluid level must always be kept between the marks.

2 On XC60 models remove the cover to check the fluid level. The MAX mark is visible with the filler cap removed.

3 If topping-up is necessary, first wipe clean the area around the filler cap to prevent dirt entering the hydraulic system. Unscrew the cap and place it on an absorbent rag.

4 Carefully add fluid, taking care not to spill it onto the surrounding components. Use only the specified fluid; mixing different types can cause damage to the system. After topping-up to the correct level, securely refit the cap and wipe off any spilt fluid.

Power steering fluid level

Before you start

✔ Park the car on level ground.
✔ Set the steering wheel straight-ahead.
✔ The engine should be cold and turned off.

HAYNES HiNT *For the check to be accurate, the steering must not be turned while the level is being checked.*

Safety first!

● The need for frequent topping-up indicates a leak, which should be investigated immediately.

1 The MAX and MIN marks are shown on the reservoir on XC60 models.

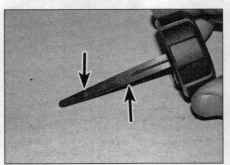

2 On XC90 models the reservoir filler cap incorporates a dipstick.

3 If topping up is necessary, wipe around the filler cap, remove the cap and top up with the specified fluid.

Tyre condition and pressure

It is very important that tyres are in good condition, and at the correct pressure - having a tyre failure at any speed is highly dangerous. Tyre wear is influenced by driving style - harsh braking and acceleration, or fast cornering, will all produce more rapid tyre wear. As a general rule, the front tyres wear out faster than the rears. Interchanging the tyres from front to rear ("rotating" the tyres) may result in more even wear. However, if this is completely effective, you may have the expense of replacing all four tyres at once!

Remove any nails or stones embedded in the tread before they penetrate the tyre to cause deflation. If removal of a nail does reveal that the tyre has been punctured, refit the nail so that its point of penetration is marked. Then immediately change the wheel, and have the tyre repaired by a tyre dealer.

Regularly check the tyres for damage in the form of cuts or bulges, especially in the sidewalls. Periodically remove the wheels, and clean any dirt or mud from the inside and outside surfaces. Examine the wheel rims for signs of rusting, corrosion or other damage. Light alloy wheels are easily damaged by "kerbing" whilst parking; steel wheels may also become dented or buckled. A new wheel is very often the only way to overcome severe damage.

New tyres should be balanced when they are fitted, but it may become necessary to re-balance them as they wear, or if the balance weights fitted to the wheel rim should fall off. Unbalanced tyres will wear more quickly, as will the steering and suspension components. Wheel imbalance is normally signified by vibration, particularly at a certain speed (typically around 50 mph). If this vibration is felt only through the steering, then it is likely that just the front wheels need balancing. If, however, the vibration is felt through the whole car, the rear wheels could be out of balance. Wheel balancing should be carried out by a tyre dealer or garage.

1 Tread Depth - visual check

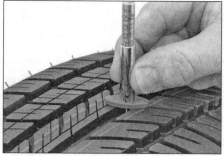

The original tyres have tread wear safety bands (B), which will appear when the tread depth reaches approximately 1.6 mm. The band positions are indicated by a triangular mark on the tyre sidewall (A).

2 Tread Depth - manual check

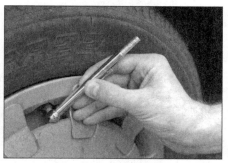

Alternatively, tread wear can be monitored with a simple, inexpensive device known as a tread depth indicator gauge.

3 Tyre Pressure Check

Check the tyre pressures regularly with the tyres cold. Do not adjust the tyre pressures immediately after the vehicle has been used, or an inaccurate setting will result.

Tyre tread wear patterns

Shoulder Wear

Underinflation (wear on both sides)
Under-inflation will cause overheating of the tyre, because the tyre will flex too much, and the tread will not sit correctly on the road surface. This will cause a loss of grip and excessive wear, not to mention the danger of sudden tyre failure due to heat build-up.
Check and adjust pressures
Incorrect wheel camber (wear on one side)
Repair or renew suspension parts
Hard cornering
Reduce speed!

Centre Wear

Overinflation
Over-inflation will cause rapid wear of the centre part of the tyre tread, coupled with reduced grip, harsher ride, and the danger of shock damage occurring in the tyre casing.
Check and adjust pressures

If you sometimes have to inflate your car's tyres to the higher pressures specified for maximum load or sustained high speed, don't forget to reduce the pressures to normal afterwards.

Uneven Wear

Front tyres may wear unevenly as a result of wheel misalignment. Most tyre dealers and garages can check and adjust the wheel alignment (or "tracking") for a modest charge.
Incorrect camber or castor
Repair or renew suspension parts
Malfunctioning suspension
Repair or renew suspension parts
Unbalanced wheel
Balance tyres
Incorrect toe setting
Adjust front wheel alignment
Note: *The feathered edge of the tread which typifies toe wear is best checked by feel.*

Washer fluid level

● Screenwash additives not only keep the windscreen clean during bad weather, they also prevent the washer system freezing in cold weather – which is when you are likely to need it most. Don't top-up using plain water, as the screenwash will become diluted, and will freeze in cold weather.

● Check the operation of the windscreen and rear window washers. Adjust the nozzles using a pin if necessary, aiming the spray to a point slightly above the centre of the swept area.

⚠ **Warning: On no account use engine coolant antifreeze in the screen washer system – this may damage the paintwork.**

1 The reservoir for the windscreen and rear window washer systems is located on the front left-hand corner of the engine compartment on XC60 models and on the front right-hand side on XC90 models. If topping-up is necessary, open the cap.

2 When topping-up the reservoir a screenwash additive should be added in the quantities recommended on the bottle.

Electrical systems

✔ Check all external lights and the horn. Refer to Chapter 12 Section 2 for details if any of the circuits are found to be inoperative.
✔ Visually check all accessible wiring connectors, harnesses and retaining clips for security, and for signs of chafing or damage.

HAYNES HINT *If you need to check your brake lights and indicators unaided, back up to a wall or garage door and operate the lights. The reflected light should show if they are working properly.*

1 If a single indicator light, stop-light or headlight has failed, it is likely that a bulb has blown and will need to be renewed. Refer to Chapter 12 for details. If both stop-lights have failed, it is possible that the switch has failed (see Chapter 9).

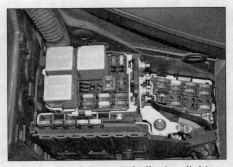

2 If more than one indicator light or headlight has failed, it is likely that either a fuse has blown or that there is a fault in the circuit (see Chapter 12). The main fuses are located under the bonnet on the left-hand side of the engine compartment. Additional fuses and relays are located on the below the glovebox (XC60) and in the left-hand side of the luggage compartment (all models).

3 XC90 models have fuses located at the right-hand end of the facia. Further fuses are located below the right-hand end of the facia.

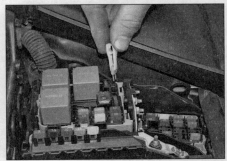

4 To renew a blown fuse, remove it using the plastic tool provided. Fit a new fuse of the same rating, available from car accessory shops. If the fuse blows repeatedly, refer to Chapter 12 to locate the fault.

Wiper blades

Check the condition of the wiper blades; if they are cracked or show any signs of deterioration, or if the glass swept area is smeared, renew them. For maximum clarity of vision, wiper blades should be renewed annually.

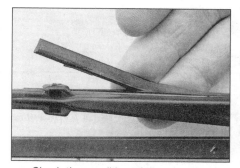

1 Check the condition of the wiper blades; if they are cracked or show any signs of deterioration, or if the glass swept area is smeared, renew them. For maximum clarity of vision, wiper blades should be renewed annually, as a matter of course.

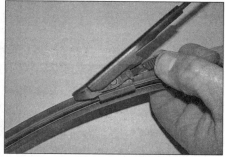

2 To remove a windscreen wiper blade, pull the arm fully away from the screen until it locks. Swivel the blade through 90°, then lift it off the wiper arm. Fit the new blade using a reversal of the removal procedure. Don't forget to check the tailgate wiper blade as well.

Battery

Caution: Before carrying out any work on the vehicle battery, read the precautions given in 'Safety first!' at the start of this manual.

✔ Make sure that the battery tray is in good condition, and that the clamp is tight. Corrosion on the tray, retaining clamp and the battery itself can be removed with a solution of water and baking soda. Thoroughly rinse all cleaned areas with water. Any metal parts damaged by corrosion should be covered with a zinc-based primer, then painted.

✔ Periodically (approximately every three months), check the charge condition of the battery, as described in Chapter 5A.

✔ If the battery is flat, and you need to jump start your vehicle, see *Roadside repairs*.

 Battery corrosion can be kept to a minimum by applying a layer of petroleum jelly to the clamps and terminals after they are reconnected.

1 On XC60 models the battery is located under a cover on the rear left-hand side of the engine compartment.

2 On XC90 models the battery is located beneath the floor in the luggage area.

3 Check the tightness of battery clamps to ensure good electrical connections. You should not be able to move them. Also check each cable for cracks and frayed conductors.

4 If corrosion (white, fluffy deposits) is evident, remove the cables from the battery terminals, clean them with a small wire brush, then refit them. Automotive stores sell a tool for cleaning the battery post . . .

5 . . . as well as the battery cable clamps.

Lubricants and fluids

Engine	Multigrade engine oil, viscosity SAE 0W-30
Cooling system	Refer to dealer
Transmission:	
Manual gearbox	Volvo oil MTF 97309
Automatic transmission	Volvo automatic transmission fluid JWS 3309
Braking and clutch systems	Hydraulic fluid to DOT 4+
Power steering system	Volvo power steering fluid M2C204-A

Tyre pressures

Note: *The tyre pressures in the table below are typical. The pressures which apply specifically to each vehicle are given on a sticker attached to the left-hand door pillar. Use the pressures on the sticker if they are different from those given here.*

Tyre pressures (cold)	Front	Rear
XC60, all models:		
Normal load...	2.4 bar (35 psi)	2.4 bar (35 psi)
Full load*....	2.7 bar (39 psi)	2.7 bar (39 psi)
XC90, 17- and 18-inch wheels:		
Normal load...	2.2 bar (32 psi)	2.2 bar (32 psi)
Full load*....	2.7 bar (39 psi)	2.7 bar (39 psi)
XC90, 19- and 20-inch wheels:		
Normal load...	2.4 bar (35 psi)	2.4 bar (35 psi)
Full load*....	2.7 bar (39 psi)	2.7 bar (39 psi)
Compact spare, all models...	4.2 bar (61 psi)	4.2 bar (61 psi)

*Full load pressure may be used under all conditions to obtain the best fuel economy, at the expense of a firmer ride when lightly laden.

Chapter 1
Routine maintenance and servicing

Contents

Degrees of difficulty

| **Easy,** suitable for novice with little experience | **Fairly easy,** suitable for beginner with some experience | **Fairly difficult,** suitable for competent DIY mechanic | **Difficult,** suitable for experienced DIY mechanic | **Very difficult,** suitable for expert DIY or professional |

Lubricants and fluids

Refer to *Lubricants and fluids* on page 0•16

Capacities*

Engine oil

Drain and refill including filter change:

2.0 litre (D5204T2/T3)	5.9 litres
2.4 litre:	
D5244T/T2/T3................................	6.5 litres
D5244T4/T5/T6/T7/T18	5.7 litres

Cooling system

XC60:	
Up to 2010	12.65 litres
From 2010...	8.9 litres
XC90:	
Up to 2011	12.5 litres
From 2011...	8.9 litres

Fuel tank

XC60..	70 litres
XC90..	68 litres

Manual transmission

M66	2.0 litres

Automatic transmission

Drain and refill	7.1 litres (approx)

Cooling system

Specified antifreeze mixture....................................	50% antifreeze/50% water

Note: *Refer to Chapter 3 for further details.*

Brakes

Brake pad minimum lining thickness	2.0 mm

Remote control battery

Type	CR 2032 3V

Torque wrench settings

	Nm	lbf ft
Automatic transmission:		
Drain plug..	35	26
Filler plug	35	26
Integrated level plug	8	6
Auxiliary drivebelt tensioner	24	18
Engine oil drain plug..	35	26
Fuel filter cover...	25	18
Oil filter cover	25	18
Roadwheel bolts...	140	103
Transfer pulley (Engines with EHPS)	24	18

* All capacities are approximate. Volvo list a considerable variation in oil capacities. Always check the engine number with the capacity stated in the owners handbook.

The maintenance intervals in this manual are provided with the assumption that you, not the dealer, will be carrying out the work. These are the average maintenance intervals recommended by the manufacturer for vehicles driven daily under normal conditions. Obviously some variation of these intervals may be expected depending on territory of use, and conditions encountered. If you wish to keep your vehicle in peak condition at all times, you may wish to perform some of these procedures more often. We encourage frequent maintenance because it enhances the efficiency, performance and resale value of your vehicle.

When the vehicle is new, it should be serviced by a dealer service department (or other workshop recognised by the vehicle manufacturer as providing the same standard of service) in order to preserve the warranty.

The vehicle manufacturer may reject warranty claims if you are unable to prove that servicing has been carried out as and when specified, using only original equipment parts or parts certified to be of equivalent quality.

If the vehicle is driven in dusty areas, used to tow a trailer, driven frequently at slow speeds (idling in traffic) or on short journeys, more frequent maintenance intervals are recommended.

Every 250 miles or weekly
☐ Refer to *Weekly checks*.

Every 9000 miles or 6 months, whichever comes first
☐ Renew the engine oil and filter – models up to 2010 (Section 3).

Note: *Although Volvo recommend that the engine oil and filter are changed at 18 000 miles or every 12 months, frequent oil and filter changes are good for the engine. We therefore recommend changing the oil more frequently.*

Every 18 000 miles or 12 months, whichever comes first
In addition to the items listed above, carry out the following:
☐ Check the condition of the brake pads (Section 4).
☐ Thoroughly inspect the engine compartment for fluid leaks (Section 5).
☐ Check the condition and security of the steering and suspension components (Section 6).
☐ Check the condition of the driveshaft gaiters (Section 7).
☐ Inspect the clutch components (Section 8).
☐ Renew the pollen filter (Section 9).
☐ Check the battery electrolyte level (Section 10).
☐ Inspect the underbody, brake hydraulic pipes and hoses, and fuel lines (Section 11).
☐ Check the condition and security of the exhaust system (Section 12).
☐ Check the handbrake (Section 13).
☐ Check the condition of the seat belts (Section 14).
☐ Lubricate the locks and hinges (Section 15).
☐ Check the headlight beam alignment (Section 16).
☐ Check the coolant antifreeze concentration (Section 17).
☐ Reset the service reminder indicator (Section 18).
☐ Road test (Section 19).
☐ Check the operation of the air conditioning system (Section 20).
☐ Drain fuel filter of water (Section 21).
☐ Renew the remote battery (Section 22).

Every 36 000 miles or 2 years, whichever comes first
In addition to the items listed above, carry out the following:
☐ Renew the air cleaner element (Section 23).
☐ Check the automatic transmission fluid level (Section 24).
☐ Renew the fuel filter (Section 25).

Every 90 000 miles or 5 years, whichever comes first
In addition to the items listed above, carry out the following:
☐ Renew the timing belt and tensioner (Section 26).
Note: *It is recommended that this interval is reduced on vehicles which are subjected to intensive use, ie, mainly short journeys or a lot of stop-start driving. The actual belt renewal interval is very much up to the individual owner, but bear in mind that severe engine damage will result if the belt breaks.*
☐ Renew the auxiliary drivebelt (Section 27).

Every 2 years, regardless of mileage
☐ Renew the brake fluid (Section 28).

Every 3 years, regardless of mileage
☐ Renew the coolant (Section 29).
Note: *This work is not included in the Volvo schedule, and should not be required if the recommended Volvo antifreeze/inhibitor is used.*

Underbonnet view – XC60 models

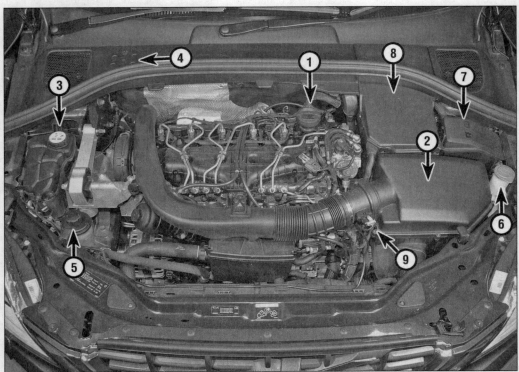

1 Engine oil filler cap
2 Air filter
3 Coolant reservoir
4 Brake fluid reservoir (under cover)
5 Power steering fluid reservoir
6 Screen washer fluid reservoir
7 Fusebox
8 Battery
9 Mass airflow meter

Underbonnet view – XC90 models

1 Engine oil level dipstick
2 Engine oil filler cap
3 Air filter
4 Coolant reservoir
5 Brake fluid reservoir
6 Power steering fluid reservoir
7 Screen washer fluid reservoir
8 Fusebox

Front underbody view – XC60 models

1   Engine oil drain plug
2   Engine oil level sensor
3   Air conditioning
    compressor
4   Engine oil cooler
5   Lower control arm
6   Steering track rod
7   Transmission drain/level
    plug
8   Brake caliper

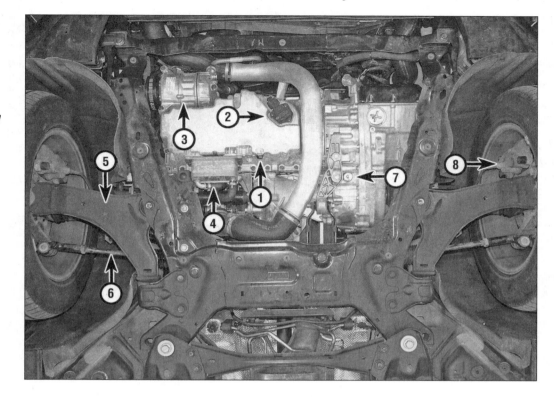

Rear underbody view – XC60 models

1   Fuel filter
2   Fuel tank
3   Rear silencer
4   Lower arm
5   Anti-roll bar
6   Track control arm
7   Propeller shaft
8   Haldex unit
9   Rear differential
10 Shock absorber
11 Driveshaft

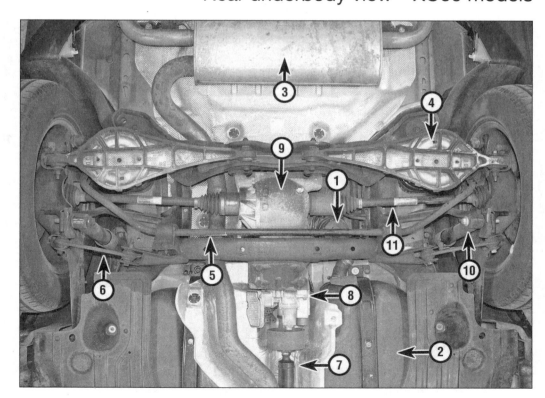

Front underbody view – XC90 models

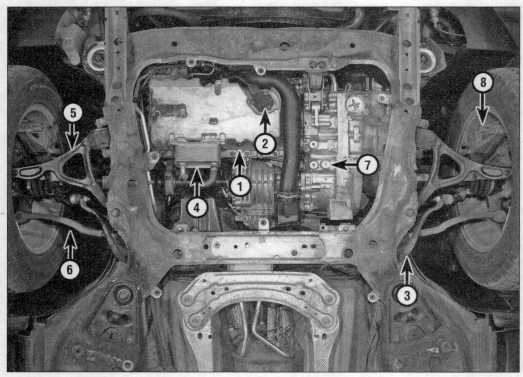

1 Engine oil drain plug
2 Engine oil level sensor
3 Anti-roll bar
4 Engine oil cooler
5 Control arm
6 Steering track rod
7 Transmission drain/level plug
8 Brake caliper

Rear underbody view – XC90 models

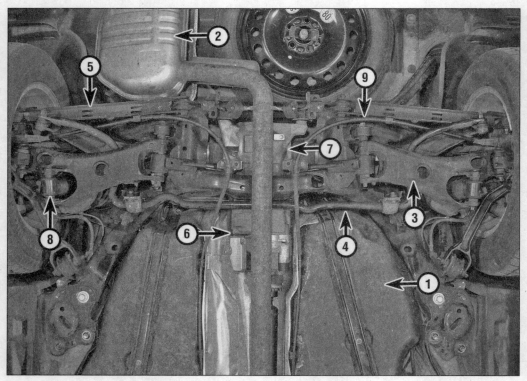

1 Fuel tank
2 Rear silencer
3 Lower arm
4 Anti-roll bar
5 Track control arm
6 Haldex unit
7 Rear differential
8 Shock absorber
9 Handbrake cable

1 Introduction

This chapter is designed to help the home mechanic maintain his/her vehicle for safety, economy, long life and peak performance.

This chapter contains a master maintenance schedule, followed by Sections dealing specifically with each task in the schedule. Visual checks, adjustments, component renewal and other helpful items are included. Refer to the accompanying illustrations of the engine compartment and the underside of the vehicle for the locations of the various components.

Servicing your vehicle in accordance with the mileage/time maintenance schedule and the following Sections will provide a planned maintenance programme which should result in a long and reliable service life. This is a comprehensive plan, so maintaining some items but not others at the specified service intervals will not produce the same results.

As you service your vehicle, you will discover that many of the procedures can – and should – be grouped together, because of the particular procedure being performed, or because of the close proximity of two otherwise unrelated components to one another. For example, if the vehicle is raised for any reason, the exhaust should be inspected at the same time as the suspension and steering components.

The first step of this maintenance programme is to prepare yourself before the actual work begins. Read through all the Sections relevant to the work to be carried out, then make a list and gather together all the parts and tools required. If a problem is encountered, seek advice from a parts specialist or a dealer service department.

Service interval display

All models are equipped with a service interval display indicator in the instrument panel. When a predetermined mileage, time period, or number of hours of engine operation has elapsed since the display was last reset, the service light will illuminate, providing a handy reminder of when the next service is required.

The display should not necessarily be used as a definitive guide to the servicing needs of your Volvo, but it is useful as a reminder, to ensure that servicing is not accidentally overlooked. Owners of older cars, or those covering a small annual mileage, may feel inclined to service their car more often, in which case the service interval display is perhaps less relevant.

Refer to Section 18 for the resetting procedure.

2 Regular maintenance

1 If, from the time the vehicle is new, the routine maintenance schedule is followed closely, and frequent checks are made of fluid levels and high-wear items, as suggested throughout this manual, the engine will be kept in relatively good running condition, and the need for additional work will be minimised.

2 It is possible that there will be some times when the engine is running poorly due to the lack of regular maintenance. This is even more likely if a used vehicle, which has not received regular and frequent maintenance checks, is purchased. In such cases, additional work may need to be carried out, outside of the regular maintenance intervals.

3 If engine wear is suspected, a compression test (as described in Chapter 2A) will provide valuable information regarding the overall performance of the main internal components. Such a test can be used as a basis to decide on the extent of the work to be carried out. If, for example, a compression test indicates serious internal engine wear, conventional maintenance as described in this Chapter will not greatly improve the performance of the engine, and may prove a waste of time and money, unless extensive overhaul work (Chapter 2B) is carried out first.

4 The following series of operations are those often required to improve the performance of a generally poor-running engine:

Primary operations

a) Clean, inspect and test the battery (See 'Weekly checks' and Section 10).
b) Check all the engine-related fluids (See 'Weekly checks').
c) Renew the auxiliary drivebelt (Section 27).
d) Check the condition of the air cleaner filter element and renew if necessary (Section 23).
e) Renew the fuel filter (Section 25).
f) Check the condition of all hoses, and check for fluid leaks (Section 5).

5 If the above operations do not prove fully effective, carry out the following operations:

Secondary operations

All the items listed under *Primary operations*, plus the following:

a) Check the charging system (Chapter 5).
b) Check the fuel system (Chapter 4A).
c) Check the preheating system (Chapter 5).

Every 9000 miles or 6 months

3 Engine oil and filter renewal

Note: *Some XC60 models do not have a conventional dipstick. On these models an electronic gauge is fitted – see below for details.*

1 Make sure that you have all the necessary tools before you begin this procedure. You should also have plenty of rags or newspapers handy, for mopping-up any spills. The oil should preferably be changed when the engine is still fully warmed-up to normal operating temperature, just after a run; warm oil and sludge will flow out more easily. Take care, however, not to touch the exhaust or any other hot parts of the engine when working under the vehicle. To avoid any possibility of scalding, and to protect yourself from possible skin irritants and other harmful contaminants in used engine oils, it is advisable to wear gloves when carrying out this work.

2 Access to the underside of the vehicle is greatly improved if the vehicle can be lifted on a hoist, driven onto ramps, or supported by axle stands (see *Jacking and vehicle support*). Whichever method is chosen, make sure that the vehicle remains level, or if it is at an angle, that the drain point is at the lowest point. Release the screws and remove the engine undershield **(see illustration)** for access to the sump and drain plug.

3 Position the draining container under the drain plug, and unscrew the plug **(see illustration)**. If possible, try to keep the plug pressed into the sump while unscrewing it by hand the last couple of turns.

4 Allow the oil to drain into the container, and

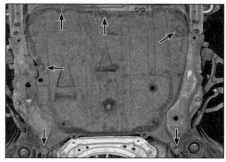

3.2 Undo the screws (arrowed) and remove the engine undershield (XC90 shown)

3.3 Undo the engine oil drain plug (arrowed)

3.5 Renew the sealing washer when fitting the drain plug

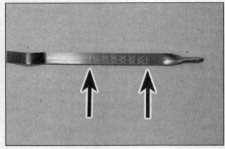

3.8a The maximum and minimum level markings are at the end of the hatched section on the dipstick (XC60 shown)

3.8b On models without a normal dipstick a small dipstick is fitted

3.12 The oil filter (arrowed)

3.13a Unscrew the filter cover...

3.13b ...and withdraw the filter element

3.15 Fit the new O-ring seal to the filter cover

discard the drain plug sealing washer. A new one must be fitted.

5 Allow some time for the old oil to drain, noting that it may be necessary to reposition the container as the oil flow slows to a trickle; when the oil has completely drained, wipe clean the drain plug and its threads in the sump and refit the plug with a new sealing washer **(see illustration)**, tightening it to the specified torque.

6 Remove the old oil and all tools from under the vehicle, then lower the vehicle to the ground.

7 Renew the oil filter as described below.

8 Remove the dipstick and the oil filler cap from the engine. Fill the engine with oil, using the correct grade and type of oil (see *Lubricants and fluids* and Specifications). Pour in half the specified quantity of oil first, then wait a few minutes for the oil to run to the sump. Continue adding oil a small quantity at a time, until the level is up to the lower mark on the dipstick. Adding approximately 1.2 litres will raise the level to the upper mark on the dipstick **(see illustrations)**.

9 Start the engine. The oil pressure warning light will take a few seconds to go out while the new filter fills with oil; do not race the engine while the light is on. Run the engine for a few minutes, while checking for leaks around the oil filter seal and the drain plug. Refit the engine undershield.

10 Switch off the engine, and wait a few minutes for the oil to settle in the sump once more. With the new oil circulated and the filter now completely full, recheck the level on the dipstick, and add more oil as necessary. On models without a traditional dipstick insert the remote key and hold the start/stop button in for approximately 2 seconds. This places the ignition in the 'on' position. Now rotate the thumbwheel on the left-hand stalk until the oil level function is displayed.

11 Dispose of the used engine oil safely and in accordance with environmental regulations (see *General repair procedures*).

Oil filter renewal

12 The oil filter is located at the front of the engine, accessible from above. Pull the plastic cover over the engine straight up to release it from the mountings **(see illustration)**.

13 Using a socket or adjustable spanner, undo the filter cover and remove it **(see illustrations)**, followed by the old filter element. Discard the filter cover O-ring seal, a new one must be fitted.

14 Using a clean, lint-free rag, wipe clean the inside of the filter housing and cover.

15 Apply a light coating of clean engine oil to the new O-ring seal and fit it to the filter cover **(see illustration)**. Insert the filter element into the cover, then screw the filter cover into position on the engine until it seats, then tighten it to the specified torque.

Every 18 000 miles or 12 months

4 Brake pad wear check

1 Jack up the front or rear of the vehicle in turn, and support it on axle stands (see *Jacking and vehicle support* in the reference section).

2 For better access to the brake calipers, remove the roadwheels.

3 Check that the thickness of the friction lining material on each of the pads is not less than the recommended minimum thickness given in the Specifications **(see illustration)**. If any one of the brake pads has worn down to, or below, the specified limit, *all four* pads at that end of the car must be renewed as

a set (ie, all the front pads or all the rear pads).

4 For a comprehensive check, the brake pads should be removed and cleaned. The operation of the brake calipers can then be checked, and the brake discs can be fully examined. Refer to Chapter 9 for details.

5 Underbonnet check for fluid leaks and hose condition

Caution: Renewal of air conditioning hoses must be left to a dealer service department or air conditioning specialist who has the equipment to depressurise the system safely. Never remove air conditioning components or hoses until the system has been depressurised.

General

1 High temperatures in the engine compartment can cause the deterioration of the rubber and plastic hoses used for engine, accessory and emission systems operation. Periodic inspection should be made for cracks, loose clamps, material hardening and leaks.

2 Carefully check the large top and bottom radiator hoses **(see Haynes Hint)**, along with the other smaller-diameter cooling system hoses and metal pipes; do not forget the heater hoses/pipes which run from the engine to the bulkhead. Inspect each hose along its entire length, renewing any that are cracked, swollen or shows signs of deterioration. Cracks may become more apparent if the hose is squeezed.

3 Make sure that all hose connections are tight. If the spring clamps that are used to secure some of the hoses appear to be slackening, they should be updated with screw-type clips to prevent the possibility of leaks.

4 Some other hoses are secured to their fittings with screw-type clips. Where screw-type clips are used, check to be sure they haven't slackened, allowing the hose to leak. If clamps or screw-type clips aren't used, make sure the hose has not expanded and/or hardened where it slips over the fitting, allowing it to leak **(see illustration)**.

5 Check all fluid reservoirs, filler caps, drain plugs and fittings, etc, looking for any signs of leakage of oil, transmission and/or brake hydraulic fluid, coolant and power steering fluid. If the vehicle is regularly parked in the same place, close inspection of the ground underneath will soon show any leaks; ignore the puddle of water which will be left if the air conditioning system is in use. As soon as a leak is detected, its source must be traced and rectified. Where oil has been leaking for some time, it is usually necessary to use a steam cleaner, pressure washer or similar, to clean away the accumulated dirt, so that the exact source of the leak can be identified.

4.3 Check the thickness of the brake pad friction material by removing a front wheel

Vacuum hoses

6 It's quite common for vacuum hoses, especially those in the emissions system, to be numbered or colour-coded, or to be identified by coloured stripes moulded into them. Various systems require hoses with different wall thicknesses, collapse resistance and temperature resistance. When renewing hoses, be sure the new ones are made of the same material.

7 Often the only effective way to check a hose is to remove it completely from the vehicle. If more than one hose is removed, be sure to label the hoses and fittings to ensure correct installation.

8 When checking vacuum hoses, be sure to include any plastic T-fittings in the check. Inspect the fittings for cracks, and check the hose where it fits over the fitting for distortion, which could cause leakage.

9 A small piece of vacuum hose can be used as a stethoscope to detect vacuum leaks. Hold one end of the hose near to your ear, and probe around vacuum hoses and fittings, listening for the hissing sound characteristic of a vacuum leak.

⚠ *Warning: When probing with the vacuum hose stethoscope, be very careful not to come into contact with moving engine components such as the auxiliary drivebelt, radiator electric cooling fan, etc.*

A leak in the cooling system will usually show up as white- or antifreeze-coloured deposits on the areas adjoining the leak.

Fuel hoses

⚠ *Warning: Before carrying out the following operation, refer to the precautions given in 'Safety first!' at the beginning of this manual, and follow them implicitly. Fuel is a highly dangerous and volatile liquid, and the precautions necessary when handling it cannot be overstressed.*

10 Check all fuel hoses for deterioration and chafing. Check especially for cracks in areas where the hose bends, and also just before fittings, such as where a hose attaches to the fuel filter.

11 High-quality fuel line, usually identified by the word 'Fluoroelastomer' printed on the hose, should be used for fuel line renewal. Never, under any circumstances, use unreinforced vacuum line, clear plastic tubing or water hose for fuel lines.

12 Spring-type clamps are commonly used on fuel lines. These clamps often lose their tension over a period of time, and can be 'sprung' during removal. Update all spring-type clamps with screw clips whenever a hose is renewed.

13 If a fuel leak is suspected, remember that any leak will be more obvious with the system at full pressure, such as when the engine is running, or shortly after switching off.

Metal lines

14 Sections of metal piping are often used for fuel line between the fuel filter and the engine. Check carefully to be sure the piping has not been bent or crimped, and that cracks have not started in the line.

15 If a section of metal fuel line must be renewed, only seamless steel piping should be used, since copper and aluminium piping don't have the strength necessary to withstand normal engine vibration.

16 Check the metal brake lines where they enter the master cylinder and ABS hydraulic unit for cracks in the lines or loose fittings. Any sign of brake fluid leakage calls for an immediate and thorough inspection of the brake system.

5.4 Check all hose connections for tightness and signs of leakage

6.2 Check the condition of the steering rack rubber gaiters

6.5 Check for wear in the wheel bearing by grasping the wheel and trying to rock it

6 Steering and suspension check

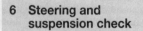

Front suspension and steering

1 Apply the handbrake, then jack up the front of the vehicle and support it on axle stands (see *Jacking and vehicle support*).

2 Visually inspect the balljoint dust covers and the steering gear gaiters for splits, chafing or deterioration **(see illustration)**. Any wear of these components will cause loss of lubricant, together with dirt and water entry, resulting in rapid deterioration of the balljoints or steering gear.

3 Check the power steering fluid hoses for chafing or deterioration, and the pipe and hose unions for fluid leaks. Also check for signs of fluid leakage under pressure from the steering gear rubber gaiters, which would indicate failed fluid seals within the steering gear.

4 Check for signs of fluid leakage around the suspension strut body, or from the rubber boot around the piston rod (where fitted). Should any fluid be noticed, the shock absorber is defective internally, and renewal is necessary.

5 Grasp the roadwheel at the 12 o'clock and 6 o'clock positions, and try to rock it **(see illustration)**. Very slight free play may be felt, but if the movement is appreciable, further investigation is necessary to determine the source. Continue rocking the wheel while an assistant depresses the footbrake. If the

7.1 Inspect the condition of the driveshaft gaiters

movement is now eliminated or significantly reduced, it is likely that the wheel bearings are at fault. If the free play is still evident with the footbrake depressed, then there is wear in the suspension joints or mountings.

6 Now grasp the wheel at the 9 o'clock and 3 o'clock positions, and try to rock it as before. Any movement felt now may again be caused by wear in the wheel bearings or the steering track rod end balljoints. If the outer track rod end is worn, the visual movement will be obvious. If the inner joint is suspect, it can be felt by placing a hand over the rack-and-pinion rubber gaiter, and gripping the track rod. If the wheel is now rocked, movement will be felt at the inner joint if wear has taken place.

7 Using a large screwdriver or flat bar, check for wear in the suspension mounting bushes by levering between the relevant suspension component and its attachment point. Some movement is to be expected as the mountings are made of rubber, but excessive wear should be obvious. Also check the condition of any visible rubber bushes, looking for splits, cracks or contamination of the rubber.

8 With the vehicle standing on its wheels, have an assistant turn the steering wheel back-and-forth, about an eighth of a turn each way. There should be very little, if any, lost movement between the steering wheel and roadwheels. If this is not the case, closely observe the joints and mountings previously described, but in addition, check the steering column universal joints for wear, and also check the rack-and-pinion steering gear itself.

9 The efficiency of the shock absorber may be checked by bouncing the car at each front corner. Generally speaking, the body will return to its normal position and stop after being depressed. If it rises and returns on a rebound, the shock absorber is probably suspect. Examine also the shock absorber upper and lower mountings for any signs of wear or fluid leakage.

Rear suspension

10 Chock the front wheels, then raise the rear of the vehicle and support it on axle stands (see *Jacking and vehicle support*).

11 Check the rear hub bearings for wear, using the method described for the front hub bearings (paragraph 5).

12 Using a large screwdriver or flat bar, check for wear in the suspension mounting bushes by levering between the relevant suspension component and its attachment point. Some movement is to be expected as the mountings are made of rubber, but excessive wear should be obvious. Check the condition of the shock absorbers as described previously.

7 Driveshaft gaiter check

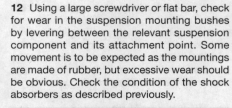

1 With the vehicle raised and securely supported on axle stands (see *Jacking and vehicle support*), turn the steering onto full lock, then slowly rotate the roadwheel. Inspect the condition of the outer constant velocity (CV) joint rubber gaiters, squeezing the gaiters to open out the folds **(see illustration)**. Check for signs of cracking, splits or deterioration of the rubber, which may allow the grease to escape, and lead to water and grit entry into the joint. Also check the security and condition of the retaining clips. Repeat these checks on the inner CV joints. If any damage or deterioration is found, the gaiters should be renewed as described in Chapter 8A.

2 At the same time, check the general condition of the CV joints themselves by first holding the driveshaft and attempting to rotate the wheel. Repeat this check by holding the inner joint and attempting to rotate the driveshaft. Any appreciable movement indicates wear in the joints, wear in the driveshaft splines, or a loose driveshaft retaining bolt/nut.

8 Clutch check

1 Check that the clutch pedal moves smoothly and easily through its full travel, and that the clutch itself functions correctly, with no trace of slip or drag.

2 Undo the two screws and remove the lower facia panel above the pedals for access to the clutch pedal, and apply a few drops of light oil to the pedal pivot. Refit the panel.

3 From within the engine compartment, check the condition of the fluid lines and hoses.

9 Pollen filter renewal

1 Undo the two screws and remove the lower facia panel from above the passenger's footwell. Disconnect the footwell lamp as the panel is removed.

2 Remove the front section of the left-hand side centre console side panel as shown in Chapter 11.

3 Pull back the carpet slightly and unclip the cover for the pollen filter. On XC90 models remove the screws from the cover. Withdraw the filter **(see illustrations)**. On XC60 models access is easier with the glovebox removed (as described in Chapter 11).

4 Slide the new filter into place, refit the cover, and refit the lower facia panel and console side panel. Note that on XC90 models the filter fits into the smaller opening. The other slot is for models fitted with an air quality sensor.

10 Battery electrolyte level check

⚠ **Warning: The electrolyte inside a battery is diluted acid – it is a good idea to wear suitable rubber gloves. When topping-up, don't overfill the cells so that the electrolyte overflows. In the event of any spillage, rinse the electrolyte off without delay. Refit the cell covers and rinse the battery with copious quantities of clean water. Don't attempt to siphon out any excess electrolyte.**

1 On XC60 models the battery is located on the left-hand side of the engine compartment. On XC90 models the battery is located below the rear load space.

2 All models covered by this manual are fitted with a maintenance-free battery as standard equipment, or may have had one fitted. If the battery in your vehicle is marked Freedom, Maintenance-Free or similar, no electrolyte level checking is required (the battery is often completely sealed, preventing any topping-up).

3 Batteries which require their electrolyte level to be checked can be recognised by the presence of removable covers over the six battery cells – the battery casing is also sometimes translucent, so that the electrolyte level can be more easily checked.

4 Remove the cell caps or covers, and either look down inside the battery to see the level web, or check the level using any markings provided on the battery casing. The electrolyte should cover the battery plates by approximately 15 mm.

5 If necessary, top-up a little at a time with distilled (de-ionised) water until the level in all six cells is correct – don't fill the cells up to the

9.3a Unclip the cover (XC60) . . .

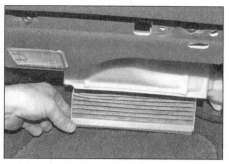

9.3b . . . and withdraw the pollen filter (XC90)

brim. Wipe up any spillage, then refit the cell covers.

6 Further information on the battery, charging and jump starting can be found at the start of this manual and in Chapter 5.

11 Underbody and fuel/brake line check

1 With the vehicle raised and supported on axle stands (see *Jacking and vehicle support*), or over an inspection pit, thoroughly inspect the underbody and wheel arches for signs of damage and corrosion. In particular, examine the bottom of the side sills, and any concealed areas where mud can collect.

2 Where corrosion and rust is evident, press and tap firmly on the panel with a screwdriver, and check for any serious corrosion which would necessitate repairs. If the panel is not seriously corroded, clean away the rust, and apply a new coating of underseal. Refer to Chapter 11 for more details of body repairs.

3 At the same time, inspect the treated lower body panels for stone damage and general condition.

4 Inspect all of the fuel and brake lines on the underbody for damage, rust, corrosion and leakage. Also make sure that they are correctly supported in their clips. Where applicable, check the PVC coating on the lines for damage **(see illustrations)**.

5 Inspect the flexible brake hoses in the vicinity of the front calipers and rear axle, where they

are subjected to most movement. Bend them between the fingers (but do not actually bend them double, or the casing may be damaged) and check that this does not reveal previously-hidden cracks, cuts or splits.

12 Exhaust system check

1 With the engine cold (at least three hours after the vehicle has been driven), check the complete exhaust system, from its starting point at the engine to the end of the tailpipe. Ideally, this should be done on a hoist, where unrestricted access is available; if a hoist is not available, raise and support the vehicle on axle stands (see *Jacking and vehicle support*).

2 Check the pipes and connections for evidence of leaks, severe corrosion, or damage. Make sure that all brackets and rubber mountings are in good condition, and tight; if any of the mountings are to be renewed, ensure that the new ones are of the correct type **(see illustration)**. Leakage at any of the joints or in other parts of the system will usually show up as a black sooty stain in the vicinity of the leak.

3 At the same time, inspect the underside of the body for holes, corrosion, open seams, etc, which may allow exhaust gases to enter the passenger compartment. Seal all body openings with silicone or body putty, with due consideration given to the heat generated by the exhaust system and gases.

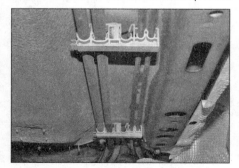

11.4a Check the condition of the fuel hoses looking for signs of leaks

11.4b Check the condition of the rubber brake hoses by bending them slightly and looking for cracks

12.2 Make sure the rubber exhaust mountings are in good condition

13.5 Remove the circlip

4 Rattles and other noises can often be traced to the exhaust system, especially the rubber mountings. Try to move the system, silencer(s) and catalytic converter. If any components can touch the body or suspension parts, secure the exhaust system with new mountings.

13 Handbrake check and adjustment

Caution: On models fitted with an electronic parking brake (EPB), adjustment of the parking brake is carried out using diagnostic equipment. This task should be entrusted to a Volvo dealer or suitably-equipped specialist.

Note: Early XC90 models were fitted with a self-adjustment system contained in the foot operated lever. If not already done so, these models should be upgraded to the later (manual adjustment) specification described below.

1 On XC90 models the parking brake can be manually adjusted.

2 Before carrying out the adjustment, drive the car slowly on a quiet road for about 400 metres with the handbrake applied by a few notches. This will clean any rust and deposits from the handbrake shoes and drum.

3 From inside the car operate the parking brake foot pedal and check that full braking effect is achieved on the rear wheels between 2 and 5 clicks of the pedal ratchet. If this is not the case, proceed as follows:

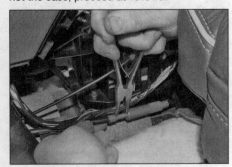

13.6 Adjust the cable with suitable pliers

4 Remove the panel from the left-hand side of the centre console and locate the cable adjuster.

5 Remove the circlip **(see illustration)** and slacken the cable by rotating it clockwise. Refit the circlip and then depress the operating pedal to the first click on the ratchet mechanism.

6 Using pliers gently prise apart the sections of the adjuster **(see illustration)**. The adjustment is correct when the rear wheels are fully locked when the foot lever is on the second to fifth teeth on the ratchet mechanism.

7 Refit the centre console side panel.

14 Seat belt check

1 Check the seat belts for satisfactory operation and condition. Inspect the webbing for fraying and cuts. Check that they retract smoothly and without binding into their reels.

2 Check the seat belt mountings, ensuring that all the bolts are securely tightened.

15 Door, tailgate and bonnet check and lubrication

1 Check that the doors, bonnet and tailgate close securely. Check that the bonnet safety catch operates correctly. Check the operation of the door check straps.

2 Lubricate the hinges, door check straps, the striker plates and the bonnet catch sparingly with a little oil or grease.

3 If any of the doors, bonnet or tailgate do not close effectively, or appear not to be flush with the surrounding panels, carry out the relevant adjustment procedures contained in Chapter 11.

16 Headlight beam alignment check

Accurate adjustment of the headlight beam is only possible using optical beam-setting equipment, and this work should therefore be carried out by a Volvo dealer or service station with the necessary facilities. All MOT test centres will have suitable equipment.

Basic adjustments can be carried out in an emergency, and further details are given in Chapter 12.

17 Coolant antifreeze concentration check

1 The cooling system should be filled with the recommended antifreeze and corrosion protection fluid. Over a period of time, the concentration of fluid may be reduced due to topping-up (this can be avoided by topping-up with the correct antifreeze mixture) or fluid loss. If loss of coolant has been evident, it is important to make the necessary repair before adding fresh fluid. The exact mixture of antifreeze-to-water which you should use depends on the relative weather conditions. The mixture should contain at least 40% antifreeze, but not more than 70%. Consult the mixture ratio chart on the antifreeze container before adding coolant. Use antifreeze which meets the vehicle manufacturer's specifications.

2 With the engine cold, carefully remove the cap from the expansion tank. If the engine is not completely cold, place a cloth rag over the cap before removing it, and remove it slowly to allow any pressure to escape.

3 Antifreeze checkers are available from car accessory shops. Draw some coolant from the expansion tank and observe how many plastic balls are floating in the checker. Usually, 2 or 3 balls must be floating for the correct concentration of antifreeze, but follow the manufacturer's instructions.

4 If the concentration is incorrect, it will be necessary to either withdraw some coolant and add antifreeze, or alternatively drain the old coolant and add fresh coolant of the correct concentration.

18 Service reminder indicator – resetting

Note: The Service Reminder Indicator (SRI) can also be reset with suitable diagnostic equipment.

XC60 models

1 Insert the remote into the facia slot.

2 Briefly press the stop/start button – this is position I.

3 Press and hold the trip reset button.

4 Press the remote fully into the slot.

5 Press and hold the stop/start button for two seconds to turn the ignition on.

6 After ten seconds the display will flash and on later models a yellow warning lamp will illuminate.

7 Release the trip reset button within four seconds. An audible chime will signal that resetting is complete.

XC90 models

8 Turn the ignition key to position I.

9 Press and hold the trip odometer reset button.

10 Within two seconds turn the key to position II.

11 Hold the reset button down until the original value has been reset. On all but very early models a yellow warning lamp will illuminate.

12 Release the reset button within four

seconds of the yellow warning lamp illuminating (or within four seconds of the odometer resetting on very early models). An audible warning will be heard when resetting is successful. Note that where the trip odometer has already been reset, then the reset button should be held in for a minimum of ten seconds and a maximum of fourteen seconds.

13 On some models an alternative procedure may be required.

14 Turn the ignition key to position I.

15 Press and hold the trip odometer reset button.

16 Turn the ignition key to position II.

17 Wait for ten seconds and then release the reset button when the information lamp starts to flash.

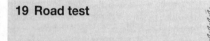

19 Road test

Braking system

1 Make sure that the vehicle does not pull to one side when braking, and that the wheels do not lock when braking hard.

2 Check that there is no vibration through the steering when braking. Note that, under heavy braking, some vibration may be felt through the brake pedal – this is a normal feature of the anti-lock braking system (ABS) operation, and does not normally indicate a fault.

3 Check that the handbrake operates correctly and that it holds the vehicle stationary on a slope.

4 With the engine switched off, test the operation of the brake servo unit as follows. Depress the footbrake four or five times to exhaust the vacuum, then start the engine. As the engine starts, there should be a noticeable give in the brake pedal as vacuum builds-up. Allow the engine to run for at least two minutes, and then switch it off. If the brake pedal is now depressed again, it should be possible to detect a hiss from the servo as the pedal is depressed. After about four or five applications, no further hissing should be heard, and the pedal should feel considerably harder.

Steering and suspension

5 Check for any abnormalities in the steering, suspension, handling or road feel.

6 Drive the vehicle, and check that there are no unusual vibrations or noises.

7 Check that the steering feels positive, with no excessive sloppiness or roughness, and check for any suspension noises when cornering and driving over bumps.

Drivetrain

8 Check the performance of the engine, transmission and driveline.

9 Check that the engine starts correctly, both when cold and hot.

10 Listen for any unusual noises from the engine and transmission.

11 Make sure that the engine runs smoothly when idling, and that there is no hesitation when accelerating.

12 On manual transmission models, check that all gears can be engaged smoothly without noise, and that the gear lever action is smooth and not abnormally vague or notchy.

13 On automatic transmission models, make sure that the drive seems smooth – there should be no jerks or 'flaring' of engine speed as gearchanges are made. Check that all the gear positions can be selected with the vehicle at rest.

Clutch

14 Check that the clutch pedal moves smoothly and easily through its full travel, and that the clutch itself functions correctly, with no trace of slip or drag. If the movement is uneven or stiff in places, check the system components with reference to Chapter 6.

Park/Neutral position switch

15 On models fitted with an automatic transmission the operation of the Park/Neutral position switch should be checked. When operating correctly the vehicle will only start with the selector lever in either the Park (P) or Neutral (N) position.

16 With both the handbrake and the footbrake applied move the selector lever to any position (other than park or neutral) and try to start the vehicle.

17 If the vehicle starts, stop immediately and check the operation of the position switch as described in Chapter 7B.

Instruments and electrical equipment

18 Check the operation of all instruments and electrical equipment.

19 Make sure that all instruments read correctly, and switch on all electrical equipment in turn, to check that it functions properly.

20 Air conditioning system check

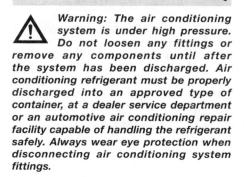

Warning: The air conditioning system is under high pressure. Do not loosen any fittings or remove any components until after the system has been discharged. Air conditioning refrigerant must be properly discharged into an approved type of container, at a dealer service department or an automotive air conditioning repair facility capable of handling the refrigerant safely. Always wear eye protection when disconnecting air conditioning system fittings.

1 The following maintenance checks should be performed on a regular basis, to ensure that the system continues to operate at peak efficiency:

a) Check the auxiliary drivebelt. If it's worn or deteriorated, renew it (see Section 27).

b) Check the system hoses. Look for cracks, bubbles, hard spots and deterioration. Inspect the hoses and all fittings for oil bubbles and seepage. If there's any evidence of wear, damage or leaks, renew the hose(s).

c) Inspect the condenser fins for leaves, insects and other debris. Use a 'fin comb' or compressed air to clean the condenser.

d) Check that the drain tube from the front of the evaporator is clear – note that it is normal to have clear fluid (water) dripping from this while the system is in operation, to the extent that quite a large puddle can be left under the vehicle when it is parked.

Warning: Wear eye protection when using compressed air.

2 It's a good idea to operate the system for about 30 minutes at least once a month, particularly during the winter. Long term non-use can cause hardening, and subsequent failure, of the seals.

3 Because of the complexity of the air conditioning system and the special equipment necessary to service it, in-depth repairs are not included in this manual, apart from those procedures covered in Chapter 3.

4 The most common cause of poor cooling is simply a low system refrigerant charge. If a noticeable drop in cool air output occurs, the following quick check will help you determine if the refrigerant level is low.

5 Warm the engine up to normal operating temperature.

6 Place the air conditioning temperature selector at the coldest setting, and put the blower at the highest setting. Open the doors – to make sure the air conditioning system doesn't cycle off as soon as it cools the passenger compartment.

7 With the compressor engaged – the compressor clutch will make an audible click, and the centre of the clutch will rotate – feel the inlet and outlet pipes at the compressor. One side should be cold, and one hot. If there's no perceptible difference between the two pipes, there's something wrong with the compressor or the system. It might be a low charge – it might be something else. Take the vehicle to a dealer service department or an automotive air conditioning specialist.

21 Fuel filter water draining

1 On both models the fuel filter is located at

21.1 Attach a length of hose and slacken the fuel filter drain screw (arrowed)

22.1a Remove the emergency key from the remote unit

22.1b Use a screwdriver to prise up the rear edge of the cover

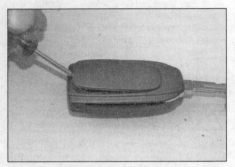

22.2 Prise up the cover

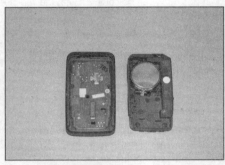

22.3a Remove the battery from the cover, noting its orientation

the rear of the vehicle, near the right-hand side rear roadwheel. On XC60 models it is within the rear suspension subframe. On XC90 models the filter is located next to the fuel tank on the right-hand side. Connect a length of hose to the drain screw and place the open end in a container. Slacken the drain screw on the underside of the filter by no more than 4 turns **(see illustration)**.
2 Drain off approximately 100 cc of fluid and tighten the drain screw.
3 Start the engine and check for leaks.

22 Remote control battery renewal

1 On XC60 models, remove the emergency key from the end of the remote, then use a small, flat-bladed screwdriver to gently prise up the rear edge of the cover **(see illustrations)**. Remove the cover.
2 On XC90 models prise the cover free **(see illustration)**.
3 Remove the battery from the control, noting its orientation **(see illustrations)**. Avoid touching the battery and contacts with bare fingers.
4 Fit the new battery into the control, refit the cover, and refit the emergency key.

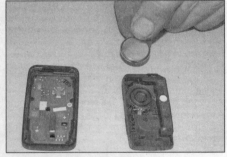

22.3b Fit the new battery into the cover on XC60 models...

22.3c ...and on XC90 models

Every 36 000 miles or 2 years

23.1 Unplug the MAF sensor

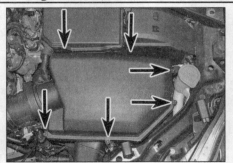

23.2 Undo the screws (arrowed) securing the air cleaner housing cover

23 Air cleaner element renewal

XC60

1 To avoid straining the MAF sensor unclip the loom and release the wiring plug from the sensor **(see illustration)**.
2 Undo the securing screws and lift up the air cleaner housing cover **(see illustration)**.
3 Lift the air cleaner element from place, noting which way around it's fitted **(see illustration)**.

4 With the filter removed, inspect the housing for debris. Remove any debris with a vacuum or remove the complete housing and invert it.

5 Fit the new element, refit the cover and tighten the securing screws.

XC90

6 Remove the cover **(see illustration)**.

7 Remove the screws from the cover and lift out the filter **(see illustrations)**.

8 With the filter removed, inspect the housing for debris. Remove any debris with a vacuum or remove the complete housing and invert it.

9 Fit the new element, refit the cover and tighten the securing screws.

23.3 Lift up the cover and remove the air cleaner element

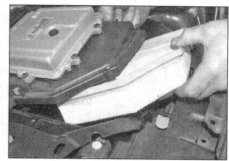

23.6 Remove the cover

---

24 Automatic transmission fluid level check and renewal

Note: *If the 'Gearbox oil change' indicator illuminates, this can only be reset using dedicated Volvo test equipment. Entrust this task to a Volvo dealer or suitably-equipped specialist.*

General

1 The need for regular topping-up of the transmission fluid indicates a leak, which should be found and rectified without delay.

2 The condition of the fluid should also be checked along with the level. If the fluid is black or a dark reddish-brown colour, or if it has a burned smell, the fluid should be changed. If you are in doubt about the condition of the fluid, purchase some new fluid, and compare the two for colour and smell.

3 If the car is used regularly for short trips, taxi work, or does a lot of towing, the transmission fluid should be renewed on a regular basis. Likewise, if a high mileage has been completed, or the history of the car is unknown, it might be worth renewing the fluid for peace of mind. Normally, however, renewal of the fluid is not a service requirement.

Fluid level check

4 The level of the automatic transmission fluid should be carefully maintained. Low fluid level can lead to slipping or loss of drive, while overfilling can cause foaming, loss of fluid and transmission damage.

5 Ideally, the transmission fluid level should be checked when the transmission is hot (50° to 60°C).

6 Park the vehicle on level ground, firmly apply the handbrake, and remove the engine transmission undershield.

7 Remove the air cleaner housing as described in Chapter 4A.

8 Clean the area on the top of the transmission around the filler plug, then using a T55 Torx bit, unscrew the filler plug **(see illustration)**.

9 Position the end of a hose in the filler aperture, and attach a funnel to the other end. Temporarily refit the air cleaner housing.

10 Start the engine. While the engine is idling,

23.7a Remove the cover screws

depress the brake pedal and move the selector lever through all gear positions (pausing in each position for 2 seconds), returning finally to the P position.

11 With the engine still running, unscrew the level plug from the centre of the transmission drain plug using a T40 Torx bit **(see illustration)**. If no fluid emerges from the level aperture, add the specified fluid (see *Lubricants and fluids*) through the funnel and hose until it does emerge. Refit the level plug and tighten it to the specified torque, using a new sealing washer. Note the fluid temperature **must not** exceed 60°C.

12 Stop the engine, remove the air cleaner housing, and tighten the fluid filler plug to the specified torque, using a new sealing washer.

13 Refit the air cleaner housing as described in Chapter 4A, then refit the engine/transmission undershield.

24.8 Unscrew the transmission filler plug (arrowed)

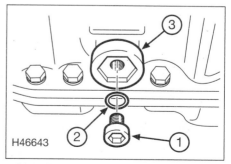

23.7b Slide out the air filter

Fluid renewal

Note: *The automatic transmission fluid does not normally require changing. It's only necessary on vehicles which are used predominantly for towing or as taxis.*

Note: *As a check when replacing the fluid, always measure the quantity of fluid removed from the transmission. This will give a good indication of the amount of fluid required to refill the transmission.*

14 Ideally, the transmission fluid level should be drained when the transmission is hot (at its normal operating temperature). Note that the fluid temperature must not be allowed to exceed 60°C, or an incorrect fluid level will result.

15 Jack up the front and rear of the vehicle and support it securely on axle stands (see *Jacking and vehicle support*). The vehicle should be level.

24.11 Transmission level plug (1), drain plug (3) and sealing washer (2)

24.18 Drain the fluid

25.2 Drain the fluid into a suitable container

25.3a Remove the housing...

25.3b ...recover the filter...

25.3c ...and seal

16 Release the screws and remove the engine undershield.

17 Position a container beneath the transmission and unscrew the level plug from the centre of the drain plug using a T40 Torx bit **(see illustration 24.11)**.

18 Unscrew the drain plug from the transmission and allow the fluid to drain **(see illustration)**. Refit the drain plug with a new seal and tighten it to the specified torque.

19 Refit the level plug, but only finger-tighten it at this stage.

20 Remove the air cleaner housing as described in Chapter 4A.

21 Clean the area on the top of the transmission around the filler plug, then using a T55 Torx bit, unscrew the filler plug **(see illustration 24.8)**.

22 Disconnect the fluid return hose from the cooler adjacent to the radiator, and attach a length of clear hose to the cooler outlet. Volvo

special tool No 999 7363 may be available for this purpose. Place the end of the hose into a container.

23 Using a funnel, add 4.0 litres of the specified fluid into the transmission casing through the filler hole.

24 Temporarily refit the air cleaner assembly. Fully apply the handbrake, and check the selector lever is in position P.

25 Start the engine, and allow it to idle. Shift through all the selector positions, pausing for 2 seconds at each position. Switch the engine off when air bubbles are visible in the clear hose attached to the cooler.

26 Add 2.0 litres of the specified fluid, then start the engine again and allow it to idle. Switch the engine off when air bubbles are visible in the clear hose.

27 Disconnect the clear hose from the cooler, and reconnect the fluid return hose.

28 Unscrew the level plug from the centre of the drain plug, and add fluid through the filler hole until It begins to run out of the level plug hole. Refit the level and filler plugs and tighten them to their specified torques.

29 Refit the air cleaner housing.

25 Fuel filter renewal

Note: *Ensure the fuel tank level is less than 3/4 full before renewing the filter.*

1 On both models the fuel filter is located at the rear of the vehicle, near the right-hand side rear roadwheel. On XC60 models it is within the rear suspension subframe. On XC90 models the filter is located next to the fuel tank on the right-hand side.

2 Place a container under the filter, then slacken the drain screw on the filter underside and allow the fluid to drain **(see illustration)**.

3 Use a strap wrench or filter removal tool to unscrew the filter from the housing **(see illustrations)**. Be prepared for fluid spillage.

4 Ensure the small O-ring seal is fitted to the top of the element, then fit the large O-ring seal to the filter housing. Fit the new element into the filter holder, then fit the assembly to the housing, ensuring the top of the element locates in the housing. Tighten the filter by hand until the seal contacts the holder, then tighten it to the specified torque.

5 Start the engine and check for leaks.

Every 90 000 miles or 5 years

26 Timing belt and tensioner renewal

Refer to Chapter 2A.

27 Auxiliary drivebelt renewal

1 The auxiliary drivebelt transmits power from

the crankshaft pulley to the alternator, steering pump and air conditioning compressor (as applicable).

2 To remove the drivebelt, first raise the front of the vehicle and support on axle stands (see *Jacking and vehicle support*). Undo the fasteners and remove the engine undershield. Remove the right-hand front wheel and the wheel arch liner. Remove the plastic cover on top of the engine.

3 The correct drivebelt tension is maintained by an automatic adjuster and tensioner assembly. This device is bolted to the front of

the engine, and incorporates a spring-loaded idler pulley. Models fitted with Electro Hydraulic Power steering (EHPS) have a separate 'stretch' belt that drives the AC compressor.

Models with EHPS

4 Using a suitable Torx bit, rotate the belt tensioner anti-clockwise and release the tension from the belt. Note the routing of the main belt and remove it **(see illustration)**. Check the tensioner pulley for any roughness or damage. Renew as necessary.

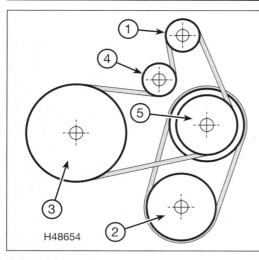

27.4 Auxiliary belt routing – models with EHPS

1 *Alternator pulley*
2 *Air conditioning compressor pulley*
3 *Crankshaft pulley*
4 *Tensioner*
5 *Transfer pulley*

27.7 Install the new belt

5 On early models release the four bolts that secure the main auxiliary drive belt pulley to the transfer pulley and then remove the pulley.
6 Cut the stretch belt with a suitable pair of side cutter pliers or a junior hacksaw.
7 Install the new belt with Volvo's own stretch belt tool (Volvo 9997250) or more conveniently use an aftermarket installation tool. We managed to work the belt onto the pulleys without the use of any special tools **(see illustration)**.
8 With the belt installed rotate the pulley several times and check that the new belt is correctly aligned in the groves of the pulley.
9 Refit the main auxiliary drive belt pulley and tighten the bolts to the specified torque.

10 Turn the main auxiliary belt tensioner anti-clockwise and fit the new belt. Release the tensioner.
11 Rotate the engine in the normal direction and check that the new belt is seated correctly.

Models with standard power steering

12 Where fitted remove the auxiliary belt cover.
13 Use Volvo tool No 999 7109, or a T60 Torx bit and spanner, to rotate the tensioner clockwise, thereby relieving the belt tension. Insert a suitable drill bit in the through the locking hole. Slip the belt off all the pulleys,

then release the tensioner and remove the belt **(see illustrations)**.
14 Check the tensioner and idler pulleys for any roughness or damage. Renew as necessary.
15 Fit the new belt loosely over the pulleys and the tensioner, ensuring that it is properly seated – leave the belt off the top (power steering pump) pulley however **(see illustration)**.
16 Rotate the tensioner clockwise, then work the drivebelt over the top pulley. Release the tensioner, which will now automatically take up the adjustment.

All models

17 Refit the inner wheel arch liner and engine undershield. Fit the engine cover.
18 Refit the wheel and lower the car to the ground. Tighten the wheel bolts to the specified torque.

27.13a Use a spanner (arrowed)…

27.13b …or a T60 torx bit to rotate the tensioner clockwise

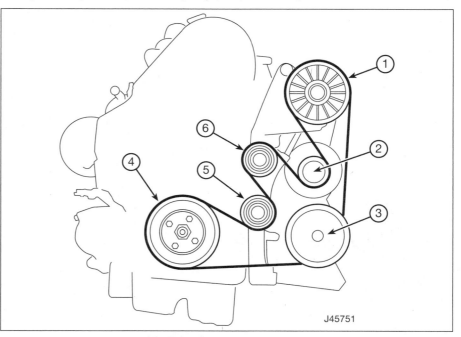

27.15 Auxiliary drivebelt routing

1 *Power steering pump pulley*
2 *Alternator pulley*
3 *Air conditioning compressor pulley*
4 *Crankshaft pulley*
5 *Tensioner*
6 *Idler pulley*

Every 2 years, regardless of mileage

28 Brake fluid renewal

 Warning: Brake hydraulic fluid can harm your eyes and damage painted surfaces, so use extreme caution when handling and pouring it. Do not use fluid that has been standing open for some time, as it absorbs moisture from the air. Excess moisture can cause a dangerous loss of braking effectiveness.

The procedure is similar to that for bleeding the hydraulic system as described in Chapter 9,

except that the brake fluid reservoir should be emptied by siphoning, and allowance should be made for the old fluid to be expelled when bleeding each section of the circuit.

Since the clutch hydraulic system uses the same fluid and reservoir as the braking system, it will probably be necessary to bleed the clutch system also (see Chapter 6).

Every 3 years, regardless of mileage

29 Coolant renewal

Note: *If genuine Volvo coolant, in the specified ratio, has been continuously maintained in the system, then coolant renewal will not normally be necessary. However, to be absolutely sure about the integrity of the antifreeze and anti-corrosion properties of the coolant, periodic renewal is to be recommended.*

 Warning: Wait until the engine is cold before starting this procedure. Do not allow antifreeze to come into contact with your skin, or with painted surfaces of the vehicle. Rinse off spills immediately with plenty of water. Never leave antifreeze lying around in an open container, or in a puddle in the driveway or on the garage floor. Children and pets are attracted by its sweet smell, but antifreeze can be fatal if ingested.

Coolant draining

1 To drain the system, first remove the expansion tank filler cap (see *Weekly checks*).
2 If the additional working clearance is required, raise the front of the vehicle and support it securely on axle stands (see *Jacking and vehicle support*).
3 Undo the screws and remove the engine undershield, then place a large drain tray underneath the radiator.
4 Slacken the drain tap at the bottom left-hand corner of the radiator, attach a length of hose to the pipe stub, and allow the coolant to drain into the tray. If no drain tap is fitted,

carefully loosen the clamp and disconnect the radiator bottom hose (see illustration).

System flushing

5 With time, the cooling system may gradually lose its efficiency, as the radiator core becomes choked with rust, scale deposits from the water, and other sediment. To minimise this, as well as using only the specified type of antifreeze and clean soft water, the system should be flushed as follows whenever any part of it is disturbed, and/or when the coolant is renewed.
6 With the coolant drained, close the drain taps and refill the system with fresh water. Refit the expansion tank filler cap, start the engine and warm it up to normal operating temperature, then stop it and (after allowing it to cool down completely) drain the system again. Repeat as necessary until only clean water can be seen to emerge, then refill finally with the specified coolant mixture.
7 If only clean, soft water and good-quality antifreeze has been used, and the coolant has been renewed at the specified intervals, the above procedure will be sufficient to keep the system clean for a considerable length of time. If, however, the system has been neglected, a more thorough operation will be required, as follows.
8 First drain the coolant, then disconnect the radiator top and bottom hoses. Insert a garden hose into the top hose, and allow water to circulate through the radiator until it runs clean from the bottom outlet.
9 To flush the engine, remove the thermostat (see Chapter 3), insert the garden hose into the thermostat housing, and allow water to circulate until it runs clear from the bottom hose. If, after a reasonable period, the water still does not run clear, the radiator should be flushed with a good proprietary cleaning agent.
10 In severe cases of contamination, reverse-flushing of the radiator may be necessary. To do this, remove the radiator (see Chapter 3), invert it, and insert the garden hose into the bottom outlet. Continue flushing until clear water runs from the top hose outlet. A similar procedure can be used to flush the heater matrix.
11 The use of chemical cleaners should be necessary only as a last resort. Normally, use

of the correct coolant will prevent excessive contamination of the system.

Coolant filling

12 With the cooling system drained and flushed, ensure that all disturbed components or hose unions are correctly fitted, and that the drain tap is securely tightened. Refit the engine undershield removed for access. If it was raised, lower the vehicle to the ground.
13 Prepare a sufficient quantity of the specified coolant mixture (see Specifications); allow for a surplus, so as to have a reserve supply for topping-up.
14 Slowly fill the system through the expansion tank; since the tank is the highest point in the system, all the air in the system should be displaced into the tank by the rising liquid. Slow pouring reduces the possibility of air being trapped and forming air-locks. It helps also if the large radiator hoses are gently squeezed during the filling procedure.
15 Continue filling until the coolant level reaches the expansion tank MAX level line, then wait for a few minutes. During this time, continue to squeeze the radiator hoses. When the level stops falling, top-up to the MAX level and refit the expansion tank cap.
16 Start the engine and run it at idle speed, until it has warmed-up to normal operating temperature. If the level in the expansion tank drops significantly, top-up to the MAX level line, to minimise the amount of air circulating in the system.
17 Stop the engine, allow it to cool down **completely** (overnight, if possible), then remove the expansion tank filler cap and top-up the tank to the MAX level line. Refit the filler cap, tightening it securely, and wash off any spilt coolant from the engine compartment and bodywork.
18 After refilling, always check carefully all components of the system (but especially any unions disturbed during draining and flushing) for signs of coolant leaks. Fresh antifreeze has a searching action, which will rapidly expose any weak points in the system.

Air-locks

19 If, after draining and refilling the system, symptoms of overheating are found which did not occur previously, then the fault is almost certainly due to trapped air at some point in the system, causing an air-lock and restricting

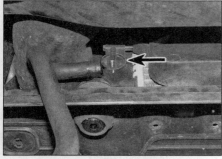
29.4 Radiator drain tap (arrowed)

the flow of coolant; usually, the air is trapped because the system was refilled too quickly.

20 If an air-lock is suspected, first try gently squeezing all visible coolant hoses. A coolant hose which is full of air feels quite different to one full of coolant, when squeezed. After refilling the system, most air-locks will clear once the system has cooled, and been topped-up.

21 While the engine is running at operating temperature, switch on the heater and heater fan, and check for heat output. Provided there is sufficient coolant in the system, lack of heat output could be due to an air-lock in the system.

22 Air-locks can have more serious effects than simply reducing heater output – a severe air-lock could reduce coolant flow around the engine. Check that the radiator top hose is hot when the engine is at operating temperature – a top hose which stays cold could be the result of an air-lock (or a non-opening thermostat).

23 If the problem persists, stop the engine and allow it to cool down **completely**, before unscrewing the expansion tank filler cap or disconnecting hoses to bleed out the trapped air. In the worst case, the system will have to be at least partially drained (this time, the coolant can be saved for re-use) and flushed to clear the problem.

Chapter 2 Part A:
Engine in-car repair procedures

Contents

Degrees of difficulty

Easy, suitable for novice with little experience 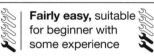	Fairly easy, suitable for beginner with some experience	Fairly difficult, suitable for competent DIY mechanic	Difficult, suitable for experienced DIY mechanic	Very difficult, suitable for expert DIY or professional

Specifications

General

Engine type.	Water-cooled, double overhead camshaft, 20 valve, in-line five cylinders, with both the cylinder block and cylinder head made from aluminium-alloy, with cast-iron cylinder sleeves
Engine codes	D5204 T2, D5204 T3 D5244 T4, D5244 T5, D5244 T10, D5244 T11, D5244 T14 and D5244 T18

Capacity:
  D5204 .... 1984 cc
  D5244 .... 2400 cc
Bore:
  D5204 .... 81.0 mm
  D5244 .... 81.0 mm
Stroke:
  D5204 .... 77.0 mm
  D5244 .... 93.15 mm

Engine code:	Power output	Torque
D5204 T2	120 kW	400 Nm at 1400 to 2750 rpm
D5204 T3	120 kW	400 Nm at 1500 to 2850 rpm
D5244 T4	136 kW	350 Nm at 1750 to 3250 rpm
D5244 T5	120 kW	340 Nm at 1750 to 3000 rpm
D5244 T10	151 kW	420 Nm at 1500 to 3000 rpm
D5244 T11	158kW	420 Nm at 1500 to 3250 rpm
D5244 T14	129 kW	420 Nm at 1500 to 2750 rpm
D5244 T16	120 kW	420 Nm at 1500 to 2500 rpm
D5244 T18	147 kW	420 Nm at 1900 to 2800 rpm

Compression ratio .... 17.3:1 to 18.0:1 depending on engine. Refer to a Volvo dealer for exact specification
Firing order.. 1-2-4-5-3
Cylinder No 1 location .... Timing belt end

Camshaft

Drive.. Toothed belt

Valves

Valve clearances .... Hydraulic compensators – no adjustment necessary

Cylinder head gasket selection

Piston protrusion over gasket face (see text):	Min	Max
1 hole	0.26 mm	0.47 mm
2 holes	0.47 mm	0.52 mm
3 holes	0.52 mm	0.57 mm
4 holes	0.57 mm	0.62 mm
5 holes	0.62 mm	0.74 mm

Lubrication system

Oil pump type.	Mounted on front of cylinder block and driven directly from crankshaft
Oil pressure – minimum (engine at operating temperature):	
At idle (at 800 rpm on 2 litre engine).	1.0 bar
At 4000 rpm	3.5 bar

Torque wrench settings

	Nm	lbf ft
Auxiliary drivebelt tensioner	24	18
Camshaft bearing cap	10	7
Camshaft cover	10	7
Camshaft end sealing/bearing caps (M7).	17	13
Camshaft position sensor	10	7
Camshaft sprocket bolt	30	22
Catalytic converter crossmember	24	18
Catalytic converter mounting screws.	10	7
Connecting rod cap:*		
Stage 1.	30	22
Stage 2.	Angle-tighten a further 90°	
Coolant temperature sensor.	22	16
Crankcase intermediate section:		
Tighten in the following sequence:		
M10*.	20	15
M10.	40	30
M8.	24	18
M7.	17	13
M10.	Angle-tighten a further 110°	
Crankshaft pulley screws:*		
Stage 1.	35	26
Stage 2.	Angle-tighten a further 50°	
Crankshaft sprocket nut.	300	221
Cylinder head bolts:*		
2.4 litre engine		
Stage 1.	20	15
Stage 2.	Slacken	
Stage 3.	20	15
Stage 4.	50	37
Stage 5.	Angle-tighten a further 90°	
Stage 6.	Angle-tighten a further 90°	
2.0 litre engine		
Stage 1.	20	15
Stage 2.	Slacken	
Stage 3.	20	15
Stage 4.	50	37
Stage 5.	Angle-tighten a further 120°	
Stage 6.	Angle-tighten a further 120°	
Driveplate:*		
Stage 1.	45	33
Stage 2.	Angle-tighten a further 50°	
Engine mountings (XC60):		
Right-hand side:*		
Mounting bracket (M12)	80	59
Mounting to cylinder head	48	35
Left-hand side:*		
Mounting bracket:		
M8.	24	18
M12.	80	59
Mounting to gearbox	175	129
Torque rod bolts*	110	81

Torque wrench settings (continued)

	Nm	lbf ft
Engine mountings (XC90):		
Front mounting (M10)	50	37
Upper mounting (on strut tower)	50	37
Upper mounting (strut brace to struts and to engine)	85	63
Upper mounting (on engine).	50	37
Rear torque rod (to transmission).	50	37
Rear torque rod (to subframe)		
Stage 1	65	48
Stage 2	Angle-tighten a further 90°	
Right hand mounting (to engine):		
M10		
Stage 1	35	26
Stage 2	Angle-tighten a further 60°	
M8		
Stage 1	20	15
Stage 2	Angle-tighten a further 60°	
Right-hand mounting (to subframe):		
Stage 1	120	88
Stage 2	Angle-tighten a further 40°	
Exhaust pipe to turbocharger	24	18
Flywheel:*		
Stage 1	45	33
Stage 2	Angle-tighten a further 65°	
Fuel injection pump	18	13
Fuel rail/injector pipe unions:*		
Stage 1	10	7
Stage 2	Angle-tighten a further 60°	
Fuel rail mounting bolts	24	18
Glow plugs.	8	6
Injector screws*	13	10
Oil cooler retaining bolts.	17	13
Oil filter.	25	18
Oil pick-up pipe	17	13
Oil pressure switch.	27	20
Oil pump bolts	10	7
Piston cooling jets	17	13
Piston cooling valve	51	38
Sump:		
Sump to transmission.	50	37
Sump to engine	17	13
Sump drain plug (engine oil).	38	28
Timing belt idler pulley	24	18
Timing belt tensioner	24	18
Torque converter bolts*	60	44
Turbocharger oil drain pipe union.	12	9
Turbocharger to manifold.	35	26
Vacuum pump	17	13

Do not re-use. Volvo specify that where a fixing requires angular tightening it must always be renewed. Any fixing retained with a thread locking compound must also be renewed. Nuts with a nylon insert must always be renewed.

1 General information

Introduction

The engines are water-cooled, double overhead camshaft, 20 valve, in-line five cylinder units of 2.0 and 2.4 litre capacities, with both the cylinder block and cylinder head made from aluminium-alloy, with cast-iron cylinder sleeves. The engine is mounted transversely at the front of the vehicle, with the transmission bolted to the left-hand end of the engine.

The cylinder head carries the camshafts, which are driven by a toothed timing belt from the crankshaft to the inlet camshaft. A toothed gear on the inlet shaft drives a corresponding gear on the exhaust camshaft. An Oldham coupling on the left-hand end of the inlet camshaft drives the low/high-pressure fuel pump, whilst the vacuum pump is driven from the left-hand end of the exhaust camshaft. The cylinder head also incorporates the 20 inlet and exhaust valves (4 per cylinder), which are closed by single coil springs, and which run in guides pressed into the cylinder head. The camshafts actuate the valves via roller type rocker arms acting upon hydraulic tappets, mounted in the cylinder head. The cylinder head contains internal oilways which supply and lubricate the hydraulic tappets.

All engines are of direct injection design where the swirl chambers are incorporated in the tops of the pistons. The cylinder head incorporates two separate inlet ports per cylinder. These ports are of different length and geometry to ensure more efficient combustion and reduced emissions.

The forged steel crankshaft is of six-bearing type, and the No 5 (from timing belt end) main bearing shells incorporate separate thrustwashers to control crankshaft endfloat. The inlet camshaft is driven by a toothed belt from the crankshaft sprocket, and the belt also drives the water pump mounted on the rear of the block.

The pistons are manufactured from aluminium-silicon alloy, with graphite

3.1 Unbolt the bracket (arrowed) on the front of the timing belt cover

coated skirts to reduce friction. The pistons incorporate cooling channels, through which oil flows, supplied by fixed jets mounted at the base of the cylinders. As each piston reaches the lower end of its stroke, the oil jet aligns with a hole in the base of the piston, and oil is forced through the cooling channel.

The engine has a full-flow lubrication system. A duocentric internal gear type oil pump is mounted on the front of the crankshaft. The oil filter is of the paper element type, mounted on the front side of the cylinder block.

Using this Chapter

This Chapter describes the repair procedures that can reasonably be carried out on the engine while it remains in the vehicle. If the engine has been removed from the vehicle and is being dismantled as described in Part B, any preliminary dismantling procedures can be ignored.

Note that, while it may be possible physically to overhaul items such as the piston/connecting rod assemblies while the engine is in the car, such tasks are not usually carried out as separate operations. Usually, several additional procedures are required (not to mention the cleaning of components and oilways); for this reason, all such tasks are classed as major overhaul procedures, and are described in Part B of this Chapter.

Part B describes the removal of the engine/transmission from the car, and the full overhaul procedures that can then be carried out.

Operations with engine in car

The following operations can be performed without removing the engine:

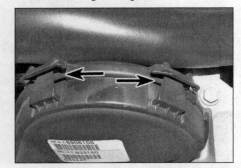

3.2 Release the clips (arrowed) securing the timing belt cover

a) Auxiliary drivebelt – removal and refitting.
b) Camshafts – removal and refitting.
c) Camshaft oil seals – renewal.
d) Camshaft sprocket – removal and refitting.
e) Coolant pump – removal and refitting (refer to Chapter 3)
f) Crankshaft oil seals – renewal.
g) Crankshaft sprocket – removal and refitting.
h) Cylinder head – removal and refitting.
i) Engine mountings – inspection and renewal.
j) Oil pump and pickup assembly – removal and refitting.
k) Sump – removal and refitting.
l) Timing belt, sprockets and cover – removal, inspection and refitting.

Note: *It is possible to remove the pistons and connecting rods (after removing the cylinder head and sump) without removing the engine from the vehicle. However, this procedure is not recommended. Work of this nature is more easily and thoroughly completed with the engine on the bench – refer to Chapter 2B.*

---

2 Compression and leakdown tests – description and interpretation

Compression test

Note: *A compression tester specifically designed for diesel engines must be used for this test.*

1 When engine performance is down, or if misfiring occurs, a compression test can provide diagnostic clues as to the engine's condition. If the test is performed regularly, it can give warning of trouble before any other symptoms become apparent.

2 A compression tester specifically intended for diesel engines must be used, because of the higher pressures involved. The tester is connected to an adapter which screws into the glow plug hole. It is unlikely to be worthwhile buying such a tester for occasional use, but it may be possible to borrow or hire one – if not, have the test performed by a garage.

3 Unless specific instructions to the contrary are supplied with the tester, observe the following points:

a) *The battery must be in a good state of charge, the air filter clean, and the engine should be at normal operating temperature.*
b) *All the glow plugs should be removed before starting the test.*
c) *The engine management ECM relay must be removed from the fuse/relay box.*

4 There is no need to hold the accelerator pedal down during the test, because the diesel engine air inlet is not throttled.

5 The manufacturers do not specify a wear limit for compression pressure. Seek the advice of a Volvo dealer or other diesel specialist if in doubt as to whether a particular pressure reading is acceptable.

6 The cause of poor compression is less easy to establish on a diesel engine than on a petrol one. The effect of introducing oil into the cylinders (wet testing) is not conclusive, because there is a risk that the oil will sit in the recess on the piston crown, instead of passing to the rings. However, the following can be used as a rough guide to diagnosis.

7 All cylinders should produce very similar pressures; a difference of more than 5.0 bars between any two cylinders indicates the existence of a fault. Note that the compression should build-up quickly in a healthy engine; low compression on the first stroke, followed by gradually-increasing pressure on successive strokes, indicates worn piston rings. A low compression reading on the first stroke, which does not build-up during successive strokes, indicates leaking valves or a blown head gasket (a cracked head could also be the cause).

8 A low reading from two adjacent cylinders is almost certainly due to the head gasket having blown between them.

Leakdown test

9 A leakdown test measures the rate at which compressed air fed into the cylinder is lost. It is an alternative to a compression test, and in many ways it is better, since the escaping air provides easy identification of where pressure loss is occurring (piston rings, valves or head gasket).

10 The equipment needed for leakdown testing is unlikely to be available to the home mechanic. If poor compression is suspected, have the test performed by a suitably-equipped garage.

---

3 Timing belt covers – removal and refitting

Removal

1 Undo the bolt and remove the pipe bracket on the front face of the timing belt cover **(see illustration)**.

2 Release the 5 securing clips and remove the cover **(see illustration)**.

Refitting

3 Refitting of the cover is a reversal of the relevant removal procedure. Ensure that all disturbed hoses are reconnected and retained by their relevant clips.

---

4 Timing belt – removal, inspection and refitting

Note: *Whenever the timing belt is renewed, the tensioner and idler pulley should also be renewed as described in Section 5.*

Removal

1 The camshaft and coolant pump sprockets

are driven by the timing belt from the crankshaft sprocket. The crankshaft and camshaft sprockets move in phase with each other to ensure correct valve timing. Should the timing belt slip or break in service, the valve timing will be disturbed and piston-to-valve contact will occur, resulting in serious engine damage.

2 The design of the engines covered in this Chapter is such that piston-to-valve contact will occur if the crankshaft is turned with the timing belt removed. For this reason, it is important that the correct phasing between the camshaft and crankshaft is preserved whilst the timing belt is off the engine. This is achieved by setting the engine in a reference condition (known as Top Dead Centre or TDC) before the timing belt is removed, and then not rotating the shafts until the belt is refitted. Similarly, if the engine has been dismantled for overhaul, the engine must be set to TDC during reassembly to ensure that the correct shaft phasing is restored.

3 TDC is the highest position a piston reaches within its respective cylinder – in a four-stroke engine, each piston reaches TDC twice per cycle, once on the compression stroke and once on the exhaust stroke. In general, TDC normally refers to No 1 cylinder on the compression stroke. The cylinders are numbered one to five, starting from the timing belt end of the engine. Note that on this particular engine, when the timing marks are aligned, the No 1 piston is positioned very slightly before TDC.

4 Before starting work, see Disconnecting the battery in Chapter 5.

5 Slacken the right-hand front roadwheel bolts, then jack up the front of the vehicle and support it securely on axle stands (see *Jacking and vehicle support*). Remove the roadwheel.

6 Remove the right-hand wheel arch liner for access to the crankshaft pulley **(see illustration)**.

7 Remove the timing belt outer cover as described in Section 3.

8 Release the return hose cable-tie from the engine cross-stay mounting bracket, then release the top clip and lift the power steering fluid reservoir from place, and move it to one side over the top of the engine. Do not disconnect the hoses.

9 Remove the auxiliary drivebelt as described in Chapter 1.

10 Undo the bolts and remove the timing belt lower cover.

11 Using a socket on the crankshaft pulley nut, rotate the crankshaft clockwise until the markings on the camshaft sprocket and timing belt rear cover align **(see illustration)**.

12 Undo the four bolts and one nut securing the crankshaft pulley to the crankshaft sprocket and remove the crankshaft pulley, leaving the sprocket in place. Note that the centre nut is very tight. In order to prevent the crankshaft from rotating on manual models, engage top gear and have an assistant fully depress the brake pedal. On automatic

4.6 Remove the wheel arch liner for access to the crankshaft pulley (arrowed)

models, remove the starter motor as described in Chapter 5, and use a large flat-bladed screwdriver wedged between the driveplate ring gear teeth and the transmission housing.

13 Check that the marks on the camshaft sprocket and timing belt rear cover are still aligned, and the lug on the oil pump housing aligns with the mark cast into crankshaft pulley mounting boss. If the marks do not align, temporarily refit two of the crankshaft pulley retaining bolts and the centre nut loosely and, using a large screwdriver/lever, rotate the crankshaft clockwise until the marks are in alignment **(see illustration)**.

14 Slacken the timing belt tensioner centre bolt slightly, and use a 6 mm Allen key to rotate the tensioner arm clockwise to the 10 o'clock position, then lightly tighten the centre bolt **(see illustration)**.

15 Remove the timing belt from the sprockets, without turning the crankshaft or camshaft.

Inspection

16 Examine the belt for evidence of contamination by coolant or lubricant. If this is the case, find the source of the contamination before progressing any further. Check the belt for signs of wear or damage, particularly around the leading edges of the belt teeth. Renew the belt if its condition is in doubt; the cost of belt renewal is negligible compared with potential cost of the engine repairs, should the belt fail in service. The belt must be renewed if it has covered the mileage stated by the manufacturer (see Chapter 1), however

4.13 The mark on the crankshaft pulley flange should align with the mark on the oil pump housing (arrowed)

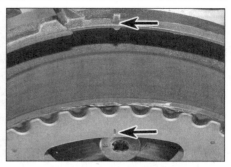
4.11 Align the mark on the camshaft sprocket with the mark on the timing belt cover (arrowed)

if it has covered less it is prudent to renew it regardless of condition, as a precautionary measure. **Note:** *If the timing belt is not going to be refitted for some time, it is a wise precaution to hang a warning label on the steering wheel, to remind yourself (and others) not to attempt to start the engine.*

17 Spin the belt tensioner and idler pulleys and listen for noise which may indicate wear in the pulley bearings. If in any doubt, renew the pulleys as described in Section 5. **Note:** *Most aftermarket belt manufacturers will not guarantee the replacement belt against failure unless a complete belt replacement kit is fitted. This will normally include the belt tensioner, idler pulleys and replacement fixings deemed necessary by the belt manufacturer.*

Refitting

18 Ensure that the crankshaft and camshaft are still aligned as described in paragraphs 11 and 13.

19 Fit the new belt around the crankshaft sprocket, idler pulley, camshaft sprocket, coolant pump sprocket, and finally, the tensioner pulley. Ensure the belt teeth seat correctly on the sprockets.

20 Ensure that the front run of the belt is taut – ie, all the slack should be in the section of the belt that passes over the tensioner roller.

21 Slacken the tensioner roller centre bolt slightly, then using a 6 mm Allen key, rotate the tensioner arm anti-clockwise until it passes the position shown, then rotate it clockwise until the indicator reaches the correct position

4.14 Use a 6 mm Allen key to position the tensioner arm (arrowed) at approximately the 10 o'clock position

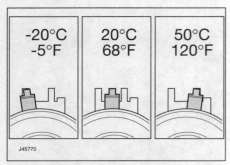

4.21 Timing belt tensioner settings at various temperatures

(see illustration). Tighten the centre bolt to the specified torque.

22 Gently press the belt between the camshaft sprocket and coolant pump sprocket, and check the tensioner arm moves freely as the belt is pressed.

23 Turn the crankshaft through two complete turns, then check that the timing marks on the crankshaft pulley boss and camshaft sprocket align correctly as described in paragraphs 11 and 13.

24 Check that the timing belt tensioner indicator is still position as described in paragraph 21. If not, repeat the operation described in paragraph 21.

25 The remainder of refitting is a reversal of removal, remembering to tighten all fasteners to their specified torque where given.

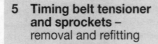
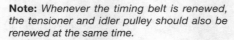

5 Timing belt tensioner and sprockets – removal and refitting

Note: *Whenever the timing belt is renewed, the tensioner and idler pulley should also be renewed at the same time.*

Timing belt tensioner

1 Remove the timing belt as described in Section 4.

2 Undo the centre bolt and remove the tensioner.

3 Spin the tensioner roller, feeling and listening for any roughness or noise, which would indicate wear in the tensioner roller bearing. If in any doubt as the condition of the tensioner, renew it.

4 Refit the tensioner and insert the bolt – do not fully tighten the bolt at this stage. Ensure the tensioner 'fork' locates correctly over the rib on the cylinder block **(see illustration).**

5 Refit and tension the timing belt as described in Section 4.

Camshaft sprocket

6 Remove the timing belt as described in Section 4.

7 Unscrew the camshaft sprocket bolts, while holding the sprocket stationary using a tool which engages the holes in the sprocket **(see illustration).** Do not allow the camshaft to rotate.

8 Remove the sprocket from the camshaft.

9 Remove the vacuum pump from the left-hand end of the exhaust camshaft as described in Chapter 9.

10 Insert a camshaft locking pin (Volvo No 999 7007) into the hole in the cylinder head and into the hole in the exhaust camshaft drivegear. If necessary, rotate the camshaft slightly to enable the pin to be inserted. If the Volvo pin is not available, a home-made equivalent can be fabricated **(see illustrations).**

11 Check the mark on the crankshaft sprocket still aligns with the mark on the oil pump housing as described in Section 4, then rotate the crankshaft clockwise (viewed from the timing belt end) approximately 15 degrees.

12 Refit the sprocket to the camshaft, but only tighten the retaining bolts sufficiently to allow the sprocket to just move independently of the camshaft. Position the sprocket so the retaining bolts are not at the ends of the slots, and the mark on the sprocket edge aligns with the mark on the timing belt inner cover **(see illustration).**

13 Unscrew the blanking plug from the front left-hand face of the cylinder block, and insert Volvo Tool No 999 7005, then rotate the crankshaft anti-clockwise (viewed from the timing belt of the engine) until the crankshaft web of No 5 cylinder comes to a stop against the tool. Check the marks on the crankshaft pulley flange and oil pump housing align. If the tool is not available, a home-made equivalent

5.4 Ensure the tensioner locates correctly over the rib (arrowed) on the cylinder block

5.7 Use a simple tool to counterhold the camshaft sprocket whilst slackening the bolts

5.10a Insert the camshaft aligning tool through the hole in the cylinder head and into the exhaust camshaft drivegear

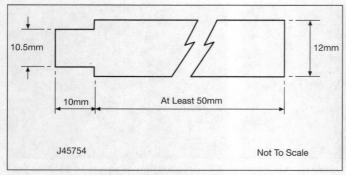

5.10b Camshaft aligning tool

5.12 Align the mark on the camshaft sprocket with the mark on the timing belt inner cover (arrowed)

may be fabricated using the dimensions shown **(see illustrations)**.

14 Refit the timing belt as described in paragraphs 18 to 23 of Section 4.

15 Ensure the marks of the crankshaft sprocket aligns with the mark on the oil pump housing, and the marks on the camshaft sprocket and timing belt inner cover align, then tighten the camshaft sprocket bolts to the specified torque, using the tool to counterhold the sprocket (see paragraph 7).

16 Remove the camshaft locking tool, crankshaft stop tool, and refit the vacuum pump as described in Chapter 9. Refit the blanking plug to the front face of the cylinder block.

17 Proceed as described from paragraph 24 of Section 4.

Crankshaft sprocket

18 Remove the timing belt as described in Section 4.

19 The crankshaft sprocket locates on a master spline on the crankshaft, and a puller may be required to work the sprocket off **(see illustration)**. Levering the sprocket off is not advisable – the rim of the sprocket itself is easily broken if care is not taken.

20 Wipe the sprocket and crankshaft mating surfaces clean.

21 Refit the sprocket to the crankshaft, and check the timing marks still align. Note the sprocket is located by means of a master spline on the crankshaft.

22 Install the timing belt around the crankshaft sprocket, idler pulley, camshaft sprocket, coolant pump, and finally the tensioner pulley.

23 Refit the pulley to the sprocket and refit the crankshaft nut, finger-tight only at this stage, then rotate the crankshaft anti-clockwise approximately 45°.

24 Stop the crankshaft from rotating and tighten the sprocket nut to the specified torque, then tighten the pulley bolts to their specified torque.

25 Tension the timing belt and complete the refitting procedure as described in Section 4.

Idler pulley

26 Remove the timing belt as described in Section 4.

27 Undo the bolt and remove the idler pulley **(see illustration)**.

28 Refitting is a reversal of removal, remembering to tighten all fasteners to their specified torque where given.

6 Cylinder head cover/inlet manifold – removal and refitting

Removal

1 The cylinder head cover is integral with the inlet manifold. Remove the plastic cover on top of the engine **(see illustration)**.

2 Remove the high-pressure fuel pipes and

5.13a Unscrew the blanking plug...

5.13b ...and insert the crankshaft stop tool

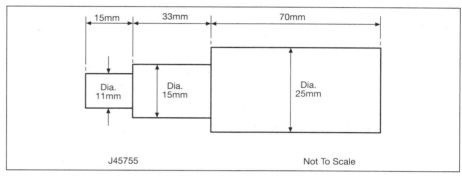
5.13c Crankshaft stop tool

the fuel injectors as described in Chapter 4A. Discard the fuel pipes as new ones must be fitted on refitting.

3 Undo the clamps and remove the air pipe

5.19 If necessary, use a puller to remove the crankshaft sprocket

6.1 Pull the engine cover straight up from its mountings

at the front of the engine, including the pipe securing bolt **(see illustrations)**.

4 Remove the crankcase ventilation hose from the cover.

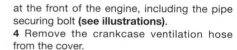

5.27 Timing belt idler pulley

6.3a Remove the air pipe over the front of the engine, undoing the clamp at the air cleaner housing...

6.3b ...unclipping the support bracket...

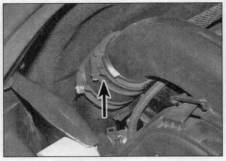

6.3c ...and undoing the clamp at the rear of the engine compartment

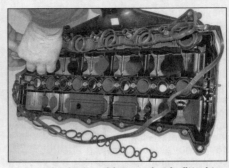

6.9 An intricate rubber gasket is fitted to the camshaft cover

5 Undo the 3 bolts and remove the oil filler neck from the cover.

6 Unplug the wiring connectors from the camshaft position sensor and the temperature sensor.

7 On XC60 models and with reference to Section 12 of this Chapter remove the engine mounting

8 Undo the remaining bolts and carefully lift the cover from place.

Refitting

9 Refit the camshaft cover by following the removal procedure in reverse, noting the following points:

a) A rubber sealing gasket is fitted to the underside of the camshaft cover **(see illustration)**. Ensure the gasket remains in place whilst the cover is refitted.

7.3a Fit the new seal using a tubular spacer which bears only on the hard, outer surface of the seal

8.2a Drill a small hole into the hard, outer edge of the seal...

b) Tighten the camshaft cover retaining nuts to the specified torque, starting from the centre and working outwards.

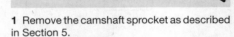
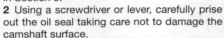

7 Camshaft oil seal – renewal

1 Remove the camshaft sprocket as described in Section 5.

2 Using a screwdriver or lever, carefully prise out the oil seal taking care not to damage the camshaft surface.

3 Clean the seating in the bearing cap, then smear a little oil on the lips of the new oil seal. Fit the new oil seal and tap it into position carefully using a tubular spacer, socket or block of wood that bears only on the hard outer surface of the seal **(see illustrations)**.

7.3b The outside edge of the seal should be flush with the outer edge of the sealing cap/cylinder head casting

8.2b ...then insert a self-tapping screw and pull the seal from place

The outside edge of the seal should be flush with the outer edge of the sealing cap/cylinder head casting.

4 Refit the camshaft sprocket as described in Section 5.

8 Crankshaft oil seals – renewal

Right-hand oil seal

1 Remove the crankshaft sprocket, with reference to Section 5.

2 The seal may be renewed without removing the oil pump by drilling a small hole, inserting a self-tapping screw, and pulling on the head of the screw with pliers **(see illustrations)**. Take great care not to mark the crankshaft surface with the drill bit.

3 Wrap some adhesive tape around the end of the crankshaft to prevent damage to the new oil seal. Dip the new seal in engine oil and drive it into the oil pump housing with a block of wood or a socket until flush. Make sure that the closed end of the seal is facing outwards **(see illustrations)**.

4 Remove the adhesive tape.

5 Refit the timing belt and crankshaft sprocket, with reference to Section 5.

Left-hand oil seal

6 Remove the flywheel/driveplate with reference to Section 11.

7 Clean the surfaces of the block and crankshaft.

8.3a Wrap tape around the shoulder on the crankshaft to protect the seal lips...

8.3b ...then use a tubular spacer or socket...

8.3c ...to drive the seal home

8.8 Drill a hole, insert a self-tapping screw and pull the crankshaft left-hand oil seal from place

8 Remove the old oil seal and fit the new one as described in paragraphs 2 to 4 above **(see illustration)**.
9 Refit the flywheel/driveplate (Section 11).

9 Cylinder head –
removal, inspection and refitting

Removal

1 Disconnect the battery negative lead - see Disconnecting the battery in Chapter 5.
2 Jack up the front of the vehicle and support it securely on axle stands (see *Jacking and vehicle support*).
3 Drain the engine oil with reference to Chapter 1.
4 Drain the cooling system with reference to Chapter 1.
5 Loosen the clips and disconnect all air, coolant and vacuum hoses from the cylinder head noting their locations.
6 Remove the air cleaner assembly as described in Chapter 4A.
7 Remove the timing belt as described in Section 4.
8 Remove the camshafts, rocker arm and hydraulic tappets as described in Section 10.
9 Remove the power steering pump support bracket from the cylinder head along with the vacuum pump and fuel pump.
10 Undo the bolts securing the fuel rail and fuel pipes to the cylinder head.
11 Undo the retaining bolts and remove the heat shield above the exhaust manifold.
12 Slacken the EGR pipe clamp at the exhaust manifold, then undo the bolts securing the EGR valve/cooler/pipe assembly to the cylinder head and move it to one side.
13 Remove the front section of the exhaust pipe, and undo the bolts securing the exhaust manifold to the cylinder head as described in Chapter 4A. Disconnect and remove the oil return and supply pipes from the turbocharger and engine block, then slacken the clamp and disconnect the turbocharger outlet pipe. Disconnect the vacuum hose from the turbocharger control valve, and the rubber intake hose from the turbocharger, then carefully lower the turbocharger and manifold

assembly onto the driveshaft and steering rack. Discard the turbocharger oil supply and return pipe sealing washers – new ones must be fitted.
14 Undo the bolts securing the coolant pipe to the cylinder head **(see illustration)**.
15 Make a final check to ensure all wiring plugs have been disconnected from the cylinder head.
16 Following the **reverse** of the tightening sequence **(see illustration 9.30)**, progressively slacken the cylinder head bolts, by half a turn at a time, until all bolts can be unscrewed by hand and removed. Discard the bolts – new ones must be fitted on reassembly.
17 Check that nothing remains connected to the cylinder head, then lift the head away from the cylinder block; seek assistance if possible, as it is heavy. Do not lay the cylinder head on the worktop face down – this may damage the sealing face.
18 Remove the gasket from the top of the block, noting the identification holes on its front edge. If the dowels are a loose fit, remove them and store them with the head for safe-keeping. Do not discard the gasket yet – it will be needed for identification purposes.
19 If the cylinder head is to be dismantled for overhaul, refer to Chapter 2B.

Inspection

20 The mating faces of the cylinder head and cylinder block/crankcase must be perfectly clean before refitting the head. Use a hard plastic or wood scraper to remove all traces of gasket and carbon; also clean the

9.14 Undo the bolt (arrowed) securing the coolant pipe to the right-hand rear corner of the cylinder head

piston crowns. Take particular care during the cleaning operations, as aluminium alloy is easily damaged. Also, make sure that the carbon is not allowed to enter the oil and water passages – this is particularly important for the lubrication system, as carbon could block the oil supply to the engine's components. Using adhesive tape and paper, seal the water, oil and bolt holes in the cylinder block/crankcase.
21 Check the mating surfaces of the cylinder block/crankcase and the cylinder head for nicks, deep scratches and other damage. If slight, they may be removed carefully with abrasive paper, but note that head machining will not be possible – refer to Chapter 2B.
22 If warpage of the cylinder head gasket surface is suspected, use a straight-edge to check it for distortion.
23 Clean out the cylinder head bolt drillings using a suitable tap. If a tap is not available, use an old head bolt with two slots cut along the length of the threads. It is most important that no oil or coolant is present in the bolts holes, otherwise the block may be cracked by the hydraulic action as the head bolts are inserted and tightened.

Refitting

24 Examine the old cylinder head gasket for manufacturer's identification markings. These are in the form of holes along the front edge of the gasket **(see illustration)**. Unless new pistons have been fitted, the new cylinder head gasket must be the same type as the old one.

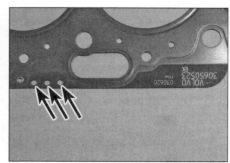

9.24 The holes (arrowed) along the edge of the cylinder head gasket indicate the thickness

9.26 Ensure the cylinder head gasket locates over the dowels in the block surface

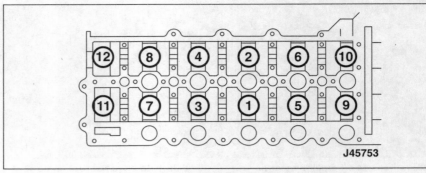

9.30 Cylinder head bolt tightening sequence

25 If new piston assemblies have been fitted as part of an engine overhaul, before purchasing the new cylinder head gasket, refer to Chapter 2B and measure the piston projection. Purchase a new gasket according to the results of the measurement.

26 Lay the new head gasket on the cylinder block, engaging it with the locating dowels **(see illustration)**. Ensure that the manufacturer's part number markings are facing upwards.

27 With the help of an assistant, place the cylinder head centrally on the cylinder block, ensuring that the locating dowels engage with the recesses in the cylinder head. Check that the head gasket is correctly seated before allowing the full weight of the cylinder head to rest on it.

28 Apply a light coating of oil to the threads and to the underside of the heads, of the new cylinder head bolts.

29 Carefully enter each bolt into its relevant

hole (*do not drop them in*) and screw in, by hand only, until finger-tight.

30 Working progressively and in the sequence shown, tighten the cylinder head bolts to their Stage 1 torque setting, using a torque wrench and socket. them slacken the bolts in sequence (Stage 2) and tighten them to the Stage 3 setting. Then working in the sequence shown tighten them to the Stage 4 setting **(see illustration)**.

31 Once all the bolts have been tightened to their Stage 4 settings, working again in the given sequence, angle-tighten the bolts through the specified Stage 5 angle, using a socket and extension bar **(see illustration)**. It is recommended that an angle-measuring gauge is used during this stage of the tightening, to ensure accuracy. If a gauge is not available, use paint to make alignment marks between the bolt head and cylinder head prior to tightening; the marks can then

be used to check the bolt has been rotated through the correct angle during tightening. Repeat the procedure, tightening the bolts to the Stage 6 angle.

32 The remainder of refitting is a reversal of removal, noting the following points:
a) *No retightening of the cylinder head bolts is required.*
b) *Tighten all fasteners to their specified torque where given.*
c) *Refill the cooling system and replenish the engine oil as described in Chapter 1.*

10 Camshafts, rocker arms and hydraulic tappets – removal, inspection and refitting

Removal

1 Remove the inlet camshaft sprocket as described in Section 5.

2 Remove the camshaft cover as described in Section 6.

3 Undo the screw securing the timing inner cover to the right-hand camshaft bearing cap **(see illustration)**.

4 Remove the vacuum pump (Chapter 9), and the fuel pump (Chapter 4A).

5 Undo the screws securing the left- and right-hand camshaft bearing/sealing caps **(see illustrations)**.

6 The camshaft bearing caps should be marked to indicate their position. If they are not, number them starting from the timing belt end **(see illustration)**. It is essential they are refitted to their original positions.

9.31 Use an angle-measuring gauge to accurately tighten the bolts

10.3 Inner timing cover screw

10.5a Undo the screws and remove the left-hand...

10.5b ...and right-hand bearing caps

10.6 The bearing caps should be numbered, starting from the timing belt end

7 Starting on the inlet camshaft, slacken each of the bearing cap screws one turn at a time until the camshaft is no longer under tension, then remove the screws and caps. The screws must be released gradually and evenly to prevent excess stress and possible damage to the camshaft. Repeat this procedure on the exhaust camshaft.

8 Lift out the camshafts, and discard the oil seal on the inlet camshaft.

9 Carefully lift the rocker arms and hydraulic tappets from the cylinder head. Lay them out on a clean, dry surface and, using paint, mark their positions in the cylinder head, eg, E1, E2 (exhaust 1, exhaust 2, etc).

Inspection

10 Unclip the hydraulic tappets from the rocker arms, and check for any signs of damage **(see illustration)**. Renew as necessary.

11 Spin the roller on each of the rocker arms and listen for any noise from the bearing **(see illustration)**. Renew as necessary.

12 Inspect the cam lobes and the camshaft bearing journals for scoring or other visible evidence of wear. Once the surface hardening of the lobes has been penetrated, wear will progress rapidly.

13 No specific bearing journal diameters or running clearances are given by Volvo for the camshafts. However, if there is a visual deterioration, then component renewal will be necessary.

Refitting

14 Clip each tappet onto the underside of their respective rocker arms.

15 Ensure the bores for the tappets in the cylinder head are clean and free of debris, then lubricate the tappets with clean engine oil, and lower them into their original positions. Check the ends of the rocker arms are correctly located over the valve stems **(see illustration)**.

16 Check to make sure the camshaft bearing positions in the cylinder head are clean, then lubricate them, and the rocker arm rollers, with clean engine oil.

17 Position the camshafts together, so the marks on the drive gears align, then lower the camshafts into position on the cylinder head **(see illustration)**. Lubricate the camshaft journals with clean engine oil.

18 Refit the camshaft bearing caps and screws into their original positions, and hand-tighten the screws evenly until the caps lie flat against the camshaft journals. Do not install the right- and left-hand bearing/sealing caps yet.

19 Tighten the bearing cap screws one turn at a time on both camshafts, until the bearing caps contact the cylinder head. It's essential the bearing caps are tightened down gradually and evenly, or damage to the camshaft may result. Finally, tighten the bearing cap screws to the specified torque.

20 Insert a camshaft locking pin (Volvo No

10.10 Unclip the tappets from the rocker arms

10.15 Ensure the end of the rocker arms are correctly located over the end of the valve stems

10.21 Apply sealant to the cylinder head/ bearing cap sealing surfaces

999 7007) though the hole in the cylinder head and into the hole in the exhaust camshaft drivegear. If necessary, rotate the camshaft slightly to enable the pin to be inserted using a large screwdriver in the camshaft end slots – do not turn the camshafts more than is absolutely necessary. If the Volvo pin is not available, a home-made equivalent can be fabricated (see Section 5).

21 Ensure the mating surfaces of the right- and left-hand camshaft bearing/sealing caps are clean and dry, then apply a light, even film of Volvo liquid sealant (Volvo No 11 61 059) to the mating surfaces **(see illustration)**. Ideally, use a short-haired roller.

22 Refit the right- and left-hand bearing/ sealing caps, and tighten the retaining screws to their specified torque.

23 Clean the oil seal seating in the bearing

10.11 Spin the roller and listen for any noise

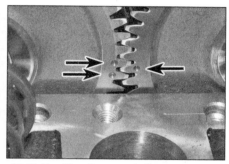

10.17 Position the camshafts together so the marks (arrowed) on the drive gears align

cap, then smear a little oil on the lips of the new camshaft oil seal. Wrap adhesive tape around the end of the camshaft, then fit the new oil seal and tap it into position carefully using a tubular bar or socket on the hard outer surface of the seal. Remove the tape on completion.

24 The remainder of refitting is a reversal of removal, noting the following points:

a) *Tighten all fasteners to the specified torque where given.*

b) *Wait a minimum of 30 minutes (or preferably, leave overnight) after fitting the hydraulic tappets before turning the engine over, to allow the tappets time to settle, otherwise the valve heads will strike the pistons.*

11 Flywheel/driveplate – removal, inspection and refitting

Removal

1 On manual transmission models, remove the gearbox (see Chapter 7A) and clutch (see Chapter 6).

2 On automatic transmission models, remove the automatic transmission as described in Chapter 7B.

3 Undo the bolts and move the engine speed sensor, complete with bracket, to one side **(see illustration)**.

4 Temporarily insert a bolt in the cylinder block, and use a wide-bladed screwdriver

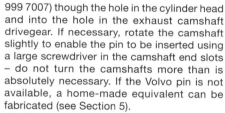

11.3 Undo the bolts and remove the engine speed sensor, complete with bracket

11.4 Ideally, make up a tool to lock the flywheel in place

11.8 Align the locating dowel in the crankshaft with the hole in the flywheel marled by the dimple (arrowed)

to hold the flywheel/driveplate, or make up a holding tool **(see illustration)**.

5 Slacken and remove the multi-spline bolts securing the flywheel/driveplate to the crankshaft, and lift the flywheel/driveplate from place – the flywheel's heavy! Discard the bolts, new ones must be fitted.

Inspection

6 Check the flywheel/driveplate for wear and damage. Examine the starter ring gear for excessive wear to the teeth. If the driveplate or ring gear are damaged, the complete driveplate must be renewed. The flywheel ring gear, however, may be renewed separately from the flywheel, but the work should be entrusted to a Volvo dealer. If the clutch friction face is discoloured or scored excessively, it may be possible to regrind it, but this work should also be entrusted to a Volvo dealer.

7 On models with a dual mass flywheel, check the radial play by turning the flywheel secondary mass one way until the spring begins to tension, then allow the flywheel to spring back – make an alignment mark between the primary and secondary masses. Now turn the flywheel in the opposite direction until the spring begins to tension – make another alignment mark between the two masses. The distance between the 2 marks must be less than 35 mm.

Refitting

8 Position the flywheel/driveplate against

the crankshaft, aligning the locating dowel with the corresponding hole in the flywheel/driveplate **(see illustration)**.

9 Insert the new bolts, and tighten them gradually and evenly, in a diagonal pattern to the Stage 1 torque setting, followed by the Stage 2 angle setting. Prevent the flywheel/driveplate from rotating using the same method as during removal.

10 The remainder of refitting is a reversal of removal.

12 Engine mountings – inspection and renewal

Inspection

1 If improved access is required, raise the front of the car and support it securely on axle stands then remove the undershield.

2 Check the mounting rubbers to see if they are cracked, hardened or separated from the metal at any point; renew the mounting if any such damage or deterioration is evident.

3 Check that all the mounting's fasteners are securely tightened; use a torque wrench to check if possible.

4 Using a large screwdriver or a crowbar, check for wear in the mounting by carefully levering against it to check for free play. Where this is not possible, enlist the aid of an assistant to move the engine/transmission back-and-forth, or from side-to-side, while

you watch the mounting. While some free play is to be expected even from new components, excessive wear should be obvious. If excessive free play is found, check first that the fasteners are correctly secured, then renew any worn components as described below.

Renewal – XC60

Right-hand mounting

5 Pull the plastic cover on the engine straight upwards and remove it from the engine compartment **(see illustration)**.

6 Remove the upper torque rod as described below.

7 Place a trolley jack under the right-hand end of the engine sump and take the weight. Position a block of wood between the jack head and sump to prevent damage to the casing.

8 Undo the 4 upper mounting bolts and the 3 lower mounting bolts **(see illustrations)**. The mounting can now be removed.

9 Refitting is a reversal of removal, tightening the mounting bolts to the correct torque.

Left-hand mounting

10 Pull the plastic cover on the engine straight upwards and remove it from the engine compartment.

11 Remove the air cleaner housing as described in Chapter 4A.

12 Remove the battery and battery tray as described in Chapter 5.

13 Move the fusebox to one side by undoing

12.5 Pull the plastic engine cover straight up from its mountings

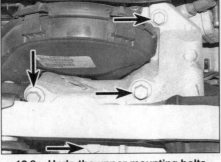

12.8a Undo the upper mounting bolts (arrowed)...

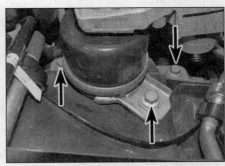

12.8b ...and the lower mounting bolts

12.13 Move the fusebox to one side

12.15a Undo the upper mounting bolts...

12.15b ...and the lower mounting bolts

the retaining bolt, releasing the clip at the base, and sliding out towards the engine **(see illustration)**.

14 Place a trolley jack under the right-hand end of the engine sump and take the weight. Position a block of wood between the jack head and sump to prevent damage to the casing.

15 Undo the 4 large nuts and the 2 small bolts on top of the mounting, then undo the 2 lower bolts **(see illustrations)**. The mounting can now be removed.

16 Refitting is a reversal of removal, tightening the mounting bolts to the correct torque.

Upper torque rod

17 Undo the bolt securing the coolant expansion tank and move the tank to one side **(see illustrations)**.

18 Undo the torque rod mounting bolt at the suspension strut turret, and at the engine mounting bracket, and manoeuvre the torque rod from place **(see illustrations)**.

19 Position the torque rod and tighten the new fasteners to the correct torque.

20 Refit the coolant expansion tank.

Lower torque rod

21 Jack up the front of the vehicle and support it securely on axle stands (see *Jacking and vehicle support*).

22 Undo the screws and remove the engine undershield.

23 Undo the bolts and manoeuvre the torque rod from place **(see illustration)**.

24 Position the torque rod and tighten the new fasteners to the correct torque.

25 Refit the undershield and lower the vehicle to the ground.

Renewal – XC90

Note: *Apart from the upper torque rod/ mounting all other mountings are attached to the subframe. To replace any of these the engine must be raised on a suitable jack, using a block of wood to spread the load on the engine sump. Failure to spread the load will damage the sump.*

26 Jack up and support the front of the vehicle -see *Jacking and vehicle support* in the reference section. Remove the engine undershield.

12.17a Undo the screw securing the coolant expansion tank...

Upper torque rod

27 Remove the engine cover.

28 Remove the strut brace by unbolting it at both strut towers and at the upper mounting.

12.18a Undo the mounting bolt at the suspension strut turret...

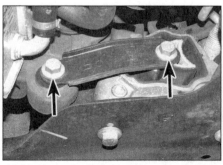

12.23 Undo the lower torque rod securing bolts (arrowed)

12.17b ...and move it to one side

29 Unbolt and remove the mounting from the engine **(see illustration)**.

30 Unbolt and remove the mountings from the strut towers **(see illustration)**.

12.18b ...and at the engine mounting bracket

12.29 The upper mounting

12.30 The strut tower mounting

12.36 The front engine mount

12.39 The rear torque rod

12.44 The right-hand mounting

31 Refitting is a reversal of removal. Tighten the bolts to the specified torque.

Front mounting

32 Remove the strut brace from the top of the engine.
33 Remove the skid pan/sump guard and then support the engine with a suitable jack.
34 Where fitted, unbolt the wiring loom from the mounting and prise free the vacuum hose.
35 Remove the lower mounting bolt – accessed through the subframe or the upper mounting nut.
36 Remove the upper mounting bolts and remove the mounting from the vehicle **(see illustration)**.
37 Refitting is a reversal of removal. Tighten the bolts to the specified torque.

Rear torque rod

38 Remove the strut brace from the top of the engine.

39 Unbolt and remove the torque rod **(see illustration)**. If necessary separate the link arm and remove it separately.
40 Refitting is a reversal of removal. Tighten the bolts to the specified torque.

Right-hand mounting

41 Remove the strut brace from the top of the engine.
42 Remove the right-hand front wheel and then partially remove the wing liner.
43 Removal of the mounting requires the engine to be raised to a reasonable height. To enable this remove the subframe mounting bolt from the front mounting and 1 of the bolts from the link arm on the rear torque rod.
44 Unbolt and remove the mounting **(see illustration)**.
45 Refitting is a reversal of removal. Tighten the bolts to the specified torque.

13 Sump – removal, inspection and refitting

Removal

1 Jack up the front of the vehicle and support it securely on axle stands (see *Jacking and vehicle support*).
2 Undo the screws and remove the engine undershield.
3 Drain the engine oil as described in Chapter 1.
4 Remove the auxiliary drivebelt as described in Chapter 1.
5 Undo the 3 bolts and move the air conditioning compressor to one side. Use wire to secure the compressor to a suitable part of the bodywork or chassis.
6 Undo the bolt/nut and pull the oil level dipstick guide tube from the sump.
7 Disconnect the wiring plug, undo the 3 bolts, and remove the oil level sensor from the sump.
8 The oil cooler (where fitted) is secured to the sump by four bolts. Undo the bolts and pull the cooler to the rear. Be prepared for oil spillage.
9 Remove the charge air pipe below the sump. Undo the clips at each end and undo the bolt securing the mounting bracket.
10 Slacken the bolts securing the sump, and remove them all, apart from one bolt in each corner.
11 Gently tap the sides and ends of the sump until the joint between the engine and sump releases. Undo the remaining bolts and remove the sump. Discard the O-rings at the right-hand end/front edge of the sump, new ones must be fitted.

Refitting

12 Clean the contact faces of the sump and block.
13 Apply a thin and even layer of Volvo sealant (No 116 1771) to the sump mating face, and position the new O-ring seals on the engine block face **(see illustrations)**. The sump must be refitted within 5 minutes of applying the sealant.
14 Refit the sump casing and refit the retaining bolts, finger-finger tight only at this stage. Note that the three longest bolts are

13.13a Apply a thin and even layer of Volvo sealant...

13.13b ...and renew the O-rings (arrowed)

13.14 The four slightly shorter bolts are fitted at the transmission end

14.2 Undo the four oil pump bolts (arrowed)

14.5 Undo the two oil pump cover screws (arrowed)

14.6a Remove the plunger...

fitted to the oil pump end, and the four slightly shorter bolts are fitted at the transmission end **(see illustration)**.

15 Refit the sump-to-transmission bolts and tighten them to the specified torque.

16 Starting from the transmission end, tighten the sump-to-engine bolts in pairs to the specified torque.

17 The remainder of refitting is a reversal of refitting, noting the following points:

   a) *Renew the oil cooler-to-sump O-ring seals.*
   b) *Tighten all fasteners to their specified torque where given.*
   c) *Fit a new engine oil filter, and refill the engine with oil as described in Chapter 1.*
   d) *Volvo recommend waiting a minimum of 2 hours before starting the engine to allow the sealant to cure fully.*

14 Oil pump – removal, inspection and refitting

Removal

1 Remove the crankshaft right-hand oil seal as described in Section 8.

2 Undo the four bolts securing the oil pump to the front of the cylinder block **(see illustration)**.

14.6b ...spring...

3 Carefully withdraw the pump assembly by levering behind the upper and lower parting lugs using a screwdriver. Remove the pump and recover the gasket.

4 Thoroughly clean the pump and cylinder block mating faces and remove all traces of old gasket. Discard the O-ring seal, a new one must be fitted.

Inspection

5 Undo the two pump cover retaining Allen screws whilst holding the two halves of the pump together, then remove the cover. Be prepared for the ejection of the pressure relief valve spring **(see illustration)**.

6 Note their fitted positions, then remove the

14.6c ...and rotors

pressure relief valve spring, plunger and pump rotors **(see illustrations)**.

7 If not already done, lever out the crankshaft oil seal.

8 Clean all the components thoroughly, then inspect the rotors, body and cover for damage or signs of wear.

9 At the time of writing, no specifications concerning the overhaul or inspection of the pump were available, and it would appear that no pump internal parts are available separately.

10 Refit the inner rotor with the marks facing the pump body **(see illustration)**.

11 Refit the outer rotor to the body, ensuring the mark on the rotor faces the cylinder block **(see illustration)**.

14.10 Fit the inner rotor with the marks (arrowed) facing the pump body...

14.11 ...and the outer rotor with the mark (arrowed) facing the cylinder block

15.3 Undo the oil cooler bolts (arrowed)

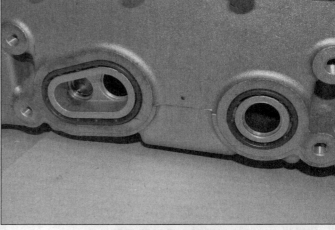

15.4 Oil cooler O-rings

12 Refit the pressure relief valve spring and plunger, and fit the cover, tightening the retaining screws securely.

Refitting

13 Using a new gasket and O-ring, fit the pump to the block. Use the pump retaining bolts as guides, and draw the pump into place with the crankshaft pulley nut and spacers. With the pump seated, tighten the retaining bolts diagonally to the specified torque.
14 Fit a new crankshaft right-hand oil seal as described in Section 8.

15 Oil cooler – removal and refitting

Removal

1 Drain the engine oil and coolant as described in Chapter 1.
2 Release the hose clamp and disconnect the coolant hoses from the cooler, located on the rear face of the sump.
3 Undo the bolts securing the cooler to the

sump, and recover the O-ring seals as the cooler is withdrawn. Be prepared for fluid spillage **(see illustration)**.

Refitting

4 Check the mating faces of the sump and oil cooler are clean, then refit the cooler using new O-ring seals. Tighten the retaining bolts securely **(see illustration)**.
5 Reconnect the coolant hoses and secure them with new clips where necessary.
6 Refill the engine oil and cooling systems as described in Chapter 1.

Chapter 2 Part B:
Engine removal and overhaul procedures

Contents

Degrees of difficulty

Easy, suitable for novice with little experience	**Fairly easy,** suitable for beginner with some experience	**Fairly difficult,** suitable for competent DIY mechanic	**Difficult,** suitable for experienced DIY mechanic	**Very difficult,** suitable for expert DIY or professional

Specifications

Cylinder head
Warp limit – maximum acceptable for use:
  Lengthways . . . . 0.05 mm
  Across. . . . . 0.02 mm
Height. . . . . 149.4 ± 0.15 mm

Inlet valves
Head diameter . . . . 28.0 ± 0.01 mm
Stem diameter . . . . 5.975 ± 0.015 mm
Length . . . . 98.1 ± 0.07 mm
Valve seat angle . . . . 45° ± 0.5°

Exhaust valves
Head diameter . . . . 26.2 ± 0.1 mm
Stem diameter . . . . 5.975 ± 0.015 mm
Length . . . . 97.7 ± 0.07 mm
Valve seat angle . . . . 45.0° ± 0.5°

Valve guides
Valve stem-to-guide clearance. . . . . 0.050 to 0.070 mm

Pistons
Piston-to-bore clearance . . . . 0.010 to 0.030 mm

Piston rings
Clearance in groove:
  Top compression . . . . 0.120 to 0.160 mm
  Second compression . . . . 0.070 to 0.110 mm
  Oil control . . . . 0.030 to 0.070 mm
End gap (measured in cylinder):
  Compression rings . . . . 0.20 to 0.40 mm
  Oil control . . . . 0.25 to 0.50 mm

Crankshaft
Endfloat . . . . 0.08 to 0.19 mm

Torque wrench settings
Refer to Chapter 2, Part A.

1 General information

Included in this Chapter are details of removing the engine/transmission from the car and general overhaul procedures for the cylinder head, cylinder block and all other engine internal components.

The information ranges from advice concerning preparation for an overhaul and the purchase of parts, to detailed step-by-step procedures covering removal, inspection, renovation and refitting of engine internal components.

After Section 5, all instructions are based on the assumption that the engine has been removed from the car. For information concerning engine in-car repair, as well as removal and installation of those external components necessary for full overhaul, refer to Chapter 2A and to Section 4. Ignore any preliminary dismantling operations described in Part A that are no longer relevant once the engine has been removed from the car.

2 Engine and transmission removal – preparation and precautions

If you have decided that an engine must be removed for overhaul or major repair work, several preliminary steps should be taken.

Locating a suitable place to work is extremely important. Adequate work space, along with storage space for the car, will be needed. If a workshop or garage is not available, at the very least, a flat, level, clean work surface is required.

If possible, clear some shelving close to the work area, and use it to store the engine components and ancillaries as they are removed and dismantled. In this manner, the components stand a better chance of staying clean and undamaged during the overhaul. Laying out components in groups together with their fixing bolts, screws, etc, will save time and avoid confusion when the engine is refitted.

Clean the engine compartment and engine/transmission before beginning the removal procedure; this will help visibility and help to keep tools clean.

The help of an assistant should be available; there are certain instances when one person cannot safely perform all of the operations required to remove the engine from the vehicle. Safety is of primary importance, considering the potential hazards involved in this kind of operation. A second person should always be in attendance to offer help in an emergency. If this is the first time you have removed an engine, advice and aid from someone more experienced would also be beneficial.

Plan the operation ahead of time. Before starting work, obtain (or arrange for the hire of) all of the tools and equipment you will need. Access to the following items will allow the task of removing and refitting the engine/transmission to be completed safely and with relative ease: an engine hoist – rated in excess of the combined weight of the engine/transmission, a heavy-duty trolley jack, complete sets of spanners and sockets as described at the rear this manual, wooden blocks, and plenty of rags and cleaning solvent for mopping-up spilled oil, coolant and fuel. A selection of different-sized plastic storage bins will also prove useful for keeping dismantled components grouped together. If any of the equipment must be hired, make sure that you arrange for it in advance, and perform all of the operations possible without it beforehand; this may save you time and money.

Plan on the vehicle being out of use for quite a while, especially if you intend to carry out an engine overhaul. Read through the whole of this Section and work out a strategy based on your own experience and the tools, time and workspace available to you. Some of the overhaul processes may have to be carried out by a Volvo dealer or an engineering works – these establishments often have busy schedules, so it would be prudent to consult them before removing or dismantling the engine, to get an idea of the amount of time required to carry out the work.

When removing the engine from the vehicle, be methodical about the disconnection of external components. Labelling cables and hoses as they removed will greatly assist the refitting process.

Always be extremely careful when lifting the engine/transmission assembly from the engine bay. Serious injury can result from careless actions. If help is required, it is better to wait until it is available rather than risk personal injury and/or damage to components by continuing alone. By planning ahead and taking your time, a job of this nature, although major, can be accomplished successfully and without incident.

On all models covered by this manual, the engine and transmission are removed as a complete assembly, upwards and out of the engine bay. The engine and transmission are then separated with the assembly on the bench.

3 Engine and transmission – removal, separation and refitting

Removal – all models

1 Open the bonnet and remove the engine cover.

2 Remove the battery and battery tray as described in Chapter 5 (XC60 only).

3 Remove the air cleaner assembly, and all air ducting, including turbocharger inlet (where applicable) with reference to the relevant part of Chapter 4A.

4 Jack up and support the front of the vehicle (see *Jacking and vehicle support* in the reference section).

5 Refer to the relevant chapters and:
a) *Drain the cooling system (Chapter 1).*
b) *If the engine is going to be dismantled, drain the engine oil (Chapter 1).*
c) *Remove the auxiliary drivebelt and tensioner (Chapter 1).*
d) *Remove the catalytic converter and particulate filter (Chapter 4B).*
e) *Remove the cooling fan (Chapter 3).*
f) *Remove the upper and lower torque rods (Chapter 2A).*
g) *Remove the alternator (Chapter 5).*
h) *Remove the propeller shaft (AWD models) (Chapter 8B).*
i) *With reference to Chapter 8A remove both front driveshafts – not required on XC90 models if the subframe is removed with the engine.*

6 Disconnect the transmission selector cables as described in Chapter 7A or 7B.

7 Move the engine bay fusebox (central electrical unit) to one side and undo the earth cables beneath the air cleaner housing **(see illustration)**.

3.7 Disconnect the earth cables beneath the air cleaner housing

3.8a Disconnect all relevant hoses...

3.8b ...and brackets

8 Disconnect all relevant wiring plugs, air pipes, and coolant hoses **(see illustrations)**.
9 On automatic transmission models, disconnect the transmission oil cooler fluid pipes at the gearbox **(see illustration)**.
10 On manual transmission models disconnect the clutch slave cylinder supply line as described in Chapter 6.
11 Remove the right-hand side wheel arch liner and disconnect the wiring plug **(see illustration)**.
12 Undo the bolts securing the power steering pump to the mounting bracket and secure it the front of the subframe using cable-ties.
13 Disconnect the air conditioning compressor wiring plug, undo the retaining bolts, and secure the compressor to a suitable point on the front panel or subframe using cable-ties. Take care not to damage the air conditioning pipes. There is no need to discharge the air conditioning refrigerant, unless the engine is to be removed out through the front of the engine bay (XC60 only).

XC60 models

Note: *Volvo suggest lifting the combined engine and transmission from the vehicle, however we found this impossible. Instead we removed the complete front end of the vehicle (radiator, condenser, intercooler and front crossmember) and pulled the engine and gearbox forward to remove.*
14 If not already done so, on models fitted with conventional power steering, remove the PAS pump from the side of the engine. Remove the support bracket from the pipe at the timing belt (right-hand) end of the engine. Move the pipe to one side.
15 Attach a lifting chain/strap to the transport brackets on the top of the engine, then manoeuvre an engine hoist/crane into position and take the weight of the engine.
16 Make a final check to ensure all hoses, pipes and electrical wiring between the engine/transmission and vehicle have been disconnected.
17 Undo the bolts securing the engine mountings as described in Chapter 2A, then lift and manoeuvre the engine/transmission assembly from the engine compartment. The aid of an assistant will be essential to support and manoeuvre the assembly without damaging the vehicle bodywork, etc.

XC90 models

Note: *The engine and transmission are removed from below on XC90 models, either complete with the front subframe or by removing the subframe first. To enable this the front of the vehicle must be raised sufficiently to allow the engine to be removed from beneath the vehicle.*
18 Where fitted disconnect the auxiliary heater wiring plug. Anticipating some spillage release the fuel pipes and coolant pipes from the heater.
19 Drill out the rivets from the front edge of the wing liner.
20 Remove the stabilizer bar from the front strut towers.

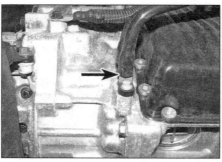

3.9 Automatic transmission oil cooler pipes (XC90 shown)

21 Lift of the PAS reservoir and expansion tank. Secure both to the top of the engine.
22 Disconnect the track rod end from the swivel hub on both sides.
23 Set the steering in the straight ahead position and measure the distance from the track rod end locking nut to a suitable fixed point on the steering rack. Remove the ignition key and then remove the pinch bolt from the steering column. Slide the column off the steering rack.
24 Once the steering column has been released **do not** allow the steering column to rotate as this will damage the SRS clock spring.
25 Install the engine crane, remembering to raise the jib first (as the engine is to be lowered, not lifted from the engine bay) **(see illustration)**.
26 Remove the bolts from the sub frame and then lower the sub frame slightly, so that the track control arms can be release from the bottom ball joints.
27 With the track control arms now free from the front hubs, hold the appropriate driveshaft outer CV joint and pull the shaft from the front hub.
28 Rest the driveshafts on the track control arms.
29 Make a final check to ensure all hoses, pipes and electrical wiring between the engine/transmission and vehicle have been disconnected.
30 Lower the engine, transmission and subframe from the vehicle.
31 Separate the engine and transmission from the subframe.

Separation

32 Remove the starter motor.
33 On AWD (All wheel Drive) models remove the support bracket from the transfer box and then unbolt and remove the transfer box.

Manual transmission models

34 Remove the bolts securing the transmission to the engine. Note the position of the bolts. They are different lengths.
35 With the aid of an assistant, draw the transmission off the engine. Once it is clear of the dowels, do not allow it to hang on the input shaft.

3.11 Disconnect the wiring plug (arrowed) behind the right-hand front wheel arch liner

Automatic transmission models

36 Rotate the crankshaft, using a socket on the sprocket nut, until one of the torque converter-to-driveplate retaining bolts becomes accessible through the opening on the rear facing side of the engine. Working through the opening, undo the bolt using a TX50 socket. Rotate the crankshaft as necessary and remove the remaining bolts in the same way. Note that new bolts will be required for refitting.
37 Remove the bolts securing the transmission to the engine. Note the position of the bolts. They are different lengths.
38 With the aid of an assistant, draw the transmission squarely off the engine dowels making sure that the torque converter remains in position on the transmission. Use the access hole in the transmission housing to hold the converter in place.

Refitting

Manual transmission models

39 Make sure that the clutch is correctly centred and that the clutch release components are fitted to the bellhousing. Do not apply any grease to the transmission input shaft, the guide sleeve, or the release bearing itself, as these components have a friction-reducing coating which does not require lubrication.
40 Manoeuvre the transmission squarely into position, and engage it with the engine dowels. Refit the bolts securing the transmission to the engine, and tighten them to the specified torque. Refit the starter motor.

3.25 Install the engine crane

5.4a Compress the valve spring with a suitable valve spring compressor

5.4b Extract the collets and release the spring compressor

Automatic transmission models

41 Before refitting the transmission, flush out the fluid cooler with fresh transmission fluid. To do this, attach a hose to the upper union, pour the specified ATF through the hose and collect it in a container positioned beneath the return hose (see *Lubricants and fluids*).

42 Clean the contact surfaces on the torque converter and driveplate, and the transmission and engine mating faces. Lightly lubricate the torque converter guide projection and the engine/transmission locating dowels with grease.

43 Manoeuvre the transmission squarely into position, and engage it with the engine dowels. Refit the bolts securing the transmission to the engine and tighten lightly first in a diagonal sequence, then again to the specified torque.

44 Attach the torque converter to the driveplate using new bolts. Rotate the crankshaft for access to the bolts as was done for removal, then rotate the torque converter by means of the access hole in the transmission housing. Fit and tighten all the bolts hand-tight first, then tighten again to the specified torque.

All models

45 The remainder of refitting is essentially a reversal of removal, noting the following points:

a) Tighten all fastenings to the specified torque and, where applicable, torque angle. Refer to the relevant Chapters of this manual for torque wrench settings not directly related to the engine.

b) Refill the engine with lubricant and coolant as necessary as described in Chapter 1.

c) Refer to Section 16 before starting the engine.

4 Engine overhaul – preliminary information

It is much easier to dismantle and work on the engine if it is mounted on a portable engine stand. These stands can often be hired from a tool hire shop. Before the engine is mounted on a stand, the flywheel/driveplate should be removed so that the stand bolts

can be tightened into the end of the cylinder block/crankcase.

If a stand is not available, it is possible to dismantle the engine with it suitably supported on a sturdy, workbench or on the floor. Be careful not to tip or drop the engine when working without a stand.

If you intend to obtain a reconditioned engine, all ancillaries must be removed first, to be transferred to the new engine (just as they will if you are doing a complete engine overhaul yourself). These components include the following:

a) Engine mountings and brackets (Chapter 2A).

b) Alternator including accessories mounting bracket (Chapter 5).

c) Starter motor (Chapter 5).

d) The fuel pump and common rail (Chapter 4A).

e) Exhaust manifold, with turbocharger if fitted (Chapter 4A).

f) Inlet manifold with fuel injection components (Chapter 4A).

g) All electrical switches, actuators and sensors, and the engine wiring harness (Chapter 12).

h) Coolant pump, thermostat, hoses, and distribution pipe (Chapter 3).

i) Clutch components – manual transmission models (Chapter 6).

j) Flywheel/driveplate(Chapter 2A).

k) Oil filter (Chapter 1).

l) Dipstick, tube and bracket.

Note: *When removing the external components from the engine, pay close attention to details that may be helpful or important during*

5.5a Remove the spring retainer...

refitting. Note the fitting positions of gaskets, seals, washers, bolts and other small items.

If you are obtaining a 'short' engine (cylinder block/crankcase, crankshaft, pistons and connecting rods all assembled), then the cylinder head, timing belt (together with tensioner, tensioner and idler pulleys and covers) and auxiliary drivebelt tensioner will have to be removed also.

If a complete overhaul is planned, the engine can be dismantled in the order given below:

a) Inlet and exhaust manifolds and turbocharger (where applicable).

b) Timing belt, sprockets, tensioner, pulleys and covers.

c) Cylinder head.

d) Oil pump.

e) Flywheel/driveplate.

f) Sump.

g) Oil pick-up pipe.

h) Intermediate section.

i) Pistons/connecting rods.

j) Crankshaft.

5 Cylinder head – dismantling, cleaning, inspection and reassembly

Note: *New and reconditioned cylinder heads are available from the manufacturer and from engine overhaul specialists. Specialist tools are required for the dismantling and inspection procedures, and new components may not be readily available. It may, therefore, be more practical and economical for the home mechanic to purchase a reconditioned head rather than dismantle, inspect and recondition the original head.*

Dismantling

1 Remove the cylinder head as described in Part A of this Chapter.

2 According to components still fitted, remove the thermostat housing (Chapter 3) and any other unions, pipes, sensors or brackets as necessary. Lift the swirl valve assembly from the top of the cylinder head.

3 Tap each valve spring smartly, using a light hammer and drift, to free the spring and associated items. **Do not** strike the head of the valve directly.

4 Fit a deep-reach type valve spring compressor to each valve in turn, and compress each spring until the collets are exposed. Lift out the collets; a small screwdriver, a magnet or a pair of tweezers may be useful **(see illustrations)**. Carefully release the spring compressor and remove it.

5 Remove the valve spring upper seat and the valve spring **(see illustrations)**. Pull the valve out of its guide.

6 Pull off the valve stem oil seal with a pair of long-nosed pliers. It may be necessary to use a tool such as a pair of electrician's wire strippers, the 'legs' of which will engage under the seal, if the seal is tight **(see illustration)**.

7 Recover the valve spring lower seat **(see illustration)**. If there is much carbon build-up round the outside of the valve guide, this will have to be scraped off before the seat can be removed.

8 It is essential that each valve is stored together with its collets, spring and seats. The valves should also be kept in their correct sequence, unless they are so badly worn or burnt that they are to be renewed. If they are going to be kept and used again, place each valve assembly in a labelled polythene bag or similar container **(see illustration)**.

9 Continue removing all the remaining valves in the same way.

Cleaning

10 Thoroughly clean all traces of old gasket material and sealing compound from the cylinder head upper and lower mating surfaces. Use a suitable liquid gasket dissolving agent together with a soft putty knife; do not use a metal scraper, or the faces will be damaged. Note that the gasket surface cannot be refaced.

11 Remove the carbon from the combustion chambers and ports, then clean all traces of oil and other deposits from the cylinder head, paying particular attention to the bearing journals, tappet bores, valve guides and oilways.

12 Wash the head thoroughly with paraffin or a suitable solvent. Take plenty of time and do a thorough job. Be sure to clean all oil holes and galleries very thoroughly, dry the head completely and coat all machined surfaces with light oil.

13 Scrape off any heavy carbon deposits that may have formed on the valves, then use a power-operated wire brush to remove deposits from the valve heads and stems.

Inspection

Note: *Be sure to perform all the following inspection procedures before concluding that the services of an engineering works are required. Make a list of all items that require attention.*

Cylinder head

14 Inspect the head very carefully for cracks, evidence of coolant leakage, and other damage. If cracks are found, a new cylinder head should be obtained.

15 Use a straight-edge and feeler blade to check that the cylinder head gasket surface is not distorted **(see illustration)**.

16 Examine the valve seats in each of the combustion chambers. If they are severely pitted, cracked or burned, then they will need to be renewed or recut by an engine overhaul specialist. If they are only slightly pitted, this can be removed by grinding-in the valve heads and seats with fine valve-grinding compound, as described below.

17 If the valve guides appear worn, indicated by a side-to-side motion of the valve, new

5.5b ...followed by the valve spring

5.7 Remove the spring seat

guides must be fitted. Verify this by mounting a dial gauge on the cylinder head, and check the side-to-side rock with the valve lifted clear of its seat **(see illustration)**. Measure the diameter of the existing valve stems (see below) and the bore of the guides, renew the valves or guides as necessary. The renewal of valve guides should be carried out by an engine overhaul specialist.

18 If the valve seats are to be recut, this must be done *only after* the guides have been renewed.

19 The threaded holes in the cylinder head must be clean to ensure accurate torque readings when tightening fixings during reassembly. Carefully run the correct size tap (which can be determined from the size of the relevant bolt which fits in the hole) into each of the holes to remove rust, corrosion, thread sealant or other contamination, and

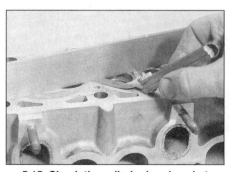

5.15 Check the cylinder head gasket surface for distortion

5.6 Pull out the valve stem oil seal with a pair of long-nosed pliers

5.8 Keep groups of components together in labelled bags or boxes

to restore damaged threads. If possible, use compressed air to clear the holes of debris produced by this operation. Do not forget to clean the threads of all bolts and nuts as well.

20 Any threads which cannot be restored in this way can often be reclaimed by the use of thread inserts. If any threaded holes are damaged, consult your dealer or engine overhaul specialist and have them install any thread inserts where necessary.

Valves

21 Examine the head of each valve for pitting, burning, cracks and general wear, and check the valve stem for scoring and wear ridges. Rotate the valve, and check for any obvious indication that it is bent. Look for pits and excessive wear on the tip of each valve stem. Renew any valve that shows any such signs of wear or damage.

22 If the valve appears satisfactory at this

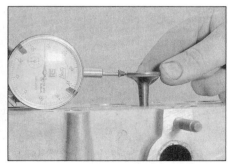

5.17 Measure the maximum deflection of the valve in its guide using a dial gauge

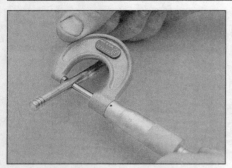

5.22 Measure the valve stem diameter with a micrometer

5.25 Grinding-in a valve

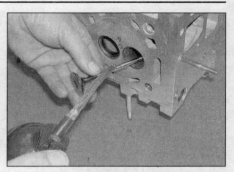

5.31 Lubricate the stem of the valve and insert it into the guide

stage, measure the valve stem diameter at several points, using a micrometer **(see illustration)**. Any significant difference in the readings obtained indicates wear of the valve stem. Should any of these conditions be apparent, the valve(s) must be renewed.

23 If the valves are in satisfactory condition, they should be ground (lapped) into their respective seats, to ensure a smooth gas-tight seal. If the seat is only lightly pitted, or if it has been recut, fine grinding compound *only* should be used to produce the required finish. Coarse valve-grinding compound should *not* be used unless a seat is badly burned or deeply pitted; if this is the case, the cylinder head and valves should be inspected by an expert, to decide whether seat recutting, or even the renewal of the valve or seat insert, is required.

24 Valve grinding is carried out as follows. Place the cylinder head upside-down on a bench, with a block of wood at each end to give clearance for the valve stems.

25 Smear a trace of (the appropriate grade) valve-grinding compound on the seat face, and press a suction grinding tool onto the valve head. With a semi-rotary action, grind the valve head to its seat, lifting the valve occasionally to redistribute the grinding compound. A light spring placed under the valve head will greatly ease this operation **(see illustration)**.

26 If coarse grinding compound is being used, work only until a dull, matt even surface is produced on both the valve seat and the valve, then wipe off the used compound, and repeat the process with fine compound. When

a smooth unbroken ring of light grey matt finish is produced on both the valve and seat, the grinding operation is complete. *Do not* grind in the valves any further than absolutely necessary, or the seat will be prematurely sunk into the cylinder head.

27 When all the valves have been ground-in, carefully wash off *all* traces of grinding compound, using paraffin or a suitable solvent, before reassembly of the cylinder head.

Valve components

28 Examine the valve springs for signs of damage and discoloration, and also measure their free length by comparing each of the existing springs with a new component.

29 Stand each spring on a flat surface, and check it for squareness. If any of the springs are damaged, distorted, or have lost their tension, obtain a complete set of new springs. It is normal to fit new springs as a matter of course if a major overhaul is being carried out.

30 Renew the valve stem oil seals regardless of their apparent condition.

Reassembly

31 Oil the stem of one valve and insert it into its guide then fit the spring lower seat **(see illustration)**.

32 The new valve stem oil seals should be supplied with a plastic fitting sleeve to protect the seal when it is fitted over the valve. If not, wrap a thin piece of polythene around the valve stem allowing it to extend about 10 mm above the end of the valve stem.

33 With the fitting sleeve, or polythene in

place around the valve, fit the valve stem oil seal, pushing it onto the valve guide as far as it will go with a suitable socket or piece of tube. Once the seal is seated, remove the protective sleeve or polythene.

34 Fit the valve spring and upper seat. Compress the spring and fit the two collets in the recesses in the valve stem. Carefully release the compressor.

35 Cover the valve stem with a cloth and tap it smartly with a light hammer to verify that the collets are properly seated.

36 Repeat these procedures on all the other valves.

37 Refit the remainder of the disturbed components then refit the cylinder head as described in Part A of this Chapter.

6 Intermediate section/ main bearing caps – removal

1 If not already done, drain the engine oil then remove the oil filter, referring to Chapter 1 if necessary.

2 Remove the oil pump as described in Part A of this Chapter.

3 On models with an oil cooler mounted on the rear face of the sump, remove the four retaining bolts and take off the cooler, if possible without disconnecting the coolant pipes **(see illustration)**.

4 Undo the bolts securing the sump to the intermediate section, noting the different bolt lengths and their locations.

5 Carefully tap the sump free using a rubber or hide mallet. Recover the O-ring seals.

6 Undo the mounting bracket bolt and remove the oil pick-up pipe **(see illustration)**. Recover the O-ring seal on the end of the pipe.

7 Remove the pistons and connecting rods as described in Section 7.

8 Undo all the M7 bolts securing the intermediate section to the cylinder block, working from the outside in. With all the M7 bolts removed, undo the M8, then the M10 bolts in the same order.

9 Carefully tap the intermediate section free using a rubber or hide mallet. Lift off the intermediate section complete with crankshaft lower main bearing shells. If any of the shells have stayed on the crankshaft, transfer them

6.3 Oil cooler mounting bolts (arrowed)

6.6 Undo the oil pick-up bracket bolt (arrowed)

to their correct locations in the intermediate section. Do not rotate the crankshaft with the intermediate section removed.

10 Remove the crankshaft left-hand oil seal.

7 Pistons and connecting rods
– removal and inspection

Removal

1 Remove the cylinder head, sump oil pump and flywheel/driveplate as described in Part A of this Chapter. Remove the intermediate section, as described in Section 6.

2 Feel inside the tops of the bores for a pronounced wear ridge. Some experts recommend that such a ridge be removed (with a scraper or ridge reamer) before attempting to remove the pistons. However, a ridge big enough to damage the pistons and/or piston rings will almost certainly mean that a rebore and new pistons/rings are needed anyway.

3 Check that there are identification numbers or marks on each connecting rod and cap; paint or punch suitable marks if necessary, so that each rod can be refitted in the same position and the same way round **(see illustration)**. Note their positions, eg, markings on the exhaust side, etc.

4 Remove the two connecting rod bolts. Tap the cap with a soft-faced hammer to free it. Remove the cap and lower bearing shell. Note that new bolts will be needed for reassembly. New shells should always be fitted.

5 Push the connecting rod and piston up and out of the bore. Recover the other half bearing shell if it is loose.

6 Refit the cap to the connecting rod, the correct way round, so that they do not get mixed up. Note that on some engines, the surface between the cap and rod is not machined, but fractured. Take great care not to damage or mark the fractured surfaces otherwise the cap will not fit properly with the shell, and new connecting rods will be required.

7 Check to see if there is an arrow on the top of the piston which should be pointing toward the timing belt end of the engine. If no arrow can be seen, make a suitable direction mark yourself.

8 Repeat the operations on the remaining connecting rods and pistons.

Inspection

9 Before the inspection process can be carried out, the piston/connecting rod assemblies must be cleaned, and the original piston rings removed from the pistons.

10 Carefully expand the old rings and remove them from the top of the pistons. The use of two or three old feeler blades will be helpful in preventing the rings dropping into empty grooves **(see illustration)**. Be careful not to scratch the pistons with the ends of the ring. The rings are brittle and will snap if they are

7.3 Connecting rod and big-end bearing cap identification marks

spread too far. They are also very sharp – protect your hands and fingers.

11 Scrape all traces of carbon from the top of the piston. A hand-held wire brush (or a piece of fine emery cloth) can be used, once the majority of the deposits have been scraped away.

12 Remove the carbon from the ring grooves in the piston, using an old ring. Break the ring in half to do this (be careful not to cut your fingers – piston rings are sharp). Be careful to remove only the carbon deposits – do not remove any metal, and do not nick or scratch the sides of the ring grooves.

13 Once the deposits have been removed, clean the piston/rod assemblies with paraffin or a suitable solvent, and dry thoroughly. Make sure the oil return holes in the ring grooves, are clear.

14 If the pistons and cylinder bores are not damaged or worn excessively, and if the cylinder block does not need to be rebored (where applicable), the original pistons can be refitted. Normal piston wear appears as even vertical wear on the piston thrust surfaces, and slight looseness of the top ring in its groove. New piston rings should always be used when the engine is reassembled.

15 Carefully inspect each piston for cracks around the skirt, around the gudgeon pin holes, and at the ring 'lands' (between the ring grooves).

16 Look for scoring and scuffing on the piston skirt, holes in the piston crown, and burned areas at the edge of the crown.

17 If the skirt is scored or scuffed, the engine may have been suffering from overheating and/or abnormal combustion, which caused

7.10 Remove the piston rings with the aid of feeler gauges

excessively-high operating temperatures. The cooling and lubrication systems should be checked thoroughly. Scorch marks on the sides of the piston show that blow-by has occurred.

18 A hole in the piston crown or burned areas at the edge of the piston crown, indicates that abnormal combustion (pre-ignition, knocking, or detonation) has been occurring.

19 If any of the above piston problems exist, the causes must be investigated and corrected, or the damage will occur again. The causes may include inlet air leaks, incorrect fuel/air mixture or an emission control system fault.

20 Corrosion of the piston, in the form of pitting, indicates that coolant has been leaking into the combustion chamber and/ or the crankcase. Again, the cause must be corrected, or the problem may persist in the rebuilt engine.

21 Examine each connecting rod carefully for signs of damage, such as cracks around the big-end and small-end bearings. Check that the rod is not bent or distorted. Damage is highly unlikely, unless the engine has been seized or badly overheated. Detailed checking of the connecting rod assembly can only be carried out by an engine overhaul specialist with the necessary equipment.

22 The gudgeon pins are of the floating type, secured in position by two circlips. Where necessary, the pistons and connecting rods can be separated as follows.

23 Remove one of the circlips which secure the gudgeon pin. Push the gudgeon pin out of piston and connecting rod **(see illustrations)**.

24 If any doubt exists concerning the condition of the pistons, have them measured

7.23a Prise out the circlip...

7.23b ...and withdraw the gudgeon pin

7.26 Measure the ring-to-groove clearance using feeler gauges

by an automotive engine reconditioning specialist. If new pistons are required, the specialist will be able to supply new pistons and rebore the cylinder block to the appropriate size (where applicable).

25 If any one of the pistons is worn, then all the pistons must be renewed. Note that if the cylinder block was rebored during a previous overhaul, oversize pistons may have been fitted.

26 Hold a new piston ring in the appropriate groove, and measure the ring-to-groove clearance using a feeler blade **(see illustration)**. Note that the rings are of different sizes, so use the correct ring for the groove. Compare the measurements with those listed in the Specifications; if the clearances are outside the tolerance range, then the pistons must be renewed.

27 Check the fit of the gudgeon pin in the connecting rod bush and in the piston. If there is perceptible play, a new bush or an oversize gudgeon pin must be fitted. Consult a Volvo dealer or engine reconditioning specialist.

28 Examine all components and obtain any new parts required. If new pistons are purchased, they will be supplied complete with gudgeon pins and circlips. Circlips can also be purchased separately.

29 Oil the gudgeon pin. Reassemble the connecting rod and piston, making sure the rod is the right way round as noted during removal, and secure the gudgeon pin with the circlip. Position the circlip so that its opening is facing downward.

30 Repeat these operations for the remaining pistons.

8.2 Check the crankshaft endfloat using a dial gauge

8 Crankshaft – removal and inspection

Note: *If no work is to be done on the pistons and connecting rods, then removal of the cylinder head and pistons will not be necessary. Instead, the pistons need only be pushed far enough up the bores so that they are positioned clear of the crankpins.*

Removal

1 With reference to Part A of this Chapter, and earlier Sections of this part as applicable, carry out the following:
   a) *Remove the oil pump.*
   b) *Remove the sump.*
   c) *Remove the clutch components and flywheel/driveplate.*
   d) *Remove the pistons and connecting rods (refer to the Note above).*

2 Before the crankshaft is removed, it is advisable to check the endfloat. To do this, mount a dial gauge with the stem in line with the crankshaft and just touching crankshaft **(see illustration)**.

3 Push the crankshaft fully away from the gauge, and zero it. Next, lever the crankshaft towards the gauge as far as possible, and check the reading obtained. The distance that the crankshaft moved is its endfloat; if it is greater than specified, check the crankshaft thrust surfaces for wear. If no wear is evident, new thrustwashers (which are integral with the main bearing shells on 2.4 litre models) should correct the endfloat.

4 Remove the intermediate section/main bearing caps, then lift out the crankshaft. Do not drop it, it is heavy.

5 Remove the upper half main bearing shells from their seats in the crankcase by pressing the end of the shell furthest from the locating tab. Keep all the shells in order.

Inspection

6 Clean the crankshaft using paraffin or a suitable solvent, and dry it, preferably with compressed air if available. Be sure to clean the oil holes with a pipe cleaner or similar probe to ensure that they are not obstructed.

 Warning: Wear eye protection when using compressed air.

7 Check the main and big-end bearing journals for uneven wear, scoring, pitting and cracking.

8 Big-end bearing wear is accompanied by distinct metallic knocking when the engine is running (particularly noticeable when the engine is pulling from low speed) and some loss of oil pressure.

9 Main bearing wear is accompanied by severe engine vibration and rumble – getting progressively worse as engine speed increases – and again by loss of oil pressure.

10 Check the bearing journal for roughness by running a finger lightly over the bearing

surface. Any roughness (which will be accompanied by obvious bearing wear) indicates that the crankshaft requires regrinding (where possible) or renewal.

11 Have the crankshaft measured and inspected by an engine reconditioning specialist. They will be able to advise concerning the availability of undersize bearings, and crankshaft reconditioning.

9 Cylinder block/crankcase – cleaning and inspection

Cleaning

1 Prior to cleaning, remove all external components and senders, and any gallery plugs or caps that may be fitted. Remove the piston cooling valve, and the cooling jets (where applicable) **(see illustration)**.

2 If any of the castings are extremely dirty, all should be steam-cleaned.

3 After the castings are returned from steam-cleaning, clean all oil holes and oil galleries one more time. Flush all internal passages with warm water until the water runs clear. If you have access to compressed air, use it to speed the drying process, and to blow out all the oil holes and galleries.

 Warning: Wear eye protection when using compressed air.

4 If the castings are not very dirty, you can do an adequate cleaning job with hot soapy water (as hot as you can stand!) and a stiff brush. Take plenty of time, and do a thorough job. Regardless of the cleaning method used, be sure to clean all oil holes and galleries very thoroughly, and to dry all components completely. Apply clean engine oil to the cylinder bores to prevent rusting.

5 The threaded holes in the cylinder block must be clean to ensure accurate torque readings when tightening fixings during reassembly. Carefully run the correct size tap (which can be determined from the size of the relevant bolt which fits in the hole) into each of the holes to remove rust, corrosion, thread sealant or other contamination, and to restore damaged threads. If possible, use compressed air to clear the holes of debris

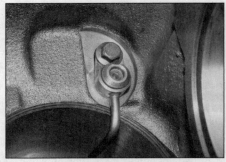

9.1 Piston cooling jets may be fitted to the base of each cylinder bore

produced by this operation. Do not forget to clean the threads of all bolts and nuts as well.

6 Any threads which cannot be restored in this way can often be reclaimed by the use of thread inserts. If any threaded holes are damaged, consult your dealer or engine overhaul specialist and have them install any thread inserts where necessary.

7 If the engine is not going to be reassembled right away, cover it with a large plastic bag to keep it clean; protect the machined surfaces as described above, to prevent rusting.

Inspection

8 Visually check the castings for cracks and corrosion. Look for stripped threads in the threaded holes. If there has been any history of internal coolant leakage, it may be worthwhile having an engine overhaul specialist check the cylinder block/crankcase for cracks with special equipment. If defects are found, have them repaired, if possible, or renew the assembly.

9 Check the condition of the cylinder head mating face and the intermediate section mating surfaces. Check the surfaces for any possible distortion using the straight-edge and feeler blade method described earlier for cylinder head inspection. If distortion is slight, consult an engine overhaul specialist as to the best course of action.

10 Check each cylinder bore for scuffing and scoring. Check for signs of a wear ridge at the top of the cylinder, indicating that the bore is excessively worn.

11 Have the bores inspected and measured by an automotive engine reconditioning specialist. They will be able to advise on possible cylinder reboring and supply appropriate pistons to match.

12 If the bores are in reasonably good condition and not excessively-worn, then it may only be necessary to renew the piston rings.

13 If this is the case, the bores should be honed, to allow the new rings to bed in correctly and provide the best possible seal. Honing is an operation that will be carried out for you by an engine reconditioning specialist.

14 After all machining operations are completed, the entire block/crankcase must be washed very thoroughly with warm soapy water to remove all traces of abrasive grit produced during the machining operations. When the cylinder block/crankcase is completely clean, rinse it thoroughly and dry it, then lightly oil all exposed machined surfaces, to prevent rusting.

15 Refit the piston cooling jets to the base of the cylinder bores, and tighten the retaining bolts to the specified torque.

16 Fit a new sealing washer to the piston cooling oil valve, or apply thread sealing compound to valve threads (as applicable), then refit the valve and tighten it to the specified torque.

10 Main and big-end bearings – inspection and selection

Inspection

1 Even though the main and big-end bearing shells should be renewed during the engine overhaul, the old shells should be retained for close examination, as they may reveal valuable information about the condition of the engine.

2 Bearing failure occurs because of lack of lubrication, the presence of dirt or other foreign particles, overloading the engine, and corrosion **(see illustration)**. Regardless of the cause of bearing failure, the cause must be corrected (where applicable) before the engine is reassembled, to prevent it from happening again.

3 When examining the bearing shells, remove them from the cylinder block/crankcase and main bearing caps, and from the connecting rods and the big-end bearing caps, then lay them out on a clean surface in the same general position as their location in the engine. This will enable you to match any bearing problems with the corresponding crankshaft journal. *Do not* touch any of the shell's bearing surface with your fingers while checking it, or the delicate surface may be scratched.

4 Dirt or other foreign matter gets into the engine in a variety of ways. It may be left in the engine during assembly, or it may pass through filters or the crankcase ventilation system. It may get into the oil, and from there into the bearings. Metal chips from machining operations and normal engine wear are often present. Abrasives are sometimes left in engine components after reconditioning, especially when parts are not thoroughly cleaned using the proper cleaning methods.

5 Whatever the source, any foreign objects often end up embedded in the soft bearing material, and are easily recognised. Large particles will not embed in the material, and will score or gouge the shell and journal. The best prevention for this cause of bearing failure is to clean all parts thoroughly, and to keep everything spotlessly-clean during engine assembly. Frequent and regular engine oil and filter changes are also recommended.

6 Lack of lubrication (or lubrication breakdown) has a number of inter-related causes. Excessive heat (which thins the oil), overloading (which squeezes the oil from the bearing face) and oil leakage (from excessive bearing clearances, worn oil pump or high engine speeds) all contribute to lubrication breakdown. Blocked oil passages, which usually are the result of misaligned oil holes in a bearing shell, will also starve a bearing of oil, and destroy it.

7 When lack of lubrication is the cause of bearing failure, the bearing material is wiped or extruded from the shell's steel backing. Temperatures may increase to the point where the steel backing turns blue from overheating.

8 Driving habits can have a definite effect on

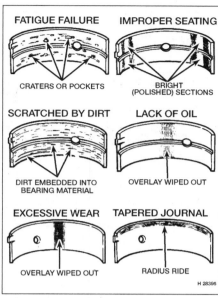

10.2 Typical bearing failures

bearing life. Full-throttle, low-speed operation (labouring the engine) puts very high loads on bearings, which tends to squeeze out the oil film. These loads cause the shells to flex, which produces fine cracks in the bearing face (fatigue failure). Eventually, the bearing material will loosen in pieces, and tear away from the steel backing.

9 Short-distance driving leads to corrosion of bearings, because insufficient engine heat is produced to drive off condensed water and corrosive gases. These products collect in the engine oil, forming acid and sludge. As the oil is carried to the engine bearings, the acid attacks and corrodes the bearing material.

10 Incorrect shell refitting during engine assembly will lead to bearing failure as well. Tight-fitting shells leave insufficient bearing running clearance, and will result in oil starvation. Dirt or foreign particles trapped behind a bearing shell result in high spots on the bearing, which lead to failure.

11 *Do not* touch any shell's bearing surface with your fingers during reassembly; there is a risk of scratching the delicate surface, or of depositing particles of dirt on it.

Bearing selection

12 Have the crankshaft measured and examined by an automotive engine reconditioning specialist, who will be able to supply the appropriate bearing shells.

11 Engine overhaul – reassembly sequence

1 Before reassembly begins, ensure that all new parts have been obtained and that all necessary tools are available. Read through the entire procedure to familiarise yourself

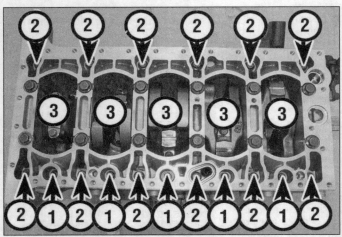

12.10 Intermediate section bolts

1 M7	2 M8	3 M10

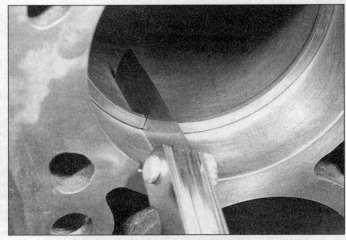

13.5 Measure the piston ring gap using feeler gauges

with the work involved, and to ensure that all items necessary for reassembly of the engine are at hand. In addition to all normal tools and materials, thread-locking compound will be needed in most areas during engine reassembly. A tube of Volvo liquid gasket solution together with a short-haired application roller will also be needed to assemble the main engine sections.

2 In order to save time and avoid problems, engine reassembly can be carried out in the following order:
  a) *Crankshaft.*
  b) *Intermediate section.*
  c) *Pistons/connecting rods.*
  d) *Sump.*
  e) *Oil pump.*
  f) *Flywheel/driveplate.*
  g) *Cylinder head.*
  h) *Camshaft and tappets.*
  i) *Timing belt, tensioner, sprockets and idler pulleys.*
  j) *Engine external components.*

3 At this stage, all engine components should be absolutely clean and dry, with all faults repaired. The components should be laid out (or in individual containers) on a completely clean work surface.

12 Crankshaft – refitting

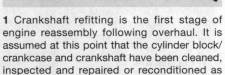

1 Crankshaft refitting is the first stage of engine reassembly following overhaul. It is assumed at this point that the cylinder block/crankcase and crankshaft have been cleaned, inspected and repaired or reconditioned as necessary, and the piston cooling jets and valve have been refitted. Position the cylinder block on a clean level work surface, with the crankcase facing upwards.

2 If they're still in place, remove the old bearing shells from the block and the intermediate section.

3 Wipe clean the main bearing shell seats in the crankcase and clean the backs of the new bearing shells. Insert the previously selected upper shells into their correct position in the crankcase. Note the shells incorporating the thrustwashers must be fitted to the No 5 bearing position. Press the shells home so that the tangs engage in the recesses provided. Note the thicker of the two shells must be fitted to the intermediate section.

4 Liberally lubricate the bearing shells in the crankcase with clean engine oil.

5 Wipe clean the crankshaft journals, then lower the crankshaft into position. Make sure that the shells are not displaced.

6 Inject oil into the crankshaft oilways, then wipe any traces of excess oil from the crankshaft and intermediate section mating faces.

7 Using the short-haired application roller, apply an even coating of Volvo liquid gasket solution (No 116 1771) to the cylinder block mating face of the intermediate section. Ensure that the whole surface is covered, but note that a thin coating is sufficient for a good seal.

8 Wipe clean the main bearing shell seats in the intermediate section and clean the backs of the bearing shells. Insert the previously selected lower shells into their correct position in the intermediate section. Press the shells home so that the tangs engage in the recesses provided.

9 Lightly lubricate the bearing shells in the intermediate section, but take care to keep the oil away from the liquid gasket solution.

10 Lay the intermediate section on the crankshaft and cylinder block, and insert the retaining bolts. Tighten the bolts in the five stages listed in the Specifications to the specified torque and torque angle, starting from the outside in **(see illustration)**.

11 Rotate the crankshaft. Slight resistance is to be expected with new components, but there must be no tight spots or binding.

12 It is a good idea at this stage to once

again check the crankshaft endfloat as described in Section 8. If the thrust surfaces of the crankshaft have been checked and new bearing shells have been fitted, then the endfloat should be within specification.

13 Lubricate the left-hand oil seal location, the crankshaft, and a new oil seal. Fit the seal, lips inwards, and use a piece of tube (or the old seal, inverted) to tap it into place until flush.

13 Pistons and piston rings – assembly

1 At this stage, it is assumed that the pistons have been correctly assembled to their respective connecting rods, and that the piston ring-to-groove clearances have been checked. If not, refer to the end of Section 7.

2 Before the rings can be fitted to the pistons, the end gaps must be checked with the rings inserted into the cylinder bores.

3 Lay out the piston assemblies and the new ring sets so the components are kept together in their groups, during and after end gap checking. Position the cylinder block on the work surface, on its side, allowing access to the top and bottom of the bores.

4 Take the No 1 piston top ring and insert it into the top of the first cylinder. Push it down the bore using the top of the piston; this will ensure that the ring remains square with the cylinder walls. Position the ring near the bottom of the cylinder bore, at the lower limit of ring travel. Note that the top and second compression rings are different. The second ring is easily identified by the step on its lower surface.

5 Measure the ring gap using feeler blades **(see illustration)**.

6 Repeat the procedure with the ring at the top of the cylinder bore, at the upper limit of its travel, and compare the measurements with the figures given in the Specifications.

7 If new rings are being fitted, it is unlikely that the end gaps will be too small. If a measurement is found to be undersize, it must be corrected, or there is the risk that the ring ends may contact each other during engine operation, possibly resulting in engine damage. Ideally, new piston rings providing the correct end gap should be fitted; however, as a last resort the end gaps can be increased by filing the ring ends very carefully with a fine file. Mount the ring in a vice equipped with soft jaws, slip the ring over the file with the ends contacting the file face, and slowly move the ring to remove material from the ends. Take care, as piston rings are sharp and are easily broken.

8 It is equally unlikely that the end gap will be too large. If the gaps are too large, check that you have the correct rings for your engine and for the cylinder bore size.

9 Repeat the checking procedure for each ring in the first cylinder, and then for the rings in the remaining cylinders. Remember to keep rings, pistons and cylinders matched up.

10 Once the ring end gaps have been checked and if necessary corrected, the rings can be fitted to the pistons.

11 Fit the piston rings using the same technique as for removal. Fit the bottom scraper ring first, and work up. Observe the text markings on one side of the top and bottom rings; this must face upwards when the rings are fitted. The middle ring is bevelled, and the bevel must face downwards when installed. Do not expand the compression rings too far, or they will break. **Note:** *Always follow any instructions supplied with the new piston ring sets – different manufacturers may specify different procedures. Do not mix up the top and second compression rings, as they have different cross-sections.*

12 When all the rings are in position, arrange the ring gaps 120° apart, with the exception of the 3-part oil scraper ring where the two plain rings should be 90° apart from each other **(see illustration).**

14 Pistons and connecting rod assemblies – refitting

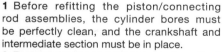

1 Before refitting the piston/connecting rod assemblies, the cylinder bores must be perfectly clean, and the crankshaft and intermediate section must be in place.

2 Remove the big-end bearing cap from No 1 cylinder connecting rod (refer to the marks noted or made on removal). Remove the original bearing shells, and wipe the bearing recesses of the connecting rod and cap with a clean, lint-free cloth. They must be kept spotlessly-clean. Ensure that new big-end bearing cap retaining bolts are available.

3 Clean the back of the new upper bearing shell, fit it to No 1 connecting rod, then fit the other shell of the bearing to the big-end bearing cap. Note that shell with the black-

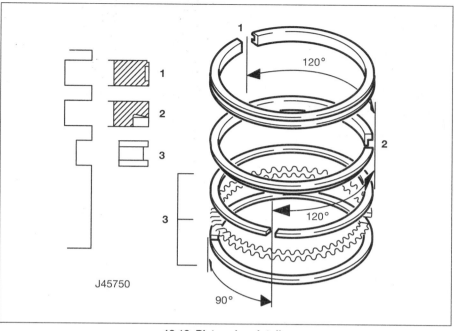

13.12 Piston ring details

1 Top compression ring   *2 2nd compression ring*   *3 Oil scraper ring assembly*

coloured size marker on its edge must be fitted to the connecting rod. On 'fractured' type rods and caps, no locating notch for the bearing shell tab is provided. On these rods/caps, simply position the shells as centrally as possible. Where tabs and notches are provided, make sure the tab on each shell fits into the notch in the rod or cap recess.

4 Position the piston ring gaps in their correct positions around the piston, lubricate the piston and rings with clean engine oil, and attach a piston ring compressor to the piston. Leave the skirt protruding slightly, to guide the piston into the cylinder bore. The rings must be compressed until they're flush with the piston.

5 Rotate the crankshaft until No 1 big-end journal is at BDC (Bottom Dead Centre), and apply a coat of engine oil to the cylinder walls.

6 Arrange the No 1 piston/connecting rod assembly so that the channel in the base of the piston aligns with the piston cooling jet at the base of the cylinder bore. Gently insert the assembly into the No 1 cylinder bore, and rest the bottom edge of the ring compressor on the engine block.

7 Tap the top edge of the ring compressor to make sure it's contacting the block around its entire circumference.

8 Gently tap on the top of the piston with the end of a wooden hammer handle while guiding the connecting rod big-end onto the crankpin. The piston rings may try to pop out of the ring compressor just before entering the cylinder bore, so keep some pressure on the ring compressor. Work slowly, and if any resistance is felt as the piston enters the cylinder, stop immediately. Find out what is binding, and fix

it before proceeding. *Do not*, for any reason, force the piston into the cylinder – you might break a ring and/or the piston. Take great care not to damage the piston cooling jets **(see illustration).**

9 Make sure the bearing surfaces are perfectly clean, then apply a uniform layer of clean engine oil to both of them. You may have to push the piston back up the cylinder bore slightly to expose the bearing surface of the shell in the connecting rod.

10 Slide the connecting rod back into place on the big-end journal, refit the big-end bearing cap. Lubricate the bolt threads, fit the bolts and tighten them in two stages to the specified torque.

11 Repeat the entire procedure for the remaining piston/connecting rod assemblies.

12 The important points to remember are:

a) *Keep the backs of the bearing shells and the recesses of the connecting rods and caps perfectly clean when assembling them.*

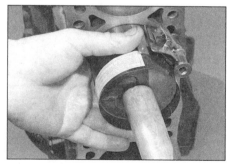

14.8 Tap the piston into the bore using a hammer handle

14.16 Measure the piston protrusion using a dial gauge

b) *Make sure you have the correct piston/ rod assembly for each cylinder.*
c) *The channel in the base of the piston must align with the piston cooling jet.*
d) *Lubricate the cylinder bores with clean engine oil.*
e) *Lubricate the bearing surfaces before fitting the big-end bearing caps.*

13 After all the piston/connecting rod assemblies have been properly installed, rotate the crankshaft a number of times by hand, to check for any obvious binding.
14 If new pistons, connecting rods, or crankshaft are fitted, or if a new short engine is installed, the projection of the piston crowns above the cylinder head surface at TDC must be measured, to determine the correct head gasket required.
15 Fit the sump as described in Section 15.
16 Anchor a DTI gauge to the cylinder block, and zero it on the head gasket mating surface. Rest the gauge probe on No 1 piston crown and turn the crankshaft slowly by hand so that the piston reaches TDC (Top Dead Centre). Measure and record the maximum projection at TDC **(see illustration)**.
17 Repeat the measurement for the remaining pistons and record.
18 If the measurements differ from piston-to-piston, take the highest figure and use this to determine the head gasket type required – refer to Chapter 2A for details.

15 Sump – refitting

See Chapter 2A, Section 13.

16 Engine – initial start-up after overhaul and reassembly

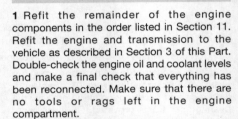

1 Refit the remainder of the engine components in the order listed in Section 11. Refit the engine and transmission to the vehicle as described in Section 3 of this Part. Double-check the engine oil and coolant levels and make a final check that everything has been reconnected. Make sure that there are no tools or rags left in the engine compartment.
2 Remove the glow plugs (Chapter 5).
3 Turn the engine over on the starter motor until the oil pressure warning light goes out. If the light fails to extinguish after several seconds of cranking, check the engine oil level and that the oil filter is fitted securely. Assuming these are correct, check the security of the oil pressure sensor wiring – do not progress any further until you are sure that oil is being pumped around the engine at sufficient pressure.
4 As applicable, refit the glow plugs, and reconnect the camshaft position sensor and fuel injector wiring connectors.
5 Start the engine, noting that this also may take a little longer than usual, due to the fuel system components being empty.
6 While the engine is idling, check for fuel, coolant and oil leaks. Don't be alarmed if there are some odd smells and smoke from parts getting hot and burning off oil deposits. Note also that it may initially be a little noisy until the hydraulic tappets fill with oil.
7 Keep the engine idling until hot water is felt circulating through the top hose, check that it idles reasonably smoothly and at the usual speed, then switch it off.
8 After a few minutes, recheck the oil and coolant levels, and top-up as necessary (see *Weekly checks*).
9 If new components such as pistons, rings or crankshaft bearings have been fitted, the engine must be run-in for the first 500 miles. Do not operate the engine at full-throttle, or allow it to labour in any gear during this period. It is recommended that the oil and filter be changed at the end of this period.

Chapter 3
Cooling, heating and air conditioning systems

Contents

Degrees of difficulty

Easy, suitable for novice with little experience	**Fairly easy,** suitable for beginner with some experience	**Fairly difficult,** suitable for competent DIY mechanic	**Difficult,** suitable for experienced DIY mechanic	**Very difficult,** suitable for expert DIY or professional

Specifications

General

System type . . . . Water-based coolant, pump-assisted circulation, thermostatically controlled

Thermostat

Opening commences. . . . . 82°C

Air conditioning system

Refrigerant R134a
Refrigerant quantity:
  XC60. . . . . 800g
  XC90 (without rear AC) 1000g
  XC90 (with rear AC) 1300g
Compressor oil. . . . . Volvo 1161627 (ISO46)
Compressor oil capacity. . . . . 70 ml
Condenser . . . . 30 ml
Evaporator . . . . 50 ml
Flexible hose . . . . 20 ml
Pipe work . . . . 10 ml
Compressor clutch clearance:
  Valeo/Zexel compressors. . . . . 0.4 to 0.6 mm
  Sanden compressors . . . . 0.4 to 0.8 mm

Torque wrench settings

	Nm	lbf ft
Auxiliary heater glow plugs	15	11
Compressor mounting bolts	24	18
Coolant pump bolts	10	7
Coolant temperature sensor	22	16
Expansion valve screws	5	4
Radiator-to-condenser bolts	5	4
Radiator support bolts	24	18
Thermostat housing:		
2.0 litre	10	7
2.4 litre	17	13

Note: *Volvo specify that where a fixing requires angular tightening it must always be renewed. Any fixing retained with a thread locking compound must also be renewed. Nuts with a nylon insert must always be renewed.*

1 General information and precautions

The cooling system is of pressurised semi-sealed type with the inclusion of an expansion tank to accept coolant displaced from the system when hot and to return it when the system cools.

Water-based coolant is circulated around the cylinder block and head by the coolant pump which is driven by the engine timing belt. As the coolant circulates around the engine it absorbs heat as it flows then, when hot, it travels out into the radiator to pass across the matrix. As the coolant flows across the radiator matrix, airflow created by the forward motion of the vehicle cools it, and it returns to the cylinder block. Airflow through the radiator matrix is assisted by a two-speed electric fan, which is controlled by the engine management system ECU.

A thermostat is fitted to control coolant flow through the radiator. When the engine is cold, the thermostat valve remains closed so that the coolant flow which occurs at normal operating temperatures through the radiator matrix is interrupted.

As the coolant warms up, the thermostat valve starts to open and allows the coolant flow through the radiator to resume.

The engine temperature will always be maintained at a constant level (according to the thermostat rating) whatever the ambient air temperature.

Most models have an oil cooler mounted on the sump – this is basically a heat exchanger with a coolant supply, to take heat away from the oil in the sump.

The vehicle interior heater operates by means of coolant from the engine cooling system. Coolant flow through the heater matrix is constant; temperature control being achieved by blending cool air from outside the vehicle with the warm air from the heater matrix, in the desired ratio.

Air entering the passenger compartment is filtered by a pleated paper filter element, sometimes known as a pollen filter. Also available instead of a pollen filer is a multifilter, which is a carbon impregnated filter which

2.3 Screw-type hose clamp (arrowed)

absorbs incoming smells, etc. With this system a pollution sensor monitors the quality of the incoming air, and opens and closes the recirculation flaps accordingly.

The standard climate control (air conditioning) systems are described in detail in Section 9.

⚠ *Warning: Do not attempt to remove the expansion tank filler cap, or to disturb any part of the cooling system, while it or the engine is hot, as there is a very great risk of scalding. If the expansion tank filler cap must be removed before the engine and radiator have fully cooled down (even though this is not recommended) the pressure in the cooling system must first be released. Cover the cap with a thick layer of cloth, to avoid scalding, and slowly unscrew the filler cap until a hissing sound can be heard. When the hissing has stopped, showing that pressure is released, slowly unscrew the filler cap further until it can be removed; if more hissing sounds are heard, wait until they have stopped before unscrewing the cap completely. At all times, keep well away from the filler opening.*

⚠ *Warning: Do not allow antifreeze to come in contact with your skin, or with the painted surfaces of the vehicle. Rinse off spills immediately with plenty of water. Never leave antifreeze lying around in an open container, or in a puddle in the driveway or on the garage floor. Children and pets are attracted by its sweet smell, but antifreeze is fatal if ingested.*

⚠ *Warning: Refer to Section 9 for precautions to be observed when working on vehicles equipped with air conditioning.*

2 Cooling system hoses – disconnection and renewal

Note: *Refer to the warnings given in Section 1 of this Chapter before proceeding. Hoses should only be disconnected once the engine has cooled sufficiently to avoid scalding.*

1 If the checks described in Chapter 1 reveal a faulty hose, it must be renewed as follows.

2 First drain the cooling system (see Chapter 1); if the antifreeze is not due for renewal, the drained coolant may be re-used, if it is collected in a clean container.

3 To disconnect any hose, use a pair of pliers to release the spring clamps (or a screwdriver to slacken screw-type clamps), then move them along the hose clear of the union **(see illustration)**. Carefully work the hose off its stubs. The hoses can be removed with relative ease when new – on an older vehicle, they may have stuck.

4 If a hose proves to be difficult to remove, try to release it by rotating it on its unions before attempting to work it off. Gently prise the end of the hose with a blunt instrument (such as a

flat-bladed screwdriver), but do not apply too much force, and take care not to damage the pipe stubs or hoses. Note in particular that the radiator hose unions are fragile; do not use excessive force when attempting to remove the hoses.

5 When refitting a hose, first slide the clamps onto the hose, then engage the hose with its unions. Work the hose into position, then check that the hose is settled correctly and is properly routed. Slide each clamp along the hose until it is behind the union flared end, before tightening it securely.

6 Refill the system with coolant (Chapter 1).

7 Check carefully for leaks as soon as possible after disturbing any part of the cooling system.

3 Antifreeze – general information

Note: *Refer to the warnings given in Section 1 of this Chapter before proceeding.*

1 The cooling system should be filled with Volvo antifreeze in a ratio of 50/50 with pure water. At this strength, the coolant will protect against freezing down to -35°C. Antifreeze also provides protection against corrosion, and increases the coolant boiling point. As the engine uses aluminium in its construction, the corrosion protection properties of the antifreeze are critical. Only Volvo antifreeze should be used in the system, and should never be mixed with different antifreeze types.

2 The cooling system should be maintained according to the schedule described in Chapter 1. Old or contaminated coolant mixtures, or antifreeze that is not to Volvo's specification, are likely to cause damage, and encourage the formation of corrosion and scale in the system.

3 Before adding antifreeze, check all hoses and hose connections, because antifreeze tends to leak through very small openings. Engines don't normally consume coolant, so if the level goes down, find the cause and correct it.

4 The specified mixture is 50% antifreeze and 50% clean soft water (by volume). Mix the required quantity in a clean container and then fill the system as described in Chapter 1 and Weekly checks. Save any surplus mixture for topping-up.

4 Radiator cooling fan – removal and refitting

Removal – all models

1 Disconnect the battery negative terminal as described in Chapter 5.

2 Disconnect the fan wiring plug from the motor and release the wiring loom from the shroud. **(see illustration)**.

4.2 Disconnect the fan motor wiring plug (XC60 shown)

4.3a Use a screwdriver to release the clips (arrowed) at the top of the radiator

4.3b Withdraw the fan assembly upwards from the engine compartment

4.3c Fan motor mounting bolts (arrowed)

4.4 Remove the inlet cowl

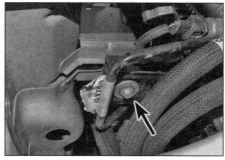

4.6 Slacken the lower bolts (arrowed)

XC60 models

3 Using a screwdriver, push back the clips at the top of the radiator on each side that secure the fan shroud to the radiator and withdraw the assembly upwards from the engine bay to remove it **(see illustrations)**.

XC90 models

4 Remove the air intake duct from the slam panel **(see illustration)**.
5 Unclip the wiring plug from the left-hand end of the radiator and then disconnect the wiring plug from the left-hand end of the radiator.
6 Slacken the combined radiator, intercooler and condenser mounting bolts. **Do not** remove them, merely slacken them enough to allow the assembly to pivot slightly **(see illustration)**.
7 Remove the 2 bolts from the top of the slam panel and then unclip the coolant hose from the shroud.
8 Remove the two upper mounting bolts release the lower retaining clips and pull the assembly upwards and out of the vehicle **(see illustrations)**.
9 If required the fan assembly can now be removed from the shroud.

Refitting

10 Refitting is the reversal of removal, ensuring that the bottom mountings locate securely in place at the bottom of the radiator. On some models it is possible for the power steering hose to foul the fan blades. Ensure the retaining clip is securely fitted. If necessary use a tie wrap to restrain the hose.

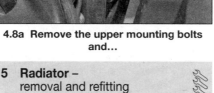

4.8a Remove the upper mounting bolts and...

5 Radiator – removal and refitting

Removal - all models

1 Undo the retaining screws and remove the engine undershield.
2 Drain the cooling system (see Chapter 1) and disconnect the upper and lower radiator hoses.
3 Remove the radiator cooling fan as described in Section 4.

XC60 models

4 Remove the front bumper cover as described in Chapter 11 and then remove the right-hand headlamp as described in Chapter 12.
5 Working through the right-hand side headlamp aperture undo the bolt and screw

4.8b ...then remove the fan

that attach the condenser to the radiator and secure the condenser to the vehicle body using cable-ties (or similar).
6 Remove the upper radiator mounts **(see illustration)**. These are only guides, but

5.6 Remove the radiator top mount securing sections

5.7a Transmission oil cooler bolt (arrowed)

5.7b Disconnect the pipe from the transmission oil cooler (arrowed)

5.7c Secure the power steering oil cooler to the vehicle body

5.8 Support the radiator assembly

5.9 Remove the support panel

5.10 Remove the air deflectors from both sides

removing them makes installation of the radiator easier.

7 Where fitted, undo the screw securing the transmission oil cooler to the radiator, and disconnect the short pipe between the cooler and the radiator. Undo the bolt securing the power steering fluid cooler to the front of the radiator, and secure the cooler to the vehicle body using cable-ties (or similar) **(see illustrations)**.

8 At this stage of the process the radiator assembly must be supported to enable the lower support panel to be removed. Volvo use a special tool to support the radiator. An alternative is to support the assembly with tie wraps and length of wood to support the load **(see illustration)**.

9 With the radiator supported in this way, and working from beneath the vehicle, the radiator support beam can be removed by undoing the 2 bolts on each side **(see illustration)**.

10 Disconnect the air pipes from the intercooler. To improve access to the pipe clamps, it may be necessary to unclip the plastic air deflectors fitted at either end of the bumper crossbeam **(see illustration)**. To improve access remove the cross member and then remove the intercooler mounting bolts. Note that the clamps are crimped to the intercooler air pipes and cannot be rotated for refitting. Remove the intercooler.

11 Using a screwdriver, push in the 2 clips securing the condenser to the bottom of the radiator. Secure the condenser to the vehicle body using cable-ties **(see illustration)**.

12 If not already done so, jack up and support the front of the vehicle (see *Jacking and vehicle support* in the reference section).

13 The radiator can now be withdrawn from beneath the car. It is worth noting that a number of items, such as pipes, brackets, and the transmission oil cooler, can obstruct the

removal of the radiator so an assistant may be helpful at this stage.

XC90 models

Note: *Removal of the radiator is considerably easier if the radiator, condenser and intercooler are removed as a complete assembly. If this option is chosen then the AC system must be drained first. Consult a Volvo garage or suitably equipped specialist and have the system drained.*

14 Remove the fan assembly as described in the previous section. Remove the bumper cover and both headlights as described in Chapter 11.

15 Disconnect the upper and lower coolant hoses. Remove the small vent hose from the top of the radiator **(see illustration)**.

16 Where fitted disconnect the gearbox oil cooler hoses. Anticipate soon coolant loss and immediately plug both the hoses and the radiator connections **(see illustration)**.

5.11 Releases the condenser – removed from the vehicle for clarity

5.15 Remove the vent hose

5.16 Remove the transmission cooler hose (arrowed)

5.18a Secure the radiator and condenser

5.18b Remove the mounting bolts

5.21 Lower the radiator

17 Jack up and support the front of the vehicle (see *Jacking and vehicle support* in the reference section) and then remove the sump guard.

18 Support the condenser and radiator with suitable straps. Remove the 4 bolts that hold the AC condenser to the radiator **(see illustrations)**.

19 Remove both intercooler hoses and disconnect the wiring plug from the boost pressure sensor.

20 Remove the 2 bolts that secure the power steering cooler and then remove the 2 main radiator mounting bolts from below.

21 With the aid of an assistant, lower the radiator and intercooler from the vehicle **(see illustration)**. Separate the intercooler from the radiator.

Refitting

22 Refit by reversing the removal operations. With reference to Chapter 1, refill the cooling system on completion.

---

6 Coolant temperature sensor – testing, removal and refitting

Testing

1 The coolant temperature sensor is located in the thermostat housing, and is used by both the engine management system and the instrument panel temperature gauge to supply an engine temperature source signal.

2 In the event of a fault in the sensor, or a loss of signal due to poor electrical connections, a fault code will be logged in the engine management system ECU, which can be read out via the diagnostic connector beneath the facia on the driver's side (using a suitable fault code reader).

3 Should a fault code be logged, a careful check should be made of the sensor wiring and the wiring connector. A simple test can be made by disconnecting the wiring plug and checking the resistance of the sensor **(see illustration)**. The ignition must be off or a fault code will be logged. Reconnect the sensor wiring plug and then run the engine up to normal operating temperature.

6.3 Checking the coolant temperature sensor resistance

Turn the ignition off and check that the sensor resistance has changed. Whilst not a definitive test, as a general rule if the sensor's resistance changes with temperature it is functioning correctly. Further checks require the use of Volvo test equipment and should be entrusted to a dealer or suitably-equipped specialist.

Removal

4 Drain the cooling system as described in Chapter 1.

5 Pull the plastic cover on the top of the engine straight up and remove it from the engine compartment.

6 Follow the steps in Section 8 (thermostat removal) for component removal until the sensor becomes accessible. The process is similar for all engines.

7 Disconnect the wiring plug. On most

7.3a Undo the mounting bolts...

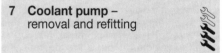

6.7 Coolant sensor wiring plug (arrowed)

models unscrew the sensor from the housing **(see illustration)**. On other models prise out the spring clip to release the sensor. Where fitted, discard the seal – a new one must be fitted.

Refitting

8 Screw (or push in) in the new sensor unit, using a smear of sealant on the threads or a new seal as applicable. Refit the spring clip on models fitted with push in sensor. Reconnect the wiring connector and then refit any components previously removed..

9 Top-up the coolant level as described in *Weekly checks*.

---

7 Coolant pump – removal and refitting

Note: *Refer to the warnings given in Section 1 of this Chapter before proceeding*.

Removal

1 Drain the cooling system as described in Chapter 1.

2 Refer to the relevant Section of Chapter 2A and remove the timing belt.

3 Undo the bolts, and remove the coolant pump from its locating dowels **(see illustrations)**. Recover the gasket, and the O-ring seal where applicable, after removing the pump.

4 Thoroughly clean all traces of old gasket from the pump and cylinder block mating faces.

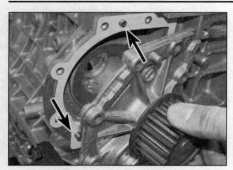

7.3b ...and remove the coolant pump from its locating dowels

Refitting

5 Using a new gasket, and O-ring seal where applicable, locate the pump in position.
6 Apply a little thread-locking compound, then tighten the bolts progressively and in a diagonal sequence to the specified torque.
7 Refit the timing belt as described in Chapter 2A and top-up the coolant as described in Chapter 1.

| 8 | Thermostat –
removal, testing and refitting |

1 As the thermostat ages, it will become slower to react to changes in water temperature. Ultimately, the unit may stick in the open or closed position, and this causes problems. A thermostat which is stuck open will result in a very slow warm-up; a thermostat which is stuck shut will lead to rapid overheating.
2 Before assuming the thermostat is to blame for a cooling system problem, check the coolant level. If the system is draining due to a leak, or has not been properly filled, there may be an air-lock in the system (see Chapter 1).
3 If the engine seems to be taking a long time to warm up (based on heater output or temperature gauge operation), the thermostat is probably stuck open.
4 Equally, a lengthy warm-up period might suggest that the thermostat is missing – it may have been removed or inadvertently omitted by a previous owner or mechanic. Don't drive the vehicle without a thermostat – the engine management system's ECU will stay

8.22 Thermostat housing bolts (arrowed, with one bolt hidden)

in warm-up mode for longer than necessary, causing emissions and fuel economy to suffer.
5 If the engine runs hot, use your hand to check the temperature of the radiator top hose. If the hose isn't hot, but the engine is, the thermostat is probably stuck closed, preventing the coolant inside the engine from escaping to the radiator – renew the thermostat. Again, this problem may also be due to an air-lock (see Chapter 1).
6 If the radiator top hose is hot, it means that the coolant is flowing and the thermostat is open. Consult the Fault diagnosis section in the Reference chapter to assist in tracing possible cooling system faults.
7 To gain a rough idea of whether the thermostat is working properly when the engine is warming up, without dismantling the system, proceed as follows.
8 With the engine completely cold, start the engine and let it idle, while checking the temperature of the radiator top hose. Periodically check the temperature indicated on the coolant temperature gauge – if overheating is indicated, switch the engine off immediately.
9 The top hose should feel cold for some time as the engine warms up, and should then get warm quite quickly as the thermostat opens.
10 The above is not a precise or definitive test of thermostat operation, but if the system does not perform as described, remove and test the thermostat as described below.

Removal

Note: *Refer to the warnings given in Section 1 of this Chapter before proceeding.*

11 The engine must be completely cold before starting this procedure – the engine should have been switched off for several hours, and ideally, left to cool overnight.
12 Drain the cooling system as described in Chapter 1.
13 Pull the plastic engine cover straight-up and remove it from the engine compartment.

XC60 models (with thermostat mounted at the rear of the engine)

14 Remove the EGR valve as described in Chapter 4B.
15 Remove the coolant hose next to the vacuum pump and then pull off the vacuum hose from the turbo control valve.
16 Release the spring clip from the main hose at the rear of the engine. Anticipate some coolant loss as the hose is removed.
17 Remove the single bolt and pull the housing free from the inlet pipe. Recover the O-ring.

XC60 models (with front mounted thermostat)

18 Remove the turbocharger inlet pipe from the top of the engine and then disconnect the wiring plug from the coolant temperature sensor.
19 Release the spring clips (or hose clips on some models) and remove the 3 coolant hoses.

20 Remove the 4 bolts and pull the housing free from the engine bloc. Recover the gasket.

XC90 models

21 Disconnect the wiring plug for the coolant temperature sensor.
22 Undo the clamps and disconnect the hose(s) from the thermostat housing. Undo the retaining bolts and remove the housing from the engine **(see illustration)**.

Testing (XC90 only)

23 Check the temperature marking stamped on the thermostat, which will typically be 82°C.
24 Using a thermometer and container of water, heat the water until the temperature corresponds with the temperature marking stamped on the thermostat.
25 Suspend the (closed) thermostat on a length of string in the water, and check that maximum opening occurs within two minutes.
26 Remove the thermostat and allow it to cool down; check that it closes fully.
27 If the thermostat does not open and close as described, or if it sticks in either position, it must be renewed.

Refitting

28 Refitting is a reversal of removal using new gaskets and seals where applicable. Top-up the cooling system as described in Chapter 1.

| 9 | Heating, ventilation and
air conditioning systems –
general information |

Manual climate control

1 On models equipped with a manual climate control system, the heater system is fitted in conjunction with a manually-controlled air conditioning unit.
2 The heater is of the fresh air type. Air enters through a grille in front of the windscreen, and passes to the various vents, a variable proportion of the air passes through the heater matrix, where it is warmed by engine coolant flowing through the matrix.
3 Distribution of air to the vents, and through or around the matrix, is controlled by flaps. These are operated by an electric motor. Separate temperature controls are provided for driver and front passenger, and these are cable-operated.
4 A variable speed electric fan is fitted to boost the airflow through the heater with a pollen filter fitted after the fan.
5 The air conditioning system works in conjunction with the heater to enable any reasonable air temperature to be achieved inside the car. It also reduces the humidity of the incoming air, aiding demisting even when cooling is not required.
6 The refrigeration side of the air conditioning system functions in a similar way to a domestic refrigerator. A compressor, belt-driven from

the crankshaft pulley, draws refrigerant in its gaseous state from an evaporator. The compound refrigerant passes through a condenser where it loses heat and enters its liquid state. After dehydration the refrigerant returns to the evaporator where it absorbs heat from air passing over the evaporator fins. The refrigerant becomes a gas again and the cycle is repeated.

7 Various subsidiary controls and sensors protect the system against excessive temperature and pressures. Additionally, engine idle speed is increased when the system is in use, to compensate for the additional load imposed by the compressor.

Automatic climate control

8 On models with automatic climate control, the temperature inside the car can be automatically maintained at the level selected by the operator, irrespective of outside temperature. The computer-controlled system operates the heater, air conditioner and fan functions as necessary to achieve this. The refrigeration side of the system is the same as for models with manual climate control; the fully automatic electronic control operates as follows.

9 An electronic control unit (ECU) receives signal inputs from sensors that detect the air duct temperatures on the driver's and passenger's side, and interior temperature on the driver's and passenger's side. A solar sensor is used to detect the presence of sunlight. Signals are also received from the dampers (air flaps) on their position at any given time. Information on engine temperature, outside temperature, whether or not the engine is running, and if so, the vehicle roadspeed, are also sent to the ECU from the engine management system.

10 When the automatic function is engaged, the ECU can establish the optimum settings needed, based on the sensor signals, for the selected temperature and air distribution. These settings can then be maintained irrespective of driving conditions and weather.

11 Distribution of air to the various vents, and the blending of hot or cold air to achieve the selected temperature, are controlled by dampers (flaps). These are operated by electric motors, which are in turn controlled by the ECU. A variable speed fan which can be manually or automatically controlled is used to boost airflow through the system.

12 Should a fault occur, the ECU stores a series of fault codes for subsequent read-out via the diagnostic connector located in the lower facia panel above the driver's pedals.

Precautions

13 When an air conditioning system is fitted, it is necessary to observe special precautions whenever dealing with any part of the system, or its associated components. If for any reason the system must be discharged, entrust this task to your Volvo dealer or a refrigeration

10.3 Climate control panel securing screws (arrowed)

engineer. It is a criminal offence to knowingly discharge refrigerant to the atmosphere.

⚠ **Warning: The refrigeration circuit contains R134a liquid refrigerant, and it is therefore dangerous to disconnect any part of the system without specialised knowledge and equipment.**

14 The refrigerant is potentially dangerous, and should only be handled by qualified persons. If it is splashed onto the skin, it can cause frostbite. It is not itself poisonous, but in the presence of a naked flame (including a cigarette) it forms a poisonous gas. Uncontrolled discharging of the refrigerant is dangerous, and potentially damaging to the environment.

---

10 Climate control system components – removal and refitting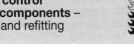

Control panel

Note: *If the control panel assembly is renewed, it will need to be programmed prior to use. This can only be carried out by a Volvo dealer or suitably-equipped specialist.*

1 Disconnect the battery (see *Disconnecting the battery* in Chapter 5). Wait at least 3 minutes before proceeding.

XC60 models

2 Remove the centre console as described in Chapter 11.

3 Remove the trim panel and then remove the four screws **(see illustration)**.

10.11a Remove the panel from the housing and...

10.7 Remove the screws (arrowed)

4 If required, prise free the switch covers, but note that these are only covers. The actual switches are integral to the control panel.

5 Refitting is a reversal of removal.

XC90 models

Note: *The audio unit and heater control assembly are removed as a single item.*

6 Prise free the gear selector trim panel, twist it slightly and move it rearwards.

7 Remove the now exposed lower screws **(see illustration)**.

8 To release the complete unit, pull out the lower edge and then pull the assembly down to free the upper edge. Disconnect the wiring plugs and remove the unit from the vehicle.

9 Turn the unit over, place it on a soft surface and remove the four screws from the rear.

10 Depress the clips on the rear and separate the audio unit from the control panel.

11 Remove two further screws and remove the control panel form the housing **(see illustrations)**.

12 Refitting is a reversal of removal.

Heater blower motor

13 Before starting work, set the ventilation system to recirculation mode. This ensures the recirculation flap on the heater unit is in the correct position.

14 Remove the facia as described in Chapter 11.

XC60 models

15 Unclip the wiring from the motor housing. Undo the 3 screws and remove the end casing containing the distribution flap motor, to gain access to the blower fan.

10.11b ...then remove the cover from the control panel

10.16a Rotate the housing...

10.16b ...and remove the fan and motor assembly

10.17 A hole (arrowed) is provided to insert a securing screw

10.21a Remove the screws (arrowed) and...

10.21b ...withdraw the motor and blower assembly

16 Disconnect the wiring plug, release the plastic tab at the motor and turn the complete motor clockwise to release it from the heater housing. Withdraw the motor from the heater housing from the side containing the fan, supporting the fan spindle as it is withdrawn **(see illustrations)**.

17 Refit by reversing the removal operations. If the plastic tab at the motor breaks on removal, a hole is provided to insert a suitable securing screw **(see illustration).**

XC90 models

18 Have the refrigerant professionally removed from the AC system and then drain the coolant as described in Chapter 1.

19 Remove the facia panel and cross member as described in Chapter 11.

20 It is now possible to access the blower motor by partially removing the heater box at the left-hand end, however having come this far it is just as easy to remove the complete heater box assembly from the vehicle and complete the work on the bench.

21 With the heater box on the bench, remove the five screws and remove the fan and motor from the housing **(see illustration)**.

22 Remove the lower cover and release the wiring plug. Remove the two screws and lift the blower motor from the housing.

23 If required remove a further two screws and remove the control unit.

24 Refitting is a reversal of removal.

XC90 Rear blower motor

25 Some XC90 models have a rear heater/AC unit fitted.

26 With reference to Chapter 11, remove the load area side panel.

27 Disconnect the wiring plug from the motor. Remove three screws and withdraw the blower motor.

28 Refitting is a reversal of removal.

Heater blower motor resistor

Note: *On XC90 models the resistor is part of the blower motor control unit and is removed after the blower motor has been removed – as described above.*

XC60 models

29 Remove the glovebox as described in Chapter 11. The resistor is located behind the pollen filter housing. Access is difficult but possible.

30 Disconnect the wiring plug, rotate the resistor anti-clockwise, and remove it from the blower motor housing **(see illustrations)**.

31 Refitting is a reversal of removal.

Heater matrix

Note: *Refer to the warnings given in Section 1 of this Chapter before proceeding.*

32 Drain the cooling system as described in Chapter 1.

33 Disconnect the battery negative terminal as described in Chapter 5.

XC60 models

34 Remove the centre console as described in Chapter 11.

35 Remove the centre air vent and move the rear air vents to one side.

36 Where fitted remove the auxiliary heater as descried in Section 11 of this Chapter.

37 Remove the upper cover from the matrix **(see illustration)**.

38 Working in the driver's footwell, undo the 2 screws and remove the plastic cover over the coolant pipes.

39 Undo the clamps and disconnect the

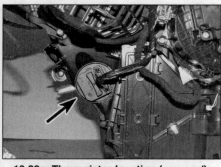

10.30a The resistor location (arrowed), with the heater removed for clarity

10.30b Rotate the resistor to remove it

10.37 Remove the screws (arrowed)

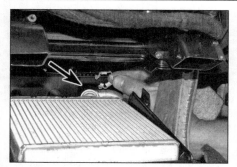

10.39 Remove the spring clips (arrowed)

10.40 Remove the matrix

10.46a Remove the spring clips (arrowed, with one hidden)

coolant pipes. Be prepared for coolant spillage **(see illustration)**.

40 Pull the matrix upwards and rearwards to remove **(see illustration)**.

41 Refit by reversing the removal operations. Use new O-rings on the heater pipes and top-up the cooling system as described in *Weekly checks* on completion.

XC90 models

42 Have the AC system professionally drained by a suitably equipped specialist.

43 Working under the bonnet, disconnect the coolant supply pipes to the heater matrix. If available clamp the pipes with suitable hose clamp pliers. Alternatively, partially drain the coolant.

44 Remove the facia as described in Chapter 11.

45 With reference to Heater housing removal (detailed below in this section) remove the cross member and then remove the heater unit from the vehicle. Anticipate some coolant spillage as the unit is removed.

46 Note the orientation of the retaining clips and then remove the clips. Release the coolant pipes from the matrix **(see illustrations)**.

47 To remove the matrix, first remove the blower motor housing by removing the screws and clips.

48 Remove the two screws and pull the matrix from the air distribution unit **(see illustration)**.

49 Refit by reversing the removal operations. Use new O-rings on the heater pipes and top-up the cooling system as described in *Weekly checks* on completion.

Air recirculation flap motor

XC60 models

50 Remove the blower motor as described above.

51 Carefully release the control flaps from the housing.

52 Remove the two screws and remove the motor from the housing

53 Refitting is a reversal of removal.

XC90 models

54 The motor is located on the left-hand side of the heater unit and can be accessed by removing the glovebox as described in Chapter 11.

10.46b Release the coolant pipes

55 Unclip the operating arm from the motor, undo the 2 screws and remove the motor **(see illustration)**. Disconnect the wiring plug.

56 Refitting is a reversal of removal.

Defroster damper motor

XC60 models

57 The motor is located on the right-hand side of the heater housing.

58 Remove the steering column as described in Chapter 10.

59 Remove the instrument panel as described in Chapter 12.

60 Disconnect the wiring plug, remove the 2 screws and release the motor.

61 Refitting is a reversal of removal.

XC90 models

62 The motor is located on the right-hand side of the heater housing.

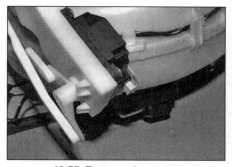

10.55 Remove the motor

10.48 Remove the matrix

63 Remove the soundproofing panel from the side of the centre console.

64 Remove the panel from below the steering column. Disconnect the footwell lamp wiring plug as the panel is removed.

65 Disconnect the wiring plug, remove the 2 screws and remove the motor.

66 Refitting is a reversal of removal.

Footwell damper motor (XC60 only)

67 The motor is located on the left-hand side of the heater housing.

68 Remove the glovebox as described in Chapter 11. The motor is the one closest to the bulkhead.

69 Disconnect the wiring plug **(see illustration)**, remove the 2 screws and withdraw the motor.

70 Refitting is a reversal of removal.

10.69 Disconnect the wiring plug

10.89 Remove and then immediately seal the AC pipes (XC60 shown)

Climate control damper motor (XC60 only)

71 The motor is located next to the footwell damper motor and is removed in a similar manner.

Temperature control motor (XC90 only)

72 2 control motors are fitted – one at each side of the heater housing. Both are the lower of the 2 motors on each side.

73 On the left-hand side remove the glovebox (as described in Chapter 11). Disconnect the wiring plug, remove the 2 mounting screws and remove the motor.

74 On the right-hand side remove the soundproofing from the side of the centre console.

75 Disconnect the wiring plug, remove the 2 screws and withdraw the motor.

76 Refitting is a reversal of removal.

10.95 Remove the central framework

10.97b Remove the end bolts from the A-pillar (arrowed)

10.90 Release the coolant hoses (XC90 shown)

Facia panel vents

Side and centre vents

77 Remove the facia end panel (on the appropriate side) by prising it free with a suitable plastic trim tool.

78 Use a suitable trim tool and release the four locking tangs from the lower vent. On XC60 models release the locking tabs from the smaller upper vent. These are locate at the base of the vent.

79 To access the centre vent on XC60 models carefully remove the trim panel. Locate the four locking tangs and release them with a trim tool. Disconnect the wiring plug from the hazard light switch. Pull the vents down and forward to release them.

80 On XC90 models use a trim tool and small screwdriver to release the centre vent, disconnect the wiring plug from the hazard warning light switch as the vent is removed.

81 Refitting is a reversal of removal.

10.97a Make alignment marks around the bolt heads (arrowed)

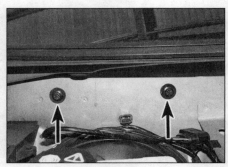

10.98 Remove the bolts (arrowed)

Heater housing

All models

Note: *Most of the main wiring loom must be unclipped and unplugged to enable removal of the heater housing. Not the location of each cable clip as the loom is removed and label each wiring plug as they are disconnected from the various electrical components.*

82 Disconnect the battery - see *Disconnecting the battery* in Chapter 5.

83 Have the air conditioning refrigerant discharged by a suitably-equipped specialist.

84 Drain the coolant as described in Section 1.

85 Remove the plenum chamber cover panel. On XC90 models remove the brace from the strut towers and then remove drain pipe from the right-hand strut tower.

86 To improve access remove the complete wiper mechanism as described in Chapter 12.

87 On some models remove the 2 bolts from the bulkhead and then remove the heat shield from above the expansion valve.

88 To allow sufficient room to disconnect the pipes from the expansion valve on XC60 models, remove the coolant expansion bottle and release the AC pipes from the clamps on the inner wing below the expansion bottle.

89 Undo the bolt securing the air conditioning pipes to the expansion valve at the bulkhead and pull the pipes towards the front of the vehicle to release them from the expansion valve. Plug the ends of the pipes to prevent the ingress of dirt, and discard the seals as new ones must be fitted on reconnection **(see illustration)**.

90 Disconnect the heater hoses at the bulkhead, below the expansion valve. Rotate the locking collar on each pipe approximately a quarter of a turn anti-clockwise, and pull from the pipe stubs **(see illustration)**.

91 Remove the centre console and facia as described in Chapter 11.

XC60 models

92 Remove the engine electronic control unit (ECU) as described in Chapter 4A.

93 Working inside the vehicle remove the ventilation ducts from the centre of the heater unit and from the top on each side.

94 Remove the 4 bolts from the heater matrix cover.

95 Remove the lower side bolts from the alloy support in the centre of the facia and then remove the remaining 8 bolts. Remove the frame from the vehicle **(see illustration)**.

96 Release the steering column lower pinch bolt and then remove the steering column as described in Chapter 10.

97 Mark the position of the cross member in relation to the A-pillars and then remove the single bolt from each A post **(see illustrations)**. The bolts can not be fully removed with the doors in place, but they can be freed from the cross member. **Do not** close the doors with the bolts removed.

98 Working in the plenum chamber, remove the 2 bolts adjacent to the brake vacuum servo **(see illustration)** and the single bolt

from behind the ECU mounting bracket. Note that this is single bolt is not fitted to all models.

99 Where fitted, remove the control module from the right-hand cross member.

100 Remove the 4 remaining bolts that secure the cross member to the vehicle body. Remove each section of the cross member **(see illustration)**.

101 Check that all sections of the wiring loom are unclipped, release the evaporator drain hose from the transmission tunnel and the (with the aid of an assistant) remove the heater unit from the vehicle **(see illustration)**.

XC90 models

102 Detach and remove the air ducts from the heater unit **(see illustration)**.

103 Working from one side to the other release the assorted wiring loom clips and cable ties from the crossmember. Note the position of the cable ties. Disconnect the various wiring plugs from the heater unit.

104 Carefully mark the position of the crossmember in relation to the A-pillars and then remove the bolts from the crossmember at the pillars **(see illustration)**.

105 Remove the bolts holding the crossmember to the transmission tunnel and to the heater housing **(see illustration)**.

106 Working under the bonnet, remove the 2 bolts from the bulkhead **(see illustration)**.

107 With the aid of an assistant hold up the loom and pull the cross member away from the bulkhead. It is not necessary to remove it from the vehicle completely, just pull it forward sufficiently to remove the heater housing **(see illustration)**.

10.100 Remove the crossmember

108 Work the heater unit free from the vehicle and remove it from the vehicle.

XC90 models (rear)

109 With reference to Chapter 11 remove the load area side panel.

110 Remove the single nut and separate the AC pipes from the heater unit. Disconnect the motor wiring plug.

111 Remove the 3 mounting bolts, unplug the drain hose and remove the unit from the side panel

Refitting – all models

112 Refitting is a reversal of removal, noting the following points:

a) If necessary replace the loom wiring clips.

b) Fit new O-ring seals to the expansion valve and air conditioning pipe connections at the engine compartment bulkhead.

c) Ensure that the evaporator drain pipe is correctly fitted and routed.

10.101 Remove the heater housing

d) Upon completion have the air conditioning system recharged, and checked for leaks.

e) Refill the cooling system and check for leaks

Evaporator

Note: *Whenever disconnecting air conditioning pipes or components, always plug the openings to prevent dirt ingress, and to prevent the receiver/drier from becoming saturated.*

All models

113 Have the air conditioning refrigerant discharged by a suitably-equipped specialist.

114 drain the cooling system and remove the heater housing as described above.

XC60 models

115 with the heater housing on the bench, remove the cover plate from the AC pipes **(see illustration)**.

10.102 Remove the ducts

10.104 Remove the bolts (arrowed)

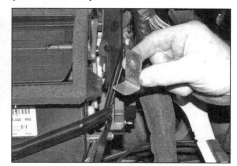

10.105 Remove the small brackets from the heater housing

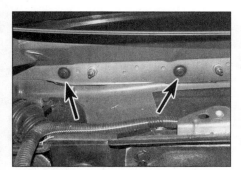

10.106 Remove the bolts (arrowed)

10.107 Pull the crossmember free

10.115 Remove the covers

10.116 Cut free the evaporator cover

10.121a Separate the housing…

10.121b …and remove the evaporator

116 Use a sharp knife (wear gloves if necessary) and cut around the seal on the evaporator **(see illustration)**. Remove the evaporator. Note that replacement evaporators are supplied with a new cover.
117 Refitting is a reversal of removal, noting the following points:
a) *Fit new O-ring seals to the expansion valve and air conditioning pipe connections at the engine compartment bulkhead.*
b) *Upon completion have the air conditioning system recharged, and checked for leaks.*

XC90 models (front)

118 Remove the foam seal and clamp from AC pipes and then remove 2 screws to access the temperature sensor. Remove the sensor.
119 Remove the 4 screws and remove the pollen filter from its housing.
120 Remove the blower motor as described in paragraphs 18 to 23.
121 Use a screwdriver to separate the locking tangs on the 2 halves of the housing. Separate the upper section from the lower section and recover the evaporator **(see illustrations)**.
122 With the evaporator on the bench, remove the 2 bolts and remove the expansion valve. Separate the pipe clamp and recover the seal.
123 Refitting is a reversal of removal, noting the following points:
a) *Fit new O-ring seals to the expansion valve and air conditioning pipe connections at the engine compartment bulkhead.*

b) *Upon completion have the air conditioning system recharged, and checked for leaks.*

XC90 models (rear)

124 Remove the rear heater unit as described above and then remove the expansion valve.
125 Work around the housing and remove the 7 screws. Remove the cover and withdraw the evaporator.
126 Refitting is a reversal of removal, noting the following points:
a) *Fit new O-ring seals to the expansion valve and air conditioning pipe connections.*
b) *Upon completion have the air conditioning system recharged, and checked for leaks.*

Condenser

Note: *Whenever disconnecting air conditioning pipes or components, always plug the openings to prevent dirt ingress, and to prevent the receiver/drier from becoming saturated.*

All models

127 Have the air conditioning system discharged by a suitably-equipped specialist. Refer to Section 5 for removal of the radiator (though note that the intercooler should not be separated at this stage), ensuring that the air conditioning pipes to the condenser are also disconnected. Note also that the radiator, condenser, and intercooler are removed from the vehicle as one unit. With the units removed, the condenser can be separated **(see illustrations)**.

128 Refitting is a reversal of removal, noting the following points:
a) *To aid refitting, disconnect the intercooler air pipes at their locations on the engine and then refit to the intercooler in the correct position. The air deflectors and brackets removed previously can then be refitted before the units are raised into position.*
b) *The units are raised into position from beneath the vehicle using a suitable jack which should be padded to prevent damage. Ensure that pipes or hoses do not become trapped as the units are raised into position. The aid of an assistant is helpful to support the units while the radiator support is refitted.*
c) *Fit new O-ring seals to the air conditioning pipe connections.*
d) *Upon completion, have the air conditioning system recharged, and checked for leaks.*
e) *Refill the cooling system.*

Expansion valve

Note: *Whenever disconnecting air conditioning pipes or components, always plug the openings to prevent dirt ingress, and to prevent the receiver/drier from becoming saturated.*

129 Have the air conditioning refrigerant discharged by a suitably-equipped specialist.

XC60 models

130 Remove the plenum cover as described in Chapter 12, Section 18 and release the clamps securing the air conditioning pipes to the valve.

10.127a Disconnect the AC pipes from the condenser (XC90 shown)

10.127b Separate the condenser from the radiator (XC60 shown)

10.127c Always seal the openings

131 Remove the coolant expansion tank (there is no need to drain the coolant) and disconnect the AC pipes from below the coolant expansion tank. Release the pipes from the pipe clamps on the inner wing. This will provide enough room to move the rigid pipes back from the expansion valve.
132 Remove the 2 bolts and pull the expansion valve from the bulk head.
133 Refitting is a reversal of removal, noting the following points:
  a) *Tighten the expansion valve screws to the specified torque.*
  b) *Renew all O-ring seals where disturbed.*
  c) *Upon completion, have the air conditioning system recharged and checked for leaks.*

XC90 models

134 Remove the support strut from the engine bay and then remove the plenum drain pipe from the right-hand side of the engine bay.
135 Release the AC pipe clamps from the right-hand inner wing and then remove the single bolt that secures the AC pipes to the expansion valve. Carefully remove the pipes from the expansion valve.
136 Remove the 2 bolts and remove the expansion valve from the bulk head.
137 Refitting is a reversal of removal, noting the following points:
  a) *Fit new O-ring seals to the expansion valve and air conditioning pipe connections at the engine compartment bulkhead.*
  b) *Upon completion have the air conditioning system recharged, and checked for leaks.*

Receiver/drier

Note: *Whenever disconnecting air conditioning pipes or components, always plug the openings to prevent dirt ingress, and to prevent the receiver/drier from becoming saturated.*

XC60 models

138 Have the air conditioning refrigerant discharged by a suitably-equipped specialist.
139 The receiver drier is located next to the condenser on the right-hand side of the engine bay.
140 Remove the single bolt and release the receiver drier from the condenser **(see illustration)**.
141 Refitting is a reversal of removal, noting the following points:
  a) *Fit new O-ring seals to the expansion valve and air conditioning pipe connections at the engine compartment bulkhead.*
  b) *Upon completion have the air conditioning system recharged, and checked for leaks.*

XC90 models

142 Have the air conditioning refrigerant discharged by a suitably-equipped specialist.
143 Remove the bumper cover as described

10.140 Remove the receiver/drier (XC60)

in Chapter 11 and then remove the shroud from the radiator/condenser assembly.
144 Raise the front of the vehicle - see *Jacking and vehicle support* in the reference section.
145 Remove the engine undershield.
146 Unbolt and remove the AC pipe from the receiver drier, disconnect the wiring plug **(see illustration)** from the pressure sensor and then remove the pressure sensor.
147 Remove the lower mounting bolt from the receiver drier and then lower the vehicle and remove the upper mounting bolt.
148 Pull up the receiver drier to unhook it from the condenser and remove it from the vehicle.
149 Refitting is a reversal of removal, noting the following points:
  a) *Fit new O-ring seals to the expansion valve and air conditioning pipe connections at the engine compartment bulkhead.*
  b) *Upon completion have the air conditioning system recharged, and checked for leaks.*

Compressor

Note: *Whenever disconnecting air conditioning pipes or components, always plug the openings to prevent dirt ingress, and to prevent the receiver/drier from becoming saturated.*

All models

150 Have the air conditioning refrigerant discharged by a suitably-equipped specialist.
151 Disconnect the battery (see *Disconnecting the battery* in Chapter 5).
152 Pull up and remove the engine cover.
153 Remove the auxiliary drivebelt as described in Chapter 1.
154 Jack up the front of the vehicle and support it securely on axle stands (see *Jacking and vehicle support*).
155 Remove the engine undershield.

XC60 models

156 Remove the intercooler hose.
157 Disconnect the wiring plug from the compressor clutch.
158 Unbolt and remove the AC pipes from the rear of the compressor.
159 Remove the 3 mounting bolts and lower the compressor from the vehicle **(see illustration)**.
160 Refitting is a reversal of removal, but to

10.146 Remove the wiring plug

avoid incorrectly aligning the compressor, note the following points:
  a) *Install the longest bolt in the rear mounting.*
  b) *Tighten the longest (rear) bolt first.*
  c) *Tighten the remaining 2 bolts.*
  d) *Fill the replacement compressor with the correct amount of compressor oil – see the specifications.*
  e) *Upon completion, have the air conditioning system recharged and checked for leaks.*

XC90 models

161 Release the clamps from the lower turbo charger supply hose and then remove the hose.
162 Protect the alternator from oil contamination and then remove the power steering fluid hose from the power steering pump.
163 Remove the AC pipes from the compressor and then disconnect the magnetic clutch wiring plug.
164 Unbolt and remove the compressor from the engine bay.
165 Refitting is a reversal of removal, but note the following:
  a) *Fill the replacement compressor with the correct amount of compressor oil – see the specifications.*
  b) *Check and if necessary top up the power steering fluid.*
  c) *Upon completion, have the air conditioning system recharged and checked for leaks.*

Solar sensor

166 The solar sensor is combined with the

10.159 Undo the three compressor mounting bolts (arrowed)

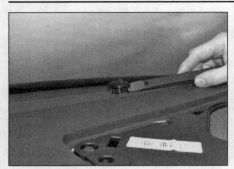

10.167 Carefully prise the solar sensor from the top of the facia

10.170 Passenger compartment temperature sensor (XC90)

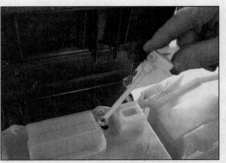

10.176 Evaporator temperature sensor (XC90)

anti-theft alarm system diode, and is located on top of the facia cover.

167 Carefully prise up the sensor using a screwdriver inserted under its base at the side (see illustration).

168 Disconnect the wiring connector and remove the sensor.

169 Refitting is a reversal of removal.

Passenger compartment and air temperature sensors

170 The passenger compartment sensor is located on the reverse of the climate control panel (see illustration). Air temperature sensors are located in the heater housing and may only be accessible with the heater housing removed. Refer to this Section for removal.

Evaporator temperature sensor

XC60

171 Remove the left-hand trim panel from the centre console.

172 Disconnect the wiring plug and pull the sensor from the housing.

173 Refitting is a reversal of removal.

XC90

174 Remove heater unit to access the temperature sensor.

175 Remove the left-hand side panel from the centre console.

176 Disconnect the wiring plug and carefully prise the sensor from position (see illustration).

177 Refitting is a reversal of removal.

11 Auxiliary heater –
general information, removal and refitting

General information

1 Some models may be fitted with an auxiliary heater. The system consists of a fuel driven coolant heater or an electrically-heated unit.

2 The fuel driven heater will always run, providing that:

a) The ambient air temperature is less than 3 degrees C.
b) The engine is running.
c) There is at least 4 litres of fuel in the tank.
d) There are no relevant diagnostic trouble codes stored in the ECU.
e) The engine coolant temperature is below 75 degrees

Removal and refitting

3 Disconnect the battery - see Disconnecting the battery in Chapter 5.

4 Partially drain the cooling system (fuel driven heaters only).

XC60 models

5 Remove the plenum chamber cover and to prevent further coolant loss, use suitable hose clamps to clamp the coolant supply and return hoses.

6 Jack up and support the front of the vehicle - see Jacking and vehicle support in the reference section. Remove the

right-hand road wheel and then remove the wing liner.

7 Remove the mountings from the exhaust pipe and then remove the exhaust from the vehicle.

8 Disconnect the wiring plug.

9 Disconnect the fuel supply line and immediately seal the fuel line.

10 Remove the 2 mounting bolts and lower the heater from the wheel arch.

11 Refitting is a reversal of removal.

XC90 models

12 Remove the front bumper cover as described in Chapter 11.

13 To prevent further coolant loss, use suitable hose clamps to clamp the coolant supply and return hoses.

14 Disconnect the fuel supply line and then unplug the wiring connector.

15 Remove the mounting bolts, unhook and then remove the heater unit.

16 Refitting is a reversal of removal.

XC60 - electrically operated fuel heater

17 Disconnect the battery negative lead as described in Chapter 5.

18 Remove the centre console as described in Chapter 11.

19 Remove the central air vent and move the rear air vents to one side.

20 Disconnect the wiring plugs on the heater unit, undo the screw on each side, and withdraw the unit (see illustrations).

21 Refitting is a reversal of removal.

11.20a Disconnect the wiring plugs for the electric auxiliary heater

11.20b Withdraw the heater

Chapter 4 Part A:
Fuel and exhaust systems

Contents

Degrees of difficulty

Easy, suitable for novice with little experience	**Fairly easy,** suitable for beginner with some experience	**Fairly difficult,** suitable for competent DIY mechanic	**Difficult,** suitable for experienced DIY mechanic	**Very difficult,** suitable for expert DIY or professional

Specifications

General

System type	Direct injection common rail with Bosch high pressure delivery pump
Fuel tank pump pressure	Unable to verify
Fuel injection pump	Tandem pump (high pressure and low pressure) driven by the inlet camshaft
Injection pressure.	Not available
Turbocharger type	Garret – variable nozzle
Turbocharger boost pressure	Not available
Idle speed:*.	720 rpm

Not adjustable – controlled by engine control module (ECM)

Torque wrench settings

	Nm	lbf ft
Exhaust manifold-to-EGR pipe nuts	24	18
Exhaust manifold to cylinder head:		
2.0 litre engine:		
End nuts:		
Stage 1	14	10
Stage 2	16	12
Top and bottom nuts:		
Stage 1	12	7
Stage 2	14	10
2.4 litre engine:		
Stage 1	15	11
Stage 2	25	18
Exhaust temperature sensor	45	34
Exhaust manifold heat shield	24	18
Fuel control valve (on rail):		
Stage 1	60	44
Stage 2	Slacken 90°	
Stage 3	80	60
Fuel injector clamp screws:*	13	10
Fuel pressure safety valve	95	70
Fuel pressure sensor:		
2.4 litre engines (D5244 T4 and T5)	70	52
Fuel pressure sensor adapter to common rail	60	44
Fuel pump mounting screws	18	13
Fuel rail-to-cylinder head bolts	24	18
Fuel sender locking ring		
2.0 litre engine	85	63
2.4 litre engine	60	44
Fuel tank restraining strap bolts	24	18
Fuel temperature sensor (on pump)	21	15
Fuel temperature/pressure sensor (on rail)	70	52
High-pressure pipe union nuts:*		
2.0 litre engine (at common rail and injector):		
Stage 1	10	8
Stage 2	Angle-tighten a further 60°	
2.0 litre engine (at high pressure pump)		
Stage 1	10	8
Stage 2	Angle-tighten a further 75°	
2.4 litre engine	28	21
Oxygen sensor	45	34
Manifold absolute pressure sensor (MAP)	10	7
Turbocharger:		
Coolant pipe to turbocharger	38	28
Oil feed to turbocharger	18	13
Oil feed to cylinder block	38	28
Oil drain from turbocharger	12	9
Turbocharger to exhaust manifold:*		
Stage 1	18	13
Stage 2	24	18
Turbocharger to turbocharger nuts	40	30

Do not re-use. Volvo specify that where a fixing requires angular tightening it must always be renewed. Any fixing retained with a thread locking compound must also be renewed. Nuts with a nylon insert must always be renewed.

1 General information and precautions

General information

Note: *The operation of the fuel injection system is described in more detail in Section 5.*

Fuel is drawn from a tank under the rear of the vehicle by a tank-immersed electric pump, and then forced through a filter to the injection pump. The inlet camshaft driven injection pump is a tandem pump – a low-pressure gear-type pump which supplies the high-pressure pump with fuel at a constant pressure, and a high-pressure piston-type pump which supplies fuel to the common fuel rail at variable pressure. Fuel is supplied from the common fuel rail to the injectors. Also inside the injection pump assembly is a pressure control valve which regulates the quantity of fuel to the high-pressure pump, and a bypass valve which returns excess fuel back to the low pressure pump. The injectors are operated by solenoids controlled by the ECM, based on information supplied by various sensors. The engine ECM also controls the preheating side of the system – refer to Chapter 5 for more details.

The EDC (electronic diesel control) system fitted, incorporates a 'drive-by-wire' system, where an accelerator pedal position sensor is fitted instead of the traditional accelerator cable. The position and rate-of-change of the accelerator pedal is reported by the position sensor to the ECM, which then adjusts the fuel injectors and fuel pressure to deliver the required amount of fuel, and optimum combustion efficiency.

The exhaust system incorporates a turbocharger, and an EGR valve. Further detail of the emission control systems can be found in Chapter 4B.

Precautions

• Avoid prolonged skin contact with diesel fuel – it can cause dermatitis. Do not expose yourself to injector spray, which can penetrate the skin.

• When working on diesel fuel system components, scrupulous cleanliness must be observed, and care must be taken not to introduce any foreign matter into fuel lines or components.

• After carrying out any work involving disconnection of fuel lines, it is advisable to check the connections for leaks; pressurise the system by cranking the engine several times.

• Electronic control units are very sensitive components, and certain precautions must be taken to avoid damage to these units as follows.

• When carrying out welding operations on the vehicle using electric welding equipment, the battery and alternator should be disconnected.

• If using welding equipment or pressure-washing equipment in the vicinity of an electronic module, take care not to direct heat, or jets of water or steam at the module. If this cannot be avoided, remove the module from the vehicle, and protect its wiring plug with a plastic bag.

• Before disconnecting any wiring, or removing components, always ensure that the ignition is switched off.

• Do not attempt to improvise ECM fault diagnosis procedures using a test lamp or multimeter, as irreparable damage could be caused to the module.

• After working on fuel injection/engine management system components, ensure that all wiring is correctly reconnected before reconnecting the battery or switching on the ignition.

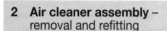

2 Air cleaner assembly – removal and refitting

Removal

1 Remove the engine cover.

XC60

2 Disconnect the mass air flow (MAF) sensor **(see illustration)** and then slacken the hose clamp from the outlet pipe.
3 Prise free the housing inlet duct **(see illustration)**.
4 Pull up and remove the filter housing. Note that the housing is a very tight fit on its mounting. Remove the housing and if necessary recover the rubber mountings from the inner wing **(see illustrations)**.

XC90

5 Disconnect the battery as described in Chapter 5.
6 Remove the cover from the main engine management ECU (Electronic Control Unit).

2.2 Disconnect the MAF sensor wiring plug

2.4a Remove the housing...

7 Disconnect the ECU wiring plugs and then remove the ECU from the top of the housing **(see illustrations)**.
8 Unbolt the inlet pipe from the bonnet slam panel and then disconnect the wiring plug from the MAF sensor **(see illustration)**.

2.7a Disconnect the wiring plugs...

2.8 Disconnect the MAF wiring plug

2.3 Remove the inlet duct

2.4b ...and recover the mountings

9 Slacken the hose clip from the housing outlet, remove the cover mounting screws (or release the spring clips) recover the air filter and then lift of the upper section of the housing **(see illustration)**.
10 Remove the mounting bolt and then

2.7b ...and then remove the ECU

2.9 Remove the upper section of the housing

2.10 Remove the main section

lift up and remove the main housing **(see illustration)**.

Refitting

11 Refitting is a reversal of removal. Make sure the outlet and intake ducts are clipped securely into position (where applicable).

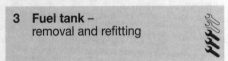

3 Fuel tank – removal and refitting

Note: *Observe the precautions in Section 1 before working on any component in the fuel system.*

Removal – all models

1 Before the tank can be removed, it must be drained of as much fuel as possible. To avoid the dangers and complications of fuel handling and storage, it is advisable to

carry out this operation with the tank almost empty.
2 Disconnect the battery negative lead (see Chapter 5).
3 Jack up and support the rear of the vehicle - see *Jacking and vehicle support* in Reference

XC60 models

4 On AWD models remove the prop shaft as described in Chapter 8B.
5 Unbolt and remove the protective covers from each side of the fuel tank.
6 With reference to Section 17 of this Chapter remove the rear section of the exhaust system.
7 Remove the heat shield from above the exhaust and then release the hose clip from the fuel filler pipe.
8 Anticipating some fluid loss, release the fuel line connections from the chassis **(see illustration)**.
9 The tank must now be supported with a suitable jack. Use a block (or blocks) of wood to spread the load.
10 Remove the retaining straps **(see illustration)** and lower the tank sufficiently to release the electrical connector(s) and the fuel filler vent pipe from the tank – where fitted. Note also the alternative method used to lower fuel tank below **(see illustrations 3.19)**.
11 With the aid of an assistant lower the tank. Note that the tank will have to be tilted slightly to clear the vehicle body work.

XC90 models

12 Remove both rear road wheels and then (with reference to Chapter 9) remove the handbrake cables.
13 With reference to Section 17 of this

Chapter remove the rear section of the exhaust system.
14 Remove the prop shaft as described in Chapter 8B.
15 The rear axle and suspension must now be removed. Use a suitable jack and support the complete rear axle and suspension. Follow the procedure as described in Chapter 10.
16 Remove the hose clips from the filler neck and breather pipe **(see illustration)**. Partially release the pipes.
17 The tank must now be supported with a suitable jack. Use a block (or blocks) of wood to spread the load.
18 With the tank supported disconnect the fuel filter connections and then unbolt and remove the tank retaining straps.
19 As an alternative solution, we swopped the tank strap bolts for lengths of threaded bar (one at a time), and then used these to lowered the tank sufficiently to release the electrical connector(s) and the fuel lines from the tank **(see illustrations)**.
20 Check that all connections have been removed and then remove the lengths of threaded bar (if fitted).
21 Lower the jack and tank, and remove the tank from under the car.

Refitting - all models

22 If the tank is contaminated with sediment or water, remove the gauge sender unit and the fuel pump (Section 7 of this Chapter). Swill the tank out with clean fuel.
23 The tank is moulded from a synthetic material and if damaged, it should be renewed. However, in certain cases it may be possible to have small leaks or minor damage repaired. Seek the advice of a dealer or suitable specialist concerning tank repair.
24 If a new tank is to be fitted, transfer all the components from the old tank to the new. Always renew the seals and plastic collars securing the fuel pump and gauge sender unit. Once used, they may not seat and seal properly on a new tank.

Refitting

25 Refitting is a reversal of removal. On completion, refill the tank with fuel and check exhaustively for signs of leakage before driving the car on the road.

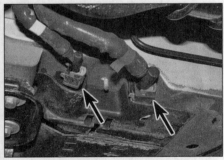

3.8 Disconnect the fuel lines (arrowed)

3.10 Remove the tank support strap bolt (arrowed)

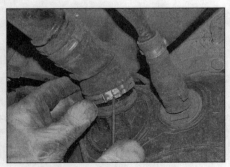

3.16 Remove the hose clips

3.19a Lower the tank on lengths of treaded bar and...

3.19b ...then remove the fuel lines and electrical connectors

4 Accelerator pedal – removal and refitting

Removal

1 Undo the two screws and remove the trim panel above the pedals in the driver's footwell.
2 Undo the 3 nuts securing the assembly to the bulkhead **(see illustrations)**.
3 Where fitted, release the cable-tie, and then disconnect the position sensor wiring plug as the pedal assembly is removed. No further dismantling of the assembly is recommended.

Refitting

4 Refit by reversing the removal operations.

5 Fuel injection system – general information

The system is under the overall control of the electronic diesel control (EDC) system, which also controls the preheating system (see Chapter 5).

Fuel is supplied from the rear-mounted fuel tank, via an electrically-powered lift pump (controlled by the central electronic module) and fuel filter, to the fuel injection pump. The fuel injection pump supplies fuel under high pressure to the common fuel rail. The fuel rail provides a reservoir of fuel under pressure ready for the injectors to deliver direct to the combustion chamber. The individual fuel injectors incorporate solenoids which, when operated, allow the high-pressure fuel to be injected. The solenoids are controlled by the EDC electric control module (ECM). The fuel injection pump purely provides high pressure fuel. The timing and duration of the injection is controlled by the ECM, based on the information received from the various sensors. In order to increase combustion efficiency and reduce combustion noise (diesel 'knock'), a small amount of fuel is injected before the main injection takes place – this is known as pre- or pilot-injection. The fuel filter may also incorporate a heater element and a temperature sensor – if so this is activated at temperatures below -3°C and deactivated at 5°C.

Additionally, the engine management ECM activates the preheating system (Chapter 5), and the exhaust gas recirculation (EGR) system (see Chapter 4B).The system uses the following sensors:
a) *Crankshaft sensor – informs the ECM of the crankshaft speed and position.*
b) *Coolant temperature sensor – informs the ECM of engine temperature.*
c) *Mass airflow/intake air temperature sensor – informs the ECM of the mass and temperature of air entering the intake tract.*

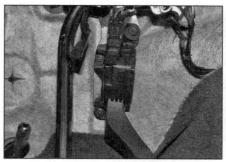

4.2a The accelerator pedal on XC60 models…

d) *Wheel speed sensor – informs the ECM of the vehicle speed.*
e) *Accelerator pedal position sensor – informs the ECM of throttle position, and the rate of throttle opening/closing.*
f) *Fuel high-pressure sensor – informs the ECM of the pressure of the fuel in the common rail.*
g) *Camshaft position sensor – informs the ECM of the camshaft position so that the engine firing sequence can be established.*
h) *Brake light switch – informs the ECM when the brakes are being applied.*
i) *Manifold absolute pressure sensor – informs the ECM of the boost pressure generated by the turbocharger.*
j) *Air conditioning pressure sensor – informs the ECM of the high-pressure side of the air conditioning circuit, in case a raised idle speed is required to compensate for compressor load.*

On all models, a 'drive-by-wire' throttle control system is used. The accelerator pedal is not physically connected to the fuel injection pump with a traditional cable, but instead is monitored by a dual potentiometer mounted on the pedal assembly, which provides the engine control module (ECM) with a signal relating to accelerator pedal movement.

The signals from the various sensors are processed by the ECM, and the optimum fuel quantity and injection timing settings are selected for the prevailing engine operating conditions.

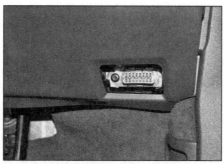

5.9 The diagnostic connector is located on the right-hand side of the facia (XC60 model shown)

4.2b …and on XC90 models

Catalytic converter(s), a particulate filter (depending on model and market) and an exhaust gas recirculation (EGR) system are fitted, to reduce harmful exhaust gas emissions. Details of this and other emissions control system equipment are given in Chapter 4B.

If there is an abnormality in any of the readings obtained from any sensor, the ECM enters its back-up mode. In this event, the ECM ignores the abnormal sensor signal, and assumes a pre-programmed value which will allow the engine to continue running (albeit at reduced efficiency). If the ECM enters this back-up mode, the warning light on the instrument panel will come on, and the relevant fault code will be stored in the ECM memory.

If the warning light comes on, the vehicle should be taken to a Volvo dealer or specialist at the earliest opportunity. A complete test of the electronic diesel control (EDC) system can then be carried out, using a special electronic test unit which is plugged into the system's diagnostic connector. The connector (or more commonly DLC – Data Link Connector) is located below the driver's side of the facia above the pedals **(see illustration)**.

6 Fuel system – priming and bleeding

1 Volvo state that no priming or bleeding is required, as the system is self-bleeding. However, if the vehicle has run out of diesel, or major parts of the fuel system have been disturbed, replenish the tank or check there is sufficient fuel in the tank.
2 On XC60 models, operate the fuel tank-mounted pump for 1 to 2 minutes by inserting the remote unit and briefly pressing the 'start/stop' button, prior to attempting to start the engine.
3 On XC90 insert the key and turn the ignition on and off several times. Do not attempt to start the engine at this point.
4 These methods should ensure sufficient fuel reaches the engine-mounted pump prior to starting.

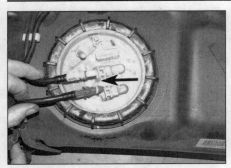

7.3 Disconnect the fuel hoses on top of the sender unit

7.4a Sender unit alignment marks

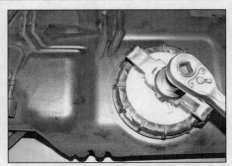

7.4b Remove the sender locking ring using a suitable tool...

7.4c ...or a home-made equivalent

7.5 Withdraw the unit from the fuel tank

7.7 Remove the blanking plate

7 Fuel gauge sender/ pump units – removal and refitting

Note: *Observe the precautions in Section 1 before working on any component in the fuel system.*

Removal

XC60

Note: *2WD models feature a combined level and pump unit, 4WD models have a separate pump and level unit - very similar to XC90 models.*

1 Disconnect the battery negative lead (see Chapter 5).

2 Remove the fuel tank as described in Section 3.

3 Make a note of the correct position, then remove any remaining wiring plugs and fuel lines. Note the position of any seals and be prepared for fuel spillage as the hoses are removed **(see illustration)**.

4 Note the alignment marks between the sender/pump unit and the tank, then remove the locking ring. Volvo use a specific tool (999 7418) but the locking ring can be removed using a suitable home-made tool or a proprietary remover purchased from a motor factors **(see illustrations)**.

5 Carefully withdraw the assembly from the tank, taking care not to bend or damage the float arm. Recover the seal between sender unit and tank **(see illustration)**.

XC 90 models

6 Disconnect the battery negative lead (see Chapter 5).

7 Open the rear doors and with reference to Chapter 11 remove the second row of seats. With the seats removed, partially release the carpet in order to gain access to the blanking plates that cover the fuel level sensors **(see illustration)**.

8 XC90 models feature a combined lift pump and level sensor in the right-hand side of the tank. A separate sensor is fitted to the left-hand side of the tank. The level sensors work in tandem, with the left-hand sensor measuring the lower fuel levels and the right-hand side measuring higher fuel levels.

9 The procedure for removing the sensors is the same as XC60 models, once the locking ring(s) have been removed. Note however if the lift pump and 'high' fuel level sensor are to be removed, the right-hand sensor must be removed first as the fuel pump pick-up pipe and the sensor wiring plug are connected to the left-hand sensor **(see illustrations)**. Take care to avoid dropping the wiring loom into the bowels of the fuel tank – connect a length of cord to the loom and tie it to the side of the tank if necessary.

7.9a Remove the locking collar

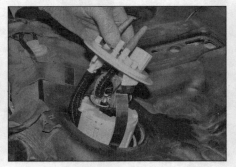

7.9b Remove the combined level/pump assembly...

7.9c ...and the level sensor from the left-hand side

Refitting

10 Refitting is a reversal of removal, bearing in mind the following points:

a) *Use a new seal, ensuring it is seated correctly, smeared with petroleum jelly.*
b) *Take care when lowering the assembly into the tank not to bend or damage the float arm.*
c) *Note the alignment marks when refitting the sender/pump **(see illustration)**.*

---

8 Fuel injection system – testing and adjustment

Testing

1 If a fault appears in the fuel injection system, first ensure that all the system wiring connectors are securely connected and free from corrosion. Ensure that the fault is not due to poor maintenance; ie, check that the air cleaner filter element is clean, that the cylinder compression pressures are correct (see Chapter 2A) and that the engine breather hoses are clear and undamaged.

2 If the engine will not start, check the condition of the glow plugs (see Chapter 5). Note however that faulty glow plugs will only hinder starting in extremely cold conditions.

3 If these checks fail to reveal the cause of the problem, the vehicle should be taken to a Volvo dealer or specialist for testing using special electronic equipment which is plugged into the diagnostic connector. The tester should locate the fault quickly and simply, avoiding the need to test all the system components individually, which is time-consuming, and also carries a risk of damaging the ECM.

Adjustment

4 The engine idle speed, maximum speed and fuel injection pump timing are all controlled by the ECM. Whilst in theory it is possible to check the settings, if they are found to be in need of adjustment, the car will have to be taken to a suitably-equipped Volvo dealer or specialist. They will have access to the necessary diagnostic equipment required to test and (where possible) adjust the settings.

---

9 Fuel injection pump – removal and refitting

Caution: Be careful not to allow dirt into the injection pump or injector pipes during this procedure.

Note: *Any rigid high-pressure fuel pipes disturbed must be renewed.*

Removal

1 Disconnect the battery negative lead (see Chapter 5). On XC60 models remove the battery as described in Chapter 5.

2 Remove the plastic cover from the top of

7.9d Disconnect the wiring loom and recover the sealing ring

the engine, by pulling it straight up from its mountings.

3 Remove the air cleaner assembly as described in Section 2.

4 Disconnect the wiring plugs from the fuel control valve and the temperature sensor.

5 Release the clamps and disconnect the supply and return hoses from the pump. If the metal hose clamps are damaged during removal, update them with traditional worm-drive clamps. Note that some later models have quick release connectors instead of hose clips **(see illustration)**. Plug or seal the pump ports to prevent dirt ingress.

6 Slacken the unions, then remove the high-pressure fuel pipe (or pipes on some models). Discard the pipe or pipes. Plug or cover the fuel rail and pump ports to prevent dirt ingress.

7 Remove the three retaining screws, and remove the fuel pump. Recover the connecting

9.5 Remove the hose connectors (arrowed)

9.7b Recover the connecting piece between the end of the camshaft and the pump drive

7.10 Align the marks on the collar and tank (arrowed)

piece between the end of the camshaft and the pump drive – this is easily lost as the pump is removed **(see illustrations)**. Discard the seal, a new one must be fitted. With the exception of the of the control valve and temperature sensor no internal components of the pump are available. If the pump is faulty, the complete unit may have to be renewed – consult a Volvo dealer or diesel specialist.

Caution: Do not rotate the pump once removed – it's important that it retains its original position if refitted.

Refitting

8 Ensure that the mating surfaces of the pump and engine are clean and dry, and fit a new O-ring seal where appropriate. Lubricate the seal with clean engine oil.

9 Position the fuel pump, ensuring any connecting piece is in place, then tighten the mounting screws to the specified torque.

9.7a Pump retaining screws

9.7c The pump connecting piece must align with the slots in the end of the inlet camshaft

9.11 Use a crow's-foot adapter to tighten the pipe union, and a second spanner to counterhold the pump port. Do not allow the pump port to rotate

10 Reconnect the fuel supply and return hoses to the pump, and secure them with new clamps.

11 Fit the new high-pressure fuel pipe between the pump and common rail, then tighten to the specified torque, using a crow's-foot adapter **(see illustration)**.

12 The remainder of refitting is a reversal of removal, bearing in mind the following points:

a) *Prior to starting the engine on XC60 models, insert the remote unit and press the 'Start' button briefly. On XC90 models insert the key and turn it to the on position. This activates the tank-mounted pump, and ensures sufficient fuel reaches the injection pump for lubrication purposes prior to starting.*

b) *Depress the accelerator pedal to the floor then start the engine as normal (this may take longer than usual – operate the starter in ten second bursts with 5 seconds rest in between each operation). Run the engine at a fast idle speed for a minute or so to purge any remaining trapped air from the fuel lines. After this time the engine should idle smoothly at a constant speed.*

c) *Once the engine has started, thoroughly check for fuel leaks from the disturbed pipes/hoses.*

10 Fuel injectors – removal and refitting

Caution: Be careful not to allow dirt into the injection pump or injector pipes during this procedure.

Removal

1 Remove the plastic cover from the top of the engine by pulling it straight up from its mountings. On XC90 models remove the strut brace and the sound proofing from the top of the engine.

2 Make sure the areas around the high-pressure fuel pipe unions from the fuel rail to the injectors are scrupulously clean and free from debris, etc. If possible, use a vacuum cleaner and a degreaser to clean the area.

3 Disconnect the wiring plugs from the top of each injector **(see illustration)**.

4 Extract the retaining clip and disconnect the leak-off pipe from each injector **(see illustration)**.

5 Undo the unions, then remove the high-pressure fuel pipes from the fuel rail to the injectors. Discard the fuel pipes, new ones must be fitted. Use a second spanner on the on the injector port to counterhold when slackening the pipe union **(see illustrations)**. Be prepared for fuel spillage, and plug/cover the ports in the injectors and fuel rail to prevent contamination.

6 On early engines mark the position of the injectors in relation to the cylinder head. Later engines have a stop provided and can only be fitted in one position.

7 Unscrew the 2 screws/nuts securing each injector (complete with spacers where fitted) and remove the injectors **(see illustration)**.

8 The injectors can be difficult to remove. Volvo use a special tool (999 2709 and 999 7009) to remove the injectors. This tool is also available from independent tool suppliers and consists of a slide hammer and collar to fit the injector.

9 Slide the washers from the end of each injector. Discard the washers – new ones must be fitted. Cover the injector hole in the cylinder head to prevent dirt ingress **(see illustration)**.

10 If the injectors are to be refitted, plug all openings, and store them upright in their original order. They must be refitted to their original positions **(see illustration)**.

Refitting

11 Ensure that the injector bores and seats

10.3 Depress the clip and disconnect the wiring plugs from the injectors

10.4 Prise out the clip and pull the return pipe from each injector

10.5a Undo the pipe union on the common rail

10.5b Use a second spanner to prevent the port on the injector from turning whilst slackening the union

10.7 Injector retaining screws (arrowed)

10.9 Slide the washer from the end of the injector

10.10 The injectors should be stored upright

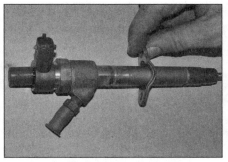

10.12a Fit the new clamp ring . . .

10.12b . . . and washer

10.12c We fabricated a tool out of sheet metal to allow the circlip to slide over the end of the injector

10.12d The circlip must locate in the groove

in the cylinder head are clean, dry and free from soot. It's essential the sealing surfaces are dirt-free, otherwise leakage will occur. Special tools are available to aid cleaning of the bores and injector seats in the cylinder head.

12 Fit new clamp rings, washers, circlips (where applicable) **(see illustrations)** and sealing washers to the injectors, and refit them to the cylinder head. On early engines use the previously made marks to correctly align the injectors. If no alignment marks were made Volvo list a special alignment tool (999 7249). On later engines fit the injectors and rotate them clockwise until they stop.

13 Fit new rigid high-pressure pipes between the common rail and the injectors. Starting at the common rail, tighten the pipe unions to the specified torque. Repeat this procedure on the pipe unions at the injectors. Use a second open-ended spanner to counterhold the injector ports whilst tightening the pipe unions.

14 The remainder of refitting is a reversal of removal, bearing in mind the following points:

a) *Check the condition of the fuel return hoses, and renew if any appear damaged or perished.*

b) *Depending on the engine fitted, different 'classes' of injector may be available as spare parts. You should refer to a Volvo dealer or parts specialist before purchasing.*

c) *If new injectors are fitted, new software may need to be downloaded to the engine management ECM from Volvo. Entrust this task to a Volvo dealer or specialist.*

d) *Depress the accelerator pedal to the floor then start the engine as normal (this may take longer than usual – operate the starter in ten second bursts with 5 seconds rest in between each operation). Run the engine at a fast idle speed for a minute or so to purge any remaining trapped air from the fuel lines. After this time the engine should idle smoothly at a constant speed.*

e) *Once the engine has started, thoroughly check for fuel leaks from the disturbed pipes/hoses.*

11 Electronic diesel control (EDC) system components – removal and refitting

Crankshaft position/speed sensor

1 Remove the EGR cooler and valve assembly, as described in Chapter 4B.

2 The sensor is located above the flywheel. Trace the wiring back from the sensor, and disconnect the wiring plug.

3 Slacken and remove the retaining bolt and carefully remove the sensor from its mounting **(see illustration)**.

4 Refitting is the reverse of removal, tightening the retaining bolt securely.

Mass airflow/intake air temperature sensor

5 Ensure the ignition is switched off then release the retaining clip and disconnect the wiring connector from the airflow sensor **(see illustration)**.

6 Undo the screws then remove the airflow sensor from the air intake pipe, along with its sealing ring where fitted.

7 Refitting is the reverse of removal, lubricating the new sealing ring.

Coolant temperature sensor

8 Refer to Chapter 3 for removal and refitting details.

Accelerator pedal position sensor

9 The sensor is secured to the accelerator

11.3 Crankshaft position sensor (arrowed)

11.5 Mass airflow sensor wiring plug (arrowed)

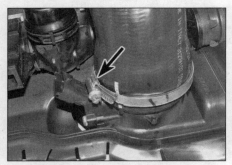

11.15 Boost pressure sensor (arrowed)

11.23a Remove the wiring plugs

11.23b release the catch – note the position of the screwdriver…

11.23c …and remove the control module

pedal. Refer to Section 4 of this Chapter on pedal removal. The sensor is part of the pedal assembly and is not available separately.

Manifold absolute pressure sensor

10 Remove the engine cover.

11 The sensor is mounted on the left-hand end of the inlet manifold, close to the oil filler cap.

12 Ensure the ignition is switched off then disconnect the wiring connector from the sensor.

13 Slacken and remove the retaining bolt and remove the sensor from the vehicle.

14 Refitting is the reverse of removal, tightening the sensor retaining securely.

Turbo boost pressure sensor

15 The sensor is mounted on the intercooler outer pipe **(see illustration)**.

16 Ensure the ignition is switched off then disconnect the wiring connector from the sensor.

17 Access on XC60 models is extremely difficult. Removal is considerably easier if the intercooler is partially removed first.

18 Slacken and remove the retaining bolt and remove the sensor from the vehicle.

19 Refitting is the reverse of removal, tightening the sensor retaining bolt securely.

Brake light switch

20 The engine control module receives a signal from the brake light switch which indicates when the brakes are being applied. Brake light switch removal and refitting details can be found in Chapter 9.

Electronic control module (ECM)

Note: *If a new control module is fitted, it must be programmed using dedicated Volvo test*

equipment. Entrust this task to a Volvo dealer or suitably-equipped specialist.

Note: *Do not touch the control module terminal pins with the bare hands – there is a danger of damage due to static electricity.*

All models

21 Disconnect the battery negative lead (see Chapter 5), then wait at least 2 minutes before commencing work, to allow any stored electrical energy to dissipate.

XC60 models

22 The ECM box is located beneath the plenum cover at the rear of the engine bay. Ensure the area around the ECM is clean to avoid debris falling inside when it is removed.

23 To remove the ECM, remove the plenum cover as described in Chapter 12, Section 18. Release the locking catches and remove the wiring plugs – a cover may be fitted over the plugs on some models. Wrap the wiring plugs in clean plastic bags to prevent the ingress of dirt. Use a small screwdriver and release the locking catch **(see illustrations)**.

24 Refitting is a reversal of removal.

XC90 models

25 Remove the cover by lifting it straight up **(see illustration)**.

26 Release both locking clamps and remove the wiring plugs **(see illustration 2.7a)**.

27 Remove the 6 screws and remove the ECM from the vehicle **(see illustration)**.

28 Fitting is a reversal of removal.

Fuel pressure sensor

29 Remove the plastic cover from the top of the engine, by pulling it straight up from its mountings.

30 Disconnect the wiring plug from the swirl valve control unit and remove the control unit – as described below.

31 Remove the wiring plug from the sensor.

32 Unscrew the pressure sensor **(see illustration)**. Plug the openings to prevent contamination.

33 Refitting is a reversal of removal, but note that new high pressure pipes must be installed. Tightening the sensor to the specified torque, where given.

Fuel control valve – on rail

34 The control valve is mounted on the

11.25 Remove the cover

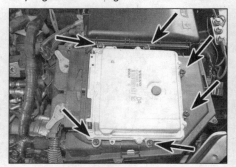

11.27 Remove the screws

11.32 The fuel pressure sensor (arrowed)

left-hand end of the fuel (common) rail **(see illustration)**.

35 Pull the plastic cover on top of the engine upwards to remove it.

36 On XC90 models remove the air filter hosing and the inlet pipe from the inlet manifold.

37 Disconnect the wiring plug from the fuel pressure sensor and the control valve.

38 Remove the crankcase breather pipe and the fuel return line(s) from the fuel rail.

39 Follow the procedure for removing the rail mounted fuel pressure sensor and then remove the high pressure pipes from the fuel rail. Seal all the openings in the rail (and the injectors) as the pipes are removed. Discard the pipes.

40 Remove the mounting bolts and manoeuvre the rail out from beneath the inlet manifold. With the rail on the bench, remove the control valve.

41 Refitting is a reversal of removal, but note that new high pressure pipes must be installed. Tightening the sensor to the specified torque, where given.

Fuel flow control valve – on pump

42 Pull the plastic cover on top of the engine upwards to remove it.

43 On XC90 models remove the air filter housing as described in Section 2 and then remove the ECM as described above.

44 Clean the area around the valve on the pump, then disconnect the valve wiring plug.

45 Undo the 2 or 3 bolts (on some models) and then remove the valve from the pump. Be prepared for fluid spillage. Plug or cover the opening to prevent contamination.

46 Refitting is a reversal of removal, lubricating the valve O-ring before fitting.

Camshaft position sensor

47 Remove the plastic cover from over the top of the engine, by pulling it straight up from its mountings at the front and right-hand edges, then pull it forwards.

48 Ensure that the ignition is switched off, and disconnect the wiring plug from the sensor, located on the right-hand side of the cylinder head cover **(see illustrations)**.

49 Undo the screw and remove the sensor.

50 To refit the sensor, ensure the mating face of the camshaft cover and sensor are clean and that the sensor is properly located on its dowels.

Swirl control valve/motor

51 Remove the plastic cover from over the top of the engine, by pulling it straight up from its mountings.

52 Pull the control arm from the valve/motor **(see illustration)**.

53 Undo the 2 bolts and remove the control valve/motor **(see illustration)**. Disconnect the wiring plug and No 1 glow plug as the assembly is withdrawn.

54 Refitting is a reversal of removal. Note

11.34 The rail mounted control valve (arrowed)

that if a new valve/motor has been fitted, the values stored in the ECM must be reset using dedicated diagnostic equipment. Entrust this task to a Volvo dealer or suitably-equipped specialist.

Turbocharger boost control

55 Depending on the engine fitted the position of the variable vane within the turbocharger (and therefore the boost output) is controlled by an either an electric motor attached to the vane control arm **(see illustration)** or by a vacuum controlled linkage attached to the control arm.

56 The motor is directly controlled by the engine management ECM. On models that use conventional vacuum control. Vacuum supply to the turbocharger boost control is controlled by an ECM controlled vacuum actuator mounted on the top of the engine.

57 To remove the vacuum actuator, first

11.52 Swirl valve motor control arm

11.55 Turbocharger and boost control motor

11.48 The camshaft position sensor (arrowed)

remove the engine cover. Mark the positions of the vacuum hoses and then remove them.

58 Disconnect the wiring plug and then unbolt and remove the vacuum actuator.

59 On models that use a motorised boost control, the control unit is removed with the turbo charger – as described in Section 12 below.

Fuel temperature sensor

60 Remove the plastic cover from over the top of the engine, by pulling it straight up from its mountings.

61 The sensor is located on the top/front edge of the high-pressure pump at the left-hand end of the cylinder head. Disconnect the sensor wiring plug **(see illustration)**.

62 Clean the area around the sensor, then unscrew it from the pump. Be prepared for fluid spillage. Plug the opening to prevent contamination.

11.53 Undo the bolts (arrowed) securing the swirl valve control motor

11.61 The fuel temperature sensor is located on the high-pressure fuel pump

11.66 Remove the throttle body and recover the gasket

63 Refitting is a reversal of removal, tightening the sensor to the specified torque.

Throttle body

64 Remove the plastic engine cover. Remove the air cleaner housing on.
65 Slacken the clamps and disconnect the air hoses from the throttle body. Move the hoses to one side.
66 Unscrew any sensors, then undo the retaining bolts and remove the throttle body. Discard the gasket, a new one must be fitted **(see illustration)**.
67 Refitting is a reversal of removal. If a new throttle body has been fitted, the stored values in the engine management ECM must be reset. Entrust this task to a Volvo dealer or suitably-equipped specialist.

12 Turbocharger –
description and precautions

Description

A turbocharger increases engine efficiency by raising the pressure in the inlet manifold above atmospheric pressure. Instead of the air simply being sucked into the cylinders, it is forced in. Additional fuel is supplied by the injection pump in proportion to the increased air intake.

Energy for the operation of the turbocharger comes from the exhaust gas. The gas flows through a specially-shaped housing (the turbine housing) and in so doing spins the turbine wheel. The turbine wheel is attached to a shaft, at the end of which is another vaned wheel known as the compressor wheel. The compressor wheel spins in its own housing and compresses the inducted air on the way to the inlet manifold.

The compressed air passes through an intercooler. This is an air-to-air heat exchanger, mounted with the radiator at the front of the vehicle. The purpose of the intercooler is to remove some of the heat gained in being compressed from the inducted air. Because cooler air is denser, removal of this heat further increases engine efficiency.

The turbocharger has adjustable guide vanes controlling the flow of exhaust gas into the turbine, the vanes being controlled by the engine management ECM. At lower engine speeds, the vanes close together, giving a smaller exhaust gas entry port, and therefore higher gas speed, which increases boost pressure at low engine speed. At high engine speed, the vanes are turned to give a larger exhaust gas entry port, and therefore lower gas speed, effectively maintaining a reasonably constant boost pressure over the engine rev range. This is known as a variable nozzle turbocharger (VNT).

The turbo shaft is pressure-lubricated by an oil feed pipe from the main oil gallery. The shaft 'floats' on a cushion of oil. A drain pipe returns the oil to the sump.

Some models also feature twin turbochargers. On these models a smaller turbocharger reacts quickly to changes in exhaust gas pressure at lower engine speeds. At engine speeds over 2,500 rpm the larger turbocharger comes into operation. An ECM controlled diverter valve controls the flow of gases between the turbochargers and a wastegate controls the boost pressure in the larger turbocharger.

A mechanical , spring loaded bypass valve is also fitted in the manifold. This ensures the correct gas flow between the turbochargers and allows a smooth transition in power output from the smaller turbocharger to the larger turbocharger.

Precautions

• The turbocharger operates at extremely high speeds and temperatures. Certain precautions must be observed to avoid premature failure of the turbo or injury to the operator.
• Do not operate the turbo with any parts exposed. Foreign objects falling onto the rotating vanes could cause excessive damage and (if ejected) personal injury.
• Do not race the engine immediately after start-up, especially if it is cold. Give the oil a few seconds to circulate.
• Always allow the engine to return to idle speed before switching it off – do not blip the throttle and switch off, as this will leave the turbo spinning without lubrication.
• Allow the engine to idle for several minutes before switching off after a high-speed run.
• Observe the recommended intervals for oil and filter changing, and use a reputable oil of the specified quality (see *Lubricants and fluids*). Neglect of oil changing, or use of inferior oil, can cause carbon formation on the turbo shaft and subsequent failure.

13 Turbocharger –
removal and refitting

Removal

1 Remove the plastic cover from over the top of the engine by pulling it straight up from its mountings.
2 Raise the front of the vehicle and support securely on axle stands (see *Jacking and vehicle support*).
3 Remove the engine undershield and drain the coolant as described in Chapter 1.
4 Remove the catalytic converter/ particulate filter as described in Chapter 4B. It is secured to the turbocharger by a clamp or by bolts **(see illustrations)**.
5 On AWD models remove the transfer box (bevel gear) as described in Chapter 8B.
6 Remove the right-hand driveshaft as described in Chapter 8A.

XC60 models

7 Unbolt, slacken the hose clamps and remove the intake pipe from the top of the engine.
8 Where fitted remove the heat shield from the exhaust manifold **(see illustration)**.
9 At the turbocharger remove the intake and output hoses.

13.4a Undo the pipe securing clamp . . .

13.4b . . . or securing bolts

13.8 Remove the heat shield

13.12 Turbocharger oil return pipe

13.17 Use pliers to release the locating peg from the grommet

13.20 Exhaust manifold/turbocharger heat shield

10 On models fitted with an electrical supply, disconnect the wiring plug. On all other models, mark the positions of the vacuum hoses and remove them.

11 Remove the banjo bolt form the oil feed supply pipe and recover the copper washers.

12 Unbolt the oil return pipe and recover the gasket **(see illustration)**.

13 On 2.0 litre models with the aid of an assistant to support the turbocharger, remove the 4 mounting bolts and lower the turbocharger from the vehicle. Recover the gasket.

14 On 2.4 litre models remove the EGR pipe from the exhaust manifold, support the exhaust manifold and then remove the manifold complete with the turbocharger.

XC60 models fitted with twin turbochargers

Note: *On models fitted with twin turbochargers access is limited. On these models removal of the engine to access the turbochargers should be considered.*

15 Remove the 3 mounting bolts, slacken the hose clamps and remove the air intake hose.

16 Locate and remove the support bracket from above the smaller turbocharger.

17 Remove the hose from the top of the engine **(see illustration)** and then remove the outlet hose from the turbocharger.

18 With difficulty remove the shorter section of inlet pipe leading to the lower turbocharger.

19 Mark the position of the vacuum hoses and remove them from the turbocharger, disconnect the wiring plug from the control valve. Remove the remaining vacuum hoses – noting their position – and unbolt and remove the control valve assembly from the top of the inlet manifold.

20 Remove the heat shields **(see illustration)** from above the turbochargers and then remove the bypass pipe from between the two turbochargers.

21 Remove the upper banjo bolt form the oil feed supply pipe and recover the copper washers.

22 Unbolt and remove the heat shield from between the turbochargers and then remove the metal hose between the EGR assembly and the turbocharger. Recover the gaskets.

23 Working from below remove the banjo bolt from the lower turbocharger and the banjo bolt from the engine block. Recover all the

washers and remove the oil feed supply pipes from both turbochargers.

24 Remove the support bracket from the lower turbocharger and then remove the oil return pipes from both turbochargers.

25 Remove the single bolt from the lower turbocharger mounting, have an assistant support the turbochargers and then remove the 12 exhaust manifold bolts. Lower the turbocharger and exhaust manifold assembly from the vehicle.

26 If required the separate the lower turbocharger from the upper turbocharger. Recover the gasket.

XC90 models

27 Remove the cross member from the suspension towers and then remove the engine ECM and air filter housing.

28 With reference to Chapter 4B, remove the EGR valve and associated pipe work,

29 Disconnect the wiring pugs from the oxygen and temperature sensors and then unbolt (but do not remove) the heat shield from above the turbocharger.

30 Remove the oil supply and coolant pipes from the turbocharger and then remove the heat shield previously unbolted.

31 Remove the wiring loom support clamp from the turbocharger and then remove intake and outlet pipes from the turbo charger **(see illustration)**.

32 Remove the oil drain pipe from the turbocharger and recover the gasket **(see illustration)**. At the engine block remove the banjo bolt, release the support clamp and remove the oil supply pipe completely.

13.31 Remove the outlet pipe

Recover the washers and discard them.

33 On RHD models remove the EGR pipe from the turbocharger.

34 Disconnect the actuator wiring plug where appropriate, any hose or vacuum pipes at the turbocharger, and unbolt any component support brackets.

35 On LHD models the turbocharger can now be removed from the exhaust manifold. On RHD models remove the exhaust manifold nuts and remove the turbocharger complete with the exhaust manifold. Discard the exhaust manifold gasket – a new one must be fitted. Separate the turbocharger from the exhaust manifold on the bench.

Refitting

36 Refitting is a reversal of removal, noting the following points:
a) *Ensure all mating surfaces are clean and dry.*
b) *Renew all O-rings, seals and gaskets.*
c) *Prime the turbocharger and oil supply pipes with clean engine oil before fitting.*
d) *Tighten all fasteners to the specified torque where available.*
e) *Fit new exhaust front section/catalytic converter-to-turbocharger nuts/bolts where appropriate.*

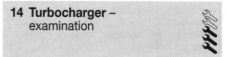

14 Turbocharger – examination

1 With the turbocharger removed, inspect the housing for cracks or other visible damage.

13.32 Remove the return pipe

15.3 Undo the radiator support beam bolts (left-hand side bolts arrowed)

2 Spin the turbine or the compressor wheel to verify that the shaft is intact and to feel for excessive shake or roughness. Some play is normal since in use the shaft is 'floating' on a film of oil. Check that the wheel vanes are undamaged.

3 The wastegate and actuator are integral with the turbocharger, and cannot be checked or renewed separately. Consult a Volvo dealer or other specialist if it is thought that the wastegate may be faulty.

4 If the exhaust or induction passages are oil-contaminated, the turbo shaft oil seals have probably failed. (On the induction side, this will also have contaminated the intercooler, where applicable, which if necessary should be flushed with a suitable solvent.)

5 No DIY repair of the turbo is possible. A new unit is available on an exchange basis.

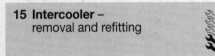

15 Intercooler –
removal and refitting

Note: *On XC90 models the intercooler is removed with the radiator as described in Chapter 3.*

1 Raise the front of the car and support securely on axle stands (see *Jacking and vehicle support*) and remove the engine undershield.

2 Remove the air deflector from below the bumper cover.

3 Support the radiator as described in Chapter 3. Undo the 2 bolts at each end and remove the radiator support beam (see illustration).

17.3a Separate the exhaust at the flange

4 Disconnect the intercooler pipes from their locations within the engine bay. Note that the hose clips are extremely difficult to access. If necessary remove the bumper cover and then partially lower the complete radiator/condenser/intercooler assembly (see Chapter 3 for further details).

5 Undo the 2 mounting bolts at the bottom of the radiator and withdraw the intercooler from beneath the vehicle. Disconnect any wiring plugs as the unit is withdrawn (see illustrations).

6 Refitting is a reversal of removal.

15.5a Undo the intercooler mounting bolts…

16 Manifolds –
removal and refitting

Inlet manifold

1 The inlet manifold is integral with the cylinder head cover – refer to Chapter 2A.

Exhaust manifold

Note: *On some models the manifold is removed with the turbocharger, on others the turbocharger is removed first – see Section 13 for details.*

2 Disconnect the battery as described in Chapter 5.

3 Where necessary, remove the turbocharger as described in Section 13.

4 Slacken and remove the nuts retaining the exhaust manifold, and remove it from the engine. Discard the gasket, a new one must be fitted.

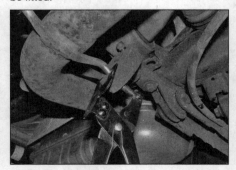

17.3b Special pliers are available to aid the removal of the exhaust rubber mountings

15.5b …and withdraw the intercooler from beneath the vehicle

5 Examine all the manifold studs for signs of damage and corrosion; remove all traces of corrosion, and repair or renew any damaged studs.

6 Ensure the mating surfaces of the exhaust manifold and cylinder head are clean and dry. Position a new gasket, and refit the exhaust manifold to the cylinder head. Tighten the nuts to the specified torque.

7 The remainder of refitting is a reversal of removal, noting the following points:

a) *Tighten all fasteners to their specified torque where available. Note that on the 2.0 litre engine, the torque value for the 2 nuts at each end of the manifold differ from the those at the top and bottom.*

b) *Check and, if necessary, top-up the oil level as described in 'Weekly checks'.*

17 Exhaust system –
general information and component renewal

General information

1 The exhaust system consists of several sections: the front pipe with the catalytic converter, and the rear section with the intermediate and rear silencers. A particulate filter is fitted to the majority of models. The particulate fitted is integrated into the catalytic converter on some models.

2 If required, the rear silencer can be renewed independently of the remainder of the system, by cutting the old silencer from the pipe, and slipping the new one over the cut end.

3 The exhaust system is joined together by a mixture of flanged, or sliding joints. Apply plenty of penetrating fluid to the fasteners prior to removal, undo the fasteners, unhook the rubber mountings, and manoeuvre the system from under the vehicle (see illustrations).

Rear silencer

4 If the rear silencer is the only part of the system requiring renewal, cut the old silencer from the rear section of the system using pipe cutters or a hacksaw. The exact point where the cut is made can differ depending on the engine fitted so you should check with a Volvo dealer before cutting the system. Free the silencer from its mountings, and remove it from the vehicle.

5 Clean up and de-burr the end of the existing exhaust pipe with a file/emery tape, etc.

6 Replacement rear silencers are available which slip over the end of the existing exhaust pipe, and are clamped in place. Slip the new silencer over the pipe, engage the rubber silencer mountings, then tighten the pipe clamp securely.

7 Each section is refitted by reversing the removal sequence, noting the following points:

a) *Ensure that all traces of corrosion have been removed from the flanges and renew all gaskets.*

b) *Inspect the rubber mountings for signs of damage or deterioration, and renew as necessary.*

c) *Prior to tightening the exhaust system fasteners to the specified torque, ensure that all rubber mountings are correctly located, and that there is adequate clearance between the exhaust system and vehicle underbody.*

18 Swirl duct – removal and refitting

Removal

1 Swirl ducts are fitted to the cylinder head to control the flow of air into the inlet tracts. The duct contains valves which alter the flow of air depending on engine speed and load. They generate a swirling motion for increased combustion efficiency and lower exhaust emissions. To remove the duct, begin by removing the cylinder head cover/inlet manifold as described in Chapter 2A.

2 Disconnect the actuating arm from the swirl control motor **(see illustration)**.

18.2 Swirl valve motor control arm

3 Undo the bolts and remove the swirl duct/valves.

Refitting

4 Refitting is a reversal of removal, tightening all fasteners securely.

Chapter 4 Part B:
Emission control systems

Contents

Degrees of difficulty

Easy, suitable for novice with little experience	**Fairly easy,** suitable for beginner with some experience	**Fairly difficult,** suitable for competent DIY mechanic	**Difficult,** suitable for experienced DIY mechanic	**Very difficult,** suitable for expert DIY or professional

Specifications

Torque wrench settings	Nm	lbf ft
Catalytic converter to turbocharger*	25	18
Exhaust front pipe to intermediate pipe	24	18
Exhaust front pipe-to-flange nuts/bolts*	50	37
Exhaust gas temperature sensor	45	33
EGR valve/cooler:		
M6 bolts	10	7
M8 bolts	24	18
M12 bolts	50	37
Oil separator bolts	20	15
Oxygen sensor	45	33

* Do not re-use. Volvo specify that where a fixing requires angular tightening it must always be renewed. Any fixing retained with a thread locking compound must also be renewed. Nuts with a nylon insert must always be renewed.

1 General information

All models covered by this manual have various features built into the fuel and exhaust systems to help minimise harmful emissions. These features fall broadly into three categories; crankcase emission control, evaporative emission control, and exhaust emission control. Additionally, most models are equipped with a particulate emission filter which uses a porous silicon carbide substrate to trap particulates of carbon as the exhaust gases pass through.

The main features of these systems are as follows.

Crankcase emission control

Crankcase gases are taken via hoses from the cylinder head and the cylinder block, into a cyclone type oil separator. Here, the gases are forced to twist past two cones. As the gases pass the cones, oil is thrown out and condenses on the walls of the separator, where it then returns to the sump. The gases are admitted into the intake system, via a pressure limiting valve.

Exhaust gas recirculation system

This system is designed to recirculate small quantities of exhaust gas into the inlet tract, and therefore into the combustion process. This reduces the level of oxides of nitrogen present in the final exhaust gas which is released into the atmosphere.

The volume of exhaust gas recirculated is controlled by an electrically-operated solenoid valve. The solenoid, valve and cooler is an assembly mounted at the left-hand end of the cylinder head between the inlet and exhaust manifold.

The EGR system is controlled by the engine management ECM, which receives information on engine operating parameters from its various sensors.

Particulate filter system

The particulate filter is combined with the catalytic converter in the exhaust system on XC60 two wheel drive models. On all other models it is a separate item, mounted downstream of the catalytic convertor. Its purpose it to trap particulates of carbon (soot) as the exhaust gases pass through, in order to comply with latest emission regulations.

The filter can be automatically regenerated (cleaned) by the system's ECM on-board the vehicle. The engine's high-pressure injection system is utilised to inject fuel into the exhaust gases during the post-injection period; this causes the filter temperature to increase sufficient to oxidise the particulates, leaving an ash residue.

Regeneration will normally take place every 1000 kilometres (or less). The exact point at which regeneration is required is determined by the ECM from data primarily gathered from the differential pressure sensors mounted at the front and rear of the filter. Note that regeneration will not take place unless the pre-filter exhaust gas temperature reaches an approximate temperature of 600 °C. On vehicles that are mainly used in an urban environment this criterion may not be reached and for this reason it is always recommended that all vehicles fitted with particulate filters should be driven at higher, constant engine speeds for a minimum of 30 minutes every 1000 kilometres or so. Assuming the vehicle has no other engine or emissions related faults, this simple course of action will enable regeneration to take place.

2 Catalytic converter – general information and precautions

The catalytic converter is a reliable and simple device, which needs no maintenance in itself, but there are some facts of which an owner should be aware if the converter is to function properly for its full service life.

a) *Always keep the fuel system well-maintained in accordance with the manufacturer's schedule (see Chapter 1).*
b) *If the engine develops a misfire, do not drive the vehicle at all (or at least as little as possible) until the fault is cured.*
c) *DO NOT push – or tow-start the vehicle – this will soak the catalytic converter in unburned fuel, causing it to overheat when the engine does start.*
d) *DO NOT switch off the ignition at high engine speeds, ie, do not blip the throttle immediately before switching off.*
e) *DO NOT use fuel or engine oil additives – these may contain substances harmful to the catalytic converter.*
f) *DO NOT continue to use the vehicle if the engine burns oil to the extent of leaving a visible trail of blue smoke.*
g) *Remember that the catalytic converter operates at very high temperatures. DO NOT, therefore, park the vehicle in dry undergrowth, over long grass or piles of dead leaves, after a long run.*

4.3 Oxygen sensor

h) *Remember that the catalytic converter is FRAGILE. Do not strike it with tools during servicing work.*
i) *The catalytic converter used on a well-maintained and well-driven vehicle should last for between 50 000 and 100 000 miles. If the converter is no longer effective, it must be renewed.*

3 Crankcase emission control system – checking and component renewal

Checking

1 The components of this system require no attention other than to check that the hoses are clear and undamaged.

Oil separator renewal

2 The oil separator is located on the front facing side of the cylinder block, below the inlet manifold. It is part of the oil filter housing.
3 Remove the clips securing the connecting hoses to the separator unit. If the clips are in less than perfect condition, obtain new clips for reassembly.
4 Undo the retaining bolts and remove the unit from the engine.
5 Refit the oil separator using a reversal of removal.

4 Exhaust emission control systems – checking and component renewal

Checking

1 Checking of the system as a whole entails a close visual inspection of all hoses, pipes and connections for condition and security. Apart from this, any known or suspected faults should be attended to by a Volvo dealer or suitably-equipped specialist.

Oxygen sensor and temperature sensor

Note: *The oxygen sensor is delicate, and will not work if it is dropped or knocked, if its power supply is disrupted, or if any cleaning materials are used on it. Both sensors are located in the exhaust manifold or front section of the exhaust system depending on the engine fitted. Some models have two temperature sensors - one fitted to the catalytic convertor and one fitted to the particulate filter.*
2 Remove the plastic engine cover.
3 Disconnect the sensor wiring connector, unscrew the sensor and collect the sealing washer (where fitted) **(see illustration)**.
4 On refitting, clean the sealing washer (where fitted) and renew it if it is damaged or worn. Apply a smear of anti-seize compound to the sensor's threads, then refit the sensor, tightening it to the specified torque. Reconnect the wiring and secure with cable-ties where applicable.

Catalytic converter

Note: *The catalytic converter is part of the exhaust system front section. On some models the converter Is combined with the particulate filter. The process for renewal differs slightly depending on the engine fitted.*

5 Remove the plastic engine cover and the engine undershield. On XC90 models remove the cross member from the suspension towers.

6 Remove the 4 EGR cover nuts and then remove the cover – where fitted.

7 Unscrew the exhaust gas temperature and oxygen sensors from the catalytic convertor and where the converter incorporates the particulate filter, mark and then disconnect the flexible pressure pipes for the differential pressure sensor **(see illustration)**.

8 On AWD models remove the propeller shaft as described in Chapter 8B and then remove the heat shield from the transmission tunnel. On some XC60 models remove the front support bar from the transmission tunnel.

9 Where fitted remove the heat shield over the exhaust manifold/turbocharger. On some models it will be necessary to partially drain the cooling system and remove the coolant hose from the turbocharger to allow the heat shield to be removed.

10 Remove the exhaust from the converter by either removing the clamp (models fitted with a combined converter and particulate filter) or by removing the 2 or 3 bolts at the connection with the particulate filter.

11 Remove the clamp at the exhaust manifold (models fitted with a combined converter and particulate filter) or remove the 3 nuts from the exhaust manifold (all other models). Some models also have another support bracket fitted. Remove this bracket (where fitted) and lower the converter from the vehicle **(see illustration)**.

12 Refitting is a reversal of removal, noting the following points:

a) *Ensure that all traces of corrosion have*

4.7 Remove the flexible pipes

been removed from the flanges and renew all gaskets.

b) *Inspect the rubber mountings for signs of damage or deterioration, and renew as necessary.*

c) *Prior to the tightening the exhaust system fasteners to the specified torque, ensure that all rubber mountings are correctly located, and that there is adequate clearance between the exhaust system and vehicle underbody.*

EGR valve/cooler

Note: *A variety of combined EGR valves and coolers are fitted to XC60 and XC90 models. They are all removed in a similar manner.*

13 Remove the engine cover and with reference to Chapter 1, drain the engine coolant.

14 On XC60 models remove the battery, battery support tray and air filter housing.

15 On XC90 models disconnect the battery and remove the ECM.

16 Disconnect the wiring plugs from the MAF sensor, EGR control valve and the throttle body. Remove the throttle body and intake hose. Remove the metal hose from exhaust manifold. This is secured by 2 bolts on some models and a clamp on others **(see illustration)**.

17 Disconnect the coolant hoses from the EGR cooler and then unbolt the cooler and control valve from the engine.

4.11 Remove the converter (XC60 shown)

18 With the EGR cooler and control valve on the bench, separate the valve from the cooler. Remove any carbon build-up from the valve stem with a solvent such as carburettor cleaner **(see illustration)**.

19 Refitting of both units is the reversal of removal, renewing any gaskets where applicable. If a new valve is fitted, it may require resetting and this task should be entrusted to a Volvo dealer or suitably-equipped specialist. Refill the cooling system as described in Chapter 1.

Particulate filter

20 See the Section above for catalytic converter renewal where the particulate filter is part of the catalytic converter.

21 On models fitted with a separate particulate filter, jack up and support the front of the vehicle - see Jacking and vehicle support in the reference section.

22 Disconnect the temperature sensor, mark the positions of the pressure sensor hoses and remove them.

23 On XC60 models remove the cross member from the transmission tunnel.

24 Remove the 2 nuts from the rear of the filter, remove the 3 nuts from the front of the filter, unhook the rubber mountings and remove the filter from the vehicle.

4.16 Remove the bolts (arrowed)

4.18 Thoroughly clean the valve (arrowed). Use a suitable solvent

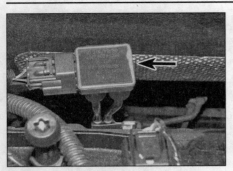

4.25 Particulate filter differential sensor (arrowed) located at the rear of the cylinder head

Particulate filter differential pressure sensor

Note: *After renewing the pressure differential sensor, the values for the sensor stored in the ECM must be adapted. This requires access to dedicated Volvo diagnostic equipment, and should be entrusted to a Volvo dealer or suitably-equipped specialist.*

25 The sensor location varies slightly depending upon the engine fitted **(see illustration)**. On all models remove the engine cover.

26 On XC60 models remove the turbocharger vacuum control as described in Chapter 4A. Disconnect the wiring plug, remove the flexible hoses and then unbolt and remove the sensor.

27 On XC90 models remove the cross member from the engine bay and then remove the cover from the EGR control valve. Disconnect the wiring plug, remove the flexible hoses and then unbolt and remove the sensor.

28 Refitting is a reversal of removal.

Chapter 5
Starting and charging systems

Contents

Degrees of difficulty

Easy, suitable for novice with little experience | **Fairly easy,** suitable for beginner with some experience | **Fairly difficult,** suitable for competent DIY mechanic | **Difficult,** suitable for experienced DIY mechanic | **Very difficult,** suitable for expert DIY or professional

Specifications

General
System type . . . . 12 volt, negative earth

Battery
Type . . . . Low-maintenance or maintenance-free sealed for life
Capacity . . . . 60 to 90 Ah (depending on model)

Alternator
Type . . . . Bosch
Output . . . . 120 or 140 A
Brush minimum length . . . . 5.0 mm

Starter motor
Type . . . . Bosch 2.0 or 2.2 kW

Torque wrench settings

	Nm	lbf ft
Alternator mounting bolts	24	18
Alternator pulley:		
Freewheel type pulley	80	59
Fixed type pulley	65	48
Glow plugs	8	6
Starter motor mounting bolts	50	37

1 General information and precautions

General information

The engine electrical system consists mainly of the charging and starting systems. Because of their engine-related functions, these components are covered separately from the body electrical devices such as the lights, instruments, etc (which are covered in Chapter 12). The electrical system is of the 12 volt negative earth type.

The battery is of the low-maintenance or maintenance-free (sealed for life) type, and is charged by the alternator, which is belt-driven from the crankshaft pulley.

The starter motor is of the pre-engaged type, incorporating an integral solenoid. On starting, the solenoid moves the drive pinion into engagement with the flywheel ring gear before the starter motor is energised. Once the engine has started, a one-way clutch prevents the motor armature being driven by the engine until the pinion disengages from the flywheel.

Further details of the various systems are given in the relevant Sections of this Chapter. While some repair procedures are given, the usual course of action is to renew the component concerned.

Precautions

Warning: It is necessary to take extra care when working on the electrical system to avoid damage to semi-conductor devices (diodes and transistors), and to avoid the risk of personal injury. In addition to the precautions given in 'Safety first!' observe the following when working on the system:

• *Always remove rings, watches, etc before working on the electrical system. Even with the battery disconnected, capacitive discharge could occur if a component's live terminal is earthed through a metal object. This could cause a shock or nasty burn.*

• *Do not reverse the battery connections. Components such as the alternator, electronic control units, or any other components having semi-conductor circuitry could be irreparably damaged.*

• *Never disconnect the battery terminals, the alternator, any electrical wiring or any test instruments when the engine is running.*

• *Do not allow the engine to turn the alternator when the alternator is not connected.*

• *Never test for alternator output by 'flashing' the output lead to earth.*
Always ensure that the battery negative lead is disconnected when working on the electrical system.
• *If the engine is being started using jump leads and a slave battery, connect the batteries positive-to-positive and negative-to-negative (see Jump starting). This also applies when connecting a battery charger.*
• *Never use an ohmmeter of the type incorporating a hand-cranked generator for circuit or continuity testing.*
• *Before using electric-arc welding equipment on the car, disconnect the battery, alternator and components such as the electronic control units (where applicable) to protect them from the risk of damage.*

2 Battery – testing and charging

Testing

Standard and low-maintenance battery

1 If the vehicle covers a small annual mileage, it is worthwhile checking the specific gravity of the electrolyte every three months to determine the state of charge of the battery. Use a hydrometer to make the check, and compare the results with the following table. Note that the specific gravity readings assume an electrolyte temperature of 15°C; for every 10°C below 15°C subtract 0.007. For every 10°C above 15°C add 0.007.

	Above 25°C	Below 25°C
Fully-charged	1.210 to 1.230	1.270 to 1.290
70% charged	1.170 to 1.190	1.230 to 1.250
Discharged	1.050 to 1.070	1.110 to 1.130

2 If the battery condition is suspect, first check the specific gravity of electrolyte in each cell. A variation of 0.040 or more between any cells indicates loss of electrolyte or deterioration of the internal plates.
3 If the specific gravity variation is 0.040 or more, the battery should be renewed. If the cell variation is satisfactory but the battery is discharged, it should be charged as described later in this Section.

Maintenance-free battery

4 In cases where a sealed for life maintenance-free battery is fitted, topping-up and testing of the electrolyte in each cell may not be possible (see Chapter 1, Section 10). The condition of the battery can therefore only be tested using a battery condition indicator or a voltmeter.
5 Certain models may be fitted with a maintenance-free battery, with a built-in charge condition indicator. The indicator is located in the top of the battery casing, and indicates the condition of the battery from its colour. The charge conditions denoted by the colour of the indicator should be printed on a label attached to the battery – if not, consult a Volvo dealer or automotive electrician for advice.
6 If testing the battery using a voltmeter, connect the voltmeter across the battery and note the voltage. The test is only accurate if the battery has not been subjected to any kind of charge for the previous six hours. If this is not the case, switch on the headlights for 30 seconds, then wait four to five minutes before testing the battery after switching off the headlights. All other electrical circuits must be switched off, so check that the doors and tailgate are fully shut when making the test.
7 If the voltage reading is less than 12.2 volts, then the battery is discharged, whilst a reading of 12.2 to 12.4 volts indicates a partially-discharged condition.
8 If the battery is to be charged, remove it from the vehicle and charge it as described later in this section.

Charging

Note: *The following is intended as a guide only. Always refer to the manufacturer's recommendations (often printed on a label attached to the battery) before charging a battery.*

Standard and low-maintenance battery

9 Charge the battery at a rate equivalent to 10% of the battery capacity (eg, for a 45 Ah battery charge at 4.5 A) and continue to charge the battery at this rate until no further rise in specific gravity is noted over a four-hour period.

10 Alternatively, a trickle charger charging at the rate of 1.5 amps can safely be used overnight.
11 Especially rapid boost charges which are claimed to restore the power of the battery in 1 to 2 hours are not recommended, as they can cause serious damage to the battery plates through overheating. If the battery is completely flat, recharging should take at least 24 hours.
12 While charging the battery, note that the temperature of the electrolyte should never exceed 38°C.

Maintenance-free battery

13 This battery type takes considerably longer to fully recharge than the standard type, the time taken being dependent on the extent of discharge, but it can take anything up to three days.
14 A constant voltage type charger is required, to be set, when connected, to 13.9 to 14.9 volts with a charger current below 25 amps. Using this method, the battery should be useable within three hours, giving a voltage reading of 12.5 volts, but this is for a partially-discharged battery and, as mentioned, full charging can take far longer.
15 If the battery is to be charged from a fully-discharged state (condition reading less than 12.2 volts), have it recharged by your Volvo dealer or local automotive electrician, as the charge rate is higher, and constant supervision during charging is necessary.

3 Battery – disconnecting, removal and refitting

Caution: Wait at least 5 minutes after turning off the ignition switch before disconnecting the battery. This is to allow sufficient time for the various control modules to shut down correctly.

Disconnecting

1 On XC60 models open the bonnet and remove the battery cover **(see illustration)**.
2 On XC90 models open the tailgate and remove the load space rear cover and then remove the metal cover plate. Remove the battery cover **(see illustrations)**.

3.1 Undo the clips and remove the battery cover

3.2a Remove the metal plate...

3.2b ...and the plastic cover

**3.3 Disconnect the earth cable
(XC90 shown)**

3.6 Remove the panel

**3.7 Disconnect the cables from the battery
positive terminal**

3 Locate the battery negative cable. This will normally be marked with a minus symbol on the battery. Slacken the terminal bolt and remove the negative ('earth') cable from the battery **(see illustration)**.
4 Move the cable away from the battery. If there is any chance of the cable making contact with the battery terminal then either tie the cable to one side or cover the battery negative with a suitable insulator – a plastic bag is ideal.

Removal

5 Disconnect the battery negative cable as previously described.
6 On XC60 models, pull up the rubber seal located on the edge of the plenum cover and remove the small section of the cowl panel **(see illustration)**.
7 Undo the 2 bolts and disconnect the cables from the positive terminal **(see illustration)**.
8 On XC60 models, unclip the cable from the battery surround box and (on all models) disconnect the breather pipe.
9 Unscrew the bolt and remove the battery retaining clamp, and lift the battery from its tray **(see illustrations)**.

Refitting

10 Position the battery in the tray, refit the retaining clamp and tighten the retaining bolt securely.
11 Reconnect the battery positive lead, followed by the negative lead. Smear a little petroleum jelly on the terminals.
12 Refit the battery cover and other associated components.
13 When switching on the engine for the first time, stand outside the vehicle and reach in to start the engine, keeping clear of the airbag operating areas.

**3.9a Remove the battery clamp
(XC90 shown)...**

**3.9b ...and lift out the battery
(XC60 shown)**

for security. If all is satisfactory, the alternator maybe at fault and should be renewed or taken to an auto-electrician for testing and repair.
2 If the ignition warning light illuminates when the engine is running, stop the engine and check that the drivebelt is correctly tensioned (see Chapter 1) and that the alternator connections are secure. If all is so far satisfactory, have the alternator checked by an auto-electrician for testing and repair.
3 If the alternator output is suspect even though the warning light functions correctly, the regulated voltage may be checked as follows.
4 Connect a voltmeter across the battery terminals and start the engine.
5 Increase the engine speed until the voltmeter reading remains steady; the reading should be between 13.5 and 14.8 volts.

**5.5 Remove the support strut bolts
(arrowed)**

6 Switch on as many electrical accessories (eg, the headlights, heated rear window and heater blower) as possible, and check that the alternator maintains the regulated voltage between 13.5 and 14.8 volts.
7 If the regulated voltage is not as stated, the fault may be due to worn brushes, weak brush springs, a faulty voltage regulator, a faulty diode, a severed phase winding, or worn or damaged slip-rings. The brushes and slip-ring may be checked (see Section 6), but if the fault persists the alternator should be renewed or taken to an auto-electrician for testing and repair.

5 Alternator and pulley – removal and refitting

Alternator

1 Disconnect the battery negative lead (see Section 3)
2 Remove the plastic cover from the top of the engine.
3 Remove the auxiliary drivebelt as described in Chapter 1.
4 On XC60 models remove the charge air pipe from the front and top of the engine.
5 On XC90 models remove the support strut from the rear of the power steering pump **(see illustration)** and then remove the power steering pump mounting bolts (accessed through the pump pulley). There is no need to completely remove the pump.
6 Disconnect the wiring multiplug and the

4 Charging system – testing

Note: *Refer to the warnings given in 'Safety first!' and in Section 1 of this Chapter before starting work.*
1 If the ignition/no-charge warning light fails to illuminate when the ignition is switched on, first check the alternator wiring connections

5.6 Disconnect the wiring plugs (arrowed)

5.8a Undo the lower mounting bolts (arrowed)…

5.8b …and the upper mounting bolt (arrowed)

5.12a Use a special tool that engages with the splines in the shaft and pulley centre

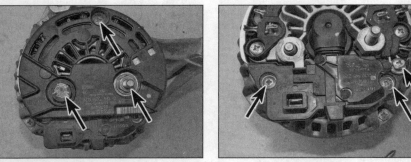

5.12b Counterhold the shaft whilst unscrewing the pulley centre

lead from the terminal stud at the rear of the alternator (see illustration)

7 On XC90 models remove the lower charge air pipe.

8 Undo the upper and lower mounting bolts and remove the alternator (see illustrations). On XC90 models tilt the power steering pump to allow sufficient room to remove the alternator.

9 Refitting is a reversal of removal, remembering to tighten the various fasteners to their specified torque where given.

Drive pulley

10 On some models the alternator drive pulley is fitted with a one-way clutch to reduce wear and stress on the auxiliary drivebelt. In order to remove the pulley, a special tool (Volvo No 999 5760) will be required to hold the alternator shaft whilst unscrewing the pulley. Equivalents to this tool are widely available from auto electrical specialists/automotive tool specialists.

11 Prise the plastic cap from the pulley.

12 Insert the special tool into the splines of the pulley, engaging the central Torx bit with the alternator shaft (see illustrations). Unscrew the pulley anti-clockwise whilst holding the shaft with the Torx bit, and remove the pulley.

13 Refitting is a reversal of removal, but tighten it securely using the special tool.

6.3 Prise off the plastic cap, undo the two nuts and one screw (arrowed), then lift off the plastic cover

6.4a Undo the three screws (arrowed)…

6 Alternator brush holder/ regulator module – renewal

1 Remove the alternator (see Section 5).

2 Place the alternator on a clean work surface, with the pulley facing down.

3 Undo the cover nuts and screws (there may be 2 or 3 depending on model), then lift the plastic cover from the rear of the alternator (see illustration).

4 Undo the screws (3 or 4 depending on model) and carefully remove the voltage regulator/brush holder from the alternator (see illustrations).

5 Measure the free length of the brushes (see illustration). Check the measurement with the Specifications; renew the module if the brushes are worn below the minimum limit.

6 Clean and inspect the surfaces of the slip-rings, at the end of the alternator shaft. If they are excessively worn, or damaged, the alternator must be renewed.

7 Reassemble the alternator by following the dismantling procedure in reverse. On completion, refer to Section 5 and refit the alternator.

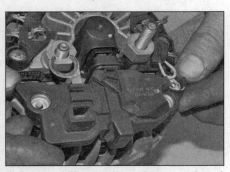

6.4b …and lift away the voltage regulator/ brush holder

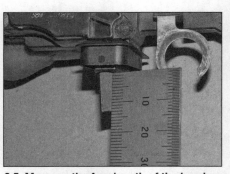

6.5 Measure the free length of the brushes

7 Starting system – testing

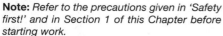

Note: *Refer to the precautions given in 'Safety first!' and in Section 1 of this Chapter before starting work.*

1 If the starter motor fails to operate when the 'Start' button is pressed or the key turned, the following possible causes may be to blame:

a) *The battery is faulty.*

b) *The electrical connections between the switch, solenoid, battery and starter motor are somewhere failing to pass the necessary current from the battery through the starter to earth.*

c) *The solenoid is faulty.*

d) *The starter motor is mechanically or electrically defective.*

2 To check the battery, switch on the headlights. If they dim after a few seconds, this indicates that the battery is discharged – recharge (see Section 2) or renew the battery. If the headlights glow brightly, operate the ignition switch and observe the lights. If they dim, then this indicates that current is reaching the starter motor, therefore the fault must lie in the starter motor. If the lights continue to glow brightly (and no clicking sound can be heard from the starter motor solenoid), this indicates that there is a fault in the circuit or solenoid – see following paragraphs. If the starter motor turns slowly when operated, but the battery is in good condition, then this indicates that either the starter motor is faulty, or there is considerable resistance somewhere in the circuit.

3 If a fault in the circuit is suspected, disconnect the battery leads (including the earth connection to the body), the starter/ solenoid wiring and the engine/transmission earth strap. Thoroughly clean the connections, and reconnect the leads and wiring, then use a voltmeter or test light to check that full battery voltage is available at the battery positive lead connection to the solenoid, and that the earth is sound. Smear petroleum jelly around the battery terminals to prevent corrosion – corroded connections are amongst the most frequent causes of electrical system faults.

4 If the battery and all connections are in good condition, check the circuit by disconnecting the wire from the solenoid blade terminal. Connect a voltmeter or test light between the wire end and a good earth (such as the battery negative terminal), and check that the wire is live when the ignition switch is turned to the start position. If it is, then the circuit is sound – if not, the circuit wiring can be checked as described in Chapter 12.

5 The solenoid contacts can be checked by connecting a voltmeter or test light between the battery positive feed connection on the starter side of the solenoid, and earth. When the ignition switch is turned to the start position, there should be a reading or lighted bulb, as applicable. If there is no reading or

8.3a Undo the starter motor mounting bolts (arrowed) and...

lighted bulb, the solenoid is faulty and should be renewed.

6 If the circuit and solenoid are proved sound, the fault must lie in the starter motor. In this event, it may be possible to have the starter motor overhauled by a specialist, but check on the cost of spares before proceeding, as it may prove more economical to obtain a new or exchange motor.

8 Starter motor – removal and refitting

Removal

1 Remove the plastic cover on top of the engine.

2 Disconnect the battery negative lead.

3 Disconnect the wiring from the starter motor solenoid, undo the mounting bolts (2 on XC60 models and 3 on XC90 models) and remove the unit **(see illustrations)**. Note the position of any locating dowels and ensure they are in position when refitting.

Refitting

4 Refitting is a reversal of removal. Tighten all fasteners to their specified torque where given.

9 Starter motor – testing and overhaul

If the starter motor is thought to be suspect, it should be removed from the vehicle and taken to an auto-electrician for testing. Most auto-electricians will be able to supply and fit brushes at a reasonable cost. However, check on the cost of repairs before proceeding, as it may prove more economical to obtain a new or exchange motor.

10 Starter control unit – removal and refitting (XC60 models only)

1 The starter control unit is located behind the facia at the rear of the remote unit aperture/ start-stop button.

2 Disconnect the battery negative terminal as described in Section 3.

8.3b ...remove the starter motor

3 Using a suitable trim tool prise free the bezel. Undo the 3 bolts (as described in Chapter 12, Section 4) pull the unit forward and disconnect the wiring plug. Remove the unit from the facia.

4 Unclip the control module from the rear of the assembly.

5 Refitting is a reversal of removal.

11 Glow plugs – general information

Glow plugs are fitted to assist cold starting and to help minimise the production of harmful emissions. Where a particulate filter is fitted the glow plugs are also used to assist with the cleaning ('regeneration') of the particulate filter. The system comprises a relay and five glow plugs. The system is controlled by the electronic diesel control (EDC) system, using information primarily provided by the coolant temperature sensor, ambient temperature sensor and altitude sensor.

The glow plugs are miniature electric heating elements, encapsulated in a metal case with a probe at one end, and an electrical connection at the other. The combustion chambers have a glow plug threaded into it. When the glow plug is energised, it heats up rapidly causing the temperature of the air charge drawn into each of the combustion chambers to rise. Each glow plug probe is positioned directly in line with the incoming spray of fuel from the injector. Hence the fuel passing over the glow plug probe is also heated, allowing its optimum combustion temperature to be achieved more readily. The glow plugs are of the low voltage type – they are only supplied with battery voltage for a maximum time of 1.5 seconds. After this time the voltage is reduced to a nominal 4.4v.

The duration of the preheating period is governed by the electronic diesel control (EDC) system control module (ECM), using information provided by the coolant temperature sensor. The ECM alters the preheating time (the length for which the glow plugs are supplied with current) to suit the prevailing conditions. Post start heating (and regeneration of the particulate filter) is also controlled by the EDC and ECM.

12.2 Release the connector

12.3 Unscrew each glow plug from the cylinder head

A warning light informs the driver that preheating is taking place. The lamp extinguishes when sufficient preheating has taken place to allow the engine to be started, but power will still be supplied to the glow plugs for a further period (post-heating) to reduce exhaust emissions. If no attempt is made to start the engine, the power supply to the glow plugs is switched off to prevent battery drain and glow plug burn-out.

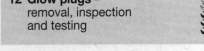

12 Glow plugs –
removal, inspection and testing

Removal

1 The glow plugs are fitted into the front or rear face of the cylinder head depending on the engine fitted. Remove the engine cover and remove components with reference to the relevant chapter until the glow plugs become accessible.

2 Unplug the wiring connector from each glow plug **(see illustration)** and where appropriate remove the wiring bracket.

3 Unscrew each plug from the cylinder head using a deep socket **(see illustration)**.

Testing

4 Inspect the glow plugs for signs of damage. Burnt or eroded glow plug tips can be caused by a bad injector spray pattern. Have the injectors checked if this sort of damage is found.

5 **Do not** attempt to test the glow plugs by applying 12v to them – this will destroy the glow plug.

6 If the glow plugs are in good condition, check their resistance with a multi-meter set to Ohms. Note that where low voltage glow plugs are fitted the electrical resistance will be low – a quality multi-meter capable of reading down to 0.1 ohms will be required.

7 A faulty glow plug will normally be found to be open circuit.

Refitting

8 Thoroughly clean the glow plugs, and the glow plug seating areas in the cylinder head.

9 Apply a smear of anti-seize compound to the glow plug threads, then refit the glow plug and tighten it to the specified torque.

10 Reconnect the wiring to the glow plug.

11 The remainder of refitting is a reversal of removal.

Chapter 6
Clutch

Contents

Degrees of difficulty

Easy, suitable for novice with little experience	**Fairly easy,** suitable for beginner with some experience	**Fairly difficult,** suitable for competent DIY mechanic	**Difficult,** suitable for experienced DIY mechanic	**Very difficult,** suitable for expert DIY or professional

Specifications

General

Clutch type . . . . Single dry plate, diaphragm spring, self-adjusting, hydraulic actuation

Pressure plate

Warp limit . . . . 0.2 mm

Torque wrench settings*

	Nm	lbf ft
Clutch cover retaining bolts	24	18
Master cylinder retaining nuts	24	18
Pedal retaining screws	24	18
Release bearing and slave cylinder mounting bolts	10	7

*Volvo specify that where a fixing requires angular tightening it must always be renewed. Any fixing retained with a thread locking compound must also be renewed. Nuts with a nylon insert must always be renewed.

1 General information

A single dry plate diaphragm spring clutch is fitted to all manual transmission models. The clutch is hydraulically-operated via a master and slave cylinder. All models have an internally-mounted slave cylinder and release bearing combined into one unit.

The main components of the clutch are the clutch cover and pressure plate, the driven plate (sometimes called the friction plate or disc) and the release bearing. The pressure plate is bolted to the flywheel, with the driven plate sandwiched between them. The centre of the driven plate carries female splines which mate with the splines on the transmission input shaft. The release bearing acts on the diaphragm spring fingers of the pressure plate.

When the engine is running and the clutch pedal is released, the diaphragm spring clamps the pressure plate, driven plate and flywheel firmly together. Drive is transmitted through the friction surfaces of the flywheel and pressure plate to the linings of the driven plate, and thus to the transmission input shaft.

The slave cylinder is incorporated into the release bearing – when the slave cylinder operates, the release bearing moves against the diaphragm spring fingers. As the spring pressure on the pressure plate is relieved, the flywheel and pressure plate spin without moving the driven plate. As the pedal is released, spring pressure is restored and the drive is gradually taken up.

The clutch hydraulic system consists of a master cylinder, a slave cylinder and the associated pipes and hoses. The fluid reservoir is shared with the brake master cylinder.

All models are fitted with a self-adjusting clutch, which compensates for driven plate wear by altering the attitude of the diaphragm spring fingers by means of a sprung mechanism within the pressure plate cover. This ensures a consistent clutch pedal 'feel' over the life of the clutch.

2 Clutch pedal – removal and refitting

Removal and refitting of the clutch pedal is included in the master cylinder removal and refitting procedure described below.

3 Clutch master cylinder – removal and refitting

⚠ *Warning: Hydraulic fluid is poisonous; wash off immediately and thoroughly in the case of skin contact, and seek immediate medical advice if any fluid is swallowed or gets into the eyes. Certain types of hydraulic fluid are inflammable, and may ignite when allowed into contact with hot components; when servicing any hydraulic system, it is safest to assume that the fluid IS inflammable, and to take precautions against the risk of fire as though it is petrol that is being handled. Hydraulic fluid is also an effective paint stripper, and will attack plastics; if any is spilt, it should be washed off immediately, using copious quantities of clean water. Finally, it is hygroscopic (it absorbs moisture from the air) – old fluid may be contaminated and unfit for further use. When topping-up or renewing the fluid, always use the recommended type, and ensure that it comes from a freshly-opened sealed container.*

Note: *Master cylinder internal components*

3.3 Prise out the clip (arrowed) and disconnect the pressure pipe union from the master cylinder

are not available separately, and therefore no repair or overhaul of the cylinder is possible. In the event of a hydraulic system fault, or any sign of visible fluid leakage on or around the master cylinder or clutch pedal, the unit should be replaced.

Removal

1 On XC60 models remove the plenum cover as described in Chapter 12, Section 18. On XC90 models remove the strut brace.
2 Disconnect the wiring plug for the clutch position sensor, located on the side of the master cylinder. On XC90 models also remove the wiring connectors from the brake servo.
3 Prise out the clip and disconnect the pressure pipe union from the master cylinder **(see illustration)**. Be prepared for further fluid spillage. Cover the open pipe union with a piece of polythene and a rubber band to keep dirt out.
4 Release the fluid supply hose from the retaining clip, then use a clamp on the hose before disconnecting it from the master cylinder. Be prepared for further fluid spillage. Cover the open pipe union with a piece of polythene and a rubber band to keep dirt out.
5 Remove the trim panel above the pedals, disconnecting the wiring plug from the footwell lamp as the panel is removed. Access cane be improved by removing the steering column lower pinch-bolt and moving the steering shaft to one side. If this does not provide adequate access, remove the steering column as described in Chapter 10.
6 Prise off the retaining clip and pull the master cylinder pushrod from the pedal **(see illustration)**. Some models do not have a

4.3 Slave cylinder fluid pipe clip

3.6 Master cylinder pushrod clip at the clutch pedal

retaining clip – on these models use a large screw driver to prise off the push rod.
7 Where fitted, remove the start inhibit switch located at the top of the pedal. Disconnect the wiring plug, release the retaining clips, and remove the switch. On XC60 models lever off and then remove the pedal return spring
8 Working under the facia, undo the 2 (or 3) nuts securing the master cylinder to the bulkhead.
9 On XC60 models rotate the master cylinder anti-clockwise (from the cabin) and separate the master cylinder from the pedal bracket. Volvo technicians use a special tool (999 7172) to rotate the master cylinder. In the absence of this tool, use a suitable wrench or adjustable spanner.
10 On XC90 models pry the master cylinder from the bulkhead. Use a screwdriver if necessary.
11 On XC60 models, manoeuvre the assembly from under the facia. No further dismantling is recommended. If faulty, the pedal and bracket must be renewed as an assembly.
12 If required , on XC90 models the pedal can now be unbolted and removed.

Refitting

13 Refit by reversing the removal operations, noting the following points:
   a) If a new master cylinder is being fitted, transfer the fluid supply hose from the old cylinder to the new one prior to installation.
   b) Tighten the master cylinder retaining nuts to the specified torque.
   c) Before refitting the start inhibit switch, ensure the plunger is fully extended.
   d) A new clip must be used when

4.4 Undo the bolts (one hidden) and remove the slave cylinder

reattaching the master cylinder pushrod to the pedal.
   e) A new seal is required where the master cylinder meets the bulkhead.
   f) Bleed the clutch hydraulic system on completion (Section 5).

4 Clutch slave cylinder – removal and refitting

Note: Refer to the warning at the beginning of Section 3 before proceeding.

Removal

1 Remove the transmission as described in Chapter 7A. The internal slave cylinder cannot be removed with the transmission in place.
2 Release the rubber seal from the transmission, and move it inwards down the pipe.
3 Prise out the clip and disconnect the fluid pipe junction from the pipe **(see illustration)**.
4 Remove the 3 mounting bolts securing the cylinder to the transmission and remove the assembly **(see illustration)**.

Refitting

5 Refit by reversing the removal operations, noting the following points:
   a) Tighten the release bearing assembly mounting bolts to the specified torque.
   b) Volvo recommend the use of new seals when refitting the quick-release pipe connections.
   c) Refit the transmission as described in Chapter 7A.
   d) Bleed the clutch hydraulic system on completion (Section 5).

5 Clutch hydraulic system – bleeding

Note: Refer to the warning at the beginning of Section 3 before proceeding.
1 Top-up the hydraulic fluid reservoir on the brake master cylinder with fresh clean fluid (see *Weekly checks*).
2 Remove the dust cap, and fit a length of clear hose over the bleed screw on the slave cylinder **(see illustration)**. Place the other end

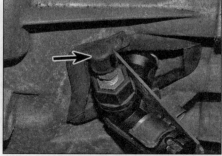

5.2 Prise off the cap (arrowed) to access the bleed screw

of the hose in a jar containing a small amount of hydraulic fluid.

3 Slacken the bleed screw, then have an assistant depress the clutch pedal. Tighten the bleed screw when the pedal is depressed. Have the assistant release the pedal, then slacken the bleed screw again.

4 Repeat the process until clean fluid, free of air bubbles, emerges from the bleed screw. Tighten the screw at the end of a pedal downstroke, and remove the hose and jar. Refit the dust cover.

5 Top-up the hydraulic fluid reservoir.

6 Pressure bleeding equipment may be used if preferred – refer to the information in Chapter 9, Section 2.

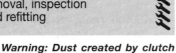

6   Clutch assembly –
     removal, inspection
     and refitting

⚠ *Warning: Dust created by clutch wear and deposited on the clutch components may contain asbestos, which is a health hazard. DO NOT blow it out with compressed air or inhale any of it. DO NOT use petrol or petroleum-based solvents to clean off the dust. Brake system cleaner or methylated spirit should be used to flush the dust into a suitable receptacle. After the clutch components are wiped clean with rags, dispose of the contaminated rags and the used cleaner in a sealed, marked container.*

Note: *Volvo tools 999 7068 and 999 5662 may be required to reset the self-adjusting mechanism and compress the diaphragm spring prior to clutch removal, although it is possible to successfully carry out the procedure using improvised home-made tools. Volvo also use a tool (999 7120), bolted to the engine mating face, to lock the flywheel in place. Again, a home-made tool or the assistance of another person will suffice.*

Removal

1 Access to the clutch may be gained in one of two ways. Either the engine/transmission assembly can be removed as described in Chapter 2B, and the transmission then separated from the engine, or the engine may be left in the car and the transmission removed independently as described in Chapter 7A. If the clutch is to be refitted, use paint or marker pen to mark the position of the clutch cover relative to the flywheel.

With Volvo special tools

2 Fit Volvo 'counterhold' tool 999 7068 to the clutch cover to reset the self-adjusting mechanism. The pins of the tool must engage in the groove in front of the adjuster springs, then hold the tool against the plate. Engage the hooks at the end of the tool springs in the centre of the three holes, located at 120° intervals along the circumference of the clutch cover.

3 Fit the Volvo compression tool 999 5662 to

the clutch cover, and compress the diaphragm spring so that the self-adjusting spring is not under tension. Ensure that hooks on the underside of the compressor engage correctly without clamping the adjuster mechanism springs. Continue to screw in the compression tool spindle until the diaphragm spring has pressed the pressure plate to a 'free' position. A distinct 'click' will be heard when the pressure plate is in the 'free' position.

With or without Volvo special tools

4 Undo the screws and remove the clutch cover/pressure plate, followed by the driven plate **(see illustration)**. Note the orientation of the driven plate.

5 It is important that no oil or grease is allowed to come into contact with the friction material or the pressure plate and flywheel faces during inspection and refitting. **Note:** *If the clutch cover/pressure plate is to be refitted, do not allow the diaphragm spring to remain in the compressed state for a long period of time, or the spring may be permanently weakened.*

Inspection

6 With the clutch assembly removed, clean off all traces of clutch dust using a dry cloth. This is best done outside or in a well-ventilated area.

7 Examine the linings of the driven plate for wear and loose rivets, and the rim for distortion, cracks, broken torsion springs and worn splines. The surface of the friction linings may be highly glazed, but, as long as the friction material pattern can be clearly seen, this is satisfactory.

8 If there is any sign of oil contamination, indicated by a continuous or patchy, shiny black discolouration, the plate must be renewed and the source of the contamination traced and rectified. This will be either a leaking crankshaft oil seal or transmission input shaft oil seal – or both.

9 The driven plate must also be renewed if the lining thickness has worn down to, or just above, the level of the rivet heads. Given the amount of dismantling work necessary to gain access to the driven plate, it may be wise to fit a new plate regardless of the old one's condition.

10 Check the machined faces of the flywheel

6.4 Undo the clutch pressure plate screws

and pressure plate. If either is grooved, or heavily scored, renewal is necessary. Providing the damage is not too serious, the flywheel can be removed as described in the Chapter 2A and taken to an engineering works, who may be able to clean up the surface by machining.

11 The pressure plate must be renewed if any cracks are apparent, if the diaphragm spring is damaged or its pressure suspect, or if there is excessive warpage of the pressure plate face.

12 With the transmission removed, check the condition of the release bearing, as described in Section 7.

Refitting

13 It is advisable to refit the clutch assembly with clean hands, and to wipe down the pressure plate and flywheel faces with a clean dry rag before assembly begins.

14 Fit an appropriate centering tool into the hole at the end of the crankshaft. The tool must be a sliding fit in the crankshaft hole and the driven plate centre.

15 Place the driven plate in position with the longer side of the centre boss towards the flywheel, or as noted on removal. Note that the new driven plate will be marked to indicate which side faces the flywheel **(see illustrations)**.

With Volvo special tools

16 Fit the counterhold tool 999 7068 to the clutch cover, ensuring the three pins engage in the grooves in front of the adjuster springs, then hold the tool against the plate. Engage the hooks at the end of the tool springs in the centre of the three holes, located at 120°

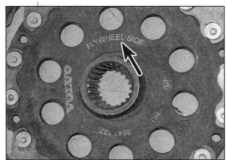

6.15a The driven plate should be marked (arrowed) to indicate which side faces the flywheel

6.15b Fit the driven plate with the longer side of the centre boss towards the flywheel

6.18a Compress the diaphragm spring fingers and the pressure plate together...

6.18b ...then rotate the adjuster ring anti-clockwise...

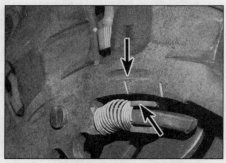

6.18c ...until the pointers align with the marks by the adjustment springs (arrowed)

intervals along the circumference of the clutch cover.

17 Fit the Volvo compression tool 999 5662 to the clutch cover, and compress the diaphragm spring so that the self-adjusting springs are not under tension. Ensure that hooks on the underside of the compressor engage correctly without clamping the adjuster mechanism springs. From the initial 'loose' state, the compressor spindle should be turned no more 5.0 turns and a distinct 'click' will be heard when the pressure plate is in the 'free' position.

Without Volvo special tools

18 Using a length of threaded rod, and some circular spacers and two nuts, compress the diaphragm spring fingers and the pressure plate together as shown. Once the fingers are compressed, use a screwdriver to move and hold the adjusting ring anti-clockwise until the pointers align with the marks by the adjustment springs **(see illustrations)**.

19 Slowly undo the nuts to uncompress the pressure plate assembly. The self-adjusting ring/spring marks should remain in the same place (see paragraph 18). Remove the threaded rod, etc.

With or without Volvo special tools

20 Position the clutch cover/pressure plate assembly over the dowels on the flywheel, aligning the previously-made marks (where applicable).

21 Working in a diagonal pattern, fit and

evenly tighten the cover retaining bolts to the specified torque.

22 Slowly release the compressor, then remove the counterhold tool from the clutch – where applicable.

23 Pull the centering tool from the plate/crankshaft, and check visually that the driven plate appears centrally located.

24 Remove the flywheel locking tool if used.

25 The engine and/or transmission can now be refitted by referring to the appropriate Chapter of this manual.

7 Clutch release bearing – removal, inspection and refitting

Removal

1 The release bearing and slave cylinder are combined into one unit, and cannot be separated. Refer to the slave cylinder removal procedure in Section 4.

Inspection

2 Check the bearing for smoothness of operation, and renew it if there is any roughness or harshness as the bearing is spun. It is a good idea to renew the bearing as a matter of course during clutch overhaul, regardless of its apparent condition, considering the amount of dismantling work necessary to gain access to it.

Refitting

3 Refer to Section 4.

8 Clutch pedal sensors – renewal

Note: *Two sensors are fitted to the clutch; a position sensor (mounted on the master cylinder) and a start inhibiter switch (mounted on the clutch pedal).*

Pedal position sensor

1 Remove the battery and battery tray as described in Chapter 5.

2 Disconnect the sensor wiring plug.

3 Volvo use a special tool (999 7402) to engage with the body of the switch and pull it from the master cylinder. However, a screwdriver or suitable flat-bladed tool can be used instead.

4 Refitting is a reversal of removal.

Start inhibit switch

5 If necessary remove the trim panel from below the steering column.

6 Disconnect the wiring plug, release the locking tang and pull up the switch to remove it.

7 Refitting is a reversal of removal, but ensure the switch plunger is fully extended before replacing the switch.

Chapter 7 Part A:
Manual transmission

Contents

Degrees of difficulty

Easy, suitable for novice with little experience	Fairly easy, suitable for beginner with some experience	Fairly difficult, suitable for competent DIY mechanic	Difficult, suitable for experienced DIY mechanic	Very difficult, suitable for expert DIY or professional

Specifications

General
Designation	M66
Type	Six forward gears and one reverse. Synchromesh on all gears

Lubrication
Lubricant type	See *Lubricants and fluids* on page 0•16
Capacity	1.9 litres

Torque wrench settings
	Nm	lbf ft
Auxiliary heater mounting nuts	25	18
Engine mounting nuts/bolts (including torque rod)	See Chapter 2A	
Gear lever housing bolts	10	7
Oil filler/drain plugs	35	26
Reversing light switch	24	18
Roadwheel bolts	140	103
Starter motor mounting bolts	See Chapter 5	
Subframe mounting bolts	See Chapter 10	
Transmission-to-engine bolts	50	37

* Do not re-use. Volvo specify that where a fixing requires angular tightening it must always be renewed. Any fixing retained with a thread locking compound must also be renewed. Nuts with a nylon insert must always be renewed.

1 General information

The manual transmission and final drive are housed in an aluminium casing, bolted directly to the left-hand side of the engine. Gear selection is by a remotely-sited lever assembly, operating the transmission selector mechanism via cables.

The input shaft contains the 6th, 5th gear idler wheels, and the 4th, 1st, and 3rd gearwheels. The two intermediate shafts contain the 5th and 6th gearwheels, 1st, 2nd, 3rd and 4th gear idler wheels, and the final drive gearwheels.

Drive from the engine is transmitted to the input shaft by the clutch. The gears on the input shaft are permanently meshed with the gears on the two layshafts, but when drive is transmitted, only one gear at a time is actually locked to its shaft, with the others freewheeling. The selection of gears is by sliding synchro units; movement of the gear lever is transmitted to selector forks, which slide the appropriate synchro unit towards the gear to be engaged, and lock it to the relevant shaft. In neutral, none of the gears are locked, all are freewheeling.

Reverse gear is obtained by locking the reverse gearwheel to the upper layshaft. Drive is transmitted through the input shaft to the reverse intermediate gearwheel on the lower layshaft, then to the reverse gearwheel and final drive pinion on the upper layshaft. Reverse is therefore obtained by transmitting power through all three shafts, instead of only two as in the case of the forward gears. By eliminating the need for a separate reverse idler gear, synchromesh can also be provided on reverse gear.

2 Gear lever housing – removal and refitting

Removal

1 Remove the centre console as described in Chapter 11.
2 Prise off the selector cable from the ball joints at the base of the gear lever. Note that on some models the cable ends may be secured by wire clips.
3 Release the outer cables from the housing.
4 Undo the four bolts securing the housing assembly to the floor. Remove the assembly form the vehicle.

3.3a Remove the cable-ends from the selector arms

3.3b Slide the locking collar forwards and unclip the cables from the bracket

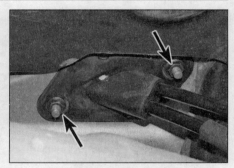

3.6 Undo the nuts (arrowed) at the grommet/cable entry at the bulkhead

Refitting

5 Refit by reversing the removal operations. Tighten the four securing bolts to the specified torque. Adjust the cables as described in Section 3 of this Chapter. Refit the centre console as described in Chapter 11.

3 Selector cables – removal and refitting

Removal

1 Refer to the relevant part of Chapter 4A and Chapter 5 and remove the air cleaner assembly. On XC60 models remove the battery and battery tray.
2 On XC60 models remove the heat shield panel at the rear of the engine bay and above the front section of the exhaust. Unclip the cable from the bulkhead.
3 Undo the clips and remove the cable-ends from the selector arms on the transmission. Slide the locking collar forwards and unclip the cables from the bracket on the transmission (see illustrations).
4 Remove the centre console as described in Chapter 11. On XC60 models, remove the central air vent and move the rear air vents to one side.
5 Disconnect the cables from the selector housing as described in Section 2.
6 Undo the nuts securing the grommet/cable entry plate to the bulkhead (see illustration).

7 Note the routing of the cables under the facia, and in the engine compartment, as an aid to refitting, then attach cords to the ends of the cables in the engine compartment. Release any adjacent components as necessary, then pull the cables one at a time into the passenger compartment. Remove the cord and remove the cables from the vehicle.

Refitting

8 From inside the car tie the replacement cables to the cord and then use the cord to pull and guide the cables into the engine bay. Ensure that the cables are routed correctly.
9 Reconnect the cables to the gear lever housing, and refit the housing as described in Section 2.
10 Refit the grommet/cable entry plate, and the carpet.
11 Adjust the cables as described below.
12 Refit the centre console (see Chapter 11).
13 Refit the battery tray, battery and air cleaner assembly as described in Chapter 5 and Chapter 4A.

Cable adjustment

XC60

14 Select fourth gear and remove the left-hand side panel from the centre console, as described in Chapter 11.
15 Release the locking collar from the selector cable and move the inner cable towards the gearbox to remove any slack in

the cable. Refit the locking collar and check that all gears can be selected. Repeat the procedure if necessary.

XC90

16 Ensure that the gear lever is in the neutral position.
17 Remove the air filter housing (as described in Chapter 4A) to gain access to the selector cables.
18 Release the ball joint from the inner cable by releasing it with a pair of long noise pliers or similar.
19 Release the adjuster from the cable and then refit the cable to the ball joint.
20 Press the adjuster into place and lock it onto the cable. Check that all gears can be selected and repeat the procedure if necessary.

4 Oil seals – renewal

Driveshaft seals

1 Remove the left- or right-hand driveshaft (as appropriate) with reference to Chapter 8A.
2 Using a large screwdriver or suitable lever, carefully prise the oil seal out of the transmission casing, taking care not to damage the casing (see illustration).
3 Wipe clean the oil seal seating in the transmission casing.
4 Apply a small amount of general-purpose grease to the new seal lips, then press it a little way into the casing by hand, making sure that it is square to its seating.
5 Using suitable tubing or a large socket, carefully drive the oil seal fully into position until it is flush with the casing edge (see illustration).
6 Refit the driveshaft(s) as described in Chapter 8A.

Input shaft oil seal

7 Remove the transmission as described in Section 7.
8 Remove the clutch release bearing/slave cylinder as described in Chapter 6.
9 Note its fitted depth, then drill a small hole in the hard outer surface of the seal, insert a

4.2 Use a piece of wood to protect the casing when levering out the driveshaft oil seal(s)

4.5 Use a socket or tubular spacer to drive in the oil seal

self-tapping screw, and use pliers to extract the seal **(see illustrations)**.

10 Lubricate the new seal with grease and fit it to the bellhousing, lips pointing to the gearbox side. Use a deep socket or suitable tubing to seat it **(see illustration)**.

11 Refit the release bearing/slave cylinder using a reversal of removal.

12 Refit the transmission as described in Section 7.

4.9a Drill a small hole in the hard outer edge of the oil seal, then insert a self-tapping screw . . .

4.9b . . . and use pliers to pull the seal from place

5 Reversing light switch – removal and refitting

Removal

1 The reversing light switch is located on the upper face of the transmission. Remove the air cleaner assembly as described in the relevant part of Chapter 4A.

2 Disconnect the wiring plug and unscrew the switch from the transmission housing **(see illustration)**.

Refitting

3 Refit by reversing the removal operations.

6 Manual transmission oil – draining and refilling

Note: *Renewal of the transmission oil is not a service requirement and will normally only be necessary if the unit is to be removed for overhaul or renewal. However, if the car has completed a high mileage, or is used under arduous conditions (eg, extensive towing or taxi work), it would be advisable to change the oil as a precaution, especially if the gearchange quality has deteriorated.*

Draining

1 Slacken the left-hand front roadwheel bolts, then jack up the front of the vehicle and support it securely on axle stands (see *Jacking and vehicle support*). Remove the roadwheel.

2 Release the screws and remove the engine undershield, then position a suitable container beneath the transmission.

3 On the side of the transmission casing, you will see the filler/level plug and the drain plug. Unscrew and remove the drain plug (the lower of the two) and allow the oil to drain into the container **(see illustration)**. Check the condition of the drain plug sealing washer, and renew if necessary.

4 When all the oil has drained, refit the drain plug and tighten it to the specified torque.

Refilling

Note: *For the level check to be accurate, the car must be completely level. If the front of the car has been jacked up, the rear should be jacked up also.*

5 Wipe clean the area around the filler/level plug, and unscrew the plug from the casing.

4.10 Use a suitable tube to drive in the seal

6 Fill the transmission through the filler/level plug hole with the correct type of oil until the oil begins to run out of the hole.

7 Refit the filler/level plug with a new seal, and tighten it to the specified torque.

8 Dispose of the old oil safely in accordance with environmental regulations.

7 Manual transmission – removal and refitting

Note: *The engine must be supported from above, to allow removal of the subframe. The best way to support the engine is an engine support bar resting on the Inner wings, with an adjustable hook appropriately placed. We used two bars to help spread the load and to control the lowering of the engine and transmission. Trolley jacks (or a suitable transmission jack) and the help of an assistant will also be required throughout the procedure.*

Removal

1 Disconnect the battery - as described in Chapter 5. Remove the engine cover and on XC90 models remove the strut brace and upper engine mount.

2 Jack up and support the front of the vehicle -see *Jacking and vehicle support* in the reference section. Remove the engine undershield. On XC90 models remove the skid plate.

3 On XC90 models, drain the cooling system as described in Chapter 1.

4 Refer to Section 6 and drain the transmission

5.2 Disconnect the reversing light switch wiring plug (arrowed)

oil. This is not absolutely essential, but will remove the potential problem of oil spillage when the driveshafts are removed, or when the transmission is moved out of the car.

5 With reference to Chapters 4A and Chapter 5, remove the battery (XC60 only) the air filter housing and the EGR control valve **(see illustration)**.

6 Remove the charge air pipe and the hose between the inter cooler and the inlet manifold.

7 On XC60 models remove the upper engine mounting bolts from the left-hand chassis leg. Do not remove the bolts from the transmission at this point.

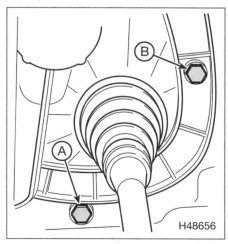

6.3 Oil drain plug (A) and filler plug (B)

7.5 Removal of the EGR valve is required to access the upper mounting bolts

8 Disconnect the gearchange cables from the transmission as described in Section 3.

9 Disconnect the wiring plug from the TCU (Transmission Control Unit) and the reverse gear sensor. Unclip the wiring loom from the bell housing.

10 Clamp the fluid supply hoses from the reservoir to the brake and clutch master cylinders, then extract the circlip and withdraw the slave cylinder supply pipe from the transmission. Have ready a container and rags to catch the fluid which will spill. Cover the open pipe union with a piece of polythene and a rubber band to keep dirt out.

11 Remove the starter motor as described in Chapter 5.

12 Undo the nut securing the earth cable to the transmission housing, and remove any brackets.

13 Where fitted remove the power steering hose support bracket from the transmission.

14 Remove both driveshafts as described in Chapter 8A.

15 On AWD (All Wheel Drive) models remove the transfer box (bevel gear) as described in Chapter 8B.

16 Undo the retaining screws and remove the wheel arch liners.

17 Arrange a suitable support for the engine – see the note at the start of this Section - and then remove the front subframe as described in Chapter 10.

18 On XC60 models, remove the left-hand side engine mounting as described in Chapter 2A.

19 The combine engine and transmission unit must now be lowered at the transmission end, so that sufficient clearance exists between the transmission and the chassis leg to allow the transmission to be removed from the engine.

20 Use a trolley jack to support the transmission and then remove the 7 bolts securing the transmission to the engine. Withdraw the transmission squarely off the engine dowels, taking care not to allow the weight of the unit to hang on the input shaft.

21 Lower the jack and remove the unit from under the car.

Refitting

22 Refitting is a reversal of removal, noting the following points:

a) *Ensure the mating surfaces between the engine and transmission are clean and free of any debris.*

b) *Apply a small amount of wheel bearing grease (Volvo 1161689) to the dowel mounting points on the engine mating surface*

c) *Ensure the input shaft is clean and free of any debris. Wipe clean if necessary and apply a small amount oil to the shaft. Do not use grease.*

d) *Tighten all fasteners to the their specified torque where given.*

e) *Top-up the gearbox oil as described in Section 6 of this Chapter.*

f) *Top-up the cooling system as described in Chapter 1.*

g) *Bleed the clutch hydraulic system as described in Chapter 6.*

h) *Reconnect the battery negative lead as described in Chapter 5A.*

8 Manual transmission overhaul – general information

Overhauling a manual transmission is a difficult job for the do-it-yourselfer. It involves the dismantling and reassembly of many small parts. Numerous clearances must be precisely measured and, if necessary, changed with selected spacers and circlips. As a result, if transmission problems arise, while the unit can be removed and refitted by a competent do-it-yourselfer, overhaul should be left to a transmission specialist. Rebuilt transmissions may be available – check with your dealer parts department, motor factors, or transmission specialists. At any rate, the time and money involved in an overhaul is almost sure to exceed the cost of a rebuilt unit.

Nevertheless, it's not impossible for an experienced mechanic to rebuild a transmission, providing the special tools are available, and the job is done in a deliberate step-by-step manner, so nothing is overlooked.

The tools necessary for an overhaul include: internal and external circlip pliers, a bearing puller, a slide hammer, a set of pin punches, a dial test indicator, and possibly a hydraulic press. In addition, a large, sturdy workbench and a vice or transmission stand will be required.

During dismantling of the transmission, make careful notes of how each part comes off, where it fits in relation to other parts, and what holds it in place.

Before taking the transmission apart for repair, it will help if you have some idea what area of the transmission is malfunctioning. Certain problems can be closely tied to specific areas in the transmission, which can make component examination and renewal easier. Refer to the Fault finding section at the rear of this manual for information regarding possible sources of trouble.

Chapter 7 Part B:
Automatic transmission

Contents

Degrees of difficulty

Easy, suitable for novice with little experience	Fairly easy, suitable for beginner with some experience	Fairly difficult, suitable for competent DIY mechanic	Difficult, suitable for experienced DIY mechanic	Very difficult, suitable for expert DIY or professional 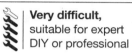

Specifications

General

Type . . . . Computer-controlled six-speed, one reverse, with torque converter lock-up on 5 highest gears
Designation: TF-8A0SC

Lubrication

Lubricant type . . . . See *Lubricants and fluids* on page 0•16
Capacity (drain and refill) . . . . 7.0 litres (approx)

Torque wrench settings

	Nm	lbf ft
Engine mounting nuts/bolts (including torque rod)	See Chapter 2A	
Engine rear mounting bracket to transmission.	50	37
Fluid drain plug.	35	26
Gear lever housing bolts	25	18
Reversing light switch	25	18
Roadwheel bolts.	140	103
Starter motor mounting bolts.	See Chapter 5	
Subframe mounting bolts.	See Chapter 10	
Torque converter to driveplate bolts*.	60	44
Transmission-to-engine bolts.	50	37

* Do not re-use. Volvo specify that where a fixing requires angular tightening it must always be renewed. Any fixing retained with a thread locking compound must also be renewed. Nuts with a nylon insert must always be renewed.

1 General information

The TF-80SC is a computer-controlled automatic transmission with 6 forward speeds, and torque converter lock-up on the 5 highest speeds. It is equipped with a Geartronic function that allows the driver to manually shift between transmission speeds in a sequential fashion – lever forward to change up, and backward to change down.

The unit is controlled by a transmission control module (TCM) which receives signal inputs from various sensors relating to transmission operating conditions. Information on engine parameters are also sent to the TCM from the engine management system. From this data, the TCM can establish the optimum gear shifting speeds and lock-up engagement points according to the driving mode selected.

Drive is taken from the engine to the transmission by a torque converter. This is a type of fluid coupling which, under certain conditions, has a torque multiplying effect. The torque converter is mechanically locked to the engine, under the control of the TCM, when the transmission is operating in the highest gears. This eliminates losses due to slip, and improves fuel economy.

The engine can only be started in position P, thanks to a safety/security feature called Shiftlock. With this system, the ignition key can only be removed from the ignition/steering lock if the selector lever is placed in position P. On restarting the car, the selector lever can only be moved from the P position once the ignition is placed in position II.

Most models with automatic transmission feature a Winter mode selector, with the switch located alongside the selector lever. In this mode, the transmission will allow starting off from rest in a higher than normal gear to avoid

wheelspin in poor road conditions. This mode can also be used to restrict gearchanging when road conditions dictate the need for more direct control of gear selection.

A kickdown facility causes the transmission to shift down a gear (subject to engine speed) when the throttle is fully depressed. This is useful when extra acceleration is required. Kickdown, like the other transmission functions, is controlled by the TCM.

In addition to control of the transmission, the TCM incorporates a built-in fault diagnosis facility. If a transmission fault occurs, the transmission warning light on the instrument panel will flash; the TCM will revert to an emergency (limp-home) programme which ensures that two forward gears and reverse will always be available, but gearchanging must be performed manually. If a fault of this nature does occur, the TCM stores a series of signals (or fault codes) which can be read and interpreted using suitable diagnostic

2.4 Depress the lock button on XC60 models

2.8 Use a screwdriver to depress the locking button

equipment, for quick and accurate fault diagnosis (see Section 7). The TCM also has a facility for recording the amount of time the gearbox fluid spends above 150°C – normally this temperature is only achieved by taxi-use, or use as a towing vehicle. Once a predetermined amount of time at or above this temperature is exceeded, the TCM will store a fault code, and illuminate a warning light on the instrument cluster, indicating that the fluid must be changed. However, changing the fluid will not extinguish the warning light – this must be carried out using dedicated Volvo test equipment.

The automatic transmission is a complex unit, but if it is not abused, it is reliable and long-lasting. Repair or overhaul operations are beyond the scope of many dealers, let alone the home mechanic; specialist advice should be sought if problems arise which cannot be solved by the procedures given in this Chapter.

2.11 Release the selector cable form the ball joint

2.5 Release the locking collar

2.9 Remove the bolts

2 Selector cable – removal, refitting and adjustment

Removal

1 Park the car on a level surface (with the transmission selector lever in position P), then refer to the relevant part of Chapter 4A and Chapter 5 and remove the air cleaner assembly, the battery, and the battery tray.
2 Remove the centre console as described in Chapter 11.

XC60

3 Working beneath the vehicle, remove the heat shields at the rear of the engine bay and above the front section of the exhaust.
4 At the transmission, release the cable from transmission control module (TCM)

2.12 Remove the outer cable

by depressing the locking button **(see illustration)**. Lift the cable from the ball joint.
5 Release the outer cable from the transmission by pulling forward the locking collar and lifting the cable from the housing **(see illustration)**.
6 Unclip the cable from the left-hand chassis leg.
7 Working in the cabin, remove the Audio unit (as described in Chapter 12) and the air distribution ducting from both sides of the transmission tunnel.
8 Release the cable at the gear lever by sliding the outer cable locking collar up and lifting the outer form the housing. With the cable outer free, depress the inner cable locking button and lift off the inner cable **(see illustration)**.
9 Remove the facia support brackets and then undo the bolts securing the cable entry cover plate to the bulkhead **(see illustration)**. Where necessary cut out a small section of the bulkhead insulation to allow the cable to be removed.
10 Note the routing of the cable under the facia and in the engine compartment, as an aid to refitting. Pull the cable into the passenger compartment and remove it from the car.

XC90

11 Use a pair of long nose pliers and free the ball joint from the transmission control unit (TCU) **(see illustration)**.
12 Release the outer cable locking collar and lift out the cable **(see illustration)**. Note that some models may have a cable tie fitted that must be cut free.
13 Jack up and support the vehicle - see *Jacking and vehicle support* in the reference section - and remove the left-hand road wheel.
14 Release the cable from the assorted retaining clips on the chassis leg and inner wing.
15 Disconnect the wiring plugs and release the selector lever upper cage - as described in Section 3 of this Chapter.
16 Use a screwdriver and prise free the outer cable from the housing and then release the inner cable **(see illustration)**.
17 To improve access remove the glovebox (as described in Chapter 11) and on vehicles fitted with rear AC release the cable clip and move the pipes to one side.

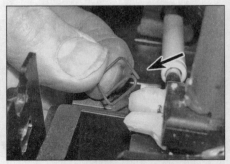

2.16 Some models have a circlip fitted to the inner cable (arrowed)

2.21 Note how the locking collar (arrowed) fits onto the cable

3.3a Unclip the cable end fitting

3.3b ...and then release the outer cable

18 Remove the bolts from the cable entry cover in the bulkhead. Before pulling the cable into the cabin secure stout cord to the cable. This can be transferred to the replacement cable and be used to pull the new cable through the bulkhead. Remove the cable.

Refitting

19 Refitting is a reversal of removal, carefully feeding the cable through into the engine compartment from inside the car, ensuring that it is correctly routed.

Adjustment

Note: *Adjustment on XC60 models is carried out at the gear lever, on XC90 models adjustment is carried out at the transmission.*

XC60

20 Ensure the gear selector lever is in the 'P' (Park) position.
21 Working at the gear lever, release the locking collar from the threaded section of the cable **(see illustration)**.
22 Remove any slack from the inner cable and refit the locking clip.

XC90

23 Slide the spring loaded collar backwards and prise up the catch - do not attempt to remove the catch.
24 The vehicle must be in the 'P' (Park) position. (The lever at the gearbox will be towards the rear of the vehicle when park is selected).
25 Confirm that the 'P' position has been correctly selected by releasing the handbrake

and attempting to push the vehicle. Only carry out this procedure on level ground.
26 Press the catch down and allow the cable to align itself.

3 Gear selector housing – removal and refitting

Removal

1 Remove the centre console as described in Chapter 11.
2 Disconnect the selector cable as described in Section 2 of this Chapter.
3 On XC90 models, note the length of the exposed threads on the interlock cable (9mm on our vehicle) and release the locking clip. Unhook the outer cable from the mounting **(see illustrations)**.

3.5a Twist the locking collar clockwise...

4 On XC60 models disconnect the wiring plug from the interlock solenoid.
5 To avoid damage to the gear lever position first remove the gear lever knob. On XC60 models, remove the gear knob by twisting the locking collar clockwise by approximately 45 degrees, pressing in the detent button, and pulling the knob upwards **(see illustration)**. On XC90 models release the gaiter and locking collar and then remove the knob by pulling it upwards with a sharp tug.
6 Disconnect the wiring connectors from the gear lever position sensor. Depress the locking tangs and remove the sensor over the gear lever **(see illustration)**. Note this procedure is not essential for simple removal of the gear selector assembly, but it avoids any possibility of damage to the sensor assembly if it is removed from the vehicle first.
7 Remove the mounting bolts and withdraw the housing from the vehicle **(see illustrations)**.

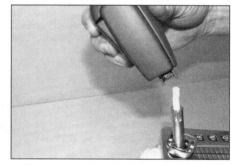

3.5b ...press in the detent button and pull up the gear knob to remove it

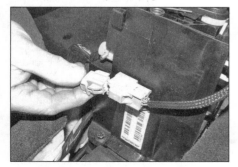

3.6a Disconnect the wiring plug...

3.6b ...and remove the position sensor

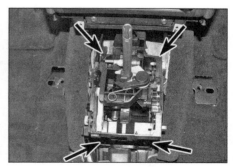

3.7a Remove the mounting bolts (arrowed)

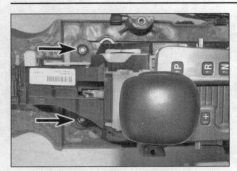

3.7b On XC60 models , remove the front bolts (arrowed)…

Refitting

8 Refitting is a reversal of removal. Check and adjust the selector cable. On XC90 models adjust the interlock cable.

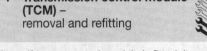

4 Transmission control module (TCM) – removal and refitting

Note: *If a new control module is fitted, it must be programmed using dedicated Volvo test equipment. Entrust this task to a Volvo dealer or suitably-equipped specialist.*

Removal

1 Disconnect the battery negative terminal as described in Chapter 5.
Caution: Wait at least two minutes after the battery negative lead has been disconnected for any residual energy to dissipate from the main system relay.
2 The transmission control module (TCM) is located on the top of the transmission casing. Remove the air cleaner assembly as described in the relevant Part of Chapter 4A.
3 Disconnect the wiring plug from the TCM **(see illustration)**.
4 Undo the nut securing the selector lever to the shaft and pull the lever upwards from position. Note the alignment marks on the TCM and selector shaft **(see illustration)**.
5 Undo the 3 bolts and remove the TCM.

Refitting

6 Ensure the selector lever is in the N (Neutral) position. Refit the TCM to the transmission

4.3 Disconnect the wiring plug

3.7c …and the rear bolts (arrowed)

casing ensuring the arrow on the shaft aligns with the arrow on the TCM **(see illustration 4.4)**. Tighten the retaining bolts securely.
7 Refit the lever to the shaft, and tighten the retaining nut securely.
8 Reconnect the wiring plug and refit the air cleaner assembly.
9 Reconnect the battery negative lead as described in Chapter 5.

5 Fluid seals – renewal

Driveshaft seals

1 The procedure is the same as that described for the manual transmission in Chapter 7A.

Input shaft/ torque converter seal

2 Remove the transmission (see Section 6).
3 Pull the torque converter squarely out of the transmission. Be careful, as it is full of fluid.
4 Pull or lever out the old seal. Clean the seat and inspect the seal rubbing surface on the torque converter.
5 Lubricate the new seal with transmission fluid and fit it, lips inwards. Seat it with a piece of tube.
6 Lubricate the torque converter sleeve with transmission fluid, and slide the converter into place, pushing it in as far as it will go.
7 Check that the torque converter is fully seated by measuring the distance from the edge of the transmission housing face to

4.4 Remove the arm. Note the alignment marks (arrowed)

the retaining bolt tabs on the converter. The dimension should be approximately 13 mm.
8 Refit the transmission as described in Section 6.

Gear shift linkage rod seal

9 Remove the transmission control module (TCM) as described in Section 4.
10 Carefully prise the old oil seal from position using a small screwdriver. Take care not to damage the linkage rod.
11 Smear the lips of the new oil seal with clean automatic transmission fluid, the guide the seal over the rod (lips towards the transmission), and seat it in place using a suitable tubular spacer.
12 Refit the TCM as described in Section 4.

All seals

13 Check the transmission fluid level as described in Chapter 1 on completion.

6 Automatic transmission – removal and refitting

Note: *The engine must be supported from above, to allow removal of the subframe. The best way to support the engine is an engine support bar resting on the Inner wings, with an adjustable hook appropriately placed. We used two bars to help spread the load and to control the lowering of the engine and transmission. Trolley jacks (or a suitable transmission jack) and the help of an assistant will also be required throughout the procedure.*

Removal

1 Disconnect the battery negative lead as described in Chapter 5. Remove the air filter housing as described in Chapter 4A
2 Slacken the front roadwheel bolts, then jack up the front of the vehicle, and support it securely on axle stands (see *Jacking and vehicle support*). Remove both front roadwheels.
3 Undo the screws and remove the engine undershield and wheel arch liners. On XC90 models remove the skid plate.
4 Refer to Chapter 1 and drain the transmission fluid.
5 Remove both driveshafts as described in Chapter 8A and then on AWD models remove the transfer box (Chapter 8B).
6 Remove the EGR valve (Chapter 4B) and the starter motor as described in Chapter 5.
7 Remove the front subframe as described in Chapter 10.
8 Disconnect the transmission control module wiring plug, undo the nut and disconnect the selector cable from the selector shaft as described in Section 4 **(see illustration)**.
9 Undo the 2 bolts securing the exhaust/ catalytic converter bracket to the transmission housing and undo the bolt securing the earth cable to the transmission housing. Remove the rear engine mounting.

6.8 To increase clearance remove the selector cable support bracket

6.10 Remove the oil cooler pipes (arrowed)

6.11 Support the transmission

10 Undo the bolts securing the transmission cooler fluid pipe unions to the transmission housing. Be prepared for some fluid leakage **(see illustration)**.
11 Securely and safely support the transmission from below on a trolley or transmission jack **(see illustration)**.
12 Rotate the crankshaft, using a socket on the pulley nut, until one of the torque converter to driveplate retaining bolts becomes accessible either through the opening on the rear facing side of the engine **(see illustration)** or through the starter motor housing. Working through the opening, undo the bolt. Rotate the crankshaft as necessary and remove the remaining bolts in the same way. Note that new bolts will be required for refitting.
13 Remove the main transmission mounting (as described in Chapter 2A) and then lower the engine/transmission sufficiently, so that the top of the transmission just clears the chassis leg. Remove the remaining 8 bolts securing the transmission to the engine. Note that the bolts are of differing length.
14 With the aid of an assistant, withdraw the transmission squarely off the engine dowels making sure that the torque converter remains in position on the transmission. Use the access hole in the transmission housing to hold the converter in place.
15 Lower the jack and remove the unit from under the car **(see illustration)**.

Refitting

16 Clean the contact surfaces on the torque converter and driveplate, and the transmission and engine mating faces. Lightly lubricate the torque converter guide projection and the engine/transmission locating dowels with grease.
17 Check that the torque converter is fully seated by measuring the distance from the edge of the transmission housing face to the retaining bolt tabs on the converter. The dimension should be approximately 13 mm.
18 The remainder of refitting is a reversal of removal, noting the following points:
 a) Tighten all fasteners to the specified torque where given.
 b) Flushing of the transmission oil cooler is advised by Volvo, and while not essential,

it is a worthwhile precaution to prevent against future contamination. Undo the lower pipe from the oil cooler and place the end in a suitable tray or container. Use an oil syringe or similar to flush fresh oil through the cooler from the upper pipe connection.
 c) *Top-up the transmission fluid as described in Chapter 1.*
 d) *Note that if a new transmission is fitted, a software download from Volvo's diagnostic system may be required. Entrust this task to a Volvo dealer or suitably-equipped specialist.*

7 Automatic transmission – fault diagnosis

The automatic transmission electronic control system incorporates an on-board diagnostic facility as an aid to fault finding and system testing. The diagnostic system is a feature of the transmission control module (TCM) which continually monitors the system components and their operation. Should a fault occur, the TCM stores a series of signals (or fault codes) for subsequent read-out.

If a fault occurs, indicated by the flashing of the warning light on the instrument panel, the on-board diagnostics can be accessed using a fault code reader for quick and accurate diagnosis. A Volvo dealer will obviously have such a reader, but they are also available

6.12 Access the torque converter bolts (arrowed)

from other suppliers. It is unlikely to be cost-effective for the private owner to purchase a fault code reader, but a well-equipped local garage or auto-electrical specialist will have one.

In many instances, the fault may be nothing more serious than a corroded, trapped or loose wiring connection, or a loose, dirty, or badly-fitted component. Remember that if the fault has appeared only a short time after any part of the vehicle has been serviced or overhauled, the first place to check is where that work was carried out, however unrelated it may appear, to ensure that no carelessly-refitted components are causing the problem.

Even if the source of the problem is found and fixed, diagnostic equipment may still be required, to erase the fault code from the TCM memory, and stop the warning light flashing.

If the fault cannot be easily cured, the only alternatives possible at this time are the substitution of a suspect component with a known good unit (where possible), or entrusting further work to a Volvo dealer or suitably-equipped specialist.

8 Emergency release of the selector lever

XC60

1 If the vehicle's battery is disconnected or discharged, it is possible to release the

6.15 With the transmission removed, secure the torque convertor in place with a simple bracket

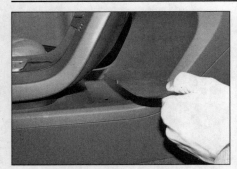

8.2 Remove the rubber mat behind the centre console panel

8.3 Insert the blade into the hole and depress while moving the gear selector to neutral

8.5 Unhook the outer cable (arrowed)

selector lever from its locked position. First, ensure the handbrake is fully applied or chock the rear wheels if it is not possible to apply the handbrake.

2 Withdraw the plastic key blade from the remote control unit, and remove the rubber mat from behind the centre console switch panel (see illustration).

3 Insert the blade into the hole revealed by the removal of the mat, and holding the blade down, move the gear lever to the neutral position (see illustration).

XC90

4 Remove the left-hand centre console side panel.

5 Unhook the (red) outer section of the interlock cable from the housing (see illustration) and move the selector lever out of the park position.

Chapter 8 Part A:
Driveshafts

Contents

Degrees of difficulty

Easy, suitable for novice with little experience	Fairly easy, suitable for beginner with some experience	Fairly difficult, suitable for competent DIY mechanic	Difficult, suitable for experienced DIY mechanic	Very difficult, suitable for expert DIY or professional

Specifications

General
Driveshaft type . . . . Equal-length solid-steel shafts, splined to inner and outer constant velocity joints. Intermediate shaft incorporated in right-hand driveshaft assembly
Outer constant velocity joint type. . . . . Ball-and-cage
Inner constant velocity joint type . . . . Tripod

Lubrication
Lubricant type . . . . Special grease supplied in repair kit, or suitable molybdenum disulphide grease – consult a Volvo dealer

Torque wrench settings

	Nm	lbf ft
ABS wheel speed sensor	See Chapter 9	
Brake caliper mounting bolts	See Chapter 9	
Driveshaft bolt (front):*		
XC60:		
Stage 1	35	26
Stage 2	Angle-tighten a further 90°	
XC90:		
Stage 1	35	26
Stage 2	Angle-tighten a further 120°	
Driveshaft bolt (rear)	50	36
Hub carrier to suspension strut	See Chapter 10	
Lower arm balljoint to hub carrier*	80	59
Right-hand driveshaft support bearing cap bolts	24	18
Roadwheel bolts	140	103

* Do not re-use. Volvo specify that where a fixing requires angular tightening it must always be renewed. Any fixing retained with a thread locking compound must also be renewed. Nuts with a nylon insert must always be renewed.

2.1 Slacken the driveshaft bolt

2.7 Undo the two bolts (arrowed) and remove the intermediate shaft support bearing cap

1 General information

Drive is transmitted from the differential to the front wheels by means of two solid-steel, equal-length driveshafts equipped with constant velocity (CV) joints at their inner and outer ends. Due to the position of the transmission, an intermediate shaft and support bearing are incorporated into the right-hand driveshaft assembly. On all wheel drive models (AWD) a transfer box (called a 'bevel gear' by Volvo) is fitted between the transmission and the right-hand driveshaft. This allows power to be deliver via the propeller shaft and differential to the rear wheels.

A ball-and-cage type CV joint is fitted to the outer end of each driveshaft. The joint has an outer member which is splined at its outer end to accept the wheel hub, and is threaded so that it can be fastened to the hub by a large bolt. The joint contains six balls within a cage, which engage with the inner member. The complete assembly is protected by a flexible gaiter secured to the driveshaft and joint outer member.

At the inner end, the driveshaft is splined to engage with a tripod type CV joint, containing needle roller bearings and cups. On the left-hand side, the driveshaft inner CV joint engages directly with the differential sun wheel. On the right-hand side, the inner joint is integral with the intermediate shaft, the inner end of which engages with the differential sun wheel. As on the outer joints, a flexible gaiter secured to the driveshaft and CV joint outer member protects the complete assembly.

2 Front driveshafts – removal and refitting

Removal

1 Working through the hole in the centre of the wheel, slacken the driveshaft bolt **(see illustration)**. This bolt is very tight. If the wheels fitted do not have a centre hole, use the spare wheel. If possible avoid slackening the bolt with the car raised.

2 Slacken the front wheel bolts, raise and support the car and remove the wheel. Remove the engine undershield and the wheel arch liner. Remove and discard the driveshaft bolt.

3 Free the driveshaft CV joint from the hub flange by tapping it inwards approximately 10 to 15 mm with a plastic or copper mallet. If this fails to free the driveshaft from the hub, the joint will have to be released using a suitable tool bolted to the hub.

XC60

4 Undo the nut securing the hub carrier lower balljoint to the suspension control arm. Pull down on the suspension arm using a stout bar to release the balljoint shank from the control arm. Take care not to damage the balljoint dust cover during and after disconnection.

5 Swivel the suspension strut and hub carrier assembly outwards, and withdraw the driveshaft CV joint from the hub flange.

6 If removing the left-hand driveshaft, free the inner CV joint from the transmission by levering between the edge of the joint and the transmission casing with a large screwdriver or similar tool. Take care not to damage the transmission oil seal or the inner CV joint gaiter. Withdraw the driveshaft from under the wheel arch.

7 If removing the right-hand driveshaft, undo the two bolts and remove the cap from the intermediate shaft support bearing **(see illustration)**. Pull the intermediate shaft out of the transmission, and remove the driveshaft assembly from under the wheel arch. **Note:** *Do not pull the outer shaft from the intermediate shaft – the coupling will separate.*

XC90

8 Unbolt the anti-roll bar drop link from the strut. Use a suitable torx key to stop the shank of the ball joint form rotating.

9 Unclip the ABS sensor wiring from the strut and the chassis leg.

10 Measure and note down the distance from the rear of the strut to the front of the hub **(see illustration)**.

11 Remove both hub to strut bolts and pivot the hub away from the strut.

12 Rotate the hub and if necessary use a lever to depress the hub. Free the driveshaft from the hub **(see illustration)**.

13 If removing the left-hand driveshaft, free the inner CV joint from the transmission by levering between the edge of the joint and the transmission casing with a large screwdriver or similar tool. Take care not to damage the transmission oil seal or the inner CV joint gaiter. Withdraw the driveshaft from under the wheel arch.

14 If removing the right-hand driveshaft, undo the two bolts and remove the cap from the intermediate shaft support bearing **(see illustration 2.7)**. Pull the intermediate shaft out of the transmission, and remove the driveshaft assembly from under the wheel arch. **Note:** *Do not pull the outer shaft from the intermediate shaft – the coupling will separate.*

Refitting

15 Refitting is a reversal of removal, but observe the following points.

a) Prior to refitting, remove all traces of rust, oil and dirt from the splines of the outer CV joint, and lubricate the splines of the inner joint with wheel bearing grease.

b) If working on the left-hand driveshaft, ensure that the inner CV joint is pushed fully into the transmission, so that the retaining circlip locks into place in the differential gear.

c) Always use a new driveshaft-to-hub retaining bolt.

d) Tighten all nuts and bolts to the specified torque (see Chapter 10 for suspension component torque settings).On XC90 models use the previously noted

2.10 Measure the distance between the back of the strut and the front of the hub

2.12 Release the driveshaft from the hub

3.10a Release the driveshaft from the hub

3.10b The hub can be secured to the bump stop

3.13 Release the left-hand driveshaft

measurement and align the hub to strut correctly.
e) *When tightening the driveshaft bolt, tighten first using a torque wrench, then further, through the specified angle, using an angle-tightening gauge.*
f) *Tighten the roadwheel bolts to the specified torque.*

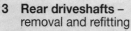
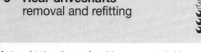

3 Rear driveshafts – removal and refitting

Note: *At the time of writing no repair kits were available for the rear driveshafts. If the shaft is faulty or the gaiters are split then the complete shaft must be replaced with an exchange (reconditioned) driveshaft.*

Removal

1 Measure the distance from the driveshaft bolt to the wheel arch and then slacken the driveshaft bolt.
2 Jack up and support the rear of the vehicle - see *Jacking and vehicle support* in the reference section. Remove the roadwheel and the driveshaft bolt.

XC60

3 Remove the appropriate spring as described in Chapter 10, Section 13.
4 Disconnect the lower shock absorber mounting, the lower arm to hub mounting, the tie rod mounting and the anti-roll bar drop link.
5 On the appropriate side remove the cover panel and then unclip the wiring loom and brake line from the trailing arm.

6 Remove the trailing arm to chassis bolts.
7 Pivot the hub assembly and pull the driveshaft from the hub.

XC90

8 Place a jack under the rear suspension arm and raise the suspension so that the gap between the hub nut and the wheel arch measures 500mm.
9 Unbolt the anti-roll bar drop link, the track rod, the control arm and the lateral link. The hub assembly should now be only held in position by the upper mountings.
10 Use a jack and raise the hub assembly sufficiently so that the driveshaft can be pulled from the hub assembly **(see illustrations)**.
11 Move the driveshaft to one side and rest it on the lower control arm.

All models

12 On the right-hand driveshaft, at the differential use a large screwdriver (or pry bar) and release the shaft from the differential. Pull the shaft straight out to avoid damaging the oil seal. Remove the shaft from the vehicle.
13 Removal of the left-hand driveshaft requires the use of Volvo special tools 9997397 and 9997398, however the driveshaft can be removed by fabricating a suitable clamp (we used an exhaust clamp) to act as a 'lip' for a suitable lever to gain purchase on **(see illustration)**.

Refitting

14 Refitting is a reversal of removal, but observe the following:
a) *Fit a new circlip to the inner joint.*
b) *Lubricate the inner shaft where it enters the differential with differential oil.*

c) *Ensure the inner joint snaps correctly it to position. Check this by pulling on the inner joint – not the shaft.*
d) *Fit the driveshaft and loosely insert its retaining bolt. Do not fully tighten it yet.*
e) *Position a trolley jack under the control arm at the point where it is attached to the hub carrier and raise the assembly until the distance from the wheel arch to the hub centre is 350mm (XC60) or 453mm (XC90). Fully tighten all the bolts to the specified torque. On XC60 models refit the spring.*
f) *Check the oil level in the differential.*

4 Outer constant velocity joint gaiter – renewal

1 Remove the driveshaft (Section 2).
2 Cut off the gaiter retaining clips, then slide the gaiter down the shaft to expose the outer constant velocity joint **(see illustration)**.
3 Scoop out as much grease as possible from the joint, then measure and note the distance from the inner groove on the shaft to the inner face of the outer CV joint **(see illustration)**.
4 Tap the exposed face of the inner ball hub with a hammer and brass drift to separate the joint from the driveshaft **(see illustration)**. Slide the gaiter off the driveshaft.
5 With the constant velocity joint removed from the driveshaft, clean the joint using paraffin, or a suitable solvent, and dry it thoroughly. This is especially important if the old gaiter was badly split, as dust and grit

4.2 Cut the old clips from the gaiter

4.3 Measure the distance from the inner groove on the shaft to the inner face of the CV joint

4.4 Use a brass drift and hammer to drive the inner joint hub from the driveshaft

4.6a Remove the balls one at a time . . .

4.6b . . . then rotate the cage 90° and lift it out

4.10 Pack the joint with half the grease supplied in the gaiter kit

4.11 Fit the new circlip to the end of the shaft

4.13 Apply the remaining grease to the inside of the gaiter

4.14a Use pincers to compress the raised section of the outer clip . . .

4.14b . . . and the inner clip

5.3 Make alignment marks between the shaft and housing

may be embedded in the lubricating grease, which will otherwise cause rapid wear of the joint. Remove the retaining circlip from the shaft, and obtain a new one for reassembly (normally supplied in the gaiter kit).

6 Move the inner splined driving member from side-to-side, and remove each ball in turn, then rotate the ball cage 90° to the upright position and lift it from the outer part of the joint **(see illustrations)**. Examine the balls for cracks, flat spots or signs of surface pitting.

7 Inspect the ball tracks on the inner and outer members. If the tracks have widened, the balls will no longer be a tight fit. At the same time, check the ball cage windows for wear or cracking between the windows. At the time of writing, it would appear that only complete exchange driveshafts are available – if the joints appear worn, complete renewal may be the only option – check with a Volvo dealer or specialist.

8 If the joint is in satisfactory condition, obtain a repair kit from your Volvo dealer, consisting of a new gaiter, retaining clips, driveshaft bolt, circlip and grease.

9 Refit the inner driving member and cage into the outer part of the joint, and insert the balls one at a time.

10 Pack the joint with the half of the grease supplied, working it well into the ball tracks, and into the driveshaft opening in the inner member **(see illustration)**.

11 Slide the rubber gaiter onto the shaft, fit the new circlip to the end of the shaft **(see illustration)**.

12 Engage the constant velocity joint with the driveshaft splines, and tap it onto the shaft until the internal circlip locates in the driveshaft groove. This can by verified by comparing the dimension with that obtained in paragraph 3.

13 Check that the circlip holds the joint securely on the driveshaft, then apply the remaining grease to the joint and the inside of the gaiter **(see illustration)**.

14 Locate the outer lip of the gaiter in the groove on the joint outer member, then fit the two retaining clips. Remove any slack in the clips by carefully compressing the raised section using a pair of pincers **(see illustrations)**.

15 Check that the constant velocity joint moves freely in all directions, then refit the driveshaft as described in Section 2.

16 Volvo recommend lubricating the gaiter once the driveshaft is refitted by applying a small amount of spray wax (Volvo 30787812) to the outside of the gaiter.

5 Inner constant velocity joint gaiter – renewal

1 Remove the driveshaft(s) as described in Section 2.

2 Cut through the metal clips, and slide the gaiter from the inner CV joint.

3 Clean out some of the grease from the joint, then make alignment marks between the housing and the shaft, to aid reassembly **(see illustration)**.

4 Carefully pull the housing from the tripod, twisting the housing so the tripod rollers come out one at a time. If necessary, use a soft-faced hammer or mallet to tap the housing off.

5 Clean the grease from the tripod and housing.

6 Remove the circlip, and carefully drive

5.6a Remove the circlip from the end of the shaft . . .

5.6b . . . then carefully drive the tripod from the shaft

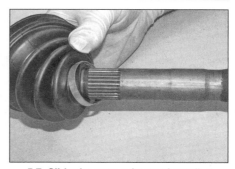

5.7 Slide the new gaiter and smaller diameter clip onto the shaft

the tripod from the end of the shaft **(see illustrations)**. Discard the circlip, a new one (supplied in the repair kit) must be fitted. Remove the gaiter if still on the shaft.

7 Slide the new gaiter onto the shaft along with the smaller clip **(see illustration)**.

8 Refit the tripod with the bevelled edge towards the driveshaft, and drive it fully into place, until the new circlip can be installed **(see illustrations)**.

9 Lubricate the tripod rollers with some of the grease supplied in the gaiter kit, then fill the housing and gaiter with the remainder.

10 Refit the housing to the tripod, tapping it gently into place using a soft-faced hammer or mallet if necessary.

11 Slide the new gaiter into place ensuring the smaller diameter of the gaiter locates over the grooves in the shaft **(see illustration)**.

12 Fit the new retaining clips and refit the driveshaft **(see illustration)**.

13 Volvo recommend lubricating the gaiter once the driveshaft is refitted by applying a small amount of spray wax (Volvo 30787812) to the outside of the gaiter.

6 Right-hand driveshaft support bearing – removal and refitting

Note: *Renewal of the bearing requires the use of special tools. This task is best entrusted to a Volvo dealer or suitably-equipped specialist.*

7 Driveshaft overhaul – general information

Road test the car, and listen for a metallic

5.8a Fit the tripod with the bevelled edge (arrowed) towards the shaft . . .

5.8b . . . then fit the new circlip

5.11 The smaller diameter of the gaiter must locate over the groove in the shaft (arrowed)

5.12 Equalise the air pressure before tightening the gaiter clip

clicking from the front as the car is driven slowly in a circle with the steering on full lock. Repeat the check on full-left and full-right lock. This noise may also be apparent when pulling away from a standstill with lock applied. If a clicking noise is heard, this indicates wear in the outer constant velocity joints.

If vibration, consistent with roadspeed, is felt through the car when accelerating, there is a possibility of wear in the inner constant velocity joints.

If the joints are worn or damaged, it would appear at the time of writing that no parts are available, other than boot kits, and the complete driveshaft must be renewed. Exchange driveshafts are available – check with a Volvo dealer or specialist.

Chapter 8 Part B:
Transfer box, propeller shaft and final drive

Contents

Degrees of difficulty

Easy, suitable for novice with little experience	Fairly easy, suitable for beginner with some experience	Fairly difficult, suitable for competent DIY mechanic	Difficult, suitable for experienced DIY mechanic	Very difficult, suitable for expert DIY or professional

Specifications

Lubricant

Active on demand coupling	Volvo 31325136 (30759648)
Transfer box oil	Volvo 31259380
Differential oil	Volvo 1161620

Torque wrench settings

	Nm	lbf ft
Active on demand coupling pinion nut	150	110
Active on demand coupling to final drive bolts	24	18
Final drive mounting bolts	80	60
Propeller shaft (6 bolts)*		
Stage 1	10	7
Stage 2	25	18
Propeller shaft (4 bolts)*		
Stage 1	16	12
Stage 2	Angle-tighten a further 120°	
Propeller shaft centre bearing	30	22
Oil plug – final drive	35	26
Oil plug – Active on demand coupling	35	26
Transfer box to transmission	75	55
Transfer box to manifold bracket*		
Stage 1	35	26
Stage 2	Angle-tighten a further 90°	
Transfer box pinion nut	180	133

Do not re-use. Volvo specify that where a fixing requires angular tightening it must always be renewed. Any fixing retained with a thread locking compound must also be renewed. Nuts with a nylon insert must always be renewed.

2.2 The centre cross member (XC90)

2.4 Make alignment marks

2.5 Use a strap wrench to lock the propeller shaft

2.6 To lock the propeller shaft at the rear on some XC60 models, a strap wrench is essential

1 General information

A transfer box (bevel gear) is located at the rear of the engine, attached to the gearbox. The transfer box permanently drives the propeller shaft. At the end of the propeller shaft is the 'Active on demand' coupling (AOC) . This is the heart of the All Wheel Drive (AWD) system. A conventional rear differential (final drive) provides power to the rear wheel through two driveshafts.

The AOC is supplied to Volvo by Haldex Traction of Sweden, hence often called a 'Haldex' unit. The AOC is a hydro-mechanical unit that controls the drive to the rear wheels. The torque to the rear wheels is controlled by an electronic module on the side of the AOC.

Hydraulic pressure is supplied by an integral electrical oil pump. The pressurised oil is then used to control the multi-plate wet clutch mounted on the output shaft. The control module varies the oil pressure supplied to the clutch and consequently the torque supplied to the rear wheels.

The control module is fully integrated into the controller area network (CAN) and receives signals from the engine control module, the brake control module, the central electrical module and the driver information module. Armed with this information the control module varies the torque supplied to the rear wheels. Full diagnostics are available via the DLC (Data Link Connector). If there is a fault with the AWD system it will be advisable to have a full diagnostic check carried out using suitable equipment before dismantling any part of the system.

3.4a Remove the mounting...

3.4b ...and then the pipe

2 Propeller shaft – removal and refitting

Removal

1 Jack up and support the vehicle see *Jacking and vehicle support* in the reference section.
2 Unclip the brake pipe and remove both front and rear cross members from the transmission tunnel **(see illustration)**.
3 Separate the exhaust system at the catalytic converter as described in Chapter 4A. Support the converter and remove the exhaust system.
4 Make alignment marks between each flange and the propeller shaft, so that the shaft can be refitted in exactly the same position **(see illustration)**.
5 Slacken and remove all but one of the bolts from the front of the propeller shaft. Volvo use a special tool (9997057) to stop the propeller shaft from rotating, we used a strap wrench instead of the special tool **(see illustration)**.
6 Repeat the procedure at the rear of the vehicle **(see illustration)**.
7 Remove the mounting bracket from the propeller shaft centre bearing and then remove the bolts from the bearing.
8 Support the propeller shaft and remove the remaining single bolts from each flange. Lower the propeller shaft from the vehicle.
9 If required the constant velocity (CV) joint can now be removed from the shaft. Remove the cover and then remove the circlip. A suitable bearing puller will now be required to pull the CV joint from the shaft.

Refitting

10 Refitting is a reversal of removal.

3 Transfer box (bevel gear) – removal and refitting

Removal

1 Jack up and support the vehicle - see *Jacking and vehicle support* in the reference section.
2 Remove the engine undershield and then remove the propeller shaft as described in Section 2.
3 Remove the right-hand front driveshaft as described in Chapter 8A.
4 On XC60 models remove the turbo charger inlet pipe and the rear engine mounting **(see illustrations)**.
5 On XC90 models (and with difficulty) remove the small section of the charge air pipe **(see illustration)**.
6 Unbolt and remove the support plate from the side of the transfer box **(see illustration)**.
7 To improve access on XC90 models we removed the particulate filter differential

3.5 Remove the pipe (XC90)

3.6 Remove the support plate

3.8 Note the location of the bolts – XC90 shown with 7 bolt holes

pressure sensor pipes and the oil return pipe from the turbo charger.

8 Anticipate some fluid spillage and then remove the 5 bolts (XC60) or 7 bolts (XC90) and pull the transfer box from the transmission. Note that the upper bolts are awkward to access. Rotate the transfer box it and remove it from the vehicle **(see illustration)**.

Refitting

9 Refitting is a reversal of removal, but in addition:

a) *Lubricate the splines between the transfer box and the transmission. Use Volvo grease 1161748.*

b) *Check the oil level in the transfer box. Replacement transfer boxes are supplied with oil, but it will always be worth checking the level.*

c) *Tighten all bolts to the correct torque*

4 Active on demand coupling (AOC) – removal and refitting

Note: *Volvo do not require the oil to be changed in the coupling.*

Removal

1 Jack up and support the vehicle - see *Jacking and vehicle support* in the reference section.

2 Separate and remove the exhaust system as described in Chapter 4A.

3 Remove the propeller shaft as described in Section 2 of this Chapter.

4 Disconnect the wiring plug from the control module **(see illustration)**.

5 Place a container below the final drive, remove the 4 mounting bolts **(see illustration)** and pull the AOC unit straight out from the rear differential.

Refitting

6 Refitting is a reversal of removal, but:

a) *Fit a new O-ring.*

b) *Check the fluid level by adding oil until the oil overflows from the filler plug (see illustration).*

c) *When the flow stops, refit the filler plug and test drive the vehicle.*

d) *Jack up and support the vehicle and then remove the filler plug and add oil until the flow stops.*

e) *When the flow stops, use a syringe and remove 40ml of fluid.*

f) *Refit the filler plug and tighten to the specified torque.*

5 Final drive (differential) – removal and refitting

Note: *Volvo do not require the oil to be changed in the final drive.*

Removal

1 Jack up and support the vehicle - see *Jacking and vehicle support* in the reference section.

2 With reference to Chapter 8A, remove both rear driveshafts.

3 Remove the spare wheel (where fitted) and then remove the rear section of the exhaust system. Ensure that the catalytic converter is adequately supported.

4 Remove the propeller shaft as described in Section 2.

5 Disconnect the wiring plug from the active on demand coupling control module. Release the wiring loom from the side of the differential.

XC60

6 Remove the 2 rear bolts **(see illustration)** and the single upper bolt. With the aid of an assistant remove the differential complete with the AOC.

XC90

7 Reach up and remove the cover plate from

4.4 Disconnect the wiring plugs (arrowed)

4.5 Remove the bolts (arrowed)

4.6 The filler plug (arrowed)

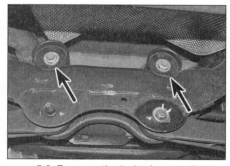

5.6 Remove the bolts (arrowed)

5.7 The upper mounting bolt

5.11 The oil level/filler plug (arrowed)

the top of the differential. Remove the single upper mounting bolt **(see illustration)**.

8 Slacken off and partially remove the 2 rear mounting bolts.

9 Support the final drive from below with a suitable jack. Use a block of wood to spread the load and then remove the front mounting bolts from the subframe. Allow the subframe assembly to pivot downwards.

10 Raise the final drive slightly and fully remove the 2 rear mounting bolts. Lower the final drive from the vehicle.

Refitting

11 Refitting is a reversal of removal, but:
a) *Check the oil level in the AOC unit, as described in Section 4.*
b) *Check the oil level in the final drive* **(see illustration).** *Top up until oil just flows from the level plug.*
c) *Tighten all nuts and bolts to the specified torques.*

Chapter 9
Braking system

Contents

Degrees of difficulty

Easy, suitable for novice with little experience	Fairly easy, suitable for beginner with some experience	Fairly difficult, suitable for competent DIY mechanic	Difficult, suitable for experienced DIY mechanic	Very difficult, suitable for expert DIY or professional

Specifications

General

System type:

Footbrake . . . . Dual-circuit hydraulic with servo assistance. Disc brakes front and rear. Anti-lock braking (ABS) on all models

Handbrake . . . . Electrically-operated on XC60 models, mechanically operated on XC90 models

Front brakes

Type . . . . Ventilated disc, with single or twin piston sliding calipers
Brake pad friction material minimum thickness . . . . 2.0 mm
Disc thickness:
New (XC60 and XC90 except 16 inch rims) . . . . 30.0 mm
Minimum thickness. 28.0mm
New (XC90 models with 16 inch rims) 28.0mm
Minimum thickness. . . . . 25.0 mm
Maximum disc run-out . . . . 0.04 mm
Maximum disc thickness variation . . . . 0.008 mm

Rear brakes

Type . . . . Solid or ventilated disc, with single-piston sliding calipers
Brake pad minimum lining thickness . . . . 2.0 mm
Disc thickness (XC60)
New:
16" Wheels . . . . 12.0 mm
17" Wheels 11.0mm
Ventilated 22.0mm
Minimum thickness
16" Wheels . . . . 10.0 mm
17" Wheels 9.0mm
Ventilated 20.0mm
Disc thickness (XC90)
New 20.0mm
Minimum thickness. 17.0mm
Maximum disc run-out . . . . 0.08 mm
Maximum disc thickness variation . . . . 0.008 mm

Torque wrench settings

	Nm	lbf ft
ABS unit mounting bolts	10	7
ABS unit pipe unions:		
6 mm diameter	14	10
8 mm diameter	18	13
ABS wheel sensor mounting bolts	5	4
Brake disc retaining bolt.	35	26
Brake pedal bolts	24	18
Flexible hose unions.	18	13
Front caliper:		
Guide pins*	28	21
Bracket bolts*		
XC60	100	74
XC90		
Stage 1	105	77
Stage 2	Angle-tighten a further 60°	
Handbrake actuator bolts.	10	7
Handbrake control module mounting bolts	7	5
Master cylinder mounting nuts.	25	18
Rear caliper:		
Guide pin bolts*	35	26
Caliper bracket bolts*		
XC60.	110	81
XC90		
Stage 1	35	26
Stage 2	Angle-tighten a further 60°	
Rigid pipe unions	14	10
Roadwheel bolts.	140	103
Steering column joint pinch-bolt	See Chapter 10	
Subframe mounting bolts:*	See Chapter 10	
Vacuum pump bolts	See Chapter 2A, 2B or 2C	
Vacuum servo unit mounting nuts	24	18

Do not re-use. Volvo specify that where a fixing requires angular tightening it must always be renewed. Any fixing retained with a thread locking compound must also be renewed. Nuts with a nylon insert must always be renewed.

1 General information

The brake pedal operates disc brakes on all four wheels by means of a dual circuit hydraulic system with servo assistance. On XC60 models, the handbrake is electrically-operated and acts on the rear brake pads by means of an actuator. On XC90 models the handbrake is mechanically operated, with a separate set of brake shoes (fitted inside the rear brake disc) providing the brake function. An anti-lock braking system (ABS) is fitted to all models, and is described in further detail in Section 20.

The hydraulic system is split into two circuits, so that in the event of failure of one circuit, the other will still provide adequate braking power (although pedal travel and effort may increase). An axle-split system is employed, in which one circuit serves the front brakes and the other circuit the rear brakes.

The brake servo is of the direct-acting type, being interposed between the brake pedal and the master cylinder. The servo magnifies the effort applied by the driver. It is vacuum-operated with a camshaft-driven vacuum pump.

Instrument panel warning lights alert the driver to low fluid level by means of a level sensor in the master cylinder reservoir. Other warning lights remind when the handbrake is applied, and indicate the presence of a fault in the ABS system.

Note: *When servicing any part of the system, work carefully and methodically; also observe scrupulous cleanliness when overhauling any part of the hydraulic system. Always renew components (in axle sets, where applicable) if in doubt about their condition, and use only genuine Volvo parts, or at least those of known good quality. Note the warnings given in 'Safety first!' and at relevant points in this Chapter concerning the dangers of asbestos dust and hydraulic fluid.*

2 Hydraulic system – bleeding

⚠️ *Warning: Hydraulic fluid is poisonous; wash off immediately and thoroughly in the case of skin contact, and seek immediate medical advice if any fluid is swallowed or gets into the eyes. Certain types of hydraulic fluid are inflammable, and may ignite when allowed into contact with hot components; when servicing any hydraulic system, it is safest to assume that the fluid IS inflammable, and to take precautions against the risk of fire as though it is petrol that is being handled. Hydraulic fluid is also an effective paint stripper, and will attack plastics; if any is spilt, it should be washed off immediately, using copious quantities of clean water. Finally, it is hygroscopic (it absorbs moisture from the air). The more moisture is absorbed by the fluid, the lower its boiling point becomes, leading to a dangerous loss of braking under hard use. Old fluid may be contaminated and unfit for further use. When topping-up or renewing the fluid, always use the recommended type, and ensure that it comes from a freshly-opened sealed container.*

General

1 The correct functioning of the brake hydraulic system is only possible after removing all air from the components and circuit; this is achieved by bleeding the system.

2 During the bleeding procedure, add only clean, fresh hydraulic fluid of the specified type; never re-use fluid that has already been bled from the system. Ensure that sufficient fluid is available before starting work.

3 If there is any possibility of incorrect fluid being used in the system, the brake lines and components must be completely flushed with uncontaminated fluid and new seals fitted to the components.

4 If brake fluid has been lost from the master

cylinder due to a leak in the system, ensure that the cause is traced and rectified before proceeding further.

5 Park the car on level ground, apply the handbrake, and switch off the ignition.

6 Check that all pipes and hoses are secure, unions tight, and bleed screws closed. Remove the dust caps and clean any dirt from around the bleed screws.

7 Unscrew the master cylinder reservoir cap, and top-up the reservoir to the MAX level line. Refit the cap loosely, and remember to maintain the fluid level at least above the MIN level line throughout the procedure, otherwise there is a risk of further air entering the system.

8 There are a number of one-man, do-it-yourself, brake bleeding kits currently available from motor accessory shops. It is recommended that one of these kits is used wherever possible, as they greatly simplify the bleeding operation, and also reduce the risk of expelled air and fluid being drawn back into the system. If such a kit is not available, the basic (two-man) method must be used, which is described in detail below.

9 If a kit is to be used, prepare the car as described previously, and follow the kit manufacturer's instructions, as the procedure may vary slightly according to the type being used; generally, they are as outlined below in the relevant sub-section.

10 Whichever method is used, the same sequence must be followed (paragraphs 11 and 12) to ensure the removal of all air from the system.

Bleeding sequence

11 If the hydraulic system has only been partially disconnected and suitable precautions were taken to minimise fluid loss, it should only be necessary to bleed that part of the system (ie, the primary or secondary circuit).

12 If the complete system is to be bled, then it should be done in the following sequence:
    a) Front left-hand brake
    b) Front right-hand brake.
    c) Rear left-hand brake.
    d) Rear right-hand brake

Bleeding

Basic (two- man) method

13 Collect a clean glass jar of reasonable size, a suitable length of plastic or rubber tubing which is a tight fit over the bleed screw, and a ring spanner to fit the screws. The help of an assistant will also be required.

14 If not already done, remove the dust cap from the bleed screw of the first wheel to be bled **(see illustration)**, and fit the spanner and bleed tube to the screw. Place the other end of the tube in the jar, and pour in sufficient fluid to cover the end of the tube.

15 Ensure that the master cylinder reservoir fluid level is maintained at least above the MIN level line throughout the procedure.

16 Have the assistant fully depress the brake

pedal several times to build-up pressure, then maintain it on the final downstroke.

17 While pedal pressure is maintained, unscrew the bleed screw (approximately one turn) and allow the compressed fluid and air to flow into the jar. The assistant should maintain pedal pressure, following it down to the floor if necessary, and should not release it until instructed to do so. When the flow stops, tighten the bleed screw again have the assistant release the pedal slowly, and recheck the reservoir fluid level.

18 Repeat the steps given in paragraphs 16 and 17 until the fluid emerging from the bleed screw is free from air bubbles. If the master cylinder has been drained and refilled, and air is being bled from the first screw in the sequence, allow approximately five seconds between cycles for the master cylinder passages to refill.

19 When no more air bubbles appear, tighten the bleed screw securely, remove the tube and spanner, and refit the dust cap. Do not overtighten the bleed screw.

20 Repeat these procedures on the remaining calipers in sequence until all air is removed from the system and the brake pedal feels firm again.

Using a one-way valve kit

21 As their name implies, these kits consist of a length of tubing with a one-way valve fitted, to prevent expelled air and fluid being drawn back into the system; some kits include a translucent container, which can be positioned so that the air bubbles can be more easily seen flowing from the end of the tube.

22 The kit is connected to the bleed screw, which is then opened **(see illustration)**. The user returns to the driver's seat, depresses the brake pedal with a smooth steady stroke, and slowly releases it; this is repeated until the expelled fluid is clear of air bubbles.

23 Note that these kits simplify work so much that it is easy to forget the master cylinder fluid level; ensure that this is maintained at least above the MIN level line at all times.

Using a pressure-bleeding kit

Note: *This is the method recommended by Volvo if the hydraulic system has been either wholly or partially drained.*

24 These kits are usually operated by the reserve of pressurised air contained in the spare tyre. However, note that it will probably be necessary to reduce the pressure to a lower level than normal; refer to the instructions supplied with the kit.

25 By connecting a pressurised, fluid-filled container to the master cylinder reservoir, bleeding is then carried out by simply opening each bleed screw in turn (in the specified sequence) and allowing the fluid to run out, until no more air bubbles can be seen in the expelled fluid.

26 This method has the advantage that the large reservoir of fluid provides an additional safeguard against air being drawn into the system during bleeding.

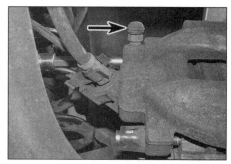

2.14 Pull the dust cap (arrowed) from the bleed screw

27 Pressure-bleeding is particularly effective when bleeding difficult systems, or when bleeding the complete system at the time of routine fluid renewal.

All methods

28 When bleeding is complete, and firm pedal feel is restored, wash off any spilt fluid, tighten the bleed screws securely, and refit their dust caps.

29 Check the hydraulic fluid level in the master cylinder reservoir, and top-up if necessary.

30 Discard any hydraulic fluid that has been bled from the system; it will not be fit for re-use.

31 Check the feel of the brake pedal. If it feels at all spongy, air must still be present in the system, and further bleeding is required. Failure to bleed satisfactorily after a reasonable repetition of the bleeding operations may be due to worn master cylinder seals.

32 Check the operation of the clutch. Any problems noted would indicate a need to bleed the clutch system also – see Chapter 6.

---

3   Hydraulic pipes and hoses –
renewal

Note: *Before starting work, refer to the warning at the beginning of Section 2 concerning the dangers of hydraulic fluid.*

1 If any pipe or hose is to be renewed, minimise hydraulic fluid loss by removing the master cylinder reservoir cap, placing a piece of plastic film over the reservoir and

2.22 Connect the kit and open the bleed screw

sealing it with an elastic band. Alternatively, flexible hoses can be sealed, if required, using a proprietary brake hose clamp; metal brake pipe unions can be plugged (if care is taken not to allow dirt into the system) or capped immediately they are disconnected. Place a wad of rag under any union that is to be disconnected, to catch any spilt fluid.

2 If a flexible hose is to be disconnected, unscrew the brake pipe union nut before removing the spring clip which secures the hose to its mounting, where applicable. Some of the flexible hose unions are protected by a rubber cover – in this case, the pipe will have to be removed from its mounting bracket first, and the cover slid down the pipe, before the nut can be unscrewed.

3 To unscrew the union nuts, it is preferable to obtain a brake pipe spanner of the correct size; these are available from most large motor accessory shops. Failing this, a close-fitting open-ended spanner will be required, though if the nuts are tight or corroded, their flats may be rounded-off if the spanner slips. In such a case, a self-locking wrench is often the only way to unscrew a stubborn union, but it follows that the pipe and the damaged nuts must be renewed on reassembly.

4 Always clean a union and surrounding area before disconnecting it. If disconnecting a component with more than one union, make a careful note of the connections before disturbing any of them.

5 If a brake pipe is to be renewed, it can be obtained, cut to length and with the union nuts and end flares in place from Volvo dealers. All that is then necessary is to bend it to shape, following the line of the original, before fitting it to the car. Alternatively, most motor accessory shops can make up brake pipes from kits, but this requires very careful measurement of the original, to ensure that the new one is of the correct length. The safest answer is usually to take the original to the shop as a pattern.

6 Before refitting, blow through the new pipe or hose with dry compressed air. Do not overtighten the union nuts. It is not necessary to exercise brute force to obtain a sound joint.

7 If flexible rubber hoses are renewed, ensure that the pipes and hoses are correctly routed, with no kinks or twists, and that they are secured in the clips or brackets provided. Original equipment flexible hoses have white lines along their length which clearly show if the hose is twisted.

8 After fitting, bleed the hydraulic system as described in Section 2, wash off any spilt fluid, and check carefully for fluid leaks.

4 Front brake pads – renewal

Warning: Disc brake pads must be renewed on both front wheels at the same time – never renew the pads on only one wheel, as uneven braking may result. Dust created by wear of the pads may contain asbestos, which is a health hazard. Never blow it out with compressed air and do not inhale any of it. DO NOT use petroleum-based solvents to clean brake parts. Use brake cleaner or methylated spirit only. DO NOT allow any brake fluid, oil or grease to contact the brake pads or disc. Also refer to the warning at the start of Section 2 concerning the dangers of hydraulic fluid.

1 Loosen the front wheel bolts and chock the rear wheels. Jack up the front of the car and support it on axle stands (see *Jacking and vehicle support*). Remove the front roadwheels.

2 Follow the accompanying photos **(illustrations 4.2a to 4.2m)** for the pad renewal procedure. Note that the sequence shows a typical brake pad replacement sequence. Volvo fit a variety of brake pads and calipers, depending on the exact model and year of manufacture, but the method of replacement is similar in all cases. Be sure to stay in order and read the caption under each illustration, and note the following points:

a) *Measure the thickness of the pad friction material (see illustration 4.2g). If any one pad has worn down to the specified minimum, all four front pads must be renewed. Do not interchange pads in an attempt to even out wear (uneven pad wear may be due to the caliper sticking on the guide pins).*

b) *Thoroughly clean the caliper guide surfaces, and apply a little silicone grease (Volvo 116 1688) to the caliper bracket where the pads contact the bracket, and to the corresponding point on the pads.*

c) *When pushing the caliper piston back to accommodate new pads, keep a close eye on the fluid level in the reservoir.*

Caution: Pushing back the piston causes a reverse-flow of brake fluid, which has been known to 'flip' the master cylinder rubber seals, resulting in a total loss of braking. To avoid this, clamp the caliper flexible hose and open the bleed screw – as the piston is pushed back, the fluid can be directed into a suitable container using a hose attached to the bleed screw. Close the screw just before the piston is pushed fully back, to ensure no air enters the system.

3 Depress the brake pedal repeatedly, until the pads are pressed into firm contact with the brake disc, and normal (non-assisted) pedal pressure is restored.

4 Repeat the above procedure on the remaining front brake caliper.

5 Refit the roadwheels, then lower the vehicle to the ground and tighten the roadwheel bolts to the specified torque.

6 Check the hydraulic fluid level as described in *Weekly checks*.

Caution: New pads will not give full braking efficiency until they have bedded-in. Be prepared for this, and avoid hard braking as far as possible for the first hundred miles or so after pad renewal.

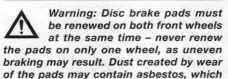

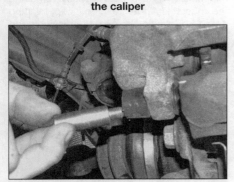

4.2a Carefully prise the spring clip from the caliper

4.2b Remove the plastic caps from the rear of the caliper . . .

4.2c . . . and unscrew the guide pins using a hex key. Note that some models require a 9mm hex key

4.2d Lift the caliper from the bracket. On this type of caliper the pads are removed with the caliper

4.2e On other models, lift out the outer brake pad . . .

4.2f . . . and unclip the inner brake pad from the caliper piston

4.2g If the thickness of the pads is less than 2 mm, all the pads should be renewed

4.2h Press the piston back into the caliper using a piston retraction tool. On twin piston models push both pistons into the caliper

4.2i Insert the new outer brake pad into the caliper bracket . . .

4.2j . . . and clip the new inner brake pad into the caliper piston

4.2k Refit the caliper, insert new guide pins, and tighten them to the specified torque

4.2l Finally fit the guide spring. Note the correct location of the spring on this XC60 model...

4.2m ...and on this XC90 model

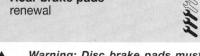

5 Rear brake pads – renewal

⚠ **Warning: Disc brake pads must be renewed on both rear wheels at the same time – never renew the pads on only one wheel as uneven braking may result. Dust created by wear of the pads may contain asbestos, which is a health hazard. Never blow it out with compressed air and do not inhale any of it. DO NOT use petroleum-based solvents to clean brake parts. Use brake cleaner or methylated spirit only. DO NOT allow any brake fluid, oil or grease to contact the brake pads or disc. Also refer to the warning at the start of Section 2 concerning the dangers of hydraulic fluid.**

1 Loosen the rear wheel bolts and chock the front wheels. Jack up the rear of the car and support it on axle stands (see *Jacking and vehicle support*). Remove the rear roadwheels.

2 On XC60 models, activate the handbrake service mode. You will need a tool similar to the one shown **(see illustration)**, which can be purchased from specialist suppliers.

5.2 Activate the handbrake service mode using a suitable tool

Alternatively, the task of changing the rear brake pads will need to be entrusted to a Volvo dealer or suitably-equipped specialist.

3 Follow the accompanying photos **(illustrations 5.3a to 5.3k)** for the pad renewal procedure. Note that the sequence shows a typical brake pad replacement sequence. Volvo fit a variety of brake pads and calipers, depending on the exact model and year of manufacture, but the method of replacement is similar in all cases. Be sure to stay in order and read the caption under each illustration, and note the following points:

a) *Thoroughly clean the caliper guide surfaces, and apply a little silicone grease (Volvo 116 1688) to the bracket where the pads contact it, and to the corresponding point on the pads.*

b) *When pushing the caliper piston back to accommodate new pads, keep a close eye on the fluid level in the reservoir.*

c) *Note that the top and bottom metal clips that secure the brake pads differ slightly so note the correct position on removal.*

Caution: Pushing back the piston causes a reverse-flow of brake fluid, which has been known to 'flip' the master cylinder rubber seals, resulting in a total loss of braking. To avoid this, clamp the caliper flexible hose and open the bleed screw – as the piston is pushed back, the fluid can be directed into a suitable container using a hose attached to the bleed screw. Close the screw just before the piston is pushed fully back, to ensure no air enters the system.

4 Depress the brake pedal repeatedly, until the pads are pressed into firm contact with the brake disc, and normal (non-assisted) pedal pressure is restored.

5 Repeat the above procedure on the remaining rear brake caliper.

6 Deactivate the handbrake service mode (see the note above).

7 Refit the roadwheels, then lower the vehicle to the ground and tighten the roadwheel bolts to the specified torque.

8 Check the hydraulic fluid level as described in *Weekly checks*.

Caution: New pads will not give full braking efficiency until they have bedded-in. Be prepared for this, and avoid hard braking as far as possible for the first hundred miles or so after pad renewal.

5.3a Where fitted remove the spring and then undo the caliper guide pin bolts. Note that some models feature hex head bolts located beneath removable caps (see illustration 4.2b)

5.3b Move the caliper from the bracket

5.3c Remove the outer brake pad . . .

5.3d . . . and the inner brake pad

5.3e Remove the lower clip . . .

5.3f . . . and the upper clip

5.3g Clean the caliper surfaces using a suitable brake cleaning agent

5.3h Fit the new upper clip . . .

5.3i . . . and lower clip

5.3j Apply a little silicone grease where the brake pads contact the bracket

6 Rear parking brake shoes – renewal (XC90 only)

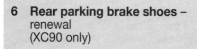

1 Loosen the rear wheel bolts and chock the front wheels. Jack up the rear of the car and support it on axle stands (see *Jacking and vehicle support*). Remove the rear roadwheels.
2 Release the parking brake and fully slacken the cable as described in Section 17. Remove the rear brake disc as described in Section 8.
3 Using a pair of long nose pliers remove both brake shoe hold down springs **(see illustration)**. Note the orientation of the hooked end of the spring as it is removed.
4 Lift the shoes from the cable operated expander and then remove the spring **(see illustration)**.

5.3k Insert the new pads and fit the caliper using new bolts tightened to the specified torque. Where fitted replace the spring and fit the guide pin covers

5 Unhook the smaller return spring and recover the forked spacer **(see illustrations)**. Remove the brake shoes.
6 Refitting is a reversal of removal, but note the following points:
a) Thoroughly clean the back plate, and apply a little silicone grease (Volvo 116 1688) to the contact points on the back plate.
b) If new shoes are being fitted, consider covering them with masking tape to avoid contaminating them until the springs are fully assembled. Remember to remove the tape before fitting the disc.
c) The hold down springs must hook into the rear back plate correctly **(see illustration)**.
d) After fitting the disc, adjust the handbrake cable as described in Section 17.

7 Front brake disc – inspection, removal and refitting

Note: *Before starting work, refer to the warning at the beginning of Section 4 concerning the dangers of asbestos dust.*

Inspection

Note: *If either disc requires renewal, BOTH should be renewed at the same time, to ensure even and consistent braking. New brake pads should also be fitted.*

1 Remove the front brake pads as described in Section 4.
2 Inspect the disc friction surfaces for cracks or deep scoring (light grooving is normal and may be ignored). A cracked disc must be renewed; a scored disc can be reclaimed by machining, provided that the thickness is not reduced below the specified minimum.
3 Check the disc run-out using a dial test indicator with its probe positioned near the outer edge of the disc. If the run-out exceeds the figures given in the Specifications, machining may be possible, otherwise disc renewal will be necessary.
4 Excessive disc thickness variation can also cause judder. Check this using a micrometer **(see illustration)**.

Removal

5 With the brake pads and caliper removed (Section 9), undo the two mounting bolts

6.3 Remove the hold down springs from both shoes

6.4 Unhook the spring from the shoe expander

6.5a Remove the spring...

6.5b ...recover the spacer and remove the shoes

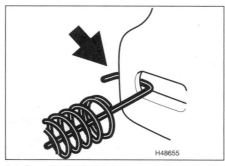

6.6 Locate the hold down springs correctly

7.4 Measure the disc thickness using a micrometer

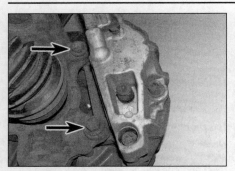

7.5 Undo the bolts (arrowed) and remove the brake caliper bracket

7.6 Front brake disc securing screw

and remove the brake caliper bracket **(see illustration)**. Note that new bolts will be required for refitting.

6 Check whether the position of the disc in relation to the hub is marked, and if not, make your own mark as an aid to refitting. Remove the screw which holds the disc to the hub, and lift off the disc **(see illustration)**. Tap it with a soft-faced mallet if necessary to free it.

Refitting

7 Ensure that the hub and disc mating faces are spotlessly clean. Clean any rustproofing compound off a new disc with degreaser and a rag.

8 Locate the disc on the hub with the orientation marks aligned, then refit and tighten the retaining screw.

9 Refit the brake caliper bracket and limiter bracket, then tighten the new bolts to the specified torque.

10 Refit the brake pads as described in Section 4.

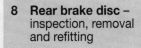

8 Rear brake disc –
inspection, removal and refitting

Note: *Before starting work, refer to the warning at the beginning of Section 5 concerning the dangers of asbestos dust.*

Inspection

Note: *If either disc requires renewal, BOTH should be renewed at the same time, to ensure*

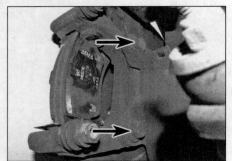

8.3 Undo the caliper bracket bolts (arrowed)

even and consistent braking. New brake pads should also be fitted.

1 Remove the rear brake pads as described in Section 5. The inspection procedures are the same as for the front brake disc, and reference should be made to Section 7.

Removal

2 If not already done, remove the rear brake pads as described in Section 5. Suitably support the caliper, or suspend it using string or wire tied to a convenient suspension component.

3 Undo the two caliper bracket bolts, and withdraw the bracket **(see illustration)**. Note that new bolts will be required for refitting.

4 Unscrew the disc retaining screw **(see illustration)**.

5 Mark the position of the disc in relation to the hub, then pull off the disc. On XC90 models it may be necessary to fully slacken the handbrake cable (as described in Section 17) to enable the disc to be removed. Tap the disc with a soft-faced mallet if necessary to free it.

Refitting

6 Ensure that the hub and disc mating faces are spotlessly clean. Clean any rustproofing compound off a new disc with degreaser and a rag.

7 Locate the disc on the hub with the orientation marks aligned, and refit the retaining screw.

8 Refit the brake caliper bracket and tighten the new bolts to the specified torque.

9 Refit the brake pads as described in Section 5.

8.4 Rear brake disc securing screw

9 Front brake caliper –
removal and refitting

Note: *Before starting work, refer to the warning at the beginning of Section 2 concerning the dangers of hydraulic fluid, and to the warning at the beginning of Section 4 concerning the dangers of asbestos dust.*

Note: *Parts are not available to service the brake caliper. Volvo and other suppliers offer new or refurbished calipers on an exchange basis.*

Removal

1 Apply the handbrake and chock the rear wheels. Loosen the front wheel bolts, then jack up the front of the car and support it on axle stands (see *Jacking and vehicle support*). Remove the roadwheel.

2 To minimise fluid loss, unscrew the master cylinder reservoir filler cap and place a piece of polythene over the filler neck. Secure the polythene with an elastic band ensuring that an airtight seal is obtained. Preferably, use a brake hose clamp, a G-clamp, or a similar tool with protected jaws, to clamp the front flexible hydraulic hose **(see illustration)**.

3 Clean the area around the hydraulic hose-to-caliper union, then slacken the hose union half a turn. Be prepared for fluid spillage.

4 Remove the brake pads as described in Section 4.

5 Unscrew the caliper from the hydraulic hose, and wipe up any spilled brake fluid immediately. Plug or cap the open unions.

6 If required, remove the caliper bracket by undoing the two bolts which secure it to the hub carrier. Note that new bolts will be required for refitting.

Refitting

7 If removed, refit the caliper bracket using new bolts tightened to the specified torque.

8 Refit the brake pads as described in Section 4, but screw the caliper onto the flexible hose before refitting it to the caliper bracket.

9 Tighten the flexible hose union ensuring that the hose is not kinked.

10 Remove the brake hose clamp or polythene, where fitted, and bleed the hydraulic system as described in Section 2.

9.2 Clamp the flexible brake hose

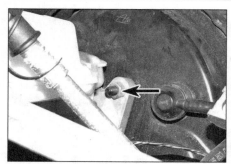

11.9a Undo the upper master cylinder nut (arrowed) . . .

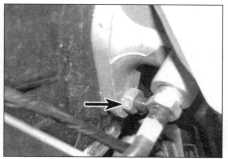

11.9b . . . and the lower master cylinder nut

11.9c On some XC90 models the heat shield must be partially released to remove the master cylinder

11 Apply the footbrake two or three times to settle the pads, then refit the roadwheel and lower the car. Tighten the wheel bolts in a diagonal sequence to the specified torque.

10 Rear brake caliper –
removal, overhaul and refitting

Note: *Before starting work, refer to the warning at the beginning of Section 2 concerning the dangers of hydraulic fluid, and to the warning at the beginning of Section 5 concerning the dangers of asbestos dust.*
Note: *Parts are not available to service the brake caliper. Volvo and other suppliers offer new or refurbished calipers on an exchange basis.*

Removal
1 To minimise fluid loss, unscrew the master cylinder reservoir filler cap, and place a piece of polythene over the filler neck. Secure the polythene with an elastic band, ensuring that an airtight seal is obtained. Preferably, use a brake hose clamp, a G-clamp, or a similar tool with protected jaws, to clamp the rear flexible hydraulic hose.
2 On XC60 models, activate the handbrake service mode.
3 Clean around the hydraulic union on the caliper, and undo. Be prepared for fluid spillage and plug or cap the open unions.
4 On XC60 models disconnect the wiring plug from the parking brake actuator.
5 Undo the 2 caliper guide pin bolts.

Refitting
6 Refit the brake caliper using new guide pin bolts.
7 Refit the brake pipe to the caliper, and tighten the union securely.
8 Remove the brake hose clamp or polythene, where fitted, and bleed the hydraulic system as described in Section 2.
9 Deactivate the handbrake service mode.
10 Apply the footbrake two or three times to settle the pads, then refit the roadwheel and lower the car. Tighten the wheel bolts in a diagonal sequence to the specified torque.

11 Brake master cylinder –
removal and refitting

Note: *Before starting work, refer to the warning at the beginning of Section 2 concerning the dangers of hydraulic fluid.*
Note: *Parts are not available to service the master cylinder. Volvo and other suppliers offer new or refurbished calipers on an exchange basis.*

Removal
1 Disconnect the battery negative lead (see Chapter 5).
2 Depress the brake pedal repeatedly to collapse any residual vacuum in the servo, then siphon as much fluid as possible from the master cylinder reservoir, using a hydrometer or old poultry baster.
3 On XC60 models remove the cover from the plenum chamber as described in Chapter 12 Section 18.
4 On XC90 models unbolt and remove the strut tower base.
Caution: Do not siphon the fluid by mouth – it is poisonous.
5 Disconnect any the wiring connector(s) from the reservoir/master cylinder low fluid level warning switch.
6 Anticipate some spillage of brake fluid and then remove the single bolt. Lift off and remove the reservoir. Recover the O-ring type seals.
7 On manual transmission models disconnect the clutch supply pipe.
8 Disconnect the hydraulic pipe unions from the master cylinder. Be prepared for further fluid spillage. Cap the open unions to keep dirt out.
9 Remove the nuts which secure the master cylinder to the servo **(see illustrations)**. Pull the master cylinder off the servo studs and remove it. Discard the O-ring seal, a new one must be fitted. Be careful not to spill hydraulic fluid on the paintwork.

Refitting
10 Place the master cylinder (with a new seal) in position on the servo unit, and secure with the nuts tightened to the specified torque.
11 Refit the brake pipes, but do not tighten the union nuts fully at this stage.
12 Refit the reservoir.

13 Reconnect the reservoir/master cylinder electrical connectors.
14 Place absorbent rags under the brake pipe unions on the master cylinder, then fill the reservoir with clean hydraulic fluid of the specified type.
15 Tighten the brake pipe unions securely when hydraulic fluid can be seen seeping out.
16 Bleed the hydraulic system as described in Section 2 on completion.
17 After the system has been bled, pressure test the master cylinder by depressing the brake pedal hard and holding it down for 30 seconds. Release the pedal and check for leaks around the master cylinder pipe unions.
18 Refitting of the remaining components is a reversal of the removal procedure.

12 Brake pedal –
removal and refitting

Removal
1 Remove the trim panel under the facia on the driver's side as described in Chapter 11. On XC90 models access can be improved by disconnecting the steering column at the lower pinch bolt and then moving the column to one side.
2 Disconnect the wiring plug from brake pedal switch and (where fitted) the brake pedal position switch and then release the retaining clip and disconnect the servo pushrod from the pedal **(see illustrations)**.

12.2a On XC60 models remove and discard the brake pedal servo rod retaining peg (arrowed)

12.2b On XC90 models remove the circlip (arrowed) and push out the pin

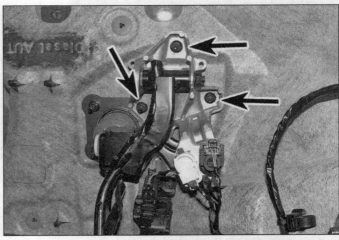

12.3 XC60 brake pedal securing nuts (arrowed)

3 Undo the nuts securing the pedal bracket to the brake servo (see illustration). Note that on some XC60 models it will be necessary to remove the instrument panel (as described in Chapter 12) to access the pedal box upper mounting. Manoeuvre the pedal box from the vehicle.

Refitting

4 Manoeuvre the pedal into position. Renew all retaining bolts and tighten to the specified torque.
5 Reconnect the servo pushrod to the pedal, and secure it with a new retaining clip or peg.
6 Refit the facia trim panel.
7 Check the operation of the brake lights.

13 Vacuum servo unit – removal and refitting

Removal

1 Disconnect the battery negative lead (see Chapter 5), then depress the brake pedal several times to dissipate any vacuum in the servo unit.
2 Remove the master cylinder as described in Section 11.
3 Disconnect the vacuum hose from the servo

and, noting their fitted positions, disconnect any wiring connectors.
4 Remove the trim panel under the facia on the driver's side as described in Chapter 11.
5 Follow the procedure described in Section 12 and partially remove the pedal box assembly. There is no need to remove the pedal box from the vehicle.
6 Manoeuvre the vacuum servo from the plenum chamber.

Refitting

7 Refitting is a reversal of removal bearing in mind the following points:
  a) Ensure that the seal is in position before fitting the servo.
  b) The nuts securing the servo to the bulkhead should be renewed. Tighten all nuts and bolts to the specified torque.
  c) Refit the master cylinder as described in Section 11.
  d) Check and bleed the hydraulic system as described in Section 2 on completion.

14 Handbrake actuator – removal and refitting (XC60 only)

1 Loosen the rear wheel bolts and chock the front wheels. Jack up the rear of the car and

support it on axle stands (see Jacking and vehicle support). Remove the rear roadwheels.
2 Activate the handbrake service mode (see Section 5).
3 Disconnect the wiring plug from the actuator (see illustration).
4 Undo the 2 screws and remove the actuator from the brake caliper (see illustration).
5 Refitting is a reversal of removal. Deactivate the handbrake service mode.

15 Handbrake switch – removal and refitting (XC60 only)

1 The switch is located to the right-hand side of the steering wheel, below the main light switch.
2 To remove, undo the 2 screws and remove the trim panel containing the switch. Undo the wiring plug as the panel is withdrawn (see illustration).
3 Refitting is a reversal of removal.

16 Handbrake module – removal and refitting (XC60 only)

1 The module is located behind the left-hand

14.3 Handbrake actuator wiring plug

14.4 Undo the two actuator securing screws (arrowed)

15.2 Remove the screws and then disconnect the wiring plug (arrowed)

16.2 Disconnect the wiring plug

17.8 Remove the circlip (arrowed)

17.9 Unhook the rear cables (arrowed)

side trim panel in the luggage area. Remove the panel as described in Chapter 11.
2 Undo the 2 bolts, disconnect the wiring plug (see illustration) and remove the control module.
3 Refitting is a reversal of removal. Note that if a new unit is fitted, suitable software will need to be downloaded and installed from Volvo. Entrust this task to a Volvo dealer or suitably-equipped specialist.

17 Parking brake cables – removal, refitting and adjustment (XC90 only)

Removal

1 Remove the left-hand centre console side panel to access the cable adjuster.
2 Prise free the circlip and rotate the barrel adjuster clockwise to slacken the cable.

Front cable

3 With reference to Chapter 11, Section 22 remove the driver's seat. There is no need to remove it from the vehicle.
4 Remove the centre console as described in Chapter 11, Section 26.
5 Remove the lower trim panel from the driver's footwell. Disconnect the wiring plug from the lamp as the panel is removed.
6 Unbolt the audio unit amplifier from below the driver's seat and then work the carpet free from the driver's footwell.
7 Remove the parking brake lever as described in the next section.

8 Turn over the lever, remove the circlip and unhook the cable from the lever (see illustration).
9 At the opposite end, unhook the rear cables from the yoke (see illustration) and pull the cable out from beneath the heater box.
10 If required the parking brake release cable can also be removed from the lever at this point.
11 To remove the release cable from the facia mounted release handle, remove the 2 screws, pull the handle forward and unhook the cable (see illustrations).

Rear cable

12 Remove the centre console as described in Chapter 11, Section 26 and then unhook the rear cable from the yoke.
13 Jack up and support the rear of the vehicle (see Jacking and vehicle support in the reference section). Remove both rear wheels.

17.11a Remove the screws...

14 With reference to Section 6 of this Chapter remove the parking brake shoes.
15 Unhook the cable inner free from the shoe expander. It will be necessary to slightly prise open the locating slot in the expander slightly in order to release the cable (see illustration).
16 Working underneath the vehicle partially release the heat shield from the transmission tunnel. Unclip and unbolt the cable from the guide brackets.
17 Prise the cable outer free from the brake back plate (see illustration).
18 Working inside the vehicle, attach stout cord to the cables and then pull them free from beneath the vehicle. As soon as the cord appears untie it from the vehicle – the cord will later be used to pull the replacement cables into position.
19 Remove the cables from the vehicle. If they are to be refitted note which side they were removed from, as they are handed.

17.11b ...and unhook the cable (arrowed) from the handle...

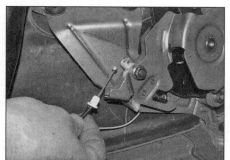

17.11c ...and the lever

17.15 Release the expander from the cable

17.17 Prise the outer cable from the back plate

17.22 Remove the circlip (arrowed)

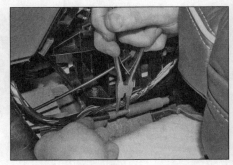

17.25 Adjust the parking brake

18.2 Remove the mounting bolts (arrowed)

Refitting

20 Refitting is a reversal of removal, but note the following:
a) *When fitting the rear cables to the expander wedge ensure they are fitted the correct way round – the pivot point must be at the top.*
b) *Carry out the cable adjustment procedure, as detailed below.*

Adjustment

Note: *Early models were fitted with a self-adjustment system contained in the foot operated lever. If not already done, these models should be upgraded to the later (manual adjustment) specification described below.*

21 Remove the side panel from the centre console.
22 If not already done so, remove the circlip **(see illustration)** and slacken the cable by rotating it clockwise.
23 Rotate the barrel anticlockwise until the groove for the circlip emerges. Refit the circlip.
24 Press the parking brake lever to the first notch on the ratchet.
25 Using pliers gently prise apart the sections of the adjuster **(see illustration)**. The adjustment is correct when the rear wheels are fully locked when the foot lever is on the second to fifth teeth on the ratchet mechanism.

26 If new parking brake shoes have been fitted, depress the parking brake pedal to the third notch on the ratchet and drive slowly for 300 metres. Fully release the parking brake and if necessary carry out the adjustment procedure again.

18 Parking brake lever – removal and refitting (XC90 only)

1 Follow the procedure, as described in the previous section to access the brake lever.
2 Remove the mounting bolts **(see illustration)**, turn the lever over and disconnect the switch wiring plug.
3 Disconnect the cables as described in the previous section and then remove the brake lever.
4 Refitting is a reversal of removal, but remember to carry out the cable adjustment procedure as described in Section 17.

19 Brake light switch – removal and refitting

Removal

1 Ensure the ignition is switched off.
2 Remove the trim panel under the facia on the driver's side as described in Chapter 11.

On XC60 models, the brake light switch is located closest to the brake pedal, adjacent to the brake diagnosis switch **(see illustration)**. Note that both units must be removed before the brake light switch can be renewed or refitted.
3 XC90 models only have a single switch fitted **(see illustration)**.
4 Disconnect the wiring plugs from the switches (or switch).
5 On XC60 models, remove the brake diagnosis switch by twisting anti-clockwise and pulling it from place. Then remove the brake light switch by twisting clockwise and pulling it from place.

Refitting

6 With the brake pedal in the rest position, insert the brake light switch and twist anti-clockwise to lock in position.
7 Insert the brake diagnosis switch and twist clockwise to lock in position. Use a feeler gauge to check the clearance between the plunger and the bracket at the rear – the gap should be between 0.5 and 1.5 mm
8 Reconnect the wiring plugs and refit the panels removed for access.

20 Anti-lock braking system (ABS) – general information

The anti-lock braking system, fitted as standard equipment on all models, monitors the rotational speed of the wheels under braking. Sudden deceleration of one wheel, indicating that lock-up is occurring, causes the hydraulic pressure to that wheel's brake to be reduced or interrupted momentarily.

The main components of the system are the wheel sensors, the electronic control module (ECM) and the hydraulic modulator assembly.

One sensor is fitted to each wheel, together with a pulse wheel carried on the wheel/driveshaft hub. The sensors monitor the rotational speeds of the wheels, and are able to detect when there is a risk of wheel locking (low rotational speed). The wheel sensors also provide vehicle speed information to the speedometer.

19.2 The brake light switch (arrowed) is located to the right of the brake pedal (XC60)

19.3 XC90 brake light switch

21.2 Front ABS sensor securing screw (arrowed)

21.4 XC60, 2WD rear ABS sensor securing screw (arrowed)

21.9 Disconnect the wiring plug (arrowed) from the side of the hydraulic modulator

Information from the sensors is fed to the ECM, which operates solenoid valves in the hydraulic modulator. The solenoid valves restrict the hydraulic fluid supply to any caliper detected to be on the verge of locking.

Should a fault develop in the system, the ECM illuminates a warning light on the instrument panel and disables the system. Normal braking will still be available, but without the anti-lock function. In the event of a fault, the ECM stores a series of signals (or fault codes) for subsequent read-out using diagnostic equipment (see Section 22).

Electronic brake force distribution (EBD) is incorporated into the ABS system, and regulates the proportion of braking force applied to the front and rear wheels.

On cars equipped with a traction control system, the ABS system performs a dual role. In addition to detecting when a wheel is locking under braking, the system also detects a wheel that is spinning under acceleration. When this condition is detected, the brake on that wheel is momentarily applied to reduce, or eliminate, the wheelspin. When the rotational speed of the spinning wheel is detected to be equal to the other wheels, the brake is released. On vehicles equipped with stability control the same sensors, solenoids and pipes are used. However, vehicles are also equipped with a combined yaw rate and lateral acceleration sensor, and a steering wheel angle sensor.

---

21 Anti-lock braking system (ABS) components – removal and refitting

Removal

Front wheel sensor

1 Loosen the appropriate front wheel bolts and chock the rear wheels. Jack up the front of the car and support it on axle stands (see *Jacking and vehicle support*). Remove the roadwheel.

2 Undo the screw which secures the sensor to the hub carrier **(see illustration)** and disconnect the wiring plug. Withdraw

---

the sensor, and unclip the wiring from any brackets.

Rear wheel sensor

3 Loosen the appropriate rear wheel bolts and chock the front wheels. Jack up the rear of the car and support it on axle stands (see *Jacking and vehicle support*). Remove the roadwheel.

4 Undo the screw which secures the sensor to the hub carrier **(see illustration)** and disconnect the wiring plug. Withdraw the sensor, and unclip the wiring from any brackets.

Hydraulic modulator

Note: *Before starting work, refer to the warning at the beginning of Section 2 concerning the dangers of hydraulic fluid.*

XC60

5 Remove the battery and battery tray as described in Chapter 5. Where fitted, undo the mounting bolts and remove the bracket below the battery tray.

6 Remove the plenum cover as described in Chapter 12, Section 18.

7 Wipe clean all the brake pipe unions at the hydraulic modulator. Place absorbent rags beneath the pipe unions to catch any spilt fluid.

8 Before disconnecting the fluid pipes from the hydraulic modulator, mark them for position (eg, by wrapping labels around the pipes). Undo the union nuts on the brake pipes on the top of the hydraulic modulator. Carefully withdraw the pipes, and cover the open unions and pipe ends.

21.14 Disconnect the wiring plug

---

9 Release the connector locking clip and disconnect the wiring plug on the side of the modulator **(see illustration)**.

10 Undo the bolts securing the hydraulic modulator mounting bracket to the bulkhead. Move the wiring aside, and lift out the modulator assembly and bracket.

11 Note that the modulator is a sealed precision assembly, and must not under any circumstances be dismantled. If the unit is knocked or dropped, it must be renewed. If a new unit is being fitted, do not remove any blanking plugs until the pipes are ready for reconnection.

XC90

12 Disconnect the battery as described in Chapter 5.

13 Remove the air filter housing as described in Chapter 4A.

14 Remove the power supply cables from the fusebox, unplug the electrical connector **(see illustration)** and then lift up and move the fusebox to one side.

15 Before disconnecting the fluid pipes from the hydraulic modulator, mark them for position (eg, by wrapping labels around the pipes). Undo the union nuts on the brake pipes on the top of the hydraulic modulator. Carefully withdraw the pipes, and cover the open unions and pipe ends.

16 Release the connector locking clip and disconnect the wiring plug on the side of the modulator.

17 Remove the 3 mounting screws from the support bracket and then lift out the modulator. Alternatively, remove the support bracket and then separate the modulator on the bench.

Brake pedal position sensor

18 Depress the brake pedal two or three times to dissipate any vacuum remaining in the servo unit.

19 Note that some models may have 2 sensors fitted. Disconnect the wiring connector from the pedal sensor located on the front face of the vacuum servo unit **(see illustration)**.

20 Open the circlip and withdraw the sensor from the servo. Recover the O-ring and spacer sleeve from the sensor if fitted.

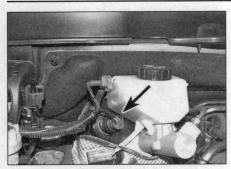

21.19 Brake pedal position sensor (arrowed)

Refitting

21 In all cases, refitting is a reversal of the removal operations but note the following points:
  a) Clean off all dirt from the wheel sensors and mounting locations before refitting with a stiff brush.
  b) Bleed the hydraulic system as described in Section 2 after refitting the hydraulic modulator.
  c) Where fitted use a new O-ring on the brake pedal position sensor, and ensure that the colour-coded spacer sleeve matches the colour code of the servo unit.

22 Anti-lock braking system (ABS) – fault diagnosis

General information

1 The anti-lock braking system incorporates an on-board diagnostic system to facilitate fault finding and system testing. Should a fault occur, the ECM stores a series of signals (or fault codes) for subsequent read-out via the diagnostic plug located under the facia, above the pedals.

2 If problems have been experienced, the on-board diagnostic system can be used to pinpoint any problem areas, but this requires special test equipment. Once this has been done, further tests may often be necessary to determine the exact nature of the fault; ie, whether a component itself has failed, or whether it is a wiring or other inter-related problem. Apart from visually checking the wiring and connections, any testing will require the use of a fault code reader at least. A Volvo dealer will obviously have such a reader, but they are also available from other suppliers. It is unlikely to be cost-effective for the private owner to purchase a fault code reader, but a well-equipped local garage or auto-electrical specialist will have one.

Preliminary checks

Note: When carrying out these checks to trace a fault, remember that if the fault has appeared only a short time after any part of the vehicle has been serviced or overhauled, the first place to check is where that work was carried out, however unrelated it may appear, to ensure that no carelessly-refitted components are causing the problem.

Note: Remember that any fault codes which have been logged will have to be cleared from the ECM memory using a dedicated fault code reader (see paragraph 2) before you can be certain the cause of the fault has been fixed.

3 Check the condition of the battery connections – remake the connections or renew the leads if a fault is found. Use the same techniques to ensure that all earth points in the engine compartment provide good electrical contact through clean, metal-to-metal joints, and that all are securely fastened.

4 Next work methodically around the engine compartment, checking all visible wiring, and the connections between sections of the wiring loom. What you are looking for at this stage is wiring that is obviously damaged by chafing against sharp edges, or against moving suspension/transmission components and/or the auxiliary drivebelt, by being trapped or crushed between carelessly-refitted components, or melted by being forced into contact with hot engine castings, coolant pipes, etc. In almost all cases, damage of this sort is caused in the first instance by incorrect routing on reassembly after previous work has been carried out (see the note at the beginning of this sub-Section).

5 Wires can break or short together inside the insulation so that no visible evidence betrays the fault, but this usually only occurs where the wiring loom has been incorrectly routed so that it is stretched taut or kinked sharply; either of these conditions should be obvious on even a casual inspection. If this is thought to have happened and the fault proves elusive, the suspect section of wiring should be checked very carefully during the more detailed checks which follow.

6 Depending on the extent of the problem, damaged wiring may be repaired by rejoining the break or splicing-in a new length of wire, using solder to ensure a good connection, and remaking the insulation with adhesive insulating tape or heat-shrink tubing, as desired. If the damage is extensive, given the implications for the vehicle's future reliability, the best long-term answer may well be to renew that entire section of the loom, however expensive this may appear.

7 When the actual damage has been repaired, ensure that the wiring loom is re-routed correctly, so that it is clear of other components, is not stretched or kinked, and is secured out of harm's way using the plastic clips, guides and ties provided.

8 Check all electrical connectors, ensuring that they are clean, securely fastened, and that each is locked by its plastic tabs or wire clip, as appropriate. If any connector shows external signs of corrosion (accumulations of white or green deposits, or streaks of 'rust'), or if any is thought to be dirty, it must be unplugged and cleaned using electrical contact cleaner. If the connector pins are severely corroded, the connector must be renewed; note that this may mean the renewal of that entire section of the loom.

9 If the cleaner completely removes the corrosion to leave the connector in a satisfactory condition, it would be wise to pack the connector with a suitable material which will exclude dirt and moisture, and prevent the corrosion from occurring again; a Volvo dealer may be able to recommend a suitable product.

10 Working methodically around the engine compartment, check carefully that all vacuum hoses and pipes are securely fastened and correctly routed, with no signs of cracks, splits or deterioration to cause air leaks, or of hoses that are trapped, kinked, or bent sharply enough to restrict airflow. Check with particular care at all connections and sharp bends, and renew any damaged or deformed lengths of hose.

11 Check the brake lines, and renew any that are found to be leaking, corroded or crushed. Check particularly the flexible hoses at the brake calipers.

12 It is possible to make a further check of the electrical connections by wiggling each electrical connector of the system in turn as the engine is idling; a faulty connector will be immediately evident from the engine's response (or that of the warning light) as contact is broken and remade. A faulty connector should be renewed to ensure that the future reliability of the system; note that this may mean the renewal of that entire section of the loom.

13 Ensure that the wiring and connections to the wheel sensors are thoroughly checked – the wheel sensors are subjected to water, road salt and general dirt, and are often responsible for the ABS warning light coming on.

14 If the preliminary checks have failed to reveal the fault, the car must be taken to a Volvo dealer or suitably-equipped garage for diagnostic testing using electronic test equipment.

23 Vacuum pump – removal and refitting

Removal

1 Pull the plastic cover from over the engine straight up from its mountings.
2 Remove the battery and battery tray as described in Chapter 5.
3 Note their fitted positions and disconnect the vacuum hoses from the pump.

23.4 Vacuum pump retaining bolts (arrowed)

23.5a Renew the vacuum pump O-rings (arrowed)

23.5b Ensure the drive lugs align with the slots in the end of the exhaust camshaft

4 Undo the retaining bolts and remove the pump from the cylinder head **(see illustration)**. Be prepared for fluid spillage. Discard the O-ring seals, new ones must be fitted. No dismantling of the pump is recommended.

Refitting

5 Fit new O-ring seals to the pump mating face, then align the pump drive lugs with the slots in the end of the exhaust camshaft, and fit the pump to the cylinder head – tighten the bolts to the specified torque **(see illustrations)**.

6 The remainder of refitting is a reversal of removal.

Chapter 10
Suspension and steering

Contents

Degrees of difficulty

Easy, suitable for novice with little experience	Fairly easy, suitable for beginner with some experience	Fairly difficult, suitable for competent DIY mechanic	Difficult, suitable for experienced DIY mechanic	Very difficult, suitable for expert DIY or professional

Specifications

Front suspension
Type . . . . Independent, with MacPherson struts incorporating coil springs and telescopic shock absorbers. Anti-roll bar fitted to all models

Rear suspension
Type . . . . Fully-independent, multi-link with coil springs and hydraulic telescopic shock absorbers. Anti-roll bar fitted to all models

Steering
Type . . . . Power-assisted rack-and-pinion
Steering fluid type . . . . See *Lubricants and fluids*

Wheel alignment and steering angles

	XC60	XC90
Front wheel:		
Camber angle	-0°38' ± 38'	0°15' ± 30'
Castor angle	3.0° 40'± 30'	4° 42' to 5°42'
Toe setting	0°12' ± 06' toe-in	0°09' 36"± 30' toe out
Rear wheel:		
Camber angle	0°12' ± 06'	-0° 20' ± 30'
Toe setting	-0°41' ± 30' toe-in	0°18'± 6' toe in

Tyres
Tyre pressures . . . . See sticker on the driver's-side B-pillar
Tyre sizes (dependent on model, market and territory) . . . . 195/65 R 15, 205/65 R 16, 215/55 R 16, 225/45 R 17, 235/40 R 18 and T125/80 R 17 (temporary spare)

Torque wrench settings	Nm	lbf ft
Front suspension		
ABS wheel sensor	See Chapter 9	
Anti-roll bar clamp bolts:		
XC60	175	129
XC90 (M10)	50	37
Anti-roll bar drop link to strut:*		
XC60	60	52
XC90 (M12)	90	66
XC90	50	37
Anti-roll bar drop link to anti-roll bar:*		
XC60	70	44
XC90	60	52
Balljoint to swivel hub bolts:*		
XC60	110	81
XC90	100	74
Ball joint mounting bolts (in swivel hub, XC90 only)	50	37
Brake caliper mounting bracket bolts	See Chapter 9	
Control arm to subframe:*		
XC60:		
Front bolt:		
Stage 1	140	103
Stage 2	Angle-tighten a further 45°	
Rear bolts	175	129
XC90:		
Front bolt (M12):		
Stage 1	65	48
Stage 2	Angle-tighten a further 90°	
Rear bolt (M14):		
Stage 1	105	78
Stage 2	Angle-tighten a further 90°	
Driveshaft bolt	See Chapter 8	
Hub balljoint to control arm nut:*		
XC60	110	81
XC90:		
To hub	50	37
To control arm	100	74
Subframe front crossmember and support brackets (XC60)	100	74
Subframe front and rear mounting bolts:*		
XC60:		
Rear bolts (M8)	24	18
Main bolts:		
Stage 1	150	111
Stage 2	Angle-tighten a further 90°	
XC90:		
Bracket bolts	50	37
Main bolts:		
Stage 1	105	78
Stage 2	Angle-tighten a further 120°	
Suspension strut to hub:*		
XC60	110	81
XC90:		
Stage 1	105	78
Stage 2	Angle-tighten a further 75°	
Suspension strut piston nut:*		
XC60	50	37
XC90	70	52
Suspension strut upper mounting to body:*		
XC60	30	22
XC90	25	19

Do not re-use. Volvo specify that where a fixing requires angular tightening it must always be renewed. Any fixing retained with a thread locking compound must also be renewed. Nuts with a nylon insert must always be renewed.

Torque wrench settings (continued)

	Nm	lbf ft
Rear suspension		
Anti-roll bar to subframe clamp bolts:		
XC60	50	37
XC90	80	59
Anti-roll bar drop link to anti-roll bar:		
XC60	15	11
XC90	80	59
Brake caliper bolts	See Chapter 9	
Hub bearing to hub:*		
XC60	110	81
XC90 (M12):		
Stage 1	20	15
Stage 2	45	33
Stage 3	Angle-tighten a further 60°	
Hub to upper arm:		
XC60	180	133
XC90 (M12)	80	59
Hub to lower arm:*		
XC60	110	81
XC90 (M12)	80	59
Hub to body trailing arm (XC60)	180	133
Lateral link arm (XC90)	80	59
Lower control arm to subframe (XC60)	90	66
Tie rod (XC90)	80	59
Shock absorber:		
XC60:		
Lower mounting bolt	175	129
Lower mounting bolt (M16)	280	206
Upper mounting bolts	30	22
XC90:		
Lower mounting bolt	80	59
Upper mounting bolt	60	44
Subframe mounting bolts:*		
XC60	110	81
XC90	100	74
Tie-rod bolts (XC60, both bolts)*	110	81
Upper control arm to subframe (XC60)*	110	81
Steering		
Power steering pipes to steering rack	18	13
Power steering pump mounting bolts	24	18
Steering column mounting bolts	24	18
Steering rack to subframe nuts/bolt:*		
XC60	140	103
XC90	50	37
Steering shaft universal joint pinch-bolts:*		
XC60	25	18
XC90	32	24
Steering wheel bolt:*		
XC60	48	35
XC90:		
Stage 1	30	22
Stage 2	Angle-tighten a further 30°	
Track rod end balljoint nuts:*		
XC60	80	59
XC90:		
Stage 1	50	37
Stage 2	Angle-tighten a further 35°	
Track rod locknuts	90	66
Roadwheels		
Wheel bolts	140	103

* Do not re-use. Volvo specify that where a fixing requires angular tightening it must always be renewed. Any fixing retained with a thread locking compound must also be renewed. Nuts with a nylon insert must always be renewed.

2.2 Undo the driveshaft bolt

2.8 With the bolt removed, pull the hub carrier downwards from the bottom of the suspension strut

1 General information

The independent front suspension is of the MacPherson strut type, incorporating coil springs and integral telescopic shock absorbers. The struts are located by transverse control arms, which are attached to the front subframe via rubber bushes at their inner ends, and incorporate a balljoint at their outer ends. The hub carriers, which carry the hub bearings, brake calipers and the hub/disc assemblies, are bolted to the MacPherson struts, and connected to the control arms through the balljoints. A front anti-roll bar is fitted to all models, and is attached to the subframe and to the MacPherson struts via link arms.

The rear suspension is of the fully independent, multilink type, consisting of an upper and lower control arm mounted via rubber bushes, to the hub carrier and rear subframe. The hub carrier is located by a lateral link arm and an upper stay each side. Coil springs are fitted between the lower control arm and the vehicle body, and there are hydraulic shock absorbers.

Power-assisted rack and pinion steering is fitted as standard equipment. Power assistance is derived from a hydraulic pump, belt-driven from the crankshaft pulley on all models except newer XC60 models. On these models power is provide by an electro hydraulic power steering pump (EHPS).

2 Front hub and bearing – removal and refitting

Note: *On XC90 models the bearing is part of the hub assembly.*

Removal – all models

1 Working through the hole in the centre of the wheel, slacken the driveshaft bolt. This bolt is very tight. If the wheels fitted do not have a centre hole, use the spare wheel. If possible avoid slackening the bolt with the car raised.

2 Slacken the front wheel bolts, raise and support the car and remove the wheel. Partially unscrew the driveshaft bolt and loosen the driveshaft in the hub by pushing or tapping the bolt inwards. Remove and discard the driveshaft bolt **(see illustration)**.

3 With reference to Chapter 9, remove the brake caliper and brake disc. Note that new bolts will be required for refitting.

4 Unbolt and remove the dust shield and then remove the ABS sensor. Unclip the sensor wiring from the support brackets and move it to one side.

5 Disconnect the anti-roll bar drop link from the control arm. Use a torx type key to counterhold the tapered joint. Repeat the procedure for the track rod end. Use a ball joint splitter to separate the track rod end from the track control arm.

6 Where fitted disconnect the headlight level control arm.

XC60 models

7 Remove the lower pinch bolt and (using a long lever) pull the lower arm from the hub. It may be necessary to use a blunt chisel to slightly open up the lower clamp on the hub.

8 Remove the bolt securing the hub carrier to the strut, and pull the hub carrier downwards from the shock absorber. Note which way the bolt is inserted – from the front **(see illustration)**.

9 Swivel the hub carrier assembly outwards, and withdraw the driveshaft from the hub flange. Support the driveshaft by securing it to the suspension strut with stout cord.

10 With the hub carrier removed, the bearing can be pressed from place. Note that this task (and subsequent renewal of the bearing) requires the use of a hydraulic press and specialist tools (Volvo part numbers 9997090, 9995686, 9997296 and 9997295).Entrust this task to a Volvo dealer or suitably equipped garage.

XC90 models

11 Before removing the hub, measure the distance from the rear of the strut to the front of the hub **(see illustration)**. Write down the measurement to ensure that the wheel camber can be maintained when the hub is reassembled. Note that this procedure *may* not be necessary for later models, as these appear to have no method of adjustment.

12 Remove the nut from the ball joint and use a ball joint splitter to separate the hub from the control arm. Lever the control arm down, pull the hub outwards and release the previously loosened driveshaft from the hub **(see illustration)**.

13 If only the hub bearing requires attention, the 4 hub mounting bolts can now be removed **(see illustration)**.

14 Remove the strut to hub bolts and remove the swivel hub assembly from the vehicle.

15 With the swivel hub assembly on the bench, if required the ball joint can now be replaced as described in Section 3.

Refitting

16 With the new bearing in place and prior to refitting the hub carrier, remove all traces of metal adhesive, rust, oil and dirt from the splines and threads of the driveshaft outer CV joint.

2.11 Measure the distance between the rear of the strut and the front of the hub

2.12 Remove the driveshaft

2.13 Remove the hub bolts (arrowed)

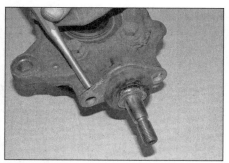

3.2 Work a drift around the old balljoint to remove it

3.4a Gently tighten the nuts...

3.4b ...whilst driving the balljoint home

17 Refit the lower arm balljoint first, then use a stout metal bar to lever down the lower arm and refit the driveshaft to the rear of the hub. Refit the hub to the bottom of the suspension strut. On XC60 models ensure that the tab on the rear of the strut engages with the slot in the hub as it is refitted.

18 On XC90 models fit the hub to the strut and adjust the hub to the previously noted measurement before fully tightening the bolts.

19 The remainder of refitting is a reversal of removal, but observe the following points:

a) *Ensure that the hub and brake disc mating faces are spotlessly clean, and refit the disc with any orientation marks aligned.*

b) *Have the front suspension geometry checked and adjusted by a Volvo dealer or suitably-equipped specialist.*

c) *Lubricate the threads of the CV joint and the driveshaft retaining bolt with engine oil before refitting the bolt. A new bolt should be used.*

d) *Tighten all nuts and bolts to the specified torque (see Chapter 9 for brake component torque settings)*

---

3 Front hub ball joint –
removal and refitting
(XC90 models only)

Note: *On XC60 models the front suspension balljoint is part of the lower control arm. If the balljoint is worn the complete arm must be replaced.*

Removal

1 Remove the swivel hub assembly as described in Section 2.

2 With the hub on the bench, remove the mounting bolts and use a suitable drift to remove the balljoint **(see illustration)**.

Refitting

3 Use a suitable wire brush and clean the housing in the hub and then apply a general purpose grease to the housing.

4 Volvo use special tools (9995781 and 9995796) to fit the new balljoint. These tools are guide pins and a drift that allow the balljoint to be driven home and correctly orientated. We used 2 lengths of threaded bar

and suitable sleeves – pipe olives in our case – and used these to align the balljoint as we gently drove it home using a combination of a drift and tightening the nuts on the threaded bars **(see illustrations)**.

5 Fit the new bolts, tighten to the specified torque and then refit the hub to the vehicle. Fit a new nut to the balljoint. Note that this should be provided with the replacement balljoint.

---

4 Front strut –
removal and refitting

Removal

1 On XC60 models, slacken the driveshaft bolt (see Section 2). On all models, slacken the front wheel bolts, raise and support the car and remove the wheel.

2 Remove the ABS wheel sensor wiring from the swivel hub.

3 Undo the retaining nut, and separate the anti-roll bar drop link from the bracket on the suspension strut. Use a Torx key to counterhold the nut **(see illustration)**. Discard the nut, a new one must be fitted.

XC60 models

4 Remove and discard the driveshaft bolt.

5 Undo the lower control arm balljoint at the hub – as described in Section 6.

6 Partially free the hub assembly from the driveshaft, such that the hub clears the lower arm balljoint.

7 Position a jack beneath the hub and raise the jack to just beneath the hub.

8 Undo the clamping bolt securing the suspension strut to the hub. If necessary use a blunt chisel to slightly open the clamp and then drive the hub from the strut using a soft faced hammer. Support the hub on the trolley jack, ensuring that the brake flexible hose is not strained. Secure the hub to the subframe with cord if necessary.

9 From within the engine compartment, remove the plenum chamber cover and then partially remove the three bolts securing the strut upper mounting to the body – **do not** attempt to loosen the centre nut **(see illustration)**. Have an assistant support the strut assembly and then fully remove the nuts. Remove the strut assembly from the wheelarch.

XC90 models

10 With reference to Section 2 measure the distance between the hub and the rear of the strut **(see illustration 2.11)**.

11 Note the orientation of the hub to strut nuts and bolts and then remove them. Lever the strut free from the hub, ensuring that the driveshaft is not dislodged or that the brake flexible hose is not strained.

12 Working under the bonnet partially remove the three bolts securing the strut upper mounting to the body – **do not** attempt to loosen the centre nut. Have an assistant support the strut assembly and then fully remove the nuts. Remove the strut assembly from the wheelarch.

4.3 Undo the nut (arrowed) securing the anti-roll drop link to the suspension strut

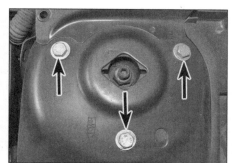

4.9 Upper strut mounting bolts (arrowed)

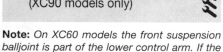

5.2 Slacken the strut mounting nut half a turn, holding the piston rod with a Torx bit

5.3 Fit the spring compressors (XC60 model shown)

5.4a Remove the piston nut

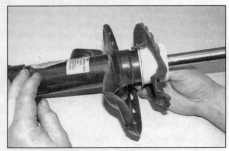

5.4b With the upper mounting and coil spring removed, the lower rubber mount can be removed

5.4c If required, the gaiter can be separated from the upper mounting…

5.4d …and the bump stop removed

Refitting

13 Refitting is a reversal of removal, but observe the following points:
a) Ensure that the ABS sensor and the sensor location in the hub carrier are perfectly clean before refitting.
b) Tighten all nuts and bolts to the specified torque, using new nuts/bolts where necessary.
c) Have the suspension geometry check and adjusted by a dealer or suitably-equipped specialist.

5 Front strut –
dimantling, inspection and reassembly

Warning: Before attempting to dismantle the suspension strut, a suitable tool to hold the coil

5.5a Remove the secondary nut…

5.5b …and then the spring seat

spring in compression must be obtained. Adjustable coil spring compressors which can be positively secured to the spring coils are readily available, and are recommended for this operation. Any attempt to dismantle the strut without such a tool is likely to result in damage or personal injury.

Dismantling

1 Remove the strut from the car as described in Section 3.
2 Slacken the strut mounting nut 1/2 a turn, while holding the protruding portion of the piston rod with a Torx bit **(see illustration)**. Do not remove the nut at this stage.
3 Fit the spring compressors to the coil springs, and tighten the compressors until the load is taken off the spring seats **(see illustration)**.
4 On XC60 models remove the piston nut, top bearing and gaiter followed by the spring and lower spring rubber mount. The upper spring

rubber mount can be removed, and the gaiter separated from the top mount if required **(see illustrations)**.
5 On XC90 models remove the upper nut, the cover plate and then the upper mounting. Remove the now exposed secondary nut and then remove the spring upper seat **(see illustrations)**. Remove the spring and if required the gaiter.

Inspection

6 With the strut assembly now completely dismantled, examine all the components for wear, damage or deformation. Renew any of the components as necessary.
7 Examine the shock absorber for signs of fluid leakage, and check the strut piston for signs of pitting along its entire length. Test the operation of the shock absorber, while holding it in an upright position, by moving the piston through a full stroke and then through short strokes of 50 to 100 mm. In both cases, the resistance felt should be smooth and continuous. If the resistance is jerky, or uneven, or if there is any visible sign of wear or damage, renewal is necessary.
8 If any doubt exists about the condition of the coil spring, gradually release the spring compressor, and check the spring for distortion and signs of cracking. Since no minimum free length is specified by Volvo, the only way to check the tension of the spring is to compare it to a new component. Renew the spring if it is damaged or distorted, or if there is any doubt as to its condition. Note that springs should always be replaced in pairs.

5.10a Ensure that the spring is fully compressed before refitting and that the spring ends are correctly located in their rubber mounts

5.10b When refitting the top mount, ensure the two plastic lugs (arrowed) align

9 If a new shock absorber is being fitted, hold it vertically and pump the piston a few times to prime it. Always replace shock absorbers in pairs.

Reassembly

10 Reassembly is a reversal of dismantling, but ensure that the spring is fully compressed before fitting. Make sure that the spring ends are correctly located in the upper and lower seats and that on XC60 models the two plastic lugs align (see illustrations). Tighten the shock absorber piston retaining nut and strut mounting nuts to the specified torque.

6 Front control arm –
removal, overhaul and refitting

Removal

1 Working through the hole in the centre of the wheel, slacken the driveshaft bolt. This bolt is very tight. If the wheels fitted do not have a centre hole, use the spare wheel. If possible avoid slackening the bolt with the car raised.
2 Slacken the front wheel bolts, raise and support the car and remove the wheel. Remove the engine undershield. Remove and discard the driveshaft bolt.
3 Follow the procedure described in Section 2 of this Chapter and release the ball joint taper from the hub. Pull the hub away from the driveshaft.
4 Where fitted unbolt the link arm for the ride height sensor from the control arm.
5 Undo the bolts securing the control arm to the subframe and remove the arm (see illustrations).

Overhaul

6 Thoroughly clean the control arm and the area around the control arm mountings. Inspect the arm for any signs of cracks, damage or distortion, and carefully check the inner pivot bushes for signs of swelling, cracks or deterioration of the rubber.

7 If either bush requires renewal, the work should be entrusted to a Volvo dealer or suitably equipped garage. A hydraulic press and suitable spacers are required to remove and refit the bushes and a setting gauge is needed for accurate positioning of the bushes in the arm.
8 On XC60 models if the ball joint is worn, then the complete control arm must be replaced as Volvo do not supply the ball joint as a separate component. An after market supplier may list the ball joint as a separate item though.

Refitting

9 Locate the arm in its mountings on the subframe, and fit the new mounting bolts. Tighten the nuts to their specified torque.
10 Engage the balljoint shank in the hub carrier, then tighten the new nut to the specified torque.
11 The remainder of refitting is a reversal of removal.

6.5a Undo the three control arm bolts (arrowed) at the subframe...

6.5b ...and then remove the control arm

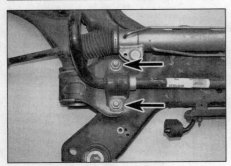

7.3a The clamps on XC60 models (arrowed)...

7 Front anti-roll bar – removal and refitting

Note: *If only the anti-roll bar bushes require replacement, complete removal of the front subframe is not necessary. The subframe must however be lowered by 50mm on XC60 models and by 110mm on XC90 models. With the subframe lowered the anti-roll bar can be raised sufficiently to allow removal of the bushes.*

Removal

1 Remove the front subframe as described in Section 9.
2 Note that on XC60 models the anti-roll bar clamps on each side of the subframe are secured by the rear 2 bolts for the lower control arm.
3 With the subframe removed, unbolt the

8.2 Remove the upper mounting (XC90)

9.8 Remove the cross member

7.3b ...and on XC90 models (arrowed)

anti-roll bar clamps **(see illustrations)** and remove the anti-roll bar.
4 Examine the anti-roll bar for signs of damage or distortion, and the connecting links and mounting bushes for signs of deterioration of the rubber.

Refitting

5 Refitting is a reversal of removal.

8 Front anti-roll bar drop link – removal and refitting

Removal

1 Loosen the front wheel bolts. Chock the rear wheels, then jack up the front of the vehicle and support it on axle stands (see *Jacking and vehicle support*). Remove the relevant roadwheel.

8.3 Counterhold the ball joint with a torx type key

9.9 Remove the rear torque mounting (left-hand shown)

2 Undo the bolt securing the link to the bottom of the suspension strut **(see illustration)**.
3 Undo the retaining nut, and separate the anti-roll bar drop link from the end of the anti-roll bar. If necessary, use a Torx bit in the end of the balljoint shank to counterhold the nut **(see illustration)**. Remove the drop link.

Refitting

4 Refitting is a reversal of removal, using new nuts and ensuring they are tightened to the specified torque.

9 Front subframe – removal and refitting

Removal

1 Drive the car forwards and park it with the steering wheels in the straight-ahead position. Remove the remote unit or the ignition key to lock the steering in this position.
2 Loosen the front wheel bolts. Chock the rear wheels then jack up the front of the vehicle and support it on axle stands (see *Jacking and vehicle support*). You will need to ensure there is adequate clearance below the vehicle. Remove both front roadwheels and both front wheel arch liners.
3 Undo the securing screws and remove the engine undershield.
4 On both sides separate the track rod end balljoints at the hub carrier.
5 On both sides undo the retaining nut, and separate the anti-roll bar connecting links on each side from the ends of the anti-roll bar. If necessary, use a Torx bit in the end of the balljoint shank to counterhold the nut.
6 Undo the steering column pinch bolt and release the column from the steering rack.

XC60

7 Remove the front bumper cover as described in Chapter 11.
8 Remove the front subframe crossmember and then remove the crossmember support brackets from both sides **(see illustration)**.
9 Undo both rear lower torque rod bolts at the engine mountings **(see illustration)**.
10 Undo the 2 bolts securing the exhaust hanger bracket to the rear of the subframe. Take care not to forcibly bend the flexible section of the exhaust. Use two lengths of wood to support the flexible section if necessary.
11 Disconnect the power steering supply and return lines. Use a suitable AC spring lock tool to release the connectors. Anticipate some spillage of fluid as the lines are disconnected.
12 Make alignment marks between the subframe and the vehicle body to aid refitting and then support the subframe from beneath using a jack (or jacks).
13 At the front of the subframe remove the outriggers from both sides **(see illustrations)**.

9.13a Unbolt and then...

9.13b ...remove both outriggers

9.14 Remove the subframe bolts

On models with EHPS (Electro Hydraulic Power Steering) it will be necessary to unbolt and move to one side the pump and reservoir assembly.

14 Undo the front subframe bolts **(see illustration)**, lower the subframe, and drag the subframe from beneath the vehicle. As the assembly is being lowered, unclip any pipes or cables and ensure that pipes or other components do not become trapped between the subframe and the vehicle body.

XC90

15 The engine must now be supported from above. To allow access to the subframe we used 2 engine support bars **(see illustration)**. It should also be possible to support the engine with a suitable engine crane.

16 Remove the cross member from the rear and then remove the exhaust support bracket **(see illustrations)**.

17 Using a socket and extension bar remove the front and rear engine mountings **(see illustration)**.

18 Remove the torque/pendulum mounting from the front of the engine and then remove the smaller engine mount from below the crankshaft pulley **(see illustrations)**.

19 Support the subframe with a suitable jack and then remove the smaller bolts from the rear subframe support bracket **(see illustration)**.

20 Make alignment marks between the subframe and vehicle body. We also took measurements from fixed points on the vehicle body.

21 Partially release the main subframe

mounting bolts. Check that all cables and pipes are free from the subframe and then fully remove the subframe bolts. Lower the subframe on the jack and withdraw it from the vehicle.

9.15 We used two support bars hold the engine in position

9.16b ...and the exhaust support bracket

9.18a Remove the front mounting...

9.18b ...and the right-hand side engine mounting bolts (arrowed)

Refitting

22 Refitting is a reversal of removal, noting the following points:

a) *When raising the subframe into position,*

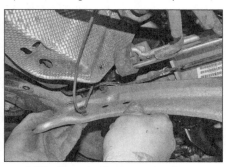
9.16a Remove the crossmember...

9.17 Access the engine mounting through the subframe

9.19 Remove the bolts (arrowed)

9.22 On XC60 models a hole is provided at the left-hand rear of the subframe to allow the fitting of an alignment tool

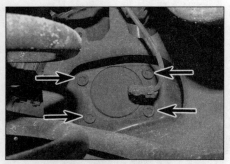

10.7a Rear hub bearing bolts (arrowed). XC60 FWD shown

ensure that pipes and other components do not become trapped between the subframe and the vehicle body.

b) Raise the front of the subframe using the jack and fit new washers and bolts, hand-tight only.

c) Ensure the alignment marks made previously **(see illustration)** are in the correct position before tightening all bolts to the specified torque.

d) Have the front wheel toe-in checked and adjusted by a Volvo dealer or suitably-equipped specialist.

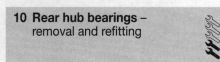

10 Rear hub bearings –
removal and refitting

Note: On both models the bearings and hubs are supplied as a complete assembly.

11.6 Remove the wiring loom and brake pipe (XC60 shown)

10.6 Raise the suspension

10.7b Remove the bearing from the hub

Removal

1 Jack up and support the rear of the vehicle - see *Jacking and vehicle support* in the reference section.

2 On AWD models have an assistant apply the brakes and slacken off the driveshaft bolt.

3 Remove the caliper and brake disc as described in Chapter 9.

4 On XC90 models, remove the bolt and with care release the ABS wheel speed sensor.

5 Use a soft faced mallet on the driveshaft bolt and partially drive the shaft into the hub. Fully remove the bolt.

6 On XC90 models place a trolley jack under the suspension lower arm and raise the rear suspension so that the distance between the centre wheel arch and the centre of the hub is 500mm **(see illustration)**.

7 Undo the four bolts and withdraw the bearing assembly from the hub carrier **(see illustrations)**. Note that on XC60 models,

11.7 Removing the lower control arm bolt (XC90)

undoing the upper bolt on the anti-roll bar connecting link will allow the anti-roll bar to be twisted slightly, improving access to the bearing assembly bolts.

Refitting

8 Refitting is a reversal of removal, noting the following:

a) Check the condition of the seal in the hub, ensuring that it is correctly located. Lubricate the seal before fitting the hub.

b) Fit the new assembly to the hub carrier then insert and tighten the new bolts (supplied in the bearing/hub kit) to the specified torque.

c) Refit the ABS wheel speed sensor and brake disc as described in Chapter 9.

11 Rear hub carrier –
removal and refitting

Removal

1 With all tyres correctly inflated measure the distance from the centre of the hub to the centre of the wheel arch. Note down the distance.

2 Jack up and support the rear of the vehicle - see *Jacking and vehicle support* in the reference section. On XC60 models remove the protective plastic cover from the rear of the floor pan

3 Remove the coil spring as described in Section 13.

4 Remove the hub bearings as described in Section 10.

5 Remove the brake backplate. If a gasket is fitted, obtain a new one if the original is in any way damaged.

6 Undo any clips that secure pipes or cables to the hub assembly **(see illustration)**.

7 Note their fitted positions then undo the bolts securing the anti-roll bar link, shock absorber, upper and lower control arms, and the tie-rod to the hub carrier **(see illustration)**. Undo the bolts securing the lateral links to the vehicle body with reference to the relevant Section in this chapter. Discard the bolts; new ones must be fitted. Withdraw the hub carrier from the vehicle.

8 If any of the various metal-elastic bushes on the hub carrier appear damaged or worn, have them renewed by a Volvo dealer or specialist, as access to special tools and a hydraulic press is required.

Refitting

9 Position the hub carrier, connect the various link arms, and fit the new bolts. Only finger-tighten the bolts at this stage.

10 On XC60 models, check the hub carrier is in the 'normal' position as described in Section 17. On XC90 models use a jack under the rear lower arm **(see illustration 10.6)** and raise the suspension, so that the distance between the hub centre and the wheel arch is the same as the previously noted distance.

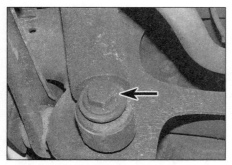

12.3a Lower shock absorber mounting bolt (arrowed)

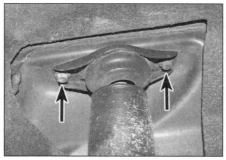

12.3b Upper shock absorber mounting bolts (arrowed)

12.7 Removing the upper mounting (shown out of the vehicle for clarity)

11 Now tighten the new mounting bolts to the specified torque where given.
12 The remainder of refitting is a reversal of removal.

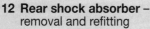
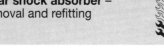

12 Rear shock absorber – removal and refitting

Note: *Shock absorbers should always be replaced in pairs.*

Removal

1 Chock the front wheels then jack up the rear of the vehicle and support it on axle stands (see *Jacking and vehicle support*). Remove the appropriate rear wheel.
2 To make removal easier, position a jack under the outer end of the lower control arm, and raise the jack sufficiently to take the load off the shock absorber.

XC60

3 Undo the shock absorber lower mounting bolt, and the 2 upper mounting bolts **(see illustrations)**.
4 Check the condition of the shock absorber and renew as necessary.

XC90

5 Slide the seat cushion back on the third row of seats and locate the outlined cutting point in the soundproofing.
6 Cut the flap with a sharp knife and remove the now exposed cover plate.
7 Using a torx socket and a crow's foot

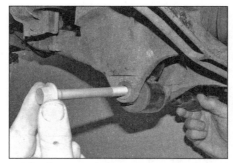

12.8a Remove the lower mounting bolt...

12.8b ...and remove the shock absorber

wrench remove the shock absorber upper mounting nut **(see illustration)**.
8 Remove the lower mounting and withdraw the shock absorber **(see illustrations)**.
9 Check the condition of the shock absorber and renew as necessary.

Refitting

10 Refitting is a reversal of removal, tightening all nuts and bolts to the specified torques.

13 Rear coil spring – removal and refitting

Removal

1 Loosen the rear wheel bolts. Chock the rear wheels, then jack up the front of the vehicle and support it on axle stands (see *Jacking*

and vehicle support). Remove the relevant roadwheel.

XC60

2 Undo the upper bolt at the anti-roll bar connecting link as described in Section 16.
3 Remove the wing liner.
4 Attach spring compressors and compress the spring **(see illustration)**.
5 Lift out the spring from its location. Note that it is also possible to remove the spring by supporting the lower suspension arm with a jack. Remove the bolt from the arm at the hub end and slowly lower the jack **(see illustrations)**. If the spring is removed by lowering the suspension arm, the spring will have to be compressed for refitting, as it is impossible to place the rear suspension in the service position (as described in Section 17) with the spring fitted.
6 Examine all the components for wear or damage, and renew as necessary.

13.4 Compress the spring

13.5a Remove the upper mounting...

13.5b ...and then remove the spring from the rear

13.5c Lower the jack and remove the spring

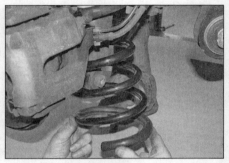

13.10 Remove the rear spring

10 Slowly lower the jack and release the tension from the spring. Remove the jack, fully lower the lower control arm and then remove the spring (see illustration).

Refitting

11 Refitting is a reversal of removal ensuring that the spring seats correctly in the lower arm. Note that on XC90 models the suspension must be in the service position as described at the end of Section 17.

14 Rear link arms – removal and refitting

XC90

7 Place a jack securely under the lower control arm and raise the suspension slightly.

8 Remove the shock absorber lower mounting

and then (where fitted) remove the link arm for the headlight levelling system.

9 Remove the bolts that locate the adjustable arm to the hub, the bolts that locate the lower arm to the hub and the bolts that locate the torque arm to the hub.

Removal

1 Loosen the rear wheel bolts. Chock the front wheels, then jack up the rear of the vehicle and support it on axle stands (see *Jacking and vehicle support*). Remove the roadwheel(s).

XC60

Tie-rod

2 Remove the coil spring as described in Section 13.

3 Where fitted, disconnect the height sensor mounting bolts.

4 Undo the bolts that secure the tie-rod to the subframe and to the trailing arm/hub carrier (see illustrations). Remove the tie-rod from the vehicle.

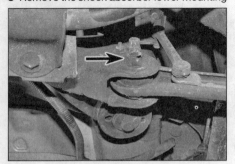

14.4a Remove the tie-rod inner mounting bolt (arrowed)...

14.4b ...and the outer mounting bolt

Upper arm

5 Remove the coil spring as described in Section 13.

6 Undo the bolts securing the upper arm to the hub carrier and to the subframe, and remove it from the vehicle (see illustrations).

Lower arm

7 Remove the coil spring as described in Section 13.

8 Undo the anti-roll bar drop link. Undo the bolts securing the inner end of the lower control arm to the subframe and to the hub carrier. Detach the lower arm (see illustrations).

XC90 models

Lower control arm

9 Remove the spring as described in Section 13

14.6a Upper arm inner bolt (arrowed)

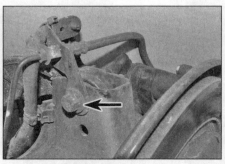

14.6b Upper arm outer bolt (arrowed) at hub carrier

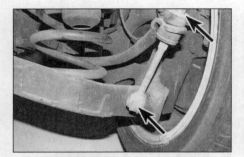

14.8a Disconnect the anti-roll bar connecting link (arrowed) before removing the lower arm

14.8b Mark the exact position of the snail cam before removing the bolt

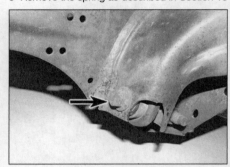

14.8c Lower arm outer bolt (arrowed)

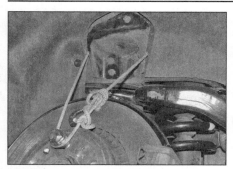
14.9 Secure the hub assembly to the bump stop bracket

14.16 Mark the position of the snail cam (arrowed)

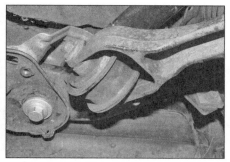
14.19 The lateral link inner mounting

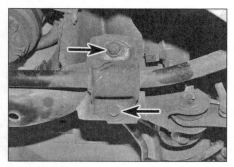
15.3 XC60 anti-roll bar clamp bolts (arrowed)

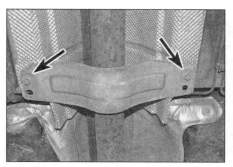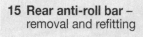
15.4 Remove the bracket bolts (arrowed)

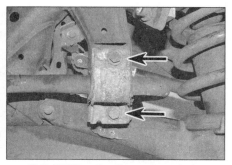
15.8 XC90 anti-roll bar clamp bolts (arrowed)

and secure the hub assembly out of the way (see illustration).
10 Remove the bolt at the subframe end and remove the control arm.

Upper control arm
11 Have an assistant operate the brake and then slacken off the driveshaft bolt. Ensure that the driveshaft moves freely in the hub and then fully remove the bolt.
12 Remove the brake caliper (see Chapter 9).
13 Slacken off the bolt for the upper control arm and using a suitable two legged puller push the hub free from the upper arm. Once the hub is free remove the bolt completely.
14 Repeat the procedure for the subframe mounting and then remove the upper control arm.

Tie rod
15 Place a suitable jack under the lower control arm and raise the suspension slightly. Where fitted unclip the handbrake guide bracket.
16 A snail cam is provided at the subframe end of the arm to allow adjustment of the rear wheel tracking. Mark the position of the cam before proceeding (see illustration).
17 Remove the bolts and remove the link from the vehicle.

Lateral link arm
18 Place a suitable jack under the lower control arm and raise the suspension slightly.
19 Remove the inner and outer mounting bolts (see illustration). Remove the arm.

Refitting
20 Refitting any of the link arms is a reversal of removal, noting the following points:

a) Always renew the link arms' mounting bolts.
b) Tighten all fasteners to their specified torque where given.
c) Before tightening any link arm mounting bolts, ensure the suspension is in the 'normal' position as described in Section 17.
d) Calibrate xenon lights – where fitted.
e) Have the tracking checked and adjusted if necessary.

15 Rear anti-roll bar – removal and refitting

Removal
1 Chock the front wheels, then jack up the rear of the vehicle and support it on axle stands (see Jacking and vehicle support).

XC60
2 Undo the bolts on each side securing the anti-roll bar to the drop link as described in Section 16.
3 Undo the bolts securing the anti-roll bar clamps to the subframe, manoeuvre the anti-roll bar past the subframe and withdraw it from the vehicle (see illustration).

XC90 models
4 Remove the support bracket at the rear of the transmission tunnel (see illustration).
5 Remove the exhaust system by separating it at the catalytic convertor. Support the converter.
6 Remove the left-hand side road spring as described in Section 13.

7 Remove the drop links at each end of the anti-roll bar, as described in Section 16 .
8 Remove the anti-roll bar bush clamps (see illustration).
9 Note the routing of the parking brake cable and remove the anti-roll bar.

Refitting
10 Refitting is a reversal of removal.

16 Rear anti-roll bar drop link – removal and refitting

1 Loosen the rear wheel bolts. Chock the front wheels, then jack up the rear of the vehicle and support it on axle stands (see Jacking and vehicle support). Remove the relevant roadwheel.
2 Undo the bolt securing the link to the lower arm (see illustration).
3 Undo the bolt securing the link to the

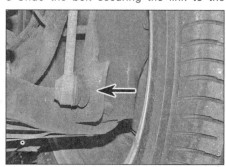
16.2 XC60 drop link lower mounting bolt (arrowed)

16.3 Use a torx key to stop the ball joint from rotating (XC90 shown)

anti-roll bar **(see illustration)**. The drop link can now be removed.

4 Refitting is a reversal of removal, using new nuts and ensuring they are tightened to the specified torque.

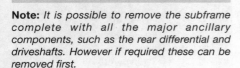

17 Rear subframe assembly – removal and refitting

Note: *It is possible to remove the subframe complete with all the major ancillary components, such as the rear differential and driveshafts. However if required these can be removed first.*

Removal

1 Before starting work measure the distance between the centre of the hub and the wheel arch at the mid point. On XC60 model this should be approximately 350mm, on XC90 models this should be approximately 453mm **(see illustration)**.

2 Jack up and support the rear of the vehicle - see *Jacking and vehicle support* in the reference section.

XC60

3 Remove both springs, as described in Section 13 of this Chapter. If refitting the old springs, make alignment marks between the spring and spring seat to aid refitting.

4 Undo the lower mounting bolts for the rear shock absorbers.

5 Undo the bolts on each side and remove the underbody panels from the floorpan.

6 Remove the bolts that secure the hub trailing arms to the vehicle body **(see illustration)**.

7 Unbolt the flexible brake hose support bracket from the chassis leg – on both sides.

8 Use a suitable diagnostic tool and activate the handbrake service mode (refer to Chapter 9). Disconnect the ABS sensor wiring plug and the wiring plug for the handbrake actuator.

9 Undo the brake caliper guide pin bolts at the hub carrier and move the calipers to one side. Unbolt the brake pipe support bracket from the hub. Suspend the calipers from the vehicle bodywork to prevent any strain on the flexible brake hose.

10 With reference to Chapter 8B, remove the propeller shaft.

11 Disconnect the wiring plug from the Haldex unit and then release the exhaust from the rubber mounting.

12 Make alignment marks between the subframe and the vehicle body and then support the subframe with a suitable jack.

13 Remove the 4 subframe mounting bolts and lower the subframe from the vehicle **(see illustration)**.

XC90

14 Have an assistant apply the brake and remove the driveshaft hub nuts. Partially free the driveshaft from the hub.

15 Remove the brake caliper, brake disc and handbrake cable as described in Chapter 9.

16 With the driveshafts partially removed, unbolt and remove the ABS wheel speed sensors from both sides.

17 Remove the rear section of the exhaust system as described in Chapter 4A and then remove the propeller shaft as described in Chapter 8B. Disconnect the wiring plug from the Haldex unit.

18 Unclip the fuel filler pipe support bracket from the top of the coil spring upper mounting **(see illustration)**.

19 Mark the position of the subframe in relation to the vehicle body. We fabricated small brackets and bolted them to the bump stops to act as alignment markers **(see illustration)**.

20 Support the subframe securely. We used a scissor type transmission jack and secured the subframe to the jack with ratchet type strap.

21 Remove the subframe mounting bolts **(see illustration)** and then with the aid of an assistant partially lower the subframe, lower the subframe from the vehicle.

22 With the subframe lowered slightly and noting the routing, remove the wiring loom and unclip the brake pipes from the support brackets.

17.1 Measure the distance from the hub centre to the wheelarch (XC60 shown)

17.6 Remove the bolts (arrowed)

17.13 Rear subframe mounting bolt

17.18 Remove the support bracket

17.19 Fabricated brackets are used to align the subframe (arrowed)

17.21 Removing the subframe mounting bolts

Refitting

23 Refitting is a reversal of removal bearing in mind the following points:

a) *Manoeuvre the subframe assembly into position using the jacks and secure with the four new mounting bolts each side, align the previously-made marks and tighten the bolts to the specified torque.*

b) *Use new bolts for the suspension and brake components as described in the relevant Sections.*

c) *On XC60 models, with the wiring plug for the handbrake actuator reconnected, deactivate the service mode.*

d) *Before finally tightening the bolts for the suspension components, the suspension needs to be in its 'normal' position. On XC60 models this should be carried out with the rear springs removed. Position a trolley jack under the control arm at the point where it is attached to the hub carrier and raise the assembly until the distance from the wheel arch to the hub centre is 350mm (XC60) or 453mm (XC90). If necessary, place some ballast in the luggage compartment to increase the weight of the vehicle, so that the suspension can be compressed enough by the jack without lifting the vehicle from the axle stands. Tighten all mounting bolts to the specified torque.*

18 Steering wheel – removal and refitting

⚠ **Warning: Handle the airbag unit with extreme care as a precaution against personal injury, and always hold it with the cover facing away from the body. If in doubt concerning any proposed work involving the airbag unit or its control circuitry, consult a Volvo dealer.**

Removal

1 Drive the car forwards and park it with the front wheels in the straight-ahead position.
2 Disconnect the battery negative lead, and wait for 10 minutes before proceeding.
3 As a precautionary measure, place a piece

of masking tape on the top of the steering wheel hub, and another piece on the top of the steering column upper shroud. Draw a pencil line across both pieces of tape to act as an alignment mark to centralise the steering wheel when refitting.
4 Remove the airbag unit from the steering wheel as described in Chapter 12.
5 Loosen the steering wheel centre retaining bolt slightly. A degree of force is required to undo the bolt and this will prevent damage to the contact reel when it is locked in place.
6 Ensure the steering wheel is in the 'straight-ahead' position and then (where fitted) remove the locking peg (for the airbag clock spring) screw from its storage position.
7 Undo the steering wheel centre retaining bolt **(see illustration)**.
8 Lift the steering wheel off the column shaft, and feed the wiring and plastic strip through the hole in the wheel. Fit the locking peg to the airbag clock spring, or alternatively tape the two sections of the clock spring together.

Refitting

9 Ensure that the front wheels are still in the straight-ahead position.
10 Feed the wiring through the hole in the steering wheel, then engage the wheel with the steering column shaft. Ensure that the marks made on removal are aligned, and that the pegs on the contact reel engage with the recesses on the steering wheel hub. Note that the upper shroud is attached to the instrument panel surround. Do not attempt to turn the steering wheel with the contact reel locked, otherwise the reel will be damaged.
11 Fit a new steering wheel retaining bolt and tighten it to the specified torque.
12 Refit the airbag unit to the steering wheel as described in Chapter 12.

19 Steering column – removal and refitting

Note: *Whilst not strictly necessary, removal of the steering wheel will make access to the column wiring and mounting bolts considerably easier.*

18.7 Removing the steering wheel

Removal

1 Disconnect the battery negative lead – see Chapter 5.
2 Fully extend the steering column then remove the steering wheel (see Section 18).
3 Remove the steering column shrouds. Unclip the flexible section below the instrument panel from the rear of the top shroud and unclip the top shroud from the lower shroud. Undo the 3 screws from under the steering column lower shroud and remove **(see illustration)**.
4 Remove the steering wheel control module. Undo the 4 screws, disconnect the wiring plug, and remove the module **(see illustration)**. Note that on refitting, the module may need to be reprogrammed using dedicated Volvo test equipment – entrust this task to a Volvo dealer or suitably-equipped specialist.
5 Where fitted disconnect the wiring plug from the key reader coil and insert the key. Turn the key to the first position, depress the locking tang and release the interlock cable from the back of the steering column lock **(see illustration)**.
6 Remove the trim panel under the facia on the driver's side. Disconnect the wiring plug from the footwell light.
7 On XC90 models, release the gaiter from the base of the column **(see illustration)**.
8 Undo the pinch-bolt at the universal joint on the intermediate steering column shaft, and pull the joint up from the lower shaft. On XC90 models this is easier if the bolt is removed from beneath the vehicle **(see illustration)**. Discard the bolt, a new one must be fitted.
9 Detach the wiring loom guide **(see**

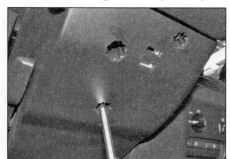

19.3 Remove the lower shroud

19.4 Remove the module

19.5 Disconnect the interlock cable (XC90 models)

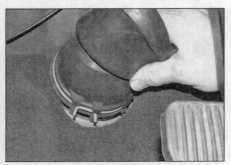

19.7 Release the gaiter

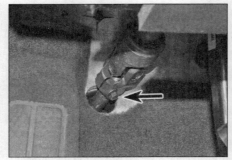

19.8 The column pinch bolt on XC60 models (arrowed)

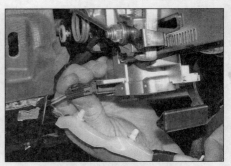

19.9 Release the wiring plug and loom

19.10a On XC60 models, remove the upper…

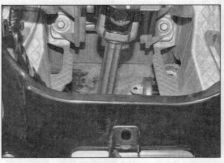

19.10b …and the lower bolts

19.10c Remove the column

illustration) from the underside of the column, and allow it to hang down.

10 Undo the four bolts securing the column to the facia, and pull the assembly rearwards, disconnecting any wiring plugs as it is withdrawn (shown with the column removed for clarity) **(see illustrations)**.

Refitting

11 Refitting is a reversal of removal, bearing in mind the following points:

a) *Lubricate the intermediate shaft splines with grease before engaging the steering column.*

b) *When refitting the column retaining bolts, tighten the rearmost bolts first.*

c) *Use a new universal joint pinch-bolt.*

20 Steering lock – removal and refitting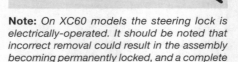

Note: *On XC60 models the steering lock is electrically-operated. It should be noted that incorrect removal could result in the assembly becoming permanently locked, and a complete new steering column would be required.*

1 Remove the steering column from the vehicle, as described in Section 19.

2 Where applicable turn the key to position one (I). The lock must be free to turn.

3 Drill out the security bolts **(see illustration)**. Use a 6mm drill bit and only drill to maximum depth of 15mm.

4 When refitting, fit new 'shear' bolts and tighten them until the heads break off.

21 Steering rack – removal and refitting

Note: *Volvo suggest that on XC60 models this task can be undertaken by lowering the rear of the front subframe. In practice, this is likely to prove difficult unless the vehicle can be raised sufficiently using a ramp or lift. Unless you have the facilities it Is strongly recommended that the front subframe Is removed with the steering rack attached.*

Removal

1 Undo the steering column pinch-bolt at the universal joint in the driver's footwell. Discard the pinch-bolt nut, a new one must be fitted.

2 Drain the power steering fluid reservoir by disconnecting the pipe at the bottom of the reservoir and collecting the fluid in a suitable container.

3 On XC60 models, wipe clean the area around the fluid pipe unions on the steering rack pinion housing, unscrew the union nut and carefully pull the pipes clear **(see illustration)**. An alternative method is to release the hose clip from the return pipe and then (where fitted) release the spring lock type connector from the supply line. This is located in front of the steering rack, adjacent to the subframe. Be prepared for some fluid leakage.

20.3 Drill out the shear bolts (arrowed)

21.3 Remove the bolt (arrowed)

4 On XC90 models disconnect the fluid delivery and return lines from the inner wing **(see illustrations)**.
5 Follow the procedure for removing the front subframe as described in Section 9.
6 Undo the 2 bolts securing the steering rack to the subframe and withdraw the assembly.

Refitting

7 Refitting is a reversal of removal, using new bolts tightened to the specified torque.
8 Refill and bleed the steering rack as described in Section 23.
9 Have the front wheel toe-in checked and adjusted by a suitably-equipped repairer.

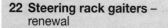

22 Steering rack gaiters – renewal

1 Count and record the number of exposed threads on the track rod from the end of the rod to the track rod end locknut.
2 Remove the track rod end on the side concerned as described in Section 26. Unscrew the locknut from the track rod.
3 Release the two clips and peel off the gaiter **(see illustrations)**.
4 Clean out any dirt and grit from the inner end of the track rod and (when accessible) the rack.
5 Wrap insulating tape around the track rod threads to protect the new gaiter whilst installing.
6 Refit the track rod end locknut, and position it so that the same number of threads counted on removal are visible.
7 Refit the track rod end as described in Section 26.

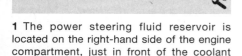

23 Steering rack – bleeding

1 The power steering fluid reservoir is located on the right-hand side of the engine compartment, just in front of the coolant expansion tank.
2 The MAX and MIN marks are indicated on the reservoir. The fluid level must be kept within the marks at all times.
3 If topping-up is necessary, wipe clean the area around the reservoir filler neck, and unscrew the filler cap from the reservoir. Use clean fluid of the specified type (see *Lubricants and fluids*).
4 After component renewal, or if the fluid level has been allowed to fall so low that air has entered the hydraulic system, bleeding must be carried out as follows.
5 Fill the reservoir to the correct level as described above.
6 Chock the rear wheels, then jack up the front of the vehicle and support it on axle stands (see *Jacking and vehicle support*).
7 Turn the steering wheel repeatedly from full

21.4a Remove the clip...

22.3a Release the inner . . .

lock one way, to full lock the other way, and top-up the fluid level as necessary.
8 Lower the car to the ground then start the engine and allow it to idle.
9 Turn the steering wheel slowly to the full-right lock position, and hold it there for 2 seconds.
10 Now turn the steering wheel slowly to the full-left lock position, and hold it there for 2 seconds.
11 Top-up the fluid level again if necessary.
12 Repeat paragraphs 9 and 10 ten. Repeatedly check and if necessary top-up the fluid level during this operation.
13 On completion, stop the engine, recheck the fluid level then refit the reservoir filler cap.

24 Steering pump – removal and refitting

Note: *All models except later XC60 models feature standard power steering with a belt driven pump. Later XC60 models feature an electro-hydraulic power steering (EHPS) pump.*

Removal – models with standard power steering

1 Pull up and remove the engine cover.
2 Remove the auxiliary drivebelt (s) as described in Chapter 1.
3 On XC60 models remove the air deflector from below the bumper and then remove the AC compressor mounting bolts. Support the compressor and move it to one side.

21.4b ...and use a spring lock tool to release the pipe

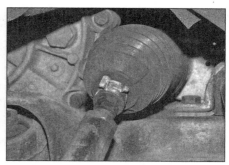
22.3b . . . and outer steering rack gaiter clips

4 Have a clean container ready and then remove the supply and pressure pipes from the side of the pump. Be prepared for fluid leakage and seal the openings of the pipes to prevent contamination **(see illustration)**.
5 Undo the bolt securing the pipe mounting bracket to the side of the pump.
6 Working through the pump pulley, undo the 3 bolts and withdraw the pump from the engine bay.

Removal – models with EHPS steering

7 Jack up and support the front of the vehicle - see *Jacking and vehicle support* in the reference section. Remove the right-hand road wheel.
8 Remove the right-hand wing liner and the bumper cover -as described in Chapter 11.
9 Have a clean container ready and then remove the return pipe and pressure pipe from

24.4 Seal the outlets from the power steering pump (XC90)

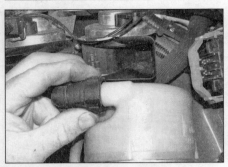

24.9a Remove the return pipe...

24.9b ...and the supply pipe (arrowed)

24.10a Disconnect the wiring plug...

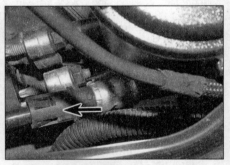

24.10b ...and remove the mounting bolts

the side of the pump (see illustrations). Be prepared for fluid leakage and seal the openings of the pipes to prevent contamination.
10 Disconnect the wiring plug and then remove the 4 mounting bolts (see illustrations).

Refitting

11 Refitting is a reversal of removal, bearing in mind the following points:
a) Use new O-ring seals where fitted.

25.4 Remove the upper radiator locating lugs

25.8 Undo the screw (arrowed) securing the power steering oil cooler to the radiator

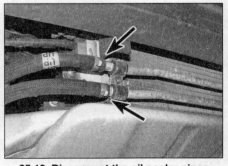

25.10 Disconnect the oil cooler pipes (arrowed)

b) Tighten the pump mounting bolts to the specified torque.
c) Refit the auxiliary drivebelt as described in Chapter 1.
d) Refill/top-up the fluid reservoir, and bleed the system as described in Section 23.
e) If a new EHPS pump has been fitted then have a Volvo dealer or suitably equipped garage install the necessary pump calibration software.

25 Steering oil cooler – removal and refitting

Removal – XC60

1 Remove both headlights as described in Chapter 12.
2 Remove the front bumper as described in Chapter 11.
3 Drain the power steering fluid reservoir by disconnecting the pipe at the bottom of the reservoir and collecting the fluid in a suitable container.
4 Undo the screws and remove the triangular plastic upper radiator locating lugs (see illustration). Gently tilt the radiator rearwards a little.
5 Working from the side of the right-hand side headlamp aperture, undo the steering fluid pipe bracket.
6 Disconnect the steering fluid pipe union adjacent to the fluid reservoir (see illustration). Be prepared for fluid spillage.
7 Working from the front of the vehicle, remove the plastic panel on the right-hand side of the radiator.
8 Undo the screw securing the oil cooler to the radiator and remove the oil cooler and pipework from the front of the radiator (see illustration).

Removal – XC90

9 Jack up and support the front of the vehicle -see *Jacking and vehicle support* in the reference section.
10 Place a large clean container below the cooler and disconnect the hoses from the cooler (see illustration).
11 Unbolt and remove the cooler.

Refitting

12 Refitting is a reversal of removal. Top-up and bleed the system as described in Section 23.

26 Track rod end – removal and refitting

Removal

1 Loosen the appropriate front wheel bolts. Chock the rear wheels, then jack up the front of the vehicle and support it on axle stands (see *Jacking and vehicle support*). Remove the roadwheel.

26.2 Slacken the track rod end locknut (arrowed)

26.3a Undo the track rod end balljoint nut...

26.3b ...and separate the balljoint using a balljoint separator

2 Counterhold the track rod, and slacken the track rod end locknut by half a turn **(see illustration)**. If the locknut is now left in this position, it will act as a guide for refitting.

3 Unscrew the track rod end balljoint nut. Separate the balljoint from the steering arm with a proprietary balljoint separator, then remove the nut and disengage the balljoint from the arm **(see illustrations)**.

4 Unscrew the track rod end from the track rod, counting the number of turns needed to remove it. Make a note of the number of turns, so that the tracking can be reset (or at least approximated) on refitting.

Refitting

5 Screw the track rod end onto the track rod by the same number of turns noted during removal.

6 Engage the balljoint in the steering arm. Fit a new nut and tighten it to the specified torque.

7 Counterhold the track rod and tighten the locknut.

8 Refit the front wheel, lower the car and tighten the wheel bolts in a diagonal sequence to the specified torque.

9 Have the front wheel toe-in (tracking) checked and adjusted by a Volvo dealer or suitably-equipped garage.

27 Wheel alignment and steering angles – general information

1 A car's steering and suspension geometry is defined in four basic settings – all angles are expressed in degrees; the relevant settings are camber, castor, steering axis inclination, and toe setting **(see illustration)**. On the models covered by this manual, only the front camber, and the front and rear wheel toe settings are adjustable. All other suspension and steering angles are set during manufacture, and no adjustment is possible. It can be assumed, therefore, that unless the vehicle has suffered accident damage, all the preset angles will be correct.

Camber

2 Camber is the angle at which the front wheels are set from the vertical when viewed from the front or rear of the car. Negative camber is the amount (in degrees) that the wheels are tilted inward at the top from the vertical.

3 The front camber angle is adjusted by slackening the hub carrier-to-suspension strut mounting bolts and repositioning the hub carrier assemblies as necessary.

Castor

4 Castor is the angle between the steering axis and a vertical line when viewed from each side of the car. Positive castor is when the steering axis is inclined rearward at the top.

Steering axis inclination

5 Steering axis inclination is the angle (when viewed from the front of the vehicle) between the vertical and an imaginary line drawn through the front suspension strut upper mounting and the control arm balljoint.

Toe

6 Toe setting is the amount by which the distance between the front inside edges of the roadwheels (measured at hub height) differs from the diametrically opposite distance measured between the rear inside edges of the roadwheels. Toe-in is when the roadwheels point inwards, towards each other at the front, while toe-out is when they splay outwards from each other at the front.

7 The front wheel toe setting is adjusted by altering the length of the steering track rods on both sides. This adjustment is normally referred to as the tracking.

8 The rear wheel toe setting is adjusted by altering the position of the rear suspension transverse arm-to-trailing arm mountings.

9 Special optical measuring equipment is necessary to accurately check and adjust the front and rear toe settings, and front camber angles, and this work should be carried out by a Volvo dealer or similar expert. Most tyre fitting centres have the expertise and equipment to carry out at least a front wheel toe setting (tracking) check for a nominal charge.

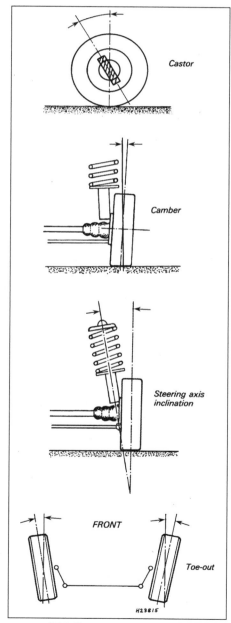

27.1 Front wheel geometry

28.3a Front height sensor retaining screws (arrowed)

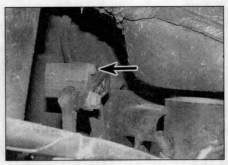

28.3b Rear height sensor retaining screw (arrowed)

28 Suspension ride height sensor – removal and refitting

Removal

1 Jack up the front or rear of the vehicle and support it securely on axle stands (see *Jacking and vehicle support*).

2 Undo the nut and disconnect the link arm from the front or rear sensor.

3 Disconnect the sensor wiring plug, undo the retaining screws and remove the sensor **(see illustrations)**.

Refitting

4 Refitting is a reversal of removal.

Chapter 11
Bodywork and fittings

Contents

Degrees of difficulty

Easy, suitable for novice with little experience	**Fairly easy,** suitable for beginner with some experience	**Fairly difficult,** suitable for competent DIY mechanic	**Difficult,** suitable for experienced DIY mechanic	**Very difficult,** suitable for expert DIY or professional

Specifications

Torque wrench settings*

	Nm	lbf ft
Bonnet hinge bolts	24	18
Door hinge bolts	24	18
Facia (to crossmember)	10	7
Centre console brackets (M8)	24	18
Front seat retaining bolts	40	30
Seat belts:		
Anchorage to front seat	45	33
All other bolts	40	30
Rear seat cushion retaining bolts	25	18
Tailgate hinge bolts	24	18

* Volvo specify that where a fixing requires angular tightening it must always be renewed. Any fixing retained with a thread locking compound must also be renewed. Nuts with a nylon insert must always be renewed.

1 General information

The bodyshell is made of pressed-steel sections, with the addition of some structural aluminium sections . Most components are welded together, but some use is made of structural adhesives. The doors and door pillars are reinforced (with high strength boron steel) against side impacts as part of the side impact protection system (SIPS).

A number of structural components and body panels are made of galvanised steel to provide a high level of protection against corrosion. Extensive use is also made of plastic materials, mainly in the interior, but also in exterior components. The front and rear bumpers are moulded from a synthetic material that is very strong and yet light. Plastic components such as wheel arch liners are fitted to the underside of the vehicle to further improve corrosion resistance.

2 Maintenance – bodywork and underframe

The general condition of a vehicle's bodywork is the one thing that significantly affects its value. Maintenance is easy but needs to be regular. Neglect, particularly after minor damage, can lead quickly to further deterioration and costly repair bills. It is important also to keep watch on those parts of the vehicle not immediately visible, for instance the underside, inside all the wheel arches and the lower part of the engine compartment.

The basic maintenance routine for the bodywork is washing preferably with a lot of water, from a hose. This will remove all the loose solids which may have stuck to the vehicle. It is important to flush these off in such a way as to prevent grit from scratching the finish. The wheel arches and underframe need washing in the same way to remove any accumulated mud which will retain moisture and tend to encourage rust. Oddly enough, the best time to clean the underframe and wheel arches is in wet weather when the mud is thoroughly wet and soft. In very wet weather the underframe is usually cleaned of large accumulations automatically and this is a good time for inspection.

Periodically, except on vehicles with a wax-based underbody protective coating, it is a good idea to have the whole of the underframe of the vehicle steam-cleaned, engine compartment included, so that a thorough inspection can be carried out to see what minor repairs and renovations are necessary. Steam-cleaning is available at many garages, and is necessary for removal of the accumulation of oily grime which

sometimes is allowed to become thick in certain areas. If steam-cleaning facilities are not available, there are one or two excellent grease solvents available which can be brush applied; the dirt can then be simply hosed off. Note that these methods should not be used on vehicles with wax-based underbody protective coating, or the coating will be removed. Such vehicles should be inspected annually, preferably just prior to winter, when the underbody should be washed down and any damage to the wax coating repaired using underseal. Ideally, a completely fresh coat should be applied. It would also be worth considering the use of such wax-based protection for injection into door panels, sills, box sections, etc, as an additional safeguard against rust damage where such protection is not provided by the vehicle manufacturer.

After washing paintwork, wipe off with a chamois leather to give an unspotted clear finish. A coat of clear protective wax polish will give added protection against chemical pollutants in the air. If the paintwork sheen has dulled or oxidised, use a cleaner/polisher combination to restore the brilliance of the shine. This requires a little effort, but such dulling is usually caused because regular washing has been neglected. Care needs to be taken with metallic paintwork, as special non-abrasive cleaner/polisher is required to avoid damage to the finish.

Always check that the door and ventilator opening drain holes and pipes are completely clear, so that water can be drained out. Brightwork should be treated in the same way as paintwork. Windscreens and windows can be kept clear of the smeary film which often appears by the use of a proprietary glass cleaner. Never use any form of wax or other body or chromium polish on glass, especially not on the windscreen or tailgate.

3 Maintenance – upholstery and carpets

Mats and carpets should be brushed or vacuum cleaned regularly to keep them free of grit. If they are badly stained, remove them from the vehicle for scrubbing or sponging, and make quite sure they are dry before refitting. Seats and interior trim panels can be kept clean by wiping with a damp cloth and a proprietary upholstery cleaner. If they do become stained (which can be more apparent on light-coloured upholstery) use a little liquid detergent and a soft nail brush to scour the grime out of the grain of the material. Do not forget to keep the headlining clean in the same way as the upholstery. When using liquid cleaners inside the vehicle, do not over-wet the surfaces being cleaned. Excessive damp could get into the seams and padded interior causing stains, offensive odours or even rot.

4 Minor body damage – repair

Minor scratches

If the scratch is very superficial, and does not penetrate to the metal of the bodywork, repair is very simple. Lightly rub the area of the scratch with a paintwork renovator, or a very fine cutting paste, to remove loose paint from the scratch, and to clear the surrounding bodywork of wax polish. Rinse the area with clean water.

In the case of metallic paint, the most commonly-found 'scratches' are not in the paint, but in the lacquer top coat, and appear white. If care is taken , these can sometimes be rendered less obvious by very careful use of paintwork renovator (which would otherwise not be used on metallic paintwork); otherwise, repair of these scratches can be achieved by applying lacquer with a fine brush.

Apply touch-up paint to the scratch using a fine paint brush; continue to apply fine layers of paint until the surface of the paint in the scratch is level with the surrounding paintwork. Allow the new paint at least two weeks to harden: then blend it into the surrounding paintwork by rubbing the scratch area with a paintwork renovator or a very fine cutting paste. Finally, apply wax polish.

Where the scratch has penetrated right through to the metal of the bodywork, causing the metal to rust, a different repair technique is required. Remove any loose rust from the bottom of the scratch with a penknife, then apply rust-inhibiting paint, to prevent the formation of rust in the future. Using a rubber or nylon applicator fill the scratch with bodystopper paste. If required, this paste can be mixed with cellulose thinners, to provide a very thin paste which is ideal for filling narrow scratches. Before the stopper-paste in the scratch hardens, wrap a piece of smooth cotton rag around the top of a finger. Dip the finger in cellulose thinners, and then quickly sweep it across the surface of the stopper-paste in the scratch; this will ensure that the surface of the stopper-paste is slightly hollowed. The scratch can now be painted over as described earlier in this Section.

Dents

When deep denting of the vehicle's bodywork has taken place, the first task is to pull the dent out, until the affected bodywork almost attains its original shape. There is little point in trying to restore the original shape completely, as the metal in the damaged area will have stretched on impact, and cannot be reshaped fully to its original contour. It is better to bring the level of the dent up to a point which is about 3 mm below the level of the surrounding bodywork. In cases where the dent is very shallow anyway, it is not worth trying to pull it out at all. If the underside of the dent is accessible, it can be hammered out gently from behind, using a mallet with a wooden or plastic head. Whilst doing this, hold a suitable block of wood firmly against the outside of the panel to absorb the impact from the hammer blows and thus prevent a large area of the bodywork from being 'belled-out'.

Should the dent be in a section of the bodywork which has a double skin or some other factor making it inaccessible from behind, a different technique is called for. Drill several small holes through the metal inside the area – particularly in the deeper section. Then screw long self-tapping screws into the holes just sufficiently for them to gain a good purchase in the metal. Now the dent can be pulled out by pulling on the protruding heads of the screws with a pair of pliers.

The next stage of the repair is the removal of the paint from the damaged area, and from an inch or so of the surrounding 'sound' bodywork. This is accomplished most easily by using a wire brush or abrasive pad on a power drill, although it can be done just as effectively by hand using sheets of abrasive paper. To complete the preparation for filling, score the surface of the bare metal with a screwdriver or the tang of a file, or alternatively, drill small holes in the affected area. This will provide a really good 'key' for the filler paste.

To complete the repair, see the Section on filling and re-spraying.

Rust holes or gashes

Remove all paint from the affected area, and from an inch or so of the surrounding 'sound' bodywork, using an abrasive pad or a wire brush on a power drill. If these are not available, a few sheets of abrasive paper will do the job just as effectively. With the paint removed, you will be able to gauge the severity of the corrosion, and therefore decide whether to renew the whole panel (if this is possible) or to repair the affected area. New body panels are not as expensive as most people think, and it is often quicker and more satisfactory to fit a new panel than to attempt to repair large areas of corrosion.

Remove all fittings from the affected area, except those which will act as a guide to the original shape of the damaged bodywork. Then, using tin snips or a hacksaw blade, remove all loose metal and any other metal badly affected by corrosion. Hammer the edges of the hole inwards in order to create a slight depression for the filler paste.

Wire-brush the affected area to remove the powdery rust from the surface of the remaining metal. Paint the affected area with rust-inhibiting paint; if the back of the rusted area is accessible treat this also.

Before filling can take place, it will be necessary to block the hole in some way. This can be achieved by the use of aluminium or plastic mesh, or aluminium tape.

Aluminium or plastic mesh or glass fibre matting is probably the best material to use for a large hole. Cut a piece to the approximate size and shape of the hole to be filled, then position it in the hole so that its edges are below the level of the surrounding bodywork. It can be retained in position by several blobs of filler paste around its periphery.

Aluminium tape should be used for small or very narrow holes. Pull a piece off the roll and trim it to the approximate size and shape required, then pull off the backing paper (if used) and stick the tape over the hole; it can be overlapped if the thickness of one piece is insufficient. Burnish down the edges of the tape with the handle of a screwdriver or similar, to ensure that the tape is securely attached to the metal underneath.

Filling and re-spraying

Before using this Section, see the Sections on dent, deep scratch, rust holes and gash repairs.

Many types of bodyfiller are available, but generally speaking those proprietary kits which contain a tin of filler paste and a tube of resin hardener are best for this type of repair; some can be used directly from the tube. A wide, flexible plastic or nylon applicator will be found invaluable for imparting a smooth and well contoured finish to the surface of the filler.

Mix up a little filler on a clean piece of card or board – measure the hardener carefully (follow the maker's instructions on the pack) otherwise the filler will set too rapidly or too slowly. Using the applicator, apply the filler paste to the prepared area; draw the applicator across the surface of the filler to achieve the correct contour and to level the filler surface. As soon as a contour that approximates to the correct one is achieved, stop working the paste – if you carry on too long the paste will become sticky and begin to 'pick up' on the applicator. Continue to add thin layers of filler paste at twenty-minute intervals until the level of the filler is just proud of the surrounding bodywork.

Once the filler has hardened, excess can be removed using a metal plane or file. From then on, progressively finer grades of abrasive paper should be used, starting with a 40-grade production paper and finishing with 400-grade wet-and-dry paper. Always wrap the abrasive paper around a flat rubber, cork, or wooden block – otherwise the surface of the filler will not be completely flat. During the smoothing of the filler surface the wet-and-dry paper should be periodically rinsed in water. This will ensure that a very smooth finish is imparted to the filler at the final stage.

At this stage the 'dent' should be surrounded by a ring of bare metal, which in turn should be encircled by the finely 'feathered' edge of the good paintwork. Rinse the repair area with clean water, until all of the dust produced by the rubbing-down operation has gone.

Spray the whole repair area with a light coat of primer – this will show up any imperfections in the surface of the filler. Repair these imperfections with fresh filler paste or bodystopper, and once more smooth the surface with abrasive paper. If bodystopper is used, it can be mixed with cellulose thinners to form a really thin paste which is ideal for filling small holes. Repeat this spray and repair procedure until you are satisfied that the surface of the filler, and the feathered edge of the paintwork are perfect. Clean the repair area with clean water and allow to dry fully.

The repair area is now ready for final spraying. Paint spraying must be carried out in a warm, dry, windless and dust free atmosphere. This condition can be created artificially if you have access to a large indoor working area, but if you are forced to work in the open, you will have to pick your day very carefully. If you are working indoors, dousing the floor in the work area with water will help to settle the dust which would otherwise be in the atmosphere. If the repair area is confined to one body panel, mask off the surrounding panels; this will help to minimise the effects of a slight mis-match in paint colours. Bodywork fittings (eg chrome strips, door handles etc) will also need to be masked off. Use genuine masking tape and several thicknesses of newspaper for the masking operations.

Before commencing to spray, agitate the aerosol can thoroughly, then spray a test area (an old tin, or similar) until the technique is mastered. Cover the repair area with a thick coat of primer; the thickness should be built up using several thin layers of paint rather than one thick one. Using 400 grade wet-and-dry paper, rub down the surface of the primer until it is really smooth. While doing this, the work area should be thoroughly doused with water, and the wet-and-dry paper periodically rinsed in water. Allow to dry before spraying on more paint.

Spray on the top coat, again building up the thickness by using several thin layers of paint. Start spraying in the centre of the repair area and then, with a single side-to-side motion, work outwards until the whole repair area and about 50 mm of the surrounding original paintwork is covered. Remove all masking material 10 to 15 minutes after spraying on the final coat of paint.

Allow the new paint at least two weeks to harden, then, using a paintwork renovator or a very fine cutting paste, blend the edges of the paint into the existing paintwork. Finally, apply wax polish.

Plastic components

With the use of more and more plastic body components by the vehicle manufacturers (eg bumpers, spoilers, and in some cases major body panels), rectification of more serious damage to such items has become a matter of either entrusting repair work to a specialist in this field, or renewing complete components. Repair of such damage by the DIY owner is not really feasible owing to the cost of the equipment and materials required for effecting such repairs. The basic technique

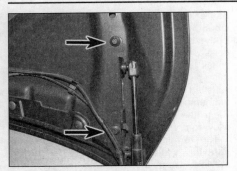

6.4 Unclip the support strut and undo the hinge bolts (arrowed)

involves making a groove along the line of the crack in the plastic using a rotary burr in a power drill. The damaged part is then welded back together by using a hot-air gun to heat up and fuse a plastic filler rod into the groove. Any excess plastic is then removed and the area rubbed down to a smooth finish. It is important that a filler rod of the correct plastic is used, as body components can be made of a variety of different types (eg polycarbonate, ABS, polypropylene).

Damage of a less serious nature (abrasions, minor cracks etc) can be repaired by the DIY owner using a two-part epoxy filler repair material. Once mixed in equal proportions, this is used in similar fashion to the bodywork filler used on metal panels. The filler is usually cured in twenty to thirty minutes, ready for sanding and painting.

If the owner is renewing a complete component himself, or if he has repaired it with epoxy filler, he will be left with the problem of finding a suitable paint for finishing which is compatible with the type of plastic used. At one time the use of a universal paint was not possible owing to the complex range of plastics encountered in body component applications. Standard paints, generally speaking, will not bond to plastic or rubber satisfactorily. However, it is now possible to obtain a plastic body parts finishing kit which consists of a pre-primer treatment, a primer and coloured top coat. Full instructions are normally supplied with a kit, but basically the method of use is to first apply the pre-primer to the component concerned and allow it to

dry for up to 30 minutes. Then the primer is applied and left to dry for about an hour before finally applying the special coloured top coat. The result is a correctly-coloured component where the paint will flex with the plastic or rubber, a property that standard paint does not normally possess.

5 Major body damage – repair

Where serious damage has occurred or large areas need renewal due to neglect, completely new sections or panels will need welding in – this is best left to professionals. If the damage is due to impact, it will also be necessary to check completely the alignment of the body shell structure. Due to the principle of construction, the strength and shape of the whole can be affected by damage to a part. In such instances, the services of a Volvo agent with specialist checking jigs are essential. If a body is left misaligned, it is first of all dangerous as the car will not handle properly and secondly uneven stresses will be imposed on the steering, engine and transmission, causing abnormal wear or complete failure. Tyre wear may also be excessive.

6 Bonnet – removal, refitting and adjustment

Removal

1 Open the bonnet, and disconnect the hoses from the washer jets, as described in Chapter 12.
2 Where applicable, disconnect the washer jet's wiring plugs and pull the loom from the bonnet.
3 Mark around the hinge bracket on the underside of the bonnet with a felt tip pen for reference when refitting. Prise out the clip and pull the support strut from place.
4 With the aid of an assistant, support the bonnet and remove the hinge bolts **(see illustration)**. Lift off the bonnet and store it in a safe place.

Refitting and adjustment

5 Before refitting, place pads of rags under the corners of the bonnet near the hinges to protect the paintwork from damage.
6 Fit the bonnet and insert the hinge bolts. Just nip the bolts up in their previously-marked positions.
7 Reconnect the washer tube and wiring plugs.
8 Shut the bonnet and check its fit. If necessary slacken the bolts and reposition the bonnet.
9 Tighten the hinge bolts securely when adjustment is correct and refit the support.

7 Bonnet release cable – removal, refitting and adjustment

Removal

1 With reference to Chapter 12 remove both front headlights.
2 On XC60 models remove the grille as described in Section 21 of this Chapter, or more easily remove the complete front bumper cover, as described in Section 20.
3 Remove the release catch from the footwell. On all models remove the single screw **(see illustrations)** and then unhook the cable.
4 Disconnect the cable from the bonnet lock - as described in the next section.
5 On left hand drive XC60 models remove the battery (Chapter 5) and then remove the air filter housing (Chapter 4A).
6 To aid refitting mark the position of the cable locating clips and then work along the cable and remove it from the assorted cable clips.
7 Feed the cable through the bulkhead, note the exact routing of the cable and remove it from the vehicle.

Refitting

8 Refit by reversing the removal operations.

8 Bonnet lock – removal and refitting

Removal

1 Remove the grille or bumper cover on XC60 models, and on XC90 models remove the air filter intake duct.
2 On XC60 models remove the air deflectors from each end of the radiator . On XC90 models remove both headlights (Chapter 12) and then (where fitted) unbolt the vacuum pump. Move the pump to one side – there is no need to remove it completely.
3 The cable must be freed from the release handle first, as described in Section 7– this will provide enough slack in the cable to enable it to be unhooked from the lock assemblies. Mark the position of the lock and then undo

7.3a Remove the single bolt from the bonnet release handle (XC90)...

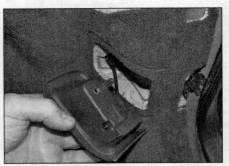

7.3b ...and remove the handle (XC60)

8.3a Remove the mounting bolts (XC60)

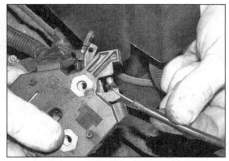

8.3b Disconnecting the cable on XC90 models...

8.3c ...and on XC60 models

the 2 bolts and remove the lock mechanism, disconnecting the cable as the assembly is withdrawn **(see illustrations)**.

Refitting and adjustment

4 Refitting is a reversal of removal. Only finger-tighten the lock retaining bolts, then shut the bonnet to centralise the catch. Tighten the retaining bolts securely.

9 Doors – removal, refitting and adjustment

Removal

1 Disconnect the battery negative lead (see Chapter 5). To aid refitting, use masking tape to make alignment marks on the door panel. As an aid to refitting, at strategic points, measure the gap between the door and the

adjacent panel and note this down **(see illustration)**.
2 Open the door and support it with a jack or axle stand, using rags to protect the paintwork.
3 Disconnect the door electrical wiring. Pull back the rubber boot, then use a small screwdriver to release the clip and unplug the connector. If removing a rear door, release the convoluted sleeve from the door pillar, pull the connector from the pillar, depress the clip and separate the two halves of the connector **(see illustrations)**.
4 Release the door check strap by undoing the bolt securing it to the door pillar **(see illustration)**.
5 Undo the upper and lower hinge bolts at the pillar **(see illustration)**. Recover and note the exact position of any spacers fitted to the door
6 With the help of an assistant, remove the door.

Refitting and adjustment

7 Refit the door by reversing the removal operations.

10 Door interior trim panel – removal and refitting

Removal

Front doors

1 Disconnect the battery (see Chapter 5). Wait at least one minute for any stored electrical energy in the SRS system to dissipate before commencing any work.
2 Carefully prise the speaker trim panel from the door mirror mounting **(see illustration)**.
3 On XC90 models, use a flat-bladed tool

9.1 Make alignment marks and measure the gap

9.3a Disconnect the wiring plug (XC90)

9.3b On XC60 models release the locking tab

9.4 Unbolt the check strap

9.5 Remove the hinge bolts (upper arrowed)

10.2 Remove the speaker panel (XC60)

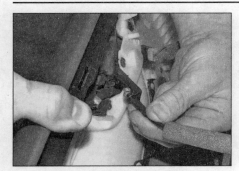

10.5a Release the cable...

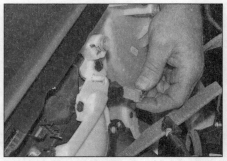

10.5b ...and disconnect the wiring plug(s)

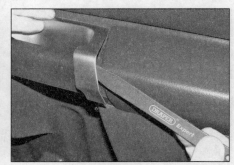

10.8a Release and...

10.8b ...and then remove the trim piece

10.8c Remove the screws (arrowed)

10.8d Remove the screws (XC60)

to prise out the trim piece from the door pull handle. Remove the now exposed screws. On XC60 models undo the two Torx bolts from below the door pull.

4 Use a broad bladed plastic trim tool and release the door panel.

5 With the clips released, pull the panel away from the door sufficiently to gain access to the speaker, electric window, and electric mirror wiring plugs and the handle release cable behind it. Noting their locations, disconnect the plugs and lift the tab on the rear of the door handle to release the cable **(see illustrations)**.

6 Lift the trim panel upwards and away from the door.

Rear doors

7 The rear door panel is removed in a very similar way to the front panel.

8 On the XC90 models remove the door pull trim panel and remove the 2 screws

from beneath. On XC60 models remove the screws from below the pull handle **(see illustrations)**.

9 Use a broad bladed plastic trim tool and release the retaining clips from the edge of the panel **(see illustration)**.

10 With the clips released, pull the panel away from the door sufficiently to gain access to the speaker wiring plug, the electric window wiring plug(s) and the inner handle release cable. Noting their locations, disconnect the plugs and lift the tab on the rear of the door handle to release the cable **(see illustrations 10.5a and 10.5b)**.

11 Lift the trim panel upwards and away from the door.

Refitting

12 Refitting is a reversal of removal. Obtain and fit new fasteners for the base/edges of the panel if any were broken during removal.

Check the operation of all switches before finally fitting the trim panel into place.

---

11 Door handle and lock components – removal and refitting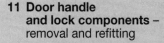

Outer handle

XC60 models

1 The operation is the same for both front and rear doors.

2 Prise out the grommet at the top of the door's rear edge **(see illustration)**.

3 Insert a torx screwdriver through the hole and loosen the screw by no more than 5 turns. The smaller section of the handle can now be removed from the door. The drivers door has the lock cylinder as part of this section of the handle **(see illustrations)**.

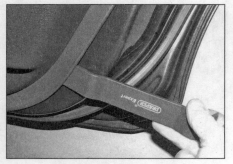

10.9 Release the door panel

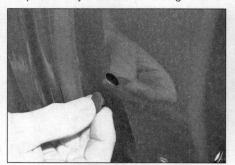

11.2 Remove the grommet

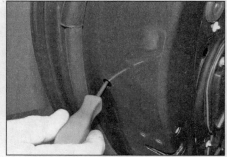

11.3a Release the locking screw...

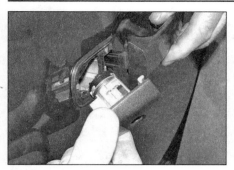

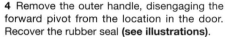
11.3b … and remove the small section of the outer handle

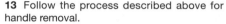
11.4a Remove the handle…

11.4b …and recover the seal

4 Remove the outer handle, disengaging the forward pivot from the location in the door. Recover the rubber seal **(see illustrations)**.

5 Models fitted with a keyless entry system have wiring connected to the outer handle. As the handle is withdrawn, gently pull the wiring connector forwards to lock it in position before separating the connector.

6 Refitting is a reversal of removal.

XC90 models

7 Remove the door inner panel from the appropriate door as described in Section 10.

8 The method of removal is similar for all doors, except for the front door on models fitted with dead locking.

9 If working on the front door (on a model fitted with dead locking) prise the rubber window guide from the channel and then drill out the guide securing rivets from the end of the door (3.5mm drill). Remove the guide channel and (if working on the drivers side door) remove the single screw from the lock/handle anti-theft cover **(see illustrations)**.

10 With difficulty, work the cover free from the door **(see illustration)**.

11 On all doors note the fitted position of the link rod and disconnect it from the handle mechanism. Reach up inside the door and slide back the spring loaded section of the mechanism to release the handle. Pull the handle free and unhook the forward edge.

12 Refitting is a reversal of removal.

Front door lock cylinder

XC60 models

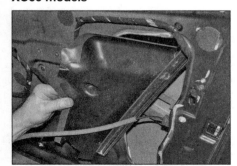
11.10 Work the cover free from the door

13 Follow the process described above for handle removal.

14 Withdraw the lock cylinder and cover from the handle. Release the 2 clips to separate the lock cylinder from the cover.

15 Refitting is a reversal of removal, noting the following points:
   a) *Make sure the lock cylinder is inserted the correct way round.*
   b) *Do not insert the key in the lock cylinder when it is being refitted, or the cylinder may be installed in the wrong position.*

XC90 models

16 Remove the outer handle as described in this section and then remove the smaller section covering the key barrel. Note that this small section will be damaged when it is removed. Volvo insist it must be replaced with a new one, however this part is only supplied painted in primer and will require painting

11.9a Drill out the rivets (arrowed)…

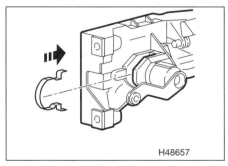
11.18 Prise out the circlip

before fitting. It may of course be possible to secure the old one in position with a suitable adhesive.

17 Remove the 2 screws from behind the now removed handle and then remove the 2 screws from the end of the door.

18 Remove the inner section of the handle assembly from the vehicle, prise out the circlip and remove the lock cylinder **(see illustration)**.

19 Refitting is a reversal of removal.

Front door latch assembly

XC60 models

20 The door latch assembly is removed at the same time as the door carrier, and is attached to the carrier by a retaining clip. Refer to Section 12 for door carrier removal. With the door carrier assembly on the bench separate the latch section from the door handle Inner section **(see illustrations)**. The latch, inner

11.9b …and remove the glass guide channel

11.20a Release the locking tab (arrowed)…

11.20b ...and disconnect the wiring plug

11.29 Remove the membrane

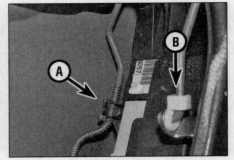

11.30 Disconnect the lock button (A) and the outer handle (B) link rods

11.32 Release the cable

section of the handle, inner handle cover and the interconnecting cables/link rod are available as separate parts.

XC90 models

21 The window must be fully closed before starting work.

22 With reference to Section 10 of this Chapter, remove the door inner panel and then using a sharp blade remove the membrane from the door panel.

23 Disconnect the link rod for the lock button and then remove the glass guide channel. This requires the drilling out of 2 rivets from the end of the door (see illustration 11.09a).

24 If working on the drivers door (and where fitted) remove the anti-theft cover from the handle/key barrel. This is held in position by a single bolt (see illustration 11.10). Unhook the link cables for the outer door handle.

25 Remove the 3 screws from the end of the door, pull the latch into the door frame and disconnect the wiring plug. Remove the latch

12.4a Remove the bolts (arrowed) from the panel

11.37 Remove the screws (arrowed)

assembly from the door. If required unhook the inner handle release cable from the latch.

26 Refitting is a reversal of removal, but fit new rivets to the guide rail.

Rear door latch assembly

27 See the note above regarding removal of the front door lock assembly on XC60 models. The procedure is the same for removal of the rear door latch. On XC90 models the procedure is identical to the removal of the front door latch, except there is no need to drill out the glass guide rail.

XC90 Rear Door latch

28 Remove the door interior panel as described in Section 10.

29 Use a sharp blade and remove the membrane (see illustration).

30 Disconnect the link arm to outer handle and to the inner lock button (see illustration).

31 Remove the screws from the end of the door and release the latch assembly. Unplug

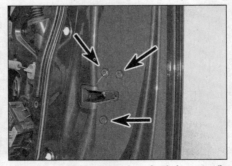

12.4b ...and from the door lock (arrowed)

the wiring connector as the latch is removed from the door.

32 With the assembly on the bench remove the inner handle cable by releasing the outer and unhooking the inner cable (see illustration).

Door interior handles

33 Note that the process is the same for both front and rear doors.

34 Remove the door trim panel as described in Section 10. Disconnect any cables and wiring plugs as the panel is withdrawn.

35 On XC60 models, use a flat-bladed tool and carefully prise off the trim piece above the inner door handle.

36 On XC60 models, the handle is held in place by several crimp type washers and a plastic plug that is bonded to the handle. Cut off the head of the plastic plug and prise off the washers to remove the handle from the door panel.

37 On XC90 models remove the 3 screws and remove the handle (see illustration).

38 On refitting or renewal, the handle should be secured to the door trim panel using locking washers (XC60 models). The remainder is a reversal of removal.

12 Door carrier (XC60 models only) – removal and refitting

Removal

Front door

1 Remove the door inner trim panel as described in Section 10.

2 Remove the outer door handle (and the lock cylinder on the driver's door) as described in Section 11.

3 Release the window glass (as described in Section 13) and secure it to the door frame with adhesive tape.

4 Release any clips securing cables to the panel and undo the 10 bolts securing the carrier to the door. Undo the 3 screws in the rear frame of the door securing the lock assembly (see illustrations). Remove the screw located on the outer door panel (beneath of the outer door handle).

5 Undo the clip and disconnect the wiring plug at the door pillar. Release the clip and

12.6 Remove the panel

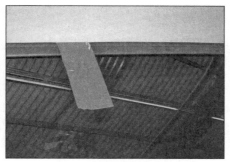

12.9 Secure the glass with tape

12.11 Remove the panel bolts (arrowed)

push the wiring connector into the door as the wiring will be withdrawn as the carrier panel is removed. Disconnect the electric mirror wiring plug and unclip it from the door frame.

6 Manoeuvre the panel assembly from the vehicle **(see illustration)**.

Rear door

7 Remove the door inner trim panel as described in Section 10.

8 Remove the outer door handle as described in Section 11.

9 Release the window glass (as described in Section 13) and secure it in the closed position with adhesive tape **(see illustration)**.

10 Undo the clip and disconnect the wiring plug at the B-pillar. Push the wiring connector into the door as the wiring will be withdrawn as the carrier panel is removed.

11 Undo the 8 bolts securing the carrier to the door **(see illustration)**. Undo the 3 screws in the rear frame of the door securing the lock assembly.

12 Undo the screw located at the pivot point of the outer door handle.

13 Remove the carrier panel, together with the lock assembly, disconnecting any cables or wiring as it is withdrawn.

Refitting

14 For both doors, refitting is a reversal of the removal procedure. Before use, the window position must be initialised, as described in Section 13.

---

13 Door window glass, motor and regulator – removal and refitting

Note: *Whenever the power supply to the electric windows is interrupted the power windows must always be initialised and synchronised on completion of the work. To do this fully lower the window and hold the switch in the down position for 5 seconds. Repeat the procedure with the window fully closed.*

Front door window glass

XC60 models

1 Lower the window until the top of the glass is 185 mm from the weather seal (measured at the rear of the door).

2 Remove the door inner trim panel as described in Section 10 and prise up the inner weather seal. *Remove the seal.*

3 Where fitted lever out the rubber cap at each end of the door carrier.

4 Use a suitable punch or screwdriver and depress the locating clips to release the glass **(see illustration)**.

5 Lift the rear edge of the glass first, and manoeuvre it upwards and out of the door frame.

6 Refitting is a reversal of removal.

XC90 models

7 Lower the window half way down. Remove the door panel as described in Section 10 of this Chapter and then (using a sharp knife) remove the membrane **(see illustration 11.29)**.

8 Remove the inner weather strip.

9 With care prise out the circlip from the slide at the bottom of the window glass **(see illustration)**.

13.4 When correctly aligned the locating peg (arrowed) can be accessed through the glass

13.10 Release the ball from the socket

10 Use a screwdriver and snap the ball joint out of the socket **(see illustration)**.

11 Remove the glass by angling it slightly and lifting it towards the inside of the door frame.

12 Refitting is a reversal of removal.

Rear door window glass

XC60 models

13 Lower the window so that the glass is 150mm above the outer weather strip – measured at the front edge of the door.

14 Remove the door panel as described in Section 10.

15 Use a flat-bladed tool to prise off the outer weather seal. Protect the paint work with masking tape if necessary.

16 Prise the seal from the glass guide channel at the rear of the door and then partially release the door seal at the rear.

17 Using a 5mm drill remove the now exposed rivets **(see illustration)**.

13.9 Remove the circlip

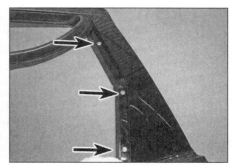

13.17 Drill out the rivets (arrowed)

13.20 Remove the panel

13.21a Remove the grommet...

13.21b ...and release the glass

13.22 Replace the drilled out rivets

13.24a Remove the upper screw...

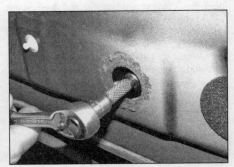

13.24b ...remove the foam cover and then the lower bolt

18 Working on the inside of the door remove the weather seal.

19 Use a 7mm drill bit and remove the single rivet adjacent to the lock button

20 The rear trim piece can now be removed from the door **(see illustration)**.

21 Remove the blanking grommet and using a suitable screwdriver or punch, depress the locating tab and release the glass **(see illustrations)**.

22 Refitting is a reversal of removal, inserting new rivets at the rear of the frame **(see illustration)**.

XC90 models

23 Fully lower the window glass and remove the inner door panel (as described in Section 10). Remove the sound proofing membrane with a sharp knife.

24 Prise out the rubber glass guide channel and then remove the inner weather strip. Remove the screw and bolt from the rear guide channel **(see illustrations)**.

25 Remove the quarter glass, complete with the guide rail by pulling it forward and then up and out from the door.

26 Disconnect the wiring plug, drill out the rivets and remove the loudspeaker.

25 Raise the window glass to the half way point. This will allow access to the glass securing rivets. One rivet is accessed through the speaker hole **(see illustration)** and the other by removing an adjacent foam blanking plug. Drill out the rivets and remove the glass from the door.

26 Refitting is a reversal of removal, but note that fitting new rivets is impossible without a rivet gun with an extremely long nose. If no suitable tool is available, the rivets should be substituted with nuts and bolts.

Front and rear window motor

XC60 models

27 Disconnect the battery negative terminal

as described in Chapter 5, and remove the door trim panel as described in Section 10.

28 Undo the 3 screws securing the motor to the door carrier and disconnect the wiring plug as the motor is withdrawn **(see illustration)**.

29 Refitting is a reversal of the removal procedure.

XC90 models

Note: *On XC90 models the regulator and motor are removed as a complete assembly. Individual parts are not available from Volvo. If there is a fault with the regulator and/or the motor, the assembly must be replaced as a complete unit.*

30 Remove the door inner panel – see Section 10. Lower the window and release the appropriate window as described above. Do not remove the window, but instead use duct tape (or similar strong tape) and secure the glass in the closed position.

31 Drill out the rivets and remove the single

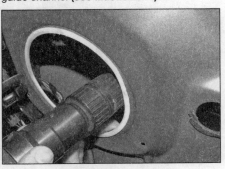

13.25 Drill out the rivet

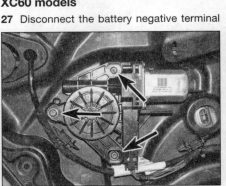

13.28 Remove the screws (arrowed)

13.31 Remove the motor and regulator

bolt (rear motor only) to release the regulator and motor assembly. Disconnect the wiring plug as the assembly is removed **(see illustration)**.
32 Refitting is a reversal of removal, but remember to fit new rivets.

Front and rear window regulator – XC60 models

33 The regulator is integral with the carrier assembly and secured by rivets or screws. Follow the instructions for removing the carrier assembly as described in Section 12, and for removing the window motor as described above. The regulator can then be removed.

14 Tailgate interior trim panel – removal and refitting

Removal

XC60 models

1 Open the tailgate and prise off the cover over the locking catch at the bottom of the tailgate **(see illustrations)**.
2 Undo the screws securing the inner handle **(see illustration)** and remove the handle.
3 Undo the screw on each side securing the upper and lower trims **(see illustration)** and then, starting at the sides and working towards the top, release the clips and remove the upper trim panel.
4 Remove the lower trim panel, releasing the clips at the sides and the bottom. Prise out the switch for the power tailgate and disconnect wiring plug (where fitted).
5 Disconnect the wiring plug for the load space lamp and then use pliers to compress the central locating peg as the panel is removed **(see illustration)**.

XC90 models – upper tailgate

6 Prise free the outer section of the interior handle and remove the single screw – this will leave the inner section of the handle in place **(see illustrations)**.
7 Use a small bladed screwdriver and remove the interior lamp. Disconnect the wiring plug and then remove the single screw **(see illustration)**.
8 Use a plastic type trim tool and fully release the lower panel.

14.1 Remove the cover

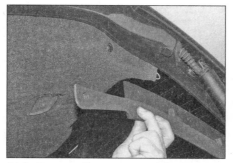
14.3 Remove the screws and then release the upper trim panel

9 Unclip the upper centre trim panel and then release the tailgate side panels

XC90 models – lower tailgate

10 Lift up the spring loaded cover panel.

14.6a Remove the outer section of the handle...

14.7 Remove the screw (arrowed)

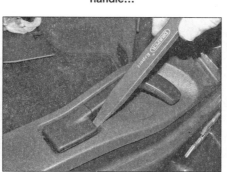
14.11a Prise off the cover...

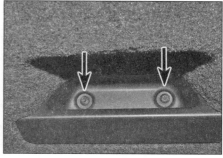
14.2 Remove the screws (arrowed)

14.5 Compress the tabs on the locating peg (panel removed for clarity)

Remove the 3 screws and then remove the main panel.
11 Prise the cover off the release handle, remove the 2 bolts and then remove the handle **(see illustrations)**.

14.6b ...and then remove the single screw (arrowed)

14.11b ...remove the bolts and then the handle

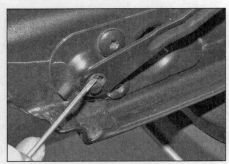

15.12a Remove the circlip...

15.12b ...and release the stay

15.13 Remove the bolts (arrowed)

12 With the main panel removed, remove the 2 outer blanking plugs and then remove the exposed screws. Remove 4 more screws from the panel and then remove the panel.

Refitting

13 Refitting is a reversal of removal.

15 Tailgate – removal and refitting

Removal

XC60 models

1 Open the tailgate, and remove the upper and lower trim panels as described in Section 14.
2 With the panels removed disconnect the assorted wiring plugs from the tailgate.
3 Pull the screen washer pipe free and then (noting the routing) release the wiring loom and washer hose from the tailgate.
4 Support the tailgate and then remove the tailgate support struts – see Section 16.
5 Mark the exact position of the Hinges and then with the aid of an assistant, remove the mounting bolts and remove the tailgate.

XC90 models – upper tailgate

6 Remove the blanking plugs and unscrew the high level brake light. Disconnect the wiring plug and the screen washer pipe as the lamp is removed.
7 Open the upper tailgate and remove the trim panels as described in Section 14.

16.6 Release the circlip

8 Disconnect the wiring plugs from the rear wiper, the rear latch, the rear screen heater and the combined rear release handle and number plate assembly.
9 Noting the routing release the wiring loom and washer hose from the tailgate. Feed the loom and hose up and out of the tailgate.
10 Support the tailgate and then remove the tailgate support struts – see Section 16.
11 Mark the exact position of the hinges and then with the aid of an assistant supporting the tailgate, remove the mounting bolts and remove the tailgate.

XC90 models – lower tailgate

12 Protect the rear bumper with a suitable old rug or blanket and then unclip the stays from each end of the tailgate **(see illustrations)**.
13 Mark the position of the hinges and then with the aid of an assistant to support the tailgate, remove the hinge mounting bolts **(see illustration)** and then remove the tailgate from the vehicle.

Refitting

14 Refitting is a reversal of removal.

16 Tailgate support struts – removal and refitting

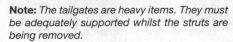

Note: *The tailgates are heavy items. They must be adequately supported whilst the struts are being removed.*

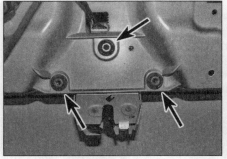

17.2 Remove the screws (arrowed)

Removal

XC60

1 Most XC60 models are fitted with a powered tailgate. Both struts are electrically powered.
2 Remove the tailgate trim panel (as described in Section 14). Disconnect the wiring plug, prise free the grommet and feed the loom out of the tailgate.
3 Support the tailgate and prise free the lower circlip and then prise free the upper clip. Remove the strut.
4 Refitting is a reversal of removal.

XC90

5 Support the tailgate with a suitable length of stout timber.
6 Use a small screwdriver and release the lower and upper locking clips **(see illustration)**. Remove the strut from the vehicle.
7 Refitting is a reversal of removal.

17 Tailgate lock components – removal and refitting

Removal

XC60

Lock assembly

1 Remove the tailgate interior upper and lower trim panels as described in Section 14.
2 Undo the 3 screws and release the cable from the tailgate lock **(see illustration)**. Note that releasing the cable is easier if the cable is removed from the closing motor first, as described below.
3 Disconnect the lock wiring plug and withdraw the lock from the tailgate.

Power tailgate closing motor

4 Follow the steps above for removing the lock assembly. Tucking the lock assembly into the tailgate will allow the cable to be removed from the motor. Undo the 3 screws, disconnect the wiring plug and withdraw the motor.
5 Unhook the operating cable **(see illustration)**.

XC90 – upper tailgate

6 Remove the trim panel as described in Section 14.

17.5 Remove the cable (arrowed)

17.9a Release the cable...

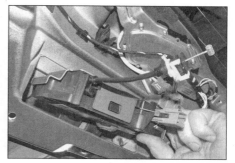

17.9b ...and remove the lock

17.13a Remove the bolts...

17.13b ...unhook the outer...

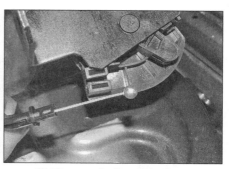

17.13c ...and release the inner

7 Disconnect the wiring plug and then remove the 3 bolts from latch assembly and partially withdraw it.
8 The Bowden cable must now be released from the handle assembly. This is considerably easier if the wiper motor is removed first (see Chapter 12 for details) although it is not essential.
9 Remove the retaining clip from Bowden cable outer and then unhook the inner cable from release handle **(see illustrations)**.
10 To remove the outer release handle, remove the wiper motor as described in Chapter 12 and then disconnect the wiring plug from the handle assembly.
11 Remove the 4 bolts from the tailgate and then remove the handle complete with the number plate lamps. This task is slightly easier if the rear number plate is removed first.

XC90 – lower tailgate

12 Remove the trim panel as described in Section 14.

13 Remove the screws (3 per latch) and lift the latch from the tailgate. Disconnect the release cable from each latch assembly **(see illustrations)**.
14 Remove the 2 bolts and remove the handle (complete with the Bowden cables) from the tailgate **(see illustration)**.

Refitting

15 Refitting is a reversal of removal.

18 Windscreen and other fixed glass – removal and refitting

Special equipment and techniques are needed for successful removal and refitting of the windscreen, rear window and side windows. Have the work carried out by a Volvo dealer or a windscreen specialist.

19 Mirrors and associated components – removal and refitting

⚠️ *Warning: If the mirror glass is broken, wear gloves to protect your hands. This is good advice, in fact, even if the glass is not broken, due to the risk of glass breakage.*

Door mirror glass

1 Pivot the mirror glass into the mirror housing as far as possible on the inside edge.
2 Insert a blunt, flat-bladed tool behind the outer edge of the glass and prise the glass from the mounting. Take care – excessive force will cause the glass to break. Disconnect the wiring plugs as the glass is withdrawn **(see illustrations)**.
3 Refitting is a reversal of removal.

17.14 Remove the handle

19.2a Release the glass at the outer edge (XC60)...

19.2b ...or from the upper edge (XC90)

19.2c Disconnect the wiring connectors

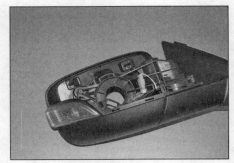

19.6 Note the location of the cover retaining clips (XC60)

19.8 Remove the cover

19.18 Remove the single screw (XC90)

20.2 Depress the centre peg to release the fixings

Door mirror cover

4 Remove the mirror glass as described previously.
5 Insert a small screwdriver into the access hole in the mirror housing and release the clips.
6 Carefully prise the cover from the mirror **(see illustration)**.
7 Refitting is a reversal of removal, ensuring the lip of the cover fits correctly around the edge of the mirror housing.

Door mirror (complete unit)

8 Remove the door interior trim panel as described in Section 10 and then remove the small cover panel **(see illustration)**. Disconnect the mirror wiring plug and release the cable from the cable clips.
9 Locate the single mounting screw on XC90 models or the 3 screws on XC60 models and remove them.

10 Support the mirror and withdraw the mirror from the door. Release the rubber grommet from the door as the mirror is withdrawn and feed the wiring through.
11 Refitting is a reversal of removal.

Interior mirror

Note: *Some models may be fitted with a proximity warning camera, in-vehicle humidity sensor, or electronic compass. Separate covers may need to be removed to gain access to the mirror mounting. Recalibration of these units may also be required on refitting and you should refer to a Volvo dealer or suitably equipped specialist.*

12 Carefully prise off the cover below the mirror to allow access to the mounting.
13 Holding the mirror at the mounting point (and not the mirror itself) rotate clockwise and remove from the mounting. Disconnect any wiring plugs as it is withdrawn.
14 Refitting is a reversal of removal.

Blind spot information system

15 An optional blind spot information system (BLIS) may be fitted to warn the driver of a vehicle in the 'blind spot' area not visible in the door mirror on both sides of the car. The system uses digital camera technology to detect a vehicle in the 'blind spot' area on each side of the car and illuminate a warning light on the inside door panel next to the mirror. A switch on the facia panel allows the driver to enable the system when required. It should be noted that the system does not react to bicycles or mopeds, and at night-time will only react to vehicles with headlamps switched on.

16 The camera is located in the door mirror lower cowl and may be removed by first removing the door mirror cover as described earlier in this Section.
17 The warning light is located on the triangular trim panel over the door mirror mounting nut, and may be removed with reference to the door interior trim panel removal procedure described in Section 10 of this Chapter.

Door mirror motor

18 Remove the mirror glass (as described above) and then remove either the single torx type screw from the centre of the motor **(see illustration)** or the 3 from the circumference.
19 Use a screwdriver and release the motor assembly from the locking tangs. Disconnect the wiring plug as the motor is withdrawn. Most of the individual components of the mirror are available as separate parts from a Volvo dealer.
20 Refitting is a reversal of removal.

20 Bumpers – removal and refitting

Note: *The bumpers consist of several sections, and once the bumper assembly has been removed as described below, further dismantling can take place. Refer to a Volvo dealer for advice on which sections are available separately.*

Front bumper

XC60 models

1 Open the bonnet and disconnect the battery as described in Chapter 5.
2 Work along the top edge of the bumper and remove the fixings **(see illustration)**.
3 Jack up and support the front of the vehicle -see *Jacking and vehicle support* in the reference section.
4 Working in the wheel arch, undo the 6 screws that attach the wheel arch liner to the rear edge of the bumper. Repeat the procedure in the other wheel arch.
5 From beneath the vehicle undo the 3 plastic screws in the centre of the bumper. Whilst not essential removal of the headlights (as described in Chapter 12) will allow the cover to be removed more easily.
6 With the help of an assistant, pull the bumper sides outwards to release the clips below the headlamps and where the bumper meets the front wing, then pull it forward and remove it from the vehicle **(see illustration)**. Note their fitted positions and disconnect the various wiring plugs as the bumper is withdrawn. On models with headlight washers, disconnect the hose at the pump on the washer reservoir.
7 Refitting is a reversal of removal, taking care to ensure that the bumper aligns correctly with surrounding body panels.

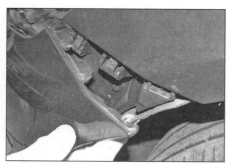

20.6 Release the bumper from the wing

20.8 Release the quarter panels

20.9a Remove the washer covers...

XC90 models

8 Remove the 2 clips (1 per side) and then remove the bumper quarter panels **(see illustration)**.

9 Where fitted remove the covers from the headlight washers and then remove the covers and screws from the mounting points at each side of the radiator **(see illustrations)**.

10 With the aid of an assistant supporting the bumper, free the bumper corners from the front wings **(see illustration)**.

11 Pull the bumper forward, disconnect the headlight washer hose (anticipate some loss of washer fluid) and unplug the wiring connector from the front fog lights. Remove the bumper.

12 Refitting is a reversal of removal.

Rear bumper

XC60 models

13 Open the tailgate and then disconnect the battery negative terminal (see Chapter 5).

14 Remove the bump stop and then undo the Torx screw at the lower corner of the opening on each side **(see illustrations)**.

15 Working in the wheel arch, undo the 5 screws that attach the wheel arch liner to the rear edge of the bumper, and undo the fixing at the top of the bumper.

16 Undo the 2 plastic bolts on the underside of the bumper in the centre.

17 With the help of an assistant, pull the bumper sides outwards to release the clips below the light units and where the bumper meets the rear wing, then pull it rearwards and remove it from the vehicle. Note their fitted positions and disconnect any wiring plugs as the bumper is withdrawn **(see illustrations)**.

20.9b ...and then the mounting bolts

18 Refitting is a reversal of removal taking care to ensure that the bumper aligns correctly with surrounding body panels.

XC90 models

19 Open both sections of the tailgate and lift up the battery compartment cover. Where fitted remove the towbar cover.

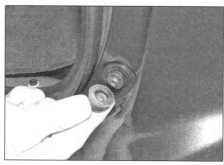

20.14a Remove the bump stop...

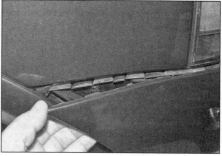

20.10 Unhook the bumper corners

20 Remove the battery as described in Chapter 5. Remove the load area rear quarter floor panels.

21 Working in the battery compartment remove the sound proofing and then remove the 4 bumper retaining nuts **(see illustration)**.

22 Remove the left-hand side load area panel

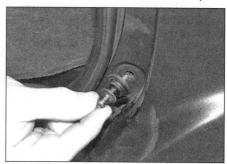

20.14b ...and the torx screw

20.17a Release the bumper...

20.17b ...and disconnect the wiring plug

20.21 Remove the mounting bolts

20.23a Release the trim panel...

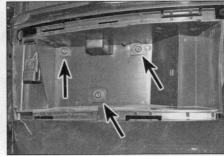

20.23b ...and remove the screws (arrowed)

26 Where fitted disconnect the wiring plugs from the side lamps and then unclip the bumper from the base of the rear wings. Ensure both sections are released as one single part **(see illustration)**.

27 Unhook the locking tangs from below the rear lamps and then remove the bumper from the vehicle.

28 Refitting is a reversal of removal, but remember to obtain and fit new rivets.

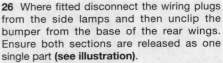

21 Front grille panel – removal and refitting

Removal

1 On X60 models Volvo suggest the grille can be removed with the bumper in place. In practice this proved difficult and there is a risk of damage to the grille and surrounding paintwork, so we recommend removing the bumper first. Using a flat-bladed tool, release the retaining clips around the edge of the grille – there are 4 at the top, 4 at the bottom, and 1 each side towards the top. Remove the grille **(see illustration)**.

2 On XC90 models partially open the bonnet and then prise free the grille **(see illustration)**.

Refitting

3 Refit by reversing the removal operations.

20.25 Drill out the rivets

20.26 Release the bumper

and disconnect the wiring plug for the rear parking sensors – where fitted.

23 On the outside edges of the bumper prise free the trim panels from below the rear lamps and remove the now exposed screws **(see illustrations)**.

24 Jack up and support the rear of the vehicle - see *Jacking and vehicle support* in the reference section.

25 Use a 6mm drill bit and remove the rivets **(see illustration)** from the lower edge of the rear wheel arches (1 per side).

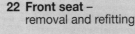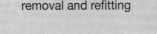

22 Front seat – removal and refitting

Note: *All models are equipped with a SIPS airbag, fitted into the side of the front seat backrest, as part of the side impact protection system; refer to Chapter 12 for further information on the SRS and SIPS systems.*

Removal

1 On all models, raise the seat base to its maximum height and move it fully forward.

2 Release the seat belt lower anchorage by either depressing the quick-release catch through the hole in the cover or by pulling back the rubber flap next to the anchorage. In both case use a small a small screwdriver to depress the clip.

3 On some XC60 models remove the seat side panels.

4 Remove the bolt covers **(see illustrations)** from the rear of the seats and then remove the bolts. Move the seats to the rearward position, remove the front bolt covers and then remove the bolts.

5 Ensure that the ignition is switched off, then disconnect the battery negative lead as described in Chapter 5. Wait at least 5 minutes for any residual electrical energy to dissipate before proceeding.

6 Undo the 7 mm bolt under the front of the seat and disconnect the wiring plug **(see illustration)**.

21.1 Detailed view of the grille locking tabs (arrowed)

21.2 Removing the grille on XC90 models

22.4a Removing the rear cover on XC60 models...

22.4b ...and on XC90 models

7 Check that all wiring plugs have been disconnected and then with the aid of an assistant lift up the seat and manoeuvre it from the vehicle.

Refitting

8 Locate the seat over the guide pins, reconnect the wiring, and insert the retaining bolts. Tighten the bolts securely and refit the bolt covers.
9 Reconnect the seat belt lower anchorage, ensuring that the catch is fully engaged.
10 Make sure that no-one is inside the car, then reconnect the battery negative lead.

23 Rear seat – removal and refitting

Note: *All seats are extremely heavy on both models. Do not attempt to remove them without the aid of an assistant.*

Removal

1 Disconnect the battery as described in Chapter 5. Wait a minimum of five minutes before beginning work

XC60 models

Seat cushion

2 Slide a screwdriver into the side of the seat, locate the catch and push the screwdriver inwards to release the seat **(see illustration)**. Pull the front edge of the seat upwards, slide the cushion towards the front of the car, and remove.

23.6a Rear seat backrest outer bolt (arrowed)

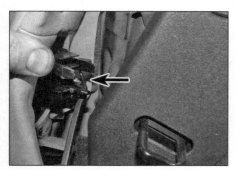
23.9 Release the clip (arrowed) at the top of the side pad

22.6 Release the wiring plug

3 If the seat is heated, slide the cushion forwards slightly and disconnect the wiring plug located at the rear, nearest the side pad. Remove the cushion.

Outer backrest

4 Remove the seat cushion and side pad as described in this Section.
5 Undo the wiring plug and securing bolt and remove the lower seat belt anchorages as appropriate.
6 Undo the bolt at the outer edge of the backrest, nearest to the door, withdraw the pivot from the base of the centre backrest and remove the backrest **(see illustrations)**.

Centre backrest/armrest

7 Remove the outer backrest as described above.
8 Pull out the plastic pivots on each side and remove the backrest/armrest **(see illustration)**.

23.6b Withdraw the pivot from the base of the centre backrest

23.11 Remove the covers

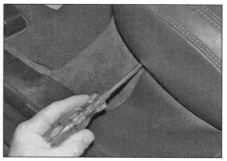
23.2 Release the seat cushion

Side pad

9 Tip the backrest forward and, using a screwdriver and a flat-bladed tool, one inserted on each side, release the clips located towards the top of the side pad **(see illustration)**.
10 Release the clip at the bottom and remove by pulling the side pad upwards and towards the centre of the car.

XC90 models

11 Slide the seat fully forward and remove the covers from the rear seat rails **(see illustration)**.
12 Unbolt the seat rails bolts at the rear and then move the seat to the rear.
13 At the front remove the covers from the seat rails and then unbolt the seat. If working on the centre seat disconnect the wiring plug **(see illustration)**. With care remove the seat from the vehicle

23.8 Pull out the plastic pivots on each side

23.13a Remove the centre cover...

23.13b ...the side cover...

23.13c ...and disconnect the wiring plug

23.15 Remove the panel

XC90 models – third row seats

14 Remove the rear luggage area side panels as described in Section 24.

15 Unbolt and remove the transverse cover panel (**see illustration**).

16 Remove the smaller panels that support the load area quarter panels (**see illustration**).

17 Remove the jack and its compartment and then remove the small polystyrene storage tray from the floor

18 Open the small storage compartment between the seats and remove the cover in the base. Remove the 2 screws and remove the trim panel from between the seats (**see illustrations**).

19 Remove a further small trim piece and then with reference to Section 25 remove the seatbelt lower mounting bolts.

20 Work round the seat frames and remove the mounting bolts – the seats are be removed as a pair.

21 Lift the seats up and angle them to remove

them through the tailgate (**see illustration**). If required the seats can now be removed from the support frames.

Refitting

22 Refit by reversing the removal operations.

24 Interior trim – removal and refitting

General

1 The interior trim panels are secured using either screws or various types of trim fasteners, usually studs or clips.

2 Check that there are no other panels overlapping the one to be removed, or other components hindering removal; usually there is a sequence that has to be followed, and this will only become obvious on close inspection.

3 Some of the interior panels will additionally be retained by the screws which are used to secure other items, such as the grab handles.

4 Remove all visible retainers, such as screws, noting that these may be hidden under small plastic caps. If the panel will not come free, it is held by internal clips or fasteners. These are usually situated around the edges of the panel, and can be prised up to release them; note, however, that they can break quite easily, so new ones should be available. The best way of releasing such clips is to use a large flat-bladed screwdriver or other wide-bladed tool. Note that in many cases, the adjacent sealing strip must be prised back to release a panel.

5 When removing a panel, **never** use excessive force or the panel may be damaged; always check carefully that all fasteners or other relevant components have been removed or released before attempting to withdraw a panel.

6 Refitting is a reversal of removal; secure the fasteners by pressing them firmly into place and ensure that all disturbed components are correctly secured to prevent rattles.

Carpets

7 The passenger compartment floor carpet is in several sections and is secured at the sides by the front and rear sill trim panels.

8 Carpet removal and refitting is reasonably straightforward, but is very time-consuming because all adjoining trim panels must be removed first, as must components such as the seats and seat belt lower anchorages.

Headlining

9 The headlining is clipped to the roof, and

23.16 Remove the support panels

23.18a Remove the cover...

23.18b ...the screws...

23.18c ...and then the panel

23.21 Remove the seats

24.11 Remove the covers to access the mounting bolts (XC90)

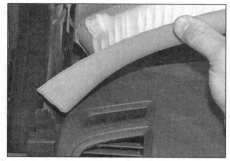

24.12 The lower trim retaining clip (XC60)

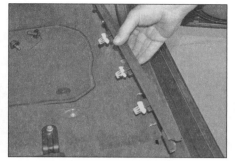

24.15 Remove the door step panel (XC60 shown)

24.18 Remove the panel (XC90)

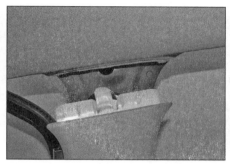

24.19a Note the upper locating tab (XC90)

24.19b Note the position of the lower trim clips (XC60)

can be withdrawn only once all fittings such as grab handles, sunvisors, sunroof (if fitted), fixed window glass, and related trim panels have been removed and the relevant sealing strips have been prised clear.

10 Note that headlining removal and refitting requires considerable skill and experience if it is to be carried out without damage, and is therefore best entrusted to a Volvo dealer or automotive upholstery specialist.

A-pillar trims

11 Prise out the airbag label and undo the bolt in the label aperture. On XC90 models remove the grab handle mounting screws (see illustration).

12 Partially release the door seal if necessary. Pull the top of the A-pillar trim inwards towards the centre of the passenger cabin to release the clips, then pull the trim from the clips at the lower edge. (see illustration).

13 If required on XC90 models the grab handle can be remove from the pillar trim.

14 If any clips are damaged, new ones should be used when refitting, so as not to impair the inflatable safety curtain performance.

B-pillar trims

15 Pull the front door sill trim panel straight up to release it from the retaining clips. Repeat the procedure on the rear door sill trim panel (see illustration).

16 Remove the cover (or move the seal on XC90 models) depress the quick-release catch at the side and remove the seat belt lower anchorage from the outside of the seat.

17 Move the front seat as far forward as

possible, then pull the rubber weatherstrips from the door apertures adjacent to the B-pillar.

18 On XC90 models (where fitted) remove the small trim piece from the base of the B-pillar (see illustration).

19 Pull the lower edge of the B-pillar trim in towards the centre of the cabin to release the clips and disengage the air ducting (where applicable), then pull it downwards at the same time as squeezing together the sides at the top of the trim to release the retaining clips located on the B-pillar below the weatherstrips (see illustrations).

20 Feed the seat belt through the panel and remove it from the cabin.

C-pillar trims

21 On XC60 models remove the rear seat side pad as described in Section 23.

22 Prise the panel free. To remove it completely on XC90 models unbolt the seatbelt

24.23 Remove the speaker cover panel

floor mounting (as described in Section 25) and feed the belt through the panel.

D-pillar trims – XC90 only

23 Prise free the inner trim panel and (where fitted) disconnect the wiring plug from the speaker (see illustration). Slip the seat belt from the panel.

24 Prise the panel free from the D-post. To remove it completely either unbolt the seat belt reel from the base of the pillar (after removing the side trim) and feeding the reel through the panel. Alternatively unbolt the seat belt from the floor mounting as described in Section 25.

Luggage area side panel

25 On all models remove the C-pillar trim as described above. On XC90 models remove the D-pillar trim panel.

26 On XC60 models remove the cant rail panel using a suitable trim tool (see illustration).

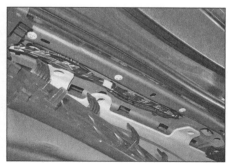

24.26 Remove the cant rail panel (XC60)

24.29a Remove the cover...

24.29b ...and then the bolt

24.30 Remove the cover to access the upper mounting bolt

24.33 Remove the trim panel (XC90)

Remove 2 screws and then prise up and remove the tailgate slam panel.

27 On XC60 models, remove the cover and guide for the rear seat belt inertia reel and then remove the spare wheel cover panel.

28 On XC90 models, remove the floor quarter panels and the side access panels.

29 On all models, prise the covers from the load securing rings and then remove the bolts **(see illustration)**.

30 Locate and remove the upper mounting bolts **(see illustration)**.

31 Pull the panel free at the top edge and then lift it up. Disconnect any wiring plugs and then remove the panel.

Glovebox

32 On XC60 models remove the end panel from the facia. Disconnect the wiring plug from the rear as the panel is removed.

33 Remove the trim panel from below the glovebox **(see illustration)** and where fitted disconnect the wiring plug from the footwell lamp.

34 Prise free the glovebox lamp and disconnect the wiring plug as the lamp is removed. Where fitted unclip the USB connector from the rear of the glovebox.

35 Remove the glovebox retaining screws. There are 8 retaining screws on XC60 models and 9 on XC90 models.

36 On XC60 models release the retain clips from the perimeter and pull the glovebox forward and remove it. There are no retaining clips on XC90 models **(see illustrations)**.

Sunvisor

37 Prise out the plastic covers and undo the bolt and screw exposed in the aperture **(see illustrations)**.

38 Unclip the sunvisor from the inboard mounting and remove it. Disconnect the wiring plug as the sunvisor is withdrawn.

39 To remove the inboard mounting, prise down the retaining tab and remove the mounting from the headlining **(see illustrations)**.

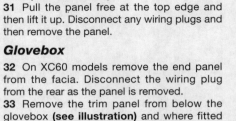

24.36a Removing the glovebox on the XC60...

24.36b ...and on the XC90

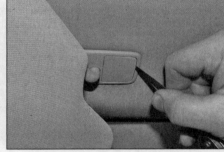

24.37a Prise out the plastic covers...

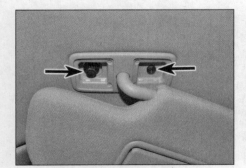

24.37b ...and undo the screw and bolt (arrowed)

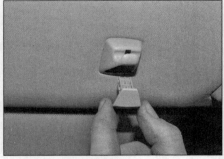

24.39a Prise down the retaining tab

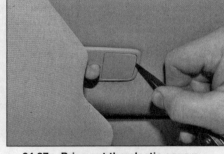

24.39b Remove the mounting from the headlining

Grab handle

40 Hold down the grab handle, prise open the plastic covers and undo the 2 retaining screws **(see illustration)**.

25 Seat belts –
general information, removal and refitting

1 All models are equipped with pyrotechnic front seat belt tensioners as part of the supplemental restraint system (SRS). The system is designed to instantaneously take up any slack in the seat belt in the case of a sudden frontal impact, therefore reducing the possibility of injury to the front seat occupants. Each front seat is fitted with the system, the tensioner being situated behind the upper B-pillar trim panel.

2 The seat belt tensioner is triggered along with the driver's and passenger's airbag, by a frontal impact above a predetermined force. Lesser impacts, including impacts from behind, will not trigger the system.

3 When the system is triggered, the explosive gas in the tensioner mechanism retracts and locks the seat belt through a cable which acts on the inertia reel. This prevents the seat belt moving, and keeps the occupant firmly in position in the seat. Once the tensioner has been triggered, the seat belt will be permanently locked and the assembly must be renewed. If any abnormal rattling noises are heard when pulling out or retracting the belt, this also indicates that the tensioner has been triggered.

4 There is a risk of injury if the system is triggered inadvertently when working on the vehicle, and it is therefore strongly recommended that any work involving the seat belt tensioner system is entrusted to a Volvo dealer or suitably equipped garage. Note the following warnings before contemplating any work on the front seat belts.

⚠ **Warning: Switch off the ignition, disconnect the battery negative lead, and wait for at least 5 minutes for any residual electrical energy to dissipate before starting work involving the seat belts.**

• *Do not expose the tensioner mechanism to temperatures in excess of 100°C.*

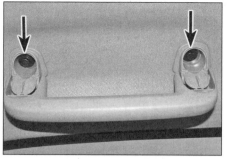

24.40 Undo the two screws (arrowed)

• *If the tensioner mechanism is dropped, it must be renewed, even it has suffered no apparent damage.*
• *Do not allow any solvents to come into contact with the tensioner mechanism.*
• *Do not attempt to open the tensioner mechanism, as it contains explosive gas.*
• *Tensioners from other vehicles, even from the same model and year, must not be fitted.*
• *Tensioners must be discharged before they are disposed of, but this task should be entrusted to a Volvo dealer or specialist.*

Removal

Front seat belts

5 Switch off the ignition then disconnect the battery negative lead as described in Chapter 5. Wait for at least 5 minutes before proceeding.

6 All models feature a quick release type

25.6 Release the seatbelt (XC60)

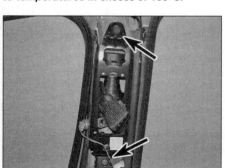

25.9a XC60 upper mounting bolts (arrowed)...

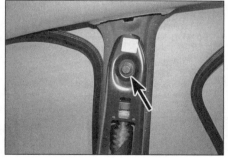

25.9b ...and the XC90 top upper (arrowed)

fitting for the lower seat belt anchor point **(see illustration)**.

7 To remove the inertia reel, remove the B-pillar trim as described in Section 24.

8 Unplug the wiring connector from the seat belt tensioner by squeezing together the two plug retaining clips **(see illustration)**.

9 Unscrew and remove the 3 inertia reel retaining bolts, and remove the seat belt reel and tensioner from the car **(see illustrations)**.

10 To remove the belt buckle, remove the seat first, as described in Section 22. Cut the cable-ties securing the wiring to the seat and disconnect the wiring plug beneath the seat. The buckles are secured with a large Torx bolt.

Rear seat belts

11 Switch off the ignition then disconnect the battery negative lead as described in Chapter 5. Wait for at least 5 minutes before proceeding.

12 To remove the inertia reel, remove the luggage compartment side panel as described In Section 24.

13 Unplug the wiring connector for the seat belt tensioner by squeezing together the two plug retaining clips **(see illustration)**.

14 Undo the bolts securing the upper belt guide and the inertia reel, and remove the inertia reel.

15 On XC60 models, to remove the lower belt anchorage remove the rear seat cushion (as described in Section 23) and the rear sill panel. If necessary, pull up the sound deadening material and fold it back until the anchorage is accessible. Undo the bolt securing the

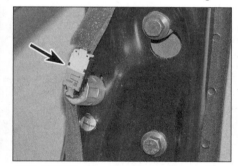

25.8 XC90 front seat belt tensioner wiring plug (arrowed)

25.13 Disconnecting the wiring plug (XC90)

25.15 XC60 buckles and lower seat belt mountings are accessible with the seat removed

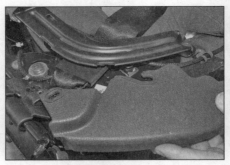

25.16a Remove the panel...

25.16b ...to expose the mounting

25.18a Remove the guide

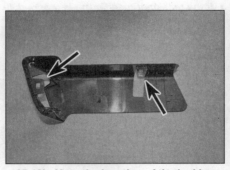

25.18b Note the location of the locking tabs (arrowed)

25.19 Remove the seat back cover

anchorage to the floorpan. The rear seat buckles can also be removed if required **(see illustration)**.

16 On XC90 models the lower seatbelt mounting has a quick release connector.

25.20a Note the location of the small trim piece

25.20b Pivot the panels to release the seat belt

Remove the sill panel and use a screwdriver to release the belt. To remove the buckle, remove the appropriate seat (as described in Section 23) and remove the seat side panel **(see illustrations)**.

Centre rear seat belt

17 On both models the centre seat belt inertia reel is incorporated into the seat back. Remove the seat from the vehicle as described in Section 23.

XC60 models

18 With the seat on the bench remove the upper belt guide and seat latch cover **(see illustrations)**.

19 Using a broad bladed plastic trim tool release the seat back cover. This is best achieved by first releasing the edge of the rear seat front cover **(see illustration)**. Some early models have 4 screws holding the seat back cover in place. Remove these.

20 Release the metal panel from the top of the seat, allowing it to pivot around the rivet. Recover the small plastic trim piece and then unscrew the belt cover from the seat back **(see illustrations)**.

XC90 models

21 With the seat on the bench, remove the belt guide from the top of the seat – 2 small torx head screws.

22 Working with care and using a broad bladed trim tool release the seat cover from the seat back. Turn the seat onto its side, remove a single screw (per side) and then partially remove the seat back from the seat frame **(see illustrations)**.

23 Unhook the outer section of the seat back release handle, push it through the handle from and then release the inner cable **(see illustration)**. Fully remove the seat back from the seat frame.

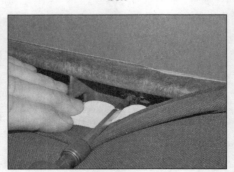

25.22a Release the cover...

25.22b ...and the now exposed screws

25.23 Unhook the cable

25.24 Unbolt the inertia reel

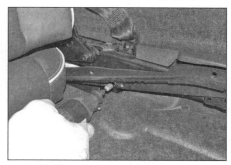
25.27a Remove a small section of the cover to…

24 Unbolt the inertia reel and disconnect the wiring plug **(see illustration)**. Remove the seat belt.
25 To remove the buckle, remove the side cover and unbolt the buckle.

Third row seats – XC90 models only

26 Raise the third row seats into the upright position.
27 To remove the lower seat rail mounting it is necessary to remove some of the plastic cover from the guide rail. We used a die grinder to remove sufficient material to allow access to the bolt **(see illustrations)**. Note that a quick release fitting is used, but this is impossible to access with the seats fitted.
28 To remove the inertia reel and upper mounting remove the appropriate luggage area side panel and the appropriate D-pillar panel as described in Section 24. Disconnect the wiring plug and the unbolt the reel and upper mounting.

Refitting

29 In all cases, refit by reversing the removal operations. Tighten the seat belt mountings to the specified torque. When refitting the seat belts, note the following points:
a) *Reconnect the quick release seat belt lower anchorages, ensuring that the catch is fully engaged They must engage with an audible click. Tug the belt to ensure it is fully engaged. Note that if the connector does not engage positively it must be replaced.*

25.27b …create enough room to fit a socket on the bolt head

b) *Make sure that no-one is inside the car. Switch on the ignition, then reconnect the battery negative lead. Switch the ignition off, then on again, and check that the airbag warning light comes on, then goes out within 15 seconds.*

26 Centre console – removal and refitting

Removal – all models

1 Fully apply the handbrake, then move the gear or selector lever to neutral – note that it may be necessary to move the gear or selector lever as the console is removed.
2 Ensure the front seats are in the fully lowered, rearmost position.

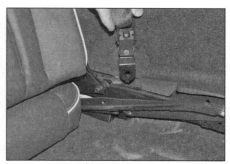
25.27c Remove the mounting

3 Disconnect the battery negative terminal as described in Chapter 5.
4 Unclip and remove the centre console side panels **(see illustration)**.

XC60 models

5 Open the cover and (where fitted) lift the lid of the cup holder and then remove the cup holder. Disconnect the wiring plug from the power socket as the holder is removed **(see illustration)**.
6 Remove the insert from beneath the rear storage compartment and then remove the 2 screws.
7 Remove the single screw from below the cup holder
8 Remove the gear selector cables as described in Chapter 7A or Chapter 7B.
9 Remove the 2 hidden screws from the rear of the console upper panel **(see illustration)**.

26.4 Removing the console side panel (XC60)

26.5 Remove the cup holder

26.9 Remove the left-hand screw. Another screw is fitted to the right-hand side

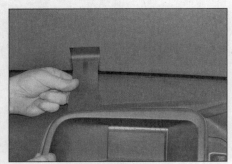

26.10a Release and then...

26.10b ...remove the air vent panel

26.11 Remove the panel and then the screws (arrowed)

26.12 Remove the panel

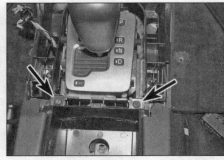

26.13 Remove the screws (arrowed)

26.16 Remove the main section of the centre console

10 Using a broad bladed trim tool remove the central air distribution vents **(see illustrations)**. Disconnect the wiring plug as the vents are removed. Remove the now exposed mounting screws

11 Remove the trim panel from the CD player **(see illustration)** and then remove the 2 screws.
12 Carefully prise free the heater control panel **(see illustration)**. Disconnect the wiring plug as the panel is removed

13 Remove the 2 screws from the front edge of the centre console **(see illustration)**.
14 Remove the 2 bolts that secure the console upper support to the facia. The left-hand bolt points to the rear of the vehicle and the right-hand bolt points towards the right-hand footwell.
15 Disconnect the wiring plugs from the console support and the gear selector housing.
16 Slide the main section of the console towards the rear of the vehicle and unhook it from the front section **(see illustration)** disconnecting the assorted wiring plugs as it is removed.
17 Remove a further 4 screws and then carefully remove the trim support panel over the gear selector **(see illustrations)**.

XC90 models

18 Remove the arm rest. On some models this simply unclips **(see illustration)** on other models there are hidden screws beneath the small rear trim panels.
19 Use a plastic trim tool and remove the now exposed cover and then remove the trim panel from around the gear selector lever **(see illustration)**.
20 Separate the outer trim panel from the inner panel and remove it **(see illustration)**. This is best done by removing the gear selector knob - with a sharp tug. This allows the panel to be turned over and released without straining the wiring.
21 Locate the 6 fixing screws and remove them from the centre console. Disconnect the

26.17a Remove the screws (arrowed)...

26.17b ...and lift off the support panel

26.18 Unclip the arm rest

26.19 Release the trim panel

wiring plugs and remove the console over the gear selector lever **(see illustration)**.

Refitting

22 Refitting is a reversal of removal.

27 Facia –
removal and refitting

⚠️ **Warning: Position the facia and airbag module in a safe place, with the mechanism facing downwards as a precaution against accidental operation. Do not attempt to open or repair the airbag module, or apply any electrical current to it. Do not re-use any airbag which is visibly damaged, or which has been tampered with.**

Note: *Removal of the facia cross member (for access to the heater assembly) is described in Chapter 3.*

Removal – all models

1 Ensure the front seats are in the rearmost positions, then disconnect the battery negative lead (see Chapter 5), and wait at least 5 minutes before proceeding to allow any residual electrical energy to dissipate.
2 Remove the centre console as described in Section 26 and then remove the glovebox (Section 24).
3 With reference to Chapter 10 and Chapter 12 remove the steering wheel, clock spring, column switches and instrument panel.
4 Remove the A-post trim panels and the

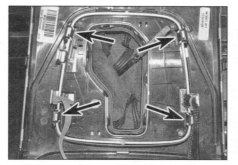

26.20 Note the position of the locating tabs (arrowed)

facia end panels. The end panels are simply clipped into place. Disconnect the wiring plug from the passenger airbag disabling (PAD) switch on the left-hand panel.
5 Remove the heating controls, audio unit and (where fitted) the driver information display/sat nav - as described in Chapter 3 and Chapter 12.
6 Prise free the solar sensor from the centre of the facia, disconnect the wiring plug and remove the sensor **(see illustration)**. Note that on XC60 models it may be necessary to disconnect the wiring plug from the rear, once the facia is partially removed

XC60 models

7 Working in the now vacant instrument panel aperture, remove the 3 mounting screws. One screw is hidden and to remove this, the air distribution duct must be partially compressed **(see illustration)**.

26.21 Removing the centre console

8 Where fitted remove the cabin temperature sensor wiring plug and 2 bolts from below the steering column aperture.
9 Remove the lighting control switch (as described in Chapter 12) and then remove the exposed screw **(see illustration)**.
10 Remove the 2 partially hidden screws from the parking brake switch. Pull the switch forward, disconnect the wiring plug and remove the switch **(see illustrations)**.
11 Where fitted, remove the cover from the diagnostic socket, remove the screw and then remove the socket from the facia. Push the socket through the facia and then release the wiring loom from the rear of the facia.
12 Where fitted remove the facia mounted loudspeaker. Prise up the cover with a trim tool or push up the cover from below **(see illustration)**. Remove the 3 fixings, disconnect the wiring plug and remove the speaker.

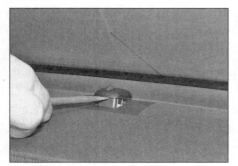

27.6 Remove the solar sensor (XC90)

27.7 Note the position of the hidden fixing and the already removed screws (arrowed)

27.9 Remove the screw

27.10a Remove the screws...

27.10b ...and disconnect the wiring plug

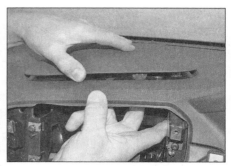

27.12 Remove the loudspeaker cover

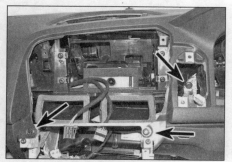

27.14 Remove the screws (arrowed)

27.16 Remove the bolts (arrowed)

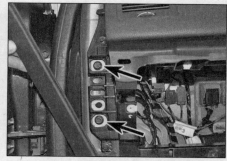

27.17a Remove the bolts (arrowed)...

27.17b ...and then remove the facia from the vehicle

27.18 Remove the lower panel

27.19 Prise free the speaker grille

13 Remove the 4 screws and release the information display unit. Disconnect the wiring plug as the display is removed.
14 Remove the 3 mounting screws from behind the information display unit **(see illustration)**.
15 Remove the cover from the ignition switch, remove the screws and then remove the switch - as described in Chapter 12. Disconnect the wiring plug as the switch is removed.
16 Working in the glovebox aperture disconnect the wiring plug from the airbag and then remove the airbag support bracket bolts **(see illustration)**.
17 Remove the A-pillar lower panels. Locate the facia mounting bolts and then mark the position of the facia in relation to the A-posts. Check that the wiring loom along the full length of the facia is full released from the

facia. Have an assistant support the panel and then remove the 4 mounting bolts (2 per side). Remove the facia from the vehicle **(see illustrations)**.

XC90 models

18 Working in both foot wells remove the insulation panel. Disconnect the wiring plug from the footwell lights as the panel is removed **(see illustration)**.
19 Prise free the central loudspeaker cover **(see illustration)**, remove the 5 screws, disconnect the wiring plug and (where fitted) remove the speaker. Reach through the speaker aperture and disconnect the wiring plug from the hazard warning light switch.
20 Unhook the handbrake cable from the release handle **(see illustrations)**.
21 Where fitted disconnect the interlock cable from the gear lever.

22 Remove the 4 gear lever mounting screws and move the complete gear shift assembly to one side. There is no need to remove it from the vehicle. Cover the exposed gear shift lever with suitable material – bubble wrap is ideal. This will avoid any chance of the gear selector lever damaging the facia as it is removed. Alternatively remove the gear selector housing completely – see Chapter 7A or Chapter 7B.
23 With reference to Section 24, remove both A-pillar trim panels and then remove the facia end panels.
24 Reach through the end of the facia and push out the lighting switch. Disconnect the wiring plug as the switch is removed.
25 Unscrew the diagnostic socket **(see illustration)** and then release the wiring loom from the facia
26 Remove the wiring plug from the

27.20a Remove the screws...

27.20b ...remove handle and unhook the cable

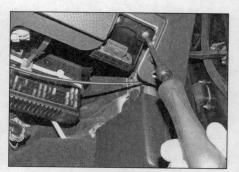

27.25 Remove the diagnostic socket

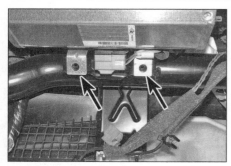

27.26 Remove the passenger airbag mounting screws (arrowed)

27.27a Remove the screws from the instrument panel aperture (arrowed)...

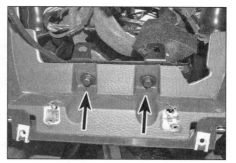

27.27b ...and from the centre of the facia (arrowed)

27.28a Make alignment marks between the facia and the A-pillar...

27.28b ...remove the bolts (arrowed)...

27.28c ...and remove the facia

passenger side airbag and then remove the 2 mounting screws (see illustration).

27 Remove the central facia mounting screws. There are 2 in the instrument panel aperture, 1 in the centre (behind the loudspeaker aperture) and 2 lower ones below the audio unit/heater control aperture (see illustrations).

28 Make alignment marks between the facia and the A-pillars. Check that all wiring connectors, cable clips and fixings have been removed and then have an assistant support the facia panel. With the panel supported remove the 4 facia mounting screws from the end of the facia panel (2 per side). Remove the panel from the vehicle (see illustrations).

Refitting

29 Refitting is a reversal of removal.

28 Sunroof –
general information

An electrically-operated sunroof is available as standard or optional equipment, according to model.

The sunroof is maintenance-free, but any adjustment or removal and refitting of the component parts should be entrusted to a dealer or specialist, due to the complexity of the unit and the need to remove much of the interior trim and headlining to gain access. The latter operation is involved, and requires care and specialist knowledge to avoid damage.

If the sunroof action becomes sluggish,

the slides and/or cables may need lubricating – consult a Volvo dealer or specialist for advice on a suitable product to use. Further checks in the event of non-operation are limited to checking the fuse and wiring, with reference to the wiring diagrams at the end of Chapter 12.

Drain tubes

It is advisable to check the sunroof water drain tubes on a periodic basis. If they become blocked, they may be cleared by probing them with a length of suitable cable (an old speedometer drive cable is ideal). The front drain tubes terminate at the front bulkhead at the rear of the engine bay. The rear drain tubes terminate ahead of the rear wheels inside the wheel arches.

Notes

Chapter 12
Body electrical system

Contents

Degrees of difficulty

Easy, suitable for novice with little experience	Fairly easy, suitable for beginner with some experience	Fairly difficult, suitable for competent DIY mechanic	Difficult, suitable for experienced DIY mechanic	Very difficult, suitable for expert DIY or professional

Specifications

General
System type . . . . 12 volt, negative earth
Fuses . . . . See wiring diagrams at end of Chapter and sticker on control box lid for specific vehicle details

Bulbs — Wattage
Brake light . . . . 21 bayonet
Door mirror ground light . . . . 6 wedge
Foglight:
    Front 35 H8
    Rear . . . . 21 bayonet
Footwell compartment illumination . . . . 5 wedge
Glovebox light . . . . 3 bayonet
Headlight:
    Halogen 55 H7
    Bi-xenon 35 D2R
High-level brake light . . . . LED type (non-renewable)
Indicator side repeater lights . . . . 5 wedge
Indicators (front and rear) . . . . 21 bayonet
Luggage compartment illumination . . . . 5 wedge
Number plate light . . . . 5 festoon
Reversing light . . . . 21 bayonet
Side marker lights:
    Front . . . . 5 wedge
    Rear . . . . 10 bayonet
Sidelights . . . . 5 capless
Tail light . . . . 5 bayonet
Vanity mirror illumination . . . . 1.2 festoon

Torque wrench settings	Nm	lbf ft
Airbag (passenger side):		
Retaining bolts	10	7
Bracket to airbag	10	7
Bracket to crossmember	6	4
Airbag control module	10	7
Airbag side crash sensors	6	4
Tailgate wiper motor bolts	10	7
Windscreen wiper linkage bolts/nuts	10	7
Windscreen wiper arm nuts	30	22

1 General information and precautions

The electrical system is of 12 volt negative earth type. Power for the lights and all electrical accessories is supplied by a lead-acid type battery, which is charged by the belt-driven alternator.

This Chapter covers repair and service procedures for the various electrical components not associated with the engine. Information on the battery, alternator and starter motor can be found in Chapter 5.

⚠️ *Warning: Before carrying out any work on the electrical system, read through the precautions given in 'Safety first!' at the beginning of this manual.*

2 Electrical system fault finding – general information

Note: *Refer to the precautions given in this Chapter before starting work. The following tests relate to testing of the main electrical circuits, and should not be used to test delicate electronic circuits, particularly where an electronic control unit/module is used.*

General

1 A typical electrical circuit consists of an electrical component, any switches, relays, motors, fuses, fusible links or circuit breakers related to that component, and the wiring and connectors which link the component to both the battery and the chassis. To help to pinpoint a problem in an electrical circuit,

wiring diagrams are included at the end of this Chapter.

2 Before attempting to diagnose an electrical fault, first study the appropriate wiring diagram, to obtain a complete understanding of the components included in the particular circuit concerned. The possible sources of a fault can be narrowed down by noting if other components related to the circuit are operating properly. If several components or circuits fail at one time, the problem is likely to be related to a shared fuse or earth connection.

3 Electrical problems usually stem from simple causes, such as loose or corroded connections, a faulty earth connection, a blown fuse, a melted fusible link, or a faulty relay. Visually inspect the condition of all fuses, wires and connections in a problem circuit before testing the components. Use the wiring diagrams to determine which terminal connections will need to be checked in order to pinpoint the trouble-spot.

4 The basic tools required for electrical fault finding include a circuit tester or voltmeter (a 12 volt bulb with a set of test leads can also be used for certain tests); an ohmmeter (to measure resistance and check for continuity); a battery and set of test leads; and a jumper wire, preferably with a circuit breaker or fuse incorporated, which can be used to bypass suspect wires or electrical components. Before attempting to locate a problem with test instruments, use the wiring diagram to determine where to make the connections.

⚠️ *Warning: Under no circumstances may live measuring instruments such as ohmmeters, voltmeters or a bulb and test leads be used to test any of the SRS airbag, SIPS bag, or pyrotechnical seat belt circuitry. Any testing of these components must be left to a Volvo dealer, as there is a danger of activating the system if the correct procedures are not followed.*
Caution: Most of the electronic control units (ECUs) are connected via a 'network' system that allows two way communication between all the control units on the network. For example, as the automatic gearbox approaches a gear ratio shift point, it signals the engine management ECU via the network. As the gearchange is made by the transmission ECU, the engine management ECU retards the ignition timing momentarily reducing engine output to ensure a smoother transition from one gear ratio to the next. Due to the design of the network system, it is not advisable to backprobe the ECUs with a

multimeter in the traditional manner. Instead, the electrical systems are equipped with a sophisticated self-diagnosis system, which can interrogate the various ECUs to reveal the stored fault codes, and help pinpoint faults. In order to access the self-diagnosis system, specialist test equipment will be required. The diagnostic tools required are commonly known as 'code readers' or 'scanners'. Code readers that can access the mandatory EOBD (European On Board Diagnostics) emissions related data are now widely available to the home mechanic (see illustration). In depth fault code diagnosis will require the use of sophisticated tools and any faults not accessible with a basic EOBD code reader should be referred to your Volvo dealer or a suitably equipped specialist.

5 To find the source of an intermittent wiring fault (usually due to a poor or dirty connection, or damaged wiring insulation), a wiggle test can be performed on the wiring. This involves wiggling the wiring by hand to see if the fault occurs as the wiring is moved. It should be possible to narrow down the source of the fault to a particular section of wiring. This method of testing can be used in conjunction with any of the tests described in the following sub-Sections.

6 Apart from problems due to poor connections, two basic types of fault can occur in an electrical circuit – open-circuit, or short-circuit.

7 Open-circuit faults are caused by a break somewhere in the circuit, which prevents current from flowing. An open-circuit fault will prevent a component from working.

8 Short-circuit faults are caused by a short somewhere in the circuit, which allows the current flowing in the circuit to escape along an alternative route, usually to earth. Short-circuit faults are normally caused by a breakdown in wiring insulation, which allows a feed wire to touch either another wire, or an earthed component such as the bodyshell. A short-circuit fault will normally cause the relevant circuit fuse to blow.

Finding an open-circuit

9 To check for an open-circuit, connect one lead of a circuit tester or the negative lead of a voltmeter either to the battery negative terminal or to a known good earth.

10 Connect the other lead to a connector in the circuit being tested, preferably nearest to the battery or fuse. At this point, battery voltage should be present, unless the lead from the

2.4 Checking for emissions related fault codes

battery or the fuse itself is faulty (bearing in mind that some circuits are live only when the ignition switch is moved to a particular position).

11 Switch on the circuit, then connect the tester lead to the connector nearest the circuit switch on the component side.

12 If voltage is present (indicated either by the tester bulb lighting or a voltmeter reading, as applicable), this means that the section of the circuit between the relevant connector and the switch is problem-free.

13 Continue to check the remainder of the circuit in the same fashion.

14 When a point is reached at which no voltage is present, the problem must lie between that point and the previous test point with voltage. Most problems can be traced to a broken, corroded or loose connection.

Finding a short-circuit

15 To check for a short-circuit, first disconnect the load(s) from the circuit (loads are the components which draw current from a circuit, such as bulbs, motors, heating elements, etc).

16 Remove the relevant fuse from the circuit, and connect a circuit tester or voltmeter to the fuse connections.

17 Switch on the circuit, bearing in mind that some circuits are live only when the ignition switch is in a particular position.

18 If voltage is present (indicated either by the tester bulb lighting or a voltmeter reading, as applicable), this means that there is a short-circuit.

19 If no voltage is present during this test, but the fuse still blows with the load(s) reconnected, this indicates an internal fault in the load(s).

Finding an earth fault

20 The battery negative terminal is connected to earth – the metal of the engine/transmission and the vehicle body – and many systems are wired so that they only receive a positive feed, the current returning via the metal of the car body **(see illustration)**. This means that the component mounting and the body form part of that circuit. Loose or corroded mountings can therefore cause a range of electrical faults, ranging from total failure of a circuit, to a puzzling partial failure. In particular, lights may shine dimly (especially when another circuit sharing the same earth point is in operation), motors (eg, wiper motors or the radiator cooling fan motor) may run slowly, and the operation of one circuit may have an apparently-unrelated effect on another.

21 Note that on many vehicles, earth straps are used between certain components, such as the engine/transmission and the body, usually where there is no metal-to-metal contact between components, due to flexible rubber mountings, etc.

22 To check whether a component is properly earthed, disconnect the battery and connect one lead of an ohmmeter to a known good earth point. Connect the other lead to the wire or earth connection being tested.

The resistance reading should be zero; if not, check the connection as follows.

23 If an earth connection is thought to be faulty, dismantle the connection, and clean both the bodyshell and the wire terminal (or the component earth connection mating surface) back to bare metal. Be careful to remove all traces of dirt and corrosion, then use a knife to trim away any paint, so that a clean metal-to-metal joint is made. On reassembly, tighten the joint fasteners securely; if a wire terminal is being refitted, use serrated washers between the terminal and the bodyshell, to ensure a clean and secure connection.

24 When the connection is remade, prevent the onset of corrosion in the future by applying a coat of petroleum jelly or silicone-based grease, or by spraying on (at regular intervals) a proprietary ignition sealer, or a water-dispersant lubricant.

3 Fuses and relays – general information

Fuses

1 Fuses are located in the central fusebox (left-hand side of the engine compartment) at the rear on the left hand side of the load area (behind the trim) and below the glovebox (XC60 models) and on XC90 models at the right-hand end of the facia **(see illustrations)**.

2 If a fuse blows, the electrical circuit(s) protected by that fuse will cease to operate. The fuse positions and the circuits protected depends on

2.20 Earth cable connections (arrowed) beneath the air cleaner housing (XC60)

vehicle specification, model year and country. Refer to the wiring diagrams at the rear of this manual, and the sticker on the fusebox lid which gives details for the particular vehicle.

3 To remove a fuse, first switch off the ignition, then lift up the cover on the central fusebox. Using the plastic removal tool provided, pull the fuse out of its terminals. The wire within the fuse should be visible; if the fuse is blown, the wire will be broken or melted.

4 Always renew a fuse with one of an identical rating; never use a fuse with a different rating from the original, or substitute anything else, as it may lead to a fire. Never renew a fuse more than once without tracing the source of the trouble. The fuse rating is stamped on top of the fuse; note that fuses are also colour-coded for easy recognition. Spare fuses are provided in the fusebox.

5 Persistent blowing of a particular fuse indicates a fault in the circuit(s) protected.

3.1a Central fusebox located on the left-hand side of the engine compartment (XC60)

3.1b XC60 fusebox located below the glovebox (wiring plug removed for clarity)

3.1c Facia mounted fusebox (XC90)

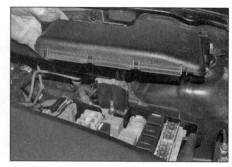

3.1d Under bonnet fusebox (XC90)

4.2a Undo the two screws (arrowed)

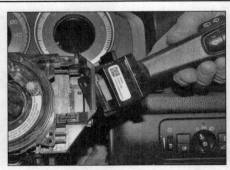

4.2b Withdraw the switch from the steering column

4.3 Remove the switch assembly

Where more than one circuit is involved, switch on one item at a time until the fuse blows, so showing in which circuit the fault lies.

6 Besides a fault in the electrical component concerned, a blown fuse can also be caused by a short-circuit in the wiring to the component. Look for trapped or frayed wires allowing a live wire to touch vehicle metal, and for loose or damaged connectors.

7 Note that **only** the blade-type fuses should ever be renewed by the home mechanic. If one of the large fusible links in the main fusebox blows, this indicates a serious electrical fault. Assuming this has not been caused by an obvious fault, such as a burnt out section of loom, then it is highly recommended that the vehicle should be taken to a Volvo dealer or automotive electrical specialist.

Relays

8 A relay is an electrically-operated switch, which is used for the following reasons:

a) A relay can switch a heavy current remotely from the circuit in which the current is flowing, allowing the use of lighter-gauge wiring and switch contacts.

b) A relay can receive more than one control input, unlike a mechanical switch.

c) A relay can have a timer function – for example an intermittent wiper delay.

9 If a circuit which includes a relay develops a fault, remember that the relay itself could be faulty. A basic test of relay operation is to have an assistant switch on the item concerned, while you listen for a click from the relay. This would at least determine whether the relay is switching or not, but is not conclusive proof that a relay is working.

10 Most relays have four or five terminals – two terminals supplying current to its solenoid winding to provide the switching, a main current input and either one or two outputs to either supply or isolate the component concerned (depending on its configuration).

Using the wiring diagrams at the end of this Chapter, test to ensure that all connections deliver the expected voltage or good earth.

11 Ultimately, testing is by substitution of a known good relay, but be careful – relays which look similar are not necessarily identical for purposes of substitution.

12 The relays are found in the fusebox, on the passenger's side of the engine compartment, and in the luggage compartment fusebox.

13 To remove a relay, make sure that the ignition is switched off, then pull the relay from its socket. Push the new relay firmly in to refit.

4   Switches – removal and refitting

Note: *When working on any electrical component always disconnect the battery negative lead, as described in Chapter 5.*

Steering column multi-function switches

1 Remove the steering column shrouds as described in Chapter 10, Section 19.

2 On XC60 models, each switch is secured by two screws. Remove the screws, disconnect the wiring plug and pull the switch out to the side carefully **(see illustrations)**.

3 On XC90 models it is necessary to remove the complete switch unit. Remove the steering wheel (Chapter 10) and the clock spring as described in Section 24 of this Chapter. Undo the 2 bolts (or screws) on the top of the steering column, disconnect the wiring plug, and slide the unit from the column **(see illustration)**.

4 Refit the relevant switch using a reversal of removal, but note that at the time of writing individual switches were not available for XC90 models.

Ignition/starter switch

XC60

5 Use a plastic type trim tool and ease of the switch cover **(see illustration)**.

6 Undo the 3 retaining bolts **(see illustration)** and disconnect the wiring plug. Pull the switch from the facia.

7 With the switch on the bench, remove the key reader and start switch **(see illustrations)**.

4.5 Remove the cover

4.6 Remove the screws (arrowed)

4.7a Remove the switch...

4.7b ...and the key reader

4.10 Remove the switch

4.11a Disconnect the wiring plug...

4.11b ...and use a small screwdriver to release the key reader coil

8 Refitting is a reversal of removal.

XC90

9 Remove the column shrouds as described in Chapter 10.

10 Disconnect the wiring plug, remove the 2 screws and remove the switch **(see illustration)**.

11 If required the key reader coil assembly can also be removed **(see illustrations)**.

12 Refitting is a reversal of removal.

Headlight switch

13 On both models remove the facia end panel **(see illustration)**.

14 On XC90 models remove the 2 screws from parking brake release lever.

15 The switch can now be pushed out from the housing in the facia **(see illustration)**. Disconnect the wiring connector as the switch is removed

16 Refitting is a reversal of removal.

Hazard warning light switch

XC60

17 Using a flat-bladed tool, carefully prise the central air distribution vent panel from the facia - as described in Chapter 11. Withdraw the complete panel from the facia and disconnect the wiring plug.

18 Squeeze together the retaining clips and press the switch from the panel **(see illustration)**.

19 Refitting is a reversal of removal.

XC90

20 Remove the facia mounted central loudspeaker by prising free the cover.

21 Use a dental mirror and a long thin screwdriver to access the spring clips at the

rear of the switch. If you are replacing the switch because it is known to be faulty, it is possible to remove it by prising it free from the facia. Note however that this will damage the switch if it is removed in this manner **(see illustration)**.

22 Refitting is a reversal of removal.

Centre panel switches

23 On XC60 models the switches are integrated into the climate control panel. Replacement switch covers are available, but at the time of writing if there is an electrical fault with the switch the climate control panel will require replacement.

24 On XC90 models remove the climate control panel as described in Chapter 3, remove the cover and then prise free the appropriate switch **(see illustrations)**.

25 Refitting is a reversal of removal.

4.13 Remove the end panel (XC60)

4.15 Push out the switch (XC90)

4.18 Remove the switch (XC60)

4.21 Note the location of the locking tabs (arrowed)

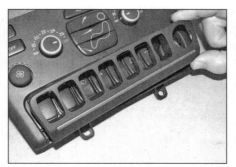

4.24a Remove the cover panel...

4.24b ...and then the appropriate switch

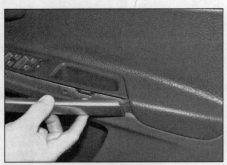

4.27a If working on XC60 models remove the trim piece…

4.27b …and push out the switch panel

4.28 Remove the screw (arrowed)

Door panel switches

Front and rear doors

26 Remove the door trim panel as described in Chapter 11.

27 Disconnect the wiring plug, press in the retaining clips and push the assembly upwards and out of the door panel **(see illustrations)**.

28 If working on the drivers door on XC90 models, remove the screw **(see illustration)** and push out the switch. All other XC90 switches are simply pushed free from the rear.

29 Refitting is a reversal of removal, but test the operation of the switch before refitting the door trim panel. To synchronise the window mechanism, operate the switch to raise the window fully and hold the switch in this position for at least 5 seconds. Then lower the window fully and hold the switch in this position for at least 5 seconds. Repeat the process for raising the window. The window mechanism should now be synchronised. **Note:** *If a new switch/module has been fitted, it may need to be programmed using dedicated Volvo test equipment – entrust this task to Volvo dealer or suitably-equipped specialist.*

Door panel switch module

Note: *This is only applicable to XC60 models. On XC90 models the module is integrated into the front door switches.*

30 The operation is the same for both front and rear doors. Remove the door trim panel as described in Chapter 11.

31 Disconnect the wiring plug, unclip and remove the module **(see illustration)**.

32 Refitting is a reversal of removal, but test the operation of the switch before refitting the door trim panel. To synchronise the window mechanism, operate the switch to raise the window fully and hold the switch in this position for at least 5 seconds. Then lower the window fully and hold the switch in this position for at least 5 seconds. Repeat the process for raising the window. The window mechanism should now be synchronised. **Note:** *If a new module has been fitted, it may need to be programmed using dedicated Volvo test equipment – entrust this task to Volvo dealer or suitably-equipped specialist.*

Brake light switch

33 Refer to Chapter 9.

Parking brake warning light switch

XC60

34 Undo the 2 screws beneath the switch and withdraw the switch from the facia. See Chapter 9, Section 15.

35 Refitting is a reversal of removal.

XC90

36 Carefully remove the driver's side floor carpet to gain access to the transmission tunnel mounted parking brake. There is no need to remove the carpet completely.

37 Remove the brake mounting bolts, lower and then turn over the assembly to access the switch mounting bolt. Remove the bolts and release the switch. Disconnect the wiring plug once the switch is removed **(see illustrations)**.

38 Refitting is a reversal of removal.

Steering wheel switches

39 Remove the driver's airbag as described in Section 24.

40 On XC60 models, use a flat-bladed tool and carefully prise the switch panel(s) from the steering wheel. On XC90 models disconnect the wiring plug remove and remove the screws to release the switch **(see illustrations)**.

4.31 The door control module (XC60 only)

4.37a Remove the parking brake assembly to access the warning light switch (arrowed)

4.37b Release the wiring plug

4.40a Remove the screw…

41 Refitting is a reversal of removal.

Sunroof switch

42 Remove the overhead courtesy light unit as described in Section 9.

43 Release the retaining clips, disconnect the wiring plug, and remove the switch.

44 Refitting is a reversal of removal.

5 Instrument panel – removal and refitting

Note: *If a new instrument panel is to be fitted, the vehicle data from the old panel must be retrieved before removal, then loaded into the new panel. This task must be entrusted to a Volvo dealer or suitably-equipped specialist.*

Removal

1 The instrument panel is linked into the Volvo on-board diagnosis system (OBD), which means that any faults occurring in the instrument panel will be logged, and can be read out using diagnostic equipment (typically, a fault code reader). It is advisable, therefore, to have any less-than-obvious faults investigated by a dealer or suitably-equipped garage in the first instance.

2 Pull out and lower the steering column as far as possible.

3 On XC60 models, unclip the trim between the upper column shroud and the base of the instrument panel **(see illustration)**.

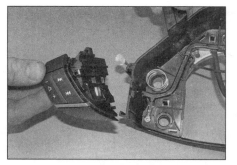

4.40b ...and release the switch

4 On XC90 models, remove the 2 screws and release the bezel **(see illustrations)**.

5 Undo the 2 upper and 2 lower screws, pull the instrument panel rearwards and disconnect the wiring connector **(see illustrations)**.

6 Remove the instrument panel completely, and recover any soundproofing material above the panel.

Refitting

7 Refitting is a reversal of removal.

6 Electrical system sensors – removal and refitting

Note: *Not all sensors are fitted to all models.*

Vehicle speed sensor

1 Vehicle speed information for the speedometer is provided by the anti-lock braking system (ABS) wheel sensors. If the speedometer does not work, therefore, this indicates a possible problem with the signal from the ABS wheel sensors. Check the wiring connections to the wheel sensors, and to the ABS control unit – if no fault is revealed, refer to a Volvo dealer or suitably-equipped garage for diagnostic testing.

Brake fluid level sensor

2 The brake fluid level sensor is a float incorporated in the master cylinder reservoir. The sensor and reservoir are an assembly; renew the reservoir if the unit is faulty – see Chapter 9.

Coolant level sensor

3 Wait until the engine is cold before starting this procedure. The cooling system need not be drained.

4 Slowly unscrew the cooling system expansion tank filler cap to release any pressure remaining in the system. Refit the cap securely.

5 Undo the retaining screw and lift the expansion tank out of its mounting, and as far as possible, turn it upside-down without disconnecting any of the hoses.

6 Disconnect the wiring connector at the sensor located in the base of the tank **(see illustration)**.

7 Taking care to avoid spilling any coolant, pull the sensor out of its sealing grommet.

8 Refitting is a reversal of removal. Top-up the

5.3 Remove the lower trim piece (XC60)

5.4a Remove the screws (arrowed)

5.4b Release the surround...

5.4c ...noting the location of the lower retaining clip (arrowed)

5.5a Remove the screws on XC60 models (arrowed)...

5.5b ...and the same on XC90 models (arrowed)

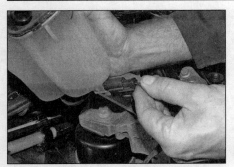

6.6 Disconnect the wiring plug (XC60)

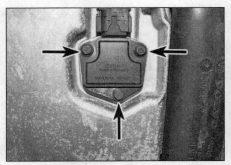

6.13 Oil level sensor retaining bolts (arrowed)

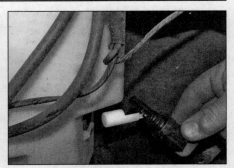

6.17 Washer fluid level sensor

expansion tank as described in *Weekly checks* if any coolant was lost.

Oil level sensor

9 The oil level sensor is located on the sump.
10 Wait until the engine is cold. Chock the rear wheels, then jack up the front of the car and support it on axle stands (see *Jacking and vehicle support*).
11 Release the screws and remove the engine undershield.
12 Drain the engine oil as described in Chapter 1.
13 Undo the 3 bolts and remove the sensor from the sump **(see illustration)**. Expect some oil spillage as the sensor is withdrawn.
14 Refitting is a reversal of removal, refilling the engine with the specified quantity of oil.
15 Refitting is a reversal of removal, tightening the sensor securely.

Washer fluid level sensor

16 Gain access to the rear of the washer reservoir as described in Section 16.
17 The sensor and float are located at the base of the reservoir. Disconnect the wiring connector and pull the sensor from the reservoir. Anticipate some fluid spillage **(see illustration)**.
18 Refitting is a reversal of removal.

Fuel level sender unit

19 Refer to Chapter 4A.

Coolant temperature sensor

20 Refer to Chapter 3.

Outside temperature sensor

21 Remove the passenger's door mirror glass and cover as described in Chapter 11.
22 Release the clips and push the sensor from the mirror housing **(see illustration)**. Disconnect the wiring plug as the sensor is withdrawn.
23 Refitting is a reversal of removal.

Air conditioning evaporator temperature sensor

24 Refer to Chapter 3, Section 10.

Clutch pedal position sensor

25 Refer to Chapter 6.

Brake master cylinder pressure sensor

26 The sensor (or sensors) are either located on the underside of the master cylinder or in the brake line close to the bulkhead. Place rags or paper towels under the sensor to collect the spilt brake fluid.
27 Disconnect the sensor wiring plug, then using a deep 24 mm socket, unscrew the sensor. Immediately plug the port in the master cylinder to limit fluid loss.
28 Refitting is a reversal of removal, remembering to tighten the sensor securely, and bleed the brakes as described in Chapter 9.

Yaw rate/lateral acceleration sensor

29 Remove the driver's seat as described in Chapter 11.

30 Remove the audio module as described in Section 20.
31 Fold the carpet to one side then undo the bolts securing the sensor to the floor **(see illustration)**. Note the sensor fitted position, and disconnect the wiring plug as the sensor is withdrawn. Take care when handling the sensor as it is easily damaged – if it is dropped, a new one must be fitted.
32 Refitting is a reversal of removal. **Note:** *If a new sensor has been fitted, it must be calibrated using Volvo dedicated test equipment. Entrust this task to a Volvo dealer or suitably-equipped specialist.*

---

7 Central electronic module (CEM) – general information, removal and refitting

General information

The central electronic module (CEM) manages the functions of a number of items including the headlights, foglights, windscreen washers, tailgate washer (where applicable), brake lights, headlamp washers (where applicable), central locking, immobiliser, headlamp range adjustment, indicators, blindspot information system, courtesy lighting, rear electric windows, fuel pump, starter motor, speed-sensitive power steering, heated seats, and the horn. It also acts as a gateway between the high-speed and low-speed communication networks. Consequently, it monitors the signals between most of the vehicle's sensors, actuators and control modules. As the CEM communicates with all other modules, it contains the vehicle's self-diagnosis system and stores any fault codes generated. The CEM also contains information specific to the vehicle: VIN, build details, and vehicle equipment options. Consequently, if the CEM needs renewing, the stored information must be retrieved prior to removal, and then programmed into the new unit.

Central electronic module

Note: *If the CEM is to be renewed, stored information must be retrieved and then programmed into the new CEM. As this task*

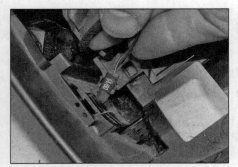

6.22 Remove the sensor (XC90)

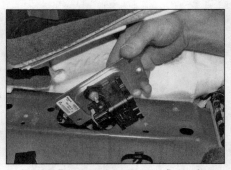

6.31 Remove the yaw rate/lateral acceleration sensor

requires the use of dedicated Volvo test equipment, entrust it to a Volvo dealer or suitably-equipped specialist.

1 Disconnect the battery negative lead as described in Chapter 5.

XC60

2 Remove the glovebox as described in Chapter 11.

3 On early models, disconnect the wiring plugs and unclip the mounting at the top of the unit. Move the unit to the left and remove from the mounting.

4 On later models, remove the cover by releasing the clip at the bottom. Disconnect the wiring plugs, and use a small screwdriver to release the top mountings. Move the unit forward and withdraw towards the right **(see illustration)**.

5 Refitting is a reversal of removal.

XC90

6 Remove the facia as described in Chapter 11.

7 Disconnect the wiring plugs from the face of the CEM and (where fitted) release the tie wrap from the unit.

8 Lower the CEM and remove the wiring plugs from the rear.

9 Locate the 2 bolts that secure the CEM and its mounting bracket to the crossmember. Remove the bolts – note that access to these bolts is restricted – and remove the CEM from the vehicle

10 Refitting is a reversal of removal, but remember to fit a new tie wrap if necessary.

---

8 Bulbs (exterior lights) – renewal

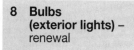

General

1 Whenever a bulb is renewed, note the following points:

a) *Remember that if the light has just been in use, the bulb may be extremely hot.*

b) *Always check the bulb contacts and holder, ensuring that there is clean metal-to-metal contact between the bulb and its live(s) and earth. Clean off any corrosion or dirt before fitting a new bulb.*

8.3 Withdraw the bulb from the light unit (XC90)

7.4 The CEM (arrowed) is located behind the glovebox (XC60)

c) *Wherever bayonet-type bulbs are fitted, ensure that the live contact(s) bear firmly against the bulb contact.*

d) *Always ensure that the new bulb is of the correct rating and that it is completely clean before fitting it; this applies particularly to headlight/foglight bulbs (see below).*

e) *With quartz halogen bulbs (headlights and similar applications), use a tissue or clean cloth when handling the bulb; do not touch the bulb glass with the fingers. Even small quantities of grease from the fingers will cause blackening and premature failure. If a bulb is accidentally touched, clean it with methylated spirit and a clean rag.*

Headlight

Note: *Headlight removal is a simple procedure*

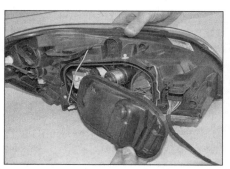

8.2a Release the wire clip and remove the cover at the rear of the headlight (XC60)...

8.7a Rotate the locking ring...

---

on all models. It is recommended that the complete headlight is always removed from the vehicle for bulb replacement.

Halogen dipped and main beam bulb

2 Remove the headlamp as described in Section 10 and then remove the cover from the rear of the unit **(see illustrations)**.

3 Disconnect the wiring plug and depending on the model either twist the bulb or release the spring clip to remove the bulb **(see illustration)**. Pliers can be used to release the dipped beam bulb from XC60 models.

4 Refitting is a reversal of removal.

Bi-xenon bulb

Caution: Xenon bulbs are pressurised to approximately 10 bar. The bulbs must be handled delicately or there is a risk of explosion. Always wear gloves and safety goggles when handling xenon bulbs.

5 Due to the high voltages (22 000 volts approximately) required by xenon gas discharge bulbs, disconnect the battery negative lead (see Chapter 5) then turn on the main and dipped beams alternately to dissipate any residual electrical energy – allow the bulb(s) to cool before commencing.

6 Remove the headlight as described in Section 10 and unclip the cover from the rear of the unit.

7 Rotate the locking ring (using a pair of long-nose pliers if necessary) and remove the bulb. Disconnect the wiring plug as the bulb is removed **(see illustrations)**.

8 Refitting is a reversal of removal.

8.2b ...or peel off the cover (XC90)

8.7b ...and carefully withdraw the xenon bulb

8.9a The parking light wedge bulb (XC60)…

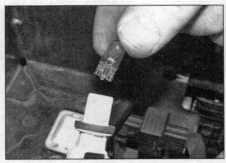

8.9b …and the daytime running bulb (XC90)

8.12a Twist the bulb holder anti-clockwise and remove it (XC60)

8.12b XC90 models feature an unusual bulb

Daytime running lights

Note: *XC60 models feature a parking light and a daytime running lamp. The daytime lamp uses LED (Light emitting diode) bulbs. If these are faulty the complete lamp must be replaced.*

9 Remove the headlight and then twist the bulb holder to remove it. Pull the wedge style bulb free from the bulb holder **(see illustrations)**.

10 Refitting is a reversal of removal.

8.16 Remove the bulb holder and then the bulb (XC90)

8.20 Remove the bulbholder and then the bulb (XC60)

8.23a Remove the bulb (XC60)

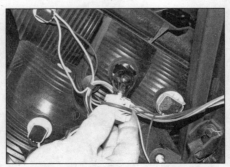

8.23b Remove the bulbholder (XC90)

Front direction indicator

11 Remove the headlamp as described in Section 10.

12 Turn the bulb holder anti-clockwise to remove it. The bulb is a bayonet type. Depress the bulb and turn it anti-clockwise to remove the bulb **(see illustrations)**.

13 Refitting is a reversal of removal.

Front foglight

14 The foglight bulb is accessed from behind the light unit – if preferred, jack up the front of the car (see *Jacking and vehicle support*).

15 On XC60 models remove the air deflector from the lower edge of the bumper cover.

16 The bulbholder has two tabs to make it easier to turn – twist the bulbholder anti-clockwise to release it from the back of the light unit **(see illustration)**.

17 Remove the bulb from the bulbholder.

18 Refitting is a reversal of removal.

Direction indicator side repeater

19 Remove the door mirror glass as described in Chapter 11.

20 Pull the bulbholder from place and then pull the wedge type bulb from the bulb holder **(see illustration)**.

21 Refitting is a reversal of removal.

Rear light cluster bulbs

Note: *On XC60 models LEDs are used for tail light illumination.*

22 On XC60 models the bulbholders can be accessed by removing the cover from the side panel, on XC90 models remove the rear lamp, as described in Section 10.

23 Rotate the appropriate bulbholder anti-clockwise and pull it from the lamp. Push in and twist the bulb anti-clockwise to remove it from the bulbholder **(see illustrations)**.

24 Refitting is a reversal of removal.

High-level brake light

25 The high-level brake light does not contain conventional light bulbs, but rather a row of LEDs (light-emitting diodes). As a result, if the high-level brake light stops working, it may ultimately be necessary to renew the light unit complete – see Section 10. Before deciding that this is necessary, however, check the fuse and all wiring, using the information in Section 2 and the wiring diagrams at the end of this Chapter.

Number plate light

26 Undo the 2 screws securing the light unit to the tailgate **(see illustration)**.

27 Carefully prise out the light unit.

28 Pull the bulb out of the holder **(see illustration)**.

29 Refitting is a reversal of removal.

Rear foglight

Note: *On XC90 models the main rear foglight is part to the rear lamp. Some models feature a bumper mounted foglight and this is removed in the same way as XC60 models.*

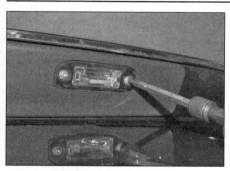

8.26 Remove the screws

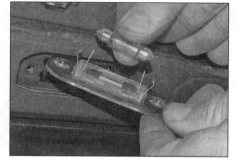

8.28 Remove the bulb

8.30 Depress the clip to release the foglight

30 On XC60 models release the lamp from the bumper – this is held in place by a clip. Removing the lamp makes bulb replacement considerable easier **(see illustration)**.
31 Rotate the bulbholder to release it **(see illustration)** and then and remove the bulb

Door mirror ground light bulb

32 Remove the door mirror glass as described in Chapter 11.
33 Remove the lens by inserting a small screwdriver into the slot and then push in to release the clip. Withdraw the lens from beneath the mirror housing and pull out the bulb holder **(see illustration)**. Remove the bulb.
34 Refitting is a reversal of removal.

8.31 Remove the foglight bulholder

8.33 Remove the bulb

back into place in the sunvisor, ensuring that the clips engage securely.

Courtesy/reading lights
Front – XC60

5 Carefully prise the unit from the headlining,

and disconnect the wiring plugs **(see illustration)**.
6 Remove the bulbholder (the bulb is integral with the holder and cannot be renewed separately) **(see illustration)**.
7 Refitting is a reversal of removal.

9 Bulbs (interior lights) – renewal

General

1 Whenever a bulb is renewed, note the following points:
 a) Remember that if the light has just been in use, the bulb may be extremely hot.
 b) Always check the bulb contacts and holder, ensuring that there is clean metal-to-metal contact between the bulb and its live(s) and earth. Clean off any corrosion or dirt before fitting a new bulb.
 c) Wherever bayonet-type bulbs are fitted, ensure that the live contact(s) bear firmly against the bulb contact.
 d) Always ensure that the new bulb is of the correct rating and that it is completely clean before fitting it.
2 Some switch illumination/pilot bulbs are integral with their switches, and cannot be renewed separately.

Vanity mirror lights

3 Using a suitable flat-bladed tool or a small screwdriver, prise the mirror housing from the sunvisor. This should be undertaken carefully as the component is easily broken. With the mirror housing removed, the bulbs can be pulled from their holders **(see illustrations)**.
4 To refit the mirror housing, almost close the mirror cover and carefully push the housing

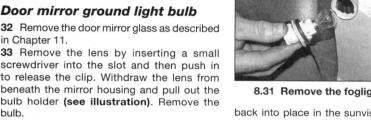

9.3a Carefully release and...

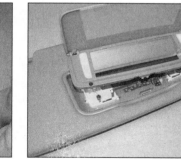

9.3b ...remove the mirror

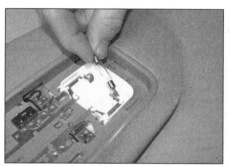

9.3c Remove the bulb

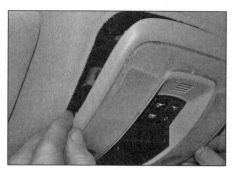

9.5 Carefully prise the light unit from the headlining

9.6 Rotate the bulb holder anti-clockwise by 90° and remove from the unit

9.8 Unclip the centre section

9.9 Remove the bulb

9.10 Prise the lamp from the headlining

9.11 Disconnect the wiring plug as the lamp is withdrawn

9.13 Prise the lamp free

Front – XC90

8 Prise free the centre section of the lamp (see illustration).

9 Release the locking tangs and remove the cover. Remove the appropriate festoon type

9.14a Remove the reflector and...

bulb by pulling it from the bulb holder (see illustration).

Rear – XC60

10 Carefully prise the lens/cover assembly from the headlining (see illustration).

9.14b ...prise out the bulb

11 Rotate the bulbholders anti-clockwise by 90 degrees and remove from the unit (see illustration).

12 Refitting is a reversal of removal.

Rear – XC90

13 Prise the lamp from the headlining (see illustration).

14 Release the reflector and pull free the festoon type bulb (see illustrations).

15 Refitting is a reversal of removal.

Glovebox light

16 Carefully prise the light unit from the glovebox (see illustration).

17 Pull the festoon bulb from the contacts (see illustration).

18 Refitting is a reversal of removal.

Heater control/switch panel illumination –XC90 only

Note: XC60 models do not have replaceable bulbs fitted.

19 Remove the control panel as described in Chapter 3.

20 Use a suitable screwdriver and rotate the bulb holder 90 degrees and remove it (see illustration). Note that the bulb is part of the bulb holder and must be replaced as a complete assembly.

Automatic transmission selector illumination

21 The selector panel is illuminated by LEDs. If faulty the entire panel must be renewed.

Instrument panel bulbs

22 The panel is illuminated by LEDs, which

9.16 Prise free the lamp (XC60)

9.17 Remove the bulb (XC90)

cannot be renewed independently of the instrument panel. In the event of a failure, refer to a Volvo dealer.

Luggage area illumination

23 Carefully prise the light unit from position.
24 Remove the bulb from the holder.
25 Refitting is a reversal of removal.

Footwell lights

26 Taking care not to damage the facia trim, prise out the inner edge of the light unit, then disconnect its wiring plug and remove it.
27 Pull the festoon bulb from the contacts.
28 Refitting is a reversal of removal.

10 Exterior light units – removal and refitting

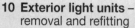
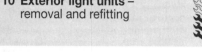

Caution: Ensure the ignition is turned off before proceeding

Headlight

1 Pull up the 2 sliding levers located on the lock panel above the headlights and disconnect the wiring plug as the unit is withdrawn from the front of the car **(see illustrations)**.
2 Refitting is a reversal of removal. Have the headlight beam alignment checked on completion (see Section 11).

Front foglight

3 Apply the handbrake, chock the rear wheels, then jack up the front of the car and support it securely on axle stands.

9.20 Use a screwdriver to remove the bulbs

XC60

4 From the rear of the bumper, undo the clips that secure the foglight grille surround. From the front, undo the retaining bolt, disconnect the wiring plug, then remove the foglight.
5 Refitting is a reversal of removal.

XC90

6 Disconnect the wiring plug from the rear.
7 Remove the 3 mounting screws and withdraw the lamp from the rear **(see illustration)**.

Rear light clusters

XC60

8 Remove the load area side trim panel as described in Chapter 11, Section 14.
9 On the appropriate side partially remove the bumper cover (as described in Chapter 11) and then remove the support panel from below the lamp **(see illustration)**.

10 Working inside the D-pillar locate and remove the 3 mounting points **(see illustration)**.
11 Withdraw the lamp and unplug the bulbholders and wiring plug as the lamp is removed
12 Refitting is a reversal of removal.

XC90

13 Open both sections of the rear tailgate and remove the load area floor quarter panels. Remove the load area rear side panels.
14 Remove the 2 nuts at the rear and release the lamp **(see illustration)**. Note the positions of the bulb holders and then remove them.
15 If the bulb holders are damaged and require replacement, then remove the rear side trim panel as described in Chapter 11. Disconnect the wiring multi-plug mounted on the D-post.
16 If required the upper lamp section can now be removed, note however that this purely cosmetic and does not contain any bulbs.
17 Refitting is a reversal of removal.

High-level brake light

18 Remove the tailgate interior trim panels as described in Chapter 11.

XC60

19 Remove the 3 blanking plugs and then remove the 3 mounting bolts.
20 Lift of the brake lamp and disconnect the wiring plug.
21 Refitting is a reversal of removal.

10.1a Pull up the two levers on the lock panel

10.1b Disconnect the wiring plug

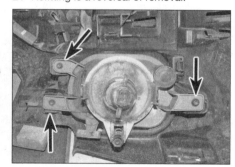

10.7 Remove the screws (arrowed)

10.9 Remove the panel mounting bolts (arrowed)

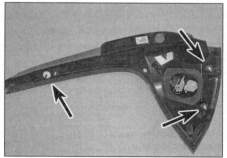

10.10 With the lamp removed note the location of the mounting points (arrowed)

10.14 Remove the mounting bolts (arrowed)

10.22 Remove the blanking plugs

10.23 Remove the rear screen washer hose

10.27 Remove the lamp (XC60)

10.31a Remove the screw…

10.31b …and manoeuvre the lamp out through the headlamp opening

XC90

22 Remove the blanking plugs. We used a piece of sticky tape to 'pluck' the blanking plug from the lamp (see illustration).
23 Remove the mounting screws. Withdraw the lamp, disconnect the wiring plug and prise off the screen washer hose (see illustration). Note that apart from the screen washer jet, no individual parts are available.

Number plate light

24 Undo the screws securing the relevant light unit to the tailgate (see illustration 8.26).
25 Carefully prise/slide out the light unit and disconnect the wiring plug as it is withdrawn.
26 Refitting is a reversal of removal.

Door mirror indicator lamp

27 Remove the door mirror outer cover

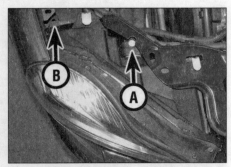

11.2 Headlight adjustment points (XC90)

A Vertical adjustment
B Horizontal adjustment

as described in Chapter 11. Use a small screwdriver to depress the plastic tab at the end of the lens and withdraw the lens from the mirror housing (see illustrations).
28 Refitting is a reversal of removal.

Daytime running lamp – XC60 only

29 Remove the headlight as described in paragraph 1.
30 Partially free the appropriate corner section of the bumper cover by removing the plastic rivets from the slam panel.
31 Remove the single screw and with care work the lamp free from the rear of the bumper cover (see illustrations). Unplug the wiring connector and remove the lamp.

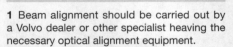

11 Headlight beam alignment – checking and adjusting

1 Beam alignment should be carried out by a Volvo dealer or other specialist heaving the necessary optical alignment equipment.
2 For reference, the headlights can be adjusted by means of the vertical and horizontal adjuster controls at the top of the headlight unit (see illustration).
3 All models are equipped with an electrically-operated headlight beam adjustment system which is controlled through the switch on the facia. Ensure that the switch is set to the 'off' position before adjusting the headlight aim.

12 Headlight height control motor – removal and refitting

Note: XC90 models only.

Removal

1 Remove the headlamp (see Section 10), and remove the cover from the rear of the unit.
2 Disconnect the wiring connector at the motor, rotate the body of the motor and withdraw the control motor from the headlamp unit (see illustration).

Refitting

3 Refitting is a reversal of removal.
4 Have the beam adjustment checked, and if necessary adjusted, by a dealer or specialist.

13 Headlight control module – removal and refitting

Removal

XC60

1 The headlamp control module is located beneath the headlight.
2 Remove the headlight, place the headlight upside down on a soft surface and remove the 3 screws. Remove the control unit.

XC90

3 Remove the front left-hand seat as described in Chapter 11.

12.2 Remove the height control motor

4 Remove the cover panel, unclip the module and disconnect the wiring plug.

Refitting

5 Refitting is a reversal of removal.
6 Where a replacement unit has been fitted, this will require programming using suitable diagnostic equipment.

14 Horn – removal and refitting

Removal

XC60

1 Jack up and support the front of the vehicle (see *Jacking and vehicle support* in the reference section). The horns are located behind the right-hand end of the bumper cover and can be accessed from the wheel arch.
2 Turn the steering wheel hard left to access the 5 wing liner to bumper cover mounting screws.
3 Remove the 5 screws and partially release the wing liner.
4 Carefully fold back the liner to access the horns. Disconnect the wiring plug and remove the 2 bolts from the mounting bracket. Withdraw the horns from the vehicle.

XC90

5 Remove the right-hand headlight as described in Section 10.
6 Remove the inboard horn from the bracket **(see illustration)** and then remove the bracket complete with the outer horn. Disconnect the wiring plug as the horns are withdrawn.

Refitting

7 Refitting is a reversal of removal.

15 Sunroof motor – removal and refitting

Removal and refitting

1 Disconnect the battery as described in Chapter 5.

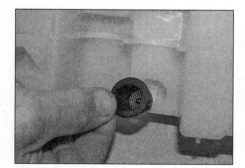

16.8 The pump seal incorporates a filter

2 Remove the front courtesy light unit as described in Section 9.
3 Undo the 3 bolts, disconnect the wiring plug, and remove the motor
4 Refitting is a reversal of removal.

Calibration

5 The motor may require calibration after refitting which should be carried out as follows.
6 With the sunroof closed, turn the ignition on.
7 Hold down the control switch and allow the roof to pen and close. The switch should be held down throughout the procedure.
8 When the roof closes calibration is complete.

16 Washer system components – removal and refitting

Washer pumps

1 The washer reservoir and pumps are located behind the front left-hand bumper cover on XC60 models and behind the front right-hand bumper cover on XC90 models.
2 The washer pumps can be accessed without removing the washer reservoir.
3 Jack up and support the front of the vehicle – see *Jacking and vehicle support* in the reference section.
4 On XC60 models, undo the plastic rivets (or screws) that secure the front of the left-hand side wheel arch liner to the front bumper, and carefully fold back the liner until the pump can be reached.

16.6a The washer pumps on XC60 models...

16.11a Remove the screw on XC60 models (arrowed)...

14.6 The horns are mounted below the right-hand headlight (XC90)

5 On XC90 models drill out the right-hand wing liner rivets and fold back the wing liner to access the pumps.
6 Note the fitted locations, then pull the hose(s) from the pump, and disconnect the pump wiring plug **(see illustrations)**.
7 Place a container under the reservoir, and be prepared for spillage.
8 Grip the washer pump and pull it out of the reservoir **(see illustration)**.
9 Refitting is a reversal of removal.

Washer reservoir

10 Remove the front bumper as described in Chapter 11.
11 Remove the single bolt and pull out the filler neck from the reservoir **(see illustrations)**.
12 Disconnect the wiring plugs from the level sensor and pump(s) on the reservoir. Undo the 3 mounting screws and lower the reservoir from position.

16.6b ...and the outer washer pump on XC90 models

16.11b ...and on XC90 models (arrowed)

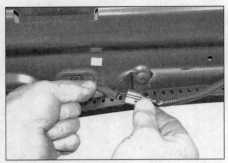

16.14 Disconnect the wiring plug

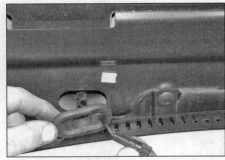

16.15a Remove the grommet...

16.15b ...and push out the washer jet (XC90 shown)

13 Refitting is a reversal of removal.

Washer jets

Windscreen

14 Open the bonnet and (where fitted)

16.18 Remove the washer jet

disconnect the washer jet wiring plug **(see illustration)**.

15 Where fitted remove the grommet and then push on the bottom of the jet to release it from the bonnet **(see illustrations)**.

16 Refitting is a reversal of removal.
17 It may be possible to adjust the jet nozzles using a pin, but if not the complete washer jet will need to be renewed.

Tailgate

18 On XC60 models prise free the washer jet and disconnect the hose **(see illustration)**.
19 On XC90 models remove the high level brake light (as described in Section 10 of this Chapter) and then prise out the washer jet **(see illustration)**.

Headlamp

20 Remove the front bumper as described in Chapter 11.
22 At the rear of the bumper undo the 2 screws securing the washer jet to its bracket and disconnect the wiring plug and washer hose. Note that the XC60 shown, but XC90 is similar **(see illustrations)**.
23 Working at the front of the bumper, unclip the body-coloured trim piece from the top of the washer jets. The unit can now be withdrawn from the rear of the bumper **(see illustrations)**.
24 Refitting is a reversal of removal.

Washer fluid level sensor

25 Refer to Section 6.

17 Wiper arms –
removal and refitting

Removal

1 Place the wipers in the normal 'park'

16.19 Prise the washer jet from high level brake light

16.22a Undo the two washer jet securing bolts (arrowed)

16.22b Disconnect the wiring plug from the washer jet...

16.22c ...and the washer hose

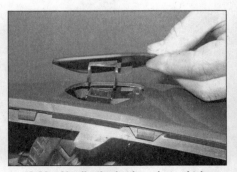

16.23a Unclip the body-coloured trim piece from the top of the bumper

16.23b Withdraw the washer jet from the rear of the bumper

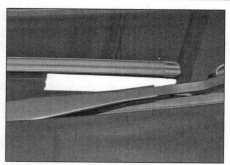

17.1 Mark the position of the wipers prior to removal

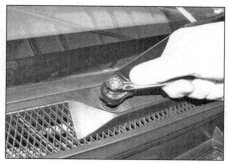

17.2 Prise off the cap and undo the wiper arm nut

17.3a Use a suitable puller if necessary . . .

17.3b . . . and remove the wiper arm from the spindle

17.4a Lift off the plastic cover, undo the nut . . .

17.4b . . . and remove the rear wiper arm from the spindle

position. Mark the position of the wipers either by using masking tape applied to the screen **(see illustration)** below the wiper, or by measuring the distance of the wiper from the bottom of the screen.

2 Lift up or prise off the cover (where applicable) then slacken the nut at the base of the wiper arm **(see illustration)**.

3 Press the front wiper arms down, and tap them gently to break the bond between the arm and spindle – use tape to protect the arm. Using a rocking motion, pull the arms off the splines. If necessary, use a puller to remove the arms **(see illustrations)**.

4 On the tailgate wiper lift up the cover and undo the nut securing the arm to the spindle. Pull the arm from the spindle using a rocking motion **(see illustrations)**.

Refitting

5 Refitting is a reversal of removal.

18.3a Remove the plastic rivets from the plenum cover

18 Windscreen wiper motor and linkage – removal and refitting

Removal

1 Switch the wipers on, then off again to ensure that the motor and linkage are parked.
2 Remove the windscreen wiper arms as described in Section 17.
3 On XC60 models remove the plenum chamber cover by first removing the battery cover which includes a section secured to the plenum cover with a plastic screw. Pull up and remove the rubber seal on the front edge of the panel, then undo the 6 plastic clips. On both sides release the small panels from the lower corners of the windscreen. Unhook the panel from the bottom edge of the screen **(see illustrations)**.
4 On XC90 models remove the 6 plastic

18.3b Remove the cover

rivets. On the 2 below the windscreen pull up the locking pin, on the others push the locking pin through the rivet. Catch the pin as it is removed. Note it may be necessary to drive the pins out with a small drift.
5 Undo the 3 bolts and remove the linkage/ frame, disconnecting the wiring plug as the unit is withdrawn **(see illustrations)**.
6 Mark the position of the motor crank arm relative to the frame, undo the nut and remove the crank arm from the motor.
7 Undo the three motor retaining bolts and remove the motor from the frame. Note that at the time of writing a replacement wiper motor was only available for XC90 models. The frame and linkage arms are an assembly, and cannot be individually renewed.

Refitting

8 Refit the motor to the frame, and secure with the 3 mounting bolts.

18.5a Remove the bolts...

18.5b ...and disconnect the wiring plug as the mechanism is removed

18.5c Mounting bolts on XC60 models (arrowed)

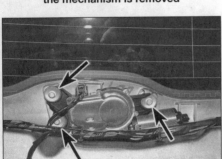

19.4a XC60 tailgate wiper motor bolts (arrowed)...

19.4b ...and XC90 wiper motor bolts (arrowed)

9 If a new motor is being fitted, temporarily reconnect the wiring connectors at the car, switch on the motor then switch it off again to ensure that it is parked.

10 Position the crank arm on the motor, with the marks made on removal aligned. Prevent the crank arm from turning by holding it with a spanner, then refit and tighten the nut.

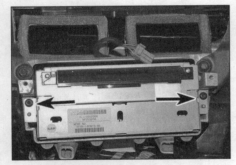

20.2a Audio unit retaining screws (arrowed)

20.2b Pull the unit forward ...

20.2c ...and disconnect the wiring plugs

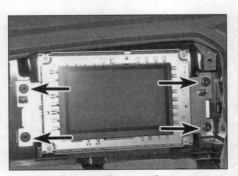

20.4a Remove the mounting screws (arrowed), pull the display out...

11 Alternatively, if a new frame and linkage are being fitted, set the motor to the park position as described previously then, when connecting the crank arm to the motor, position it so that it is parallel with the linkage arm directly above.

12 The assembled components can now be refitted using a reversal of removal, noting that the grommet at the rear of the linkage locates on a bracket below the windscreen. Ensure that the plenum cover is refitted correctly at the bottom edge of the screen.

19 Tailgate wiper motor – removal and refitting

Removal

1 Switch the wiper on then off again to ensure that the motor and linkage are parked.
2 Remove the tailgate wiper arm as described in Section 17.
3 Remove the tailgate interior trim panels as described in Chapter 11.
4 Disconnect the wiring plug, undo the three motor retaining bolts and withdraw it from the tailgate **(see illustration)**.

Refitting

5 Refit the motor to the tailgate and secure with the three mounting bolts.
6 If a new motor is being fitted, temporarily reconnect the wiring connector at the car, switch on the motor then switch it off again to ensure that it is parked.
7 Refitting is a reversal of removal.

20 Audio units – removal and refitting

Note: *If any component parts of the Volvo audio system are being replaced, software will need to be downloaded and installed from Volvo. Entrust this task to a Volvo dealer or suitably-equipped specialist.*

Facia-mounted audio units

XC60 models

1 Remove the centre console as described in Chapter 11.
2 Undo the 2 retaining screws and pull the unit from the facia until the wiring plugs are accessible **(see illustrations)**.
3 Disconnect the wiring plugs and remove the unit. Be aware that the wiring may be of the fibre optic variety and should not be bent excessively as this can cause damage.
4 If required the main information display unit can also be removed at this point **(see illustrations)**. Note that not all of the available sockets on the rear of the display will be populated – this is dependent on the vehicle trim level.
5 Refitting is a reversal of removal.

XC90 models

6 Move the gear selector lever to the rear most position and then partially remove the centre console as described in Chapter 11. There is no need to completely remove the centre console.

7 Remove the lower 2 mounting screws **(see illustration)** and then remove the heater control panel, complete with the audio unit. Disconnect the wiring plugs as the assembly is withdrawn.

8 With the complete assembly on the bench, remove the 2 screws, depress the locking tangs and then separate the audio unit from the heater control panel.

9 With the control panel removed, remove the CD player **(see illustration)**.

10 Refitting is a reversal of removal.

Audio amplifier

11 Slide the driver's seat fully rearwards and undo the 3 retaining screws.

12 Disconnect the wiring plugs as the amplifier is withdrawn **(see illustration)**.

13 Refitting is the reversal of removal.

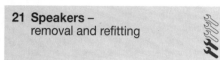

21 Speakers –
removal and refitting

Facia speaker

1 Carefully prise up the speaker/display unit grille on the top of the facia **(see illustration)**.

2 Undo the 3 screws (XC60 models) or the 5 screws (XC90 models) and lift up the speaker. Disconnect the wiring and remove the speaker.

3 Refitting is a reversal of removal, making sure the speaker is correctly located.

Door speakers

Front

4 A tweeter is located in the forward edge of the door ahead of the window. Carefully unclip the trim panel containing the speaker and disconnect the wiring plug as it is withdrawn. The speaker is integral with the trim panel so you should refer to a Volvo dealer regarding renewal **(see illustrations)**.

5 To remove the main speakers, remove the door trim panel as described in Chapter 11.

6 On XC60 models remove the screws, on XC90 models drill out the rivets **(see illustrations)**. Remove the speaker and disconnect the wiring plug .

7 Refitting is a reversal of removal, but use new rivets on XC90 models.

20.4b ...and disconnect the wiring plugs

20.9 Remove the screws

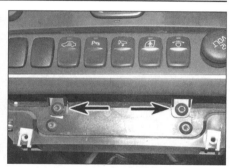

20.7 Remove the mounting screws (arrowed)

20.12 Remove the amplifier (XC90)

21.1 Prise up the speaker grille on top of the facia (XC90)

21.4a Unclip the panel...

21.4b ...and disconnect the wiring plug

21.6a On XC60 models remove the screws (arrowed)...

21.6b ...and on XC90 models drill out the rivets

21.9 Remove the speaker (XC60)

21.11 Remove the cover

21.12 Disconnect the wiring plug

Rear

8 Remove the door trim panel as described in Chapter 11.

9 On XC60 models remove the screws, on XC90 models drill out the 3 rivets securing the speaker to the door panel. Remove the speaker and disconnect the wiring plug **(see illustration)**.

10 Refitting is a reversal of removal.

D-pillar speaker (XC90 only)

11 Use a trim tool and prise the speaker cover free **(see illustration)**. Feed the seatbelt through the slot provided in the cover. Remove the cover.

12 Disconnect the wiring plug **(see illustration)** and unclip the speaker from the cover.

Subwoofer

XC60 models

13 Lift up the panel in the floor of the luggage area and using a small screwdriver, release the clip at the bottom of the gas damper. Remove the storage tray.

14 Lower the seat backs and undo the 2 bolts/screws at the front of the unit (nearest the rear seat backs) and disconnect the wiring plugs.

15 Undo the 2 bolts/screws nearest to the bumper that secure the unit to the floor of the vehicle. and carefully lift the unit from place.

16 Refitting is a reversal of removal.

XC90 models

17 Remove the leaf-hand load area side panel as described in Chapter 11.

18 Unplug the wiring connector, remove the mounting screws and remove the subwoofer from the vehicle.

19 Refitting is a reversal of removal.

22 Anti-theft alarm and immobiliser system – general information

Note: *This information is applicable only to the systems fitted by Volvo as original equipment.*

Immobiliser

The electronic immobiliser is automatically activated when the remote unit or key are removed from the starter panel or ignition lock. On XC60 models with keyless locking the system is activated when the remote is removed from the vehicle. When activated, it cuts the ignition circuit, preventing the engine from being started.

On XC60 models the system is disarmed when the remote unit is inserted into the starter panel on the facia or (where a keyless locking is fitted) as soon as the remote is in the cabin. On XC90 models the system is disarmed when the key is placed in the key barrel. It should be noted that on all models this is a 'passive' security feature. Functioning batteries in the remote or key fob are not needed to disarm the system.

It is essential that the tag showing the remote (or key number) is not lost (this will be supplied with the car when new). Any duplicate remotes or keys will have to be obtained from a Volvo dealer, who will need the number to supply a duplicate.

Any problems or work involving the immobiliser system should be entrusted to a Volvo dealer or specialist, as dedicated electronic equipment is required to diagnose faults, or to 'match' the various components.

Alarm

An anti-theft alarm system is fitted as standard equipment. The alarm has switches on all the doors (including the tailgate), and the bonnet. If the tailgate, bonnet or any of the doors are opened or the ignition switch is switched on whilst the alarm is set, the alarm horn will sound and the hazard warning lights will flash. The alarm also has an immobiliser function which makes the ignition inoperable whilst the alarm is triggered.

Signals from the alarm system switches and contacts which are integral with the door, bonnet and tailgate locks are sent to a central control unit inside the car once the system is set. The control unit monitors the signals and activates the alarm if any of the signal loops are broken, or if an attempt is made to start the car.

The status of the system is displayed by means of a flashing LED.

Should the alarm system become faulty, bear in mind the following points:

a) *As with other electrical equipment, many faults are caused by poor connections or bad earths.*

b) *Check the operation of all the door, bonnet and tailgate switches, and the operation of all interior lights.*

c) *The alarm system may behave oddly if the vehicle battery is in poor condition, or if its terminals are loose.*

d) *If the system is operating correctly, but gives too many false alarms, a Volvo dealer or specialist may be able to reduce the sensitivity of some of the system sensors.*

e) *Ultimately, the vehicle may have to be taken to a Volvo dealer or a suitably-equipped garage for examination. They will have access to a special diagnostic tester which will quickly trace any fault present in the system.*

23 Airbag system – general information and precautions

A supplemental restraint system is fitted in various forms as standard or optional equipment depending on model and territory.

The main system component is a driver's airbag, which is designed to prevent serious chest and head injuries to the driver during an accident. Similar airbags for the front seat passenger, side airbags (built into the side of the front seats), and side curtain airbags are also standard fitment. Side impact crash sensors are located on the B- and C-pillars of the vehicle, with a frontal sensor incorporated into the SRS module located under the centre console. The module incorporates a deceleration sensor, and a microprocessor ECU, to monitor the severity of the impact and trigger the airbag where necessary. The airbag is inflated by a gas generator, which forces the bag out of the module cover in the centre of the steering wheel, or out of a cover on the passenger's side of the facia/seat cover/headlining. A contact reel (clockspring) behind the steering wheel at the top of the steering column ensures that a good electrical connection is maintained with the airbag at all times as the steering wheel is turned in each direction.

In addition to the airbag units, the supplemental restraint system also incorporates pyrotechnical seat belt tensioners

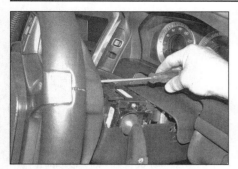

24.3a Release the spring clips at the rear of the steering wheel

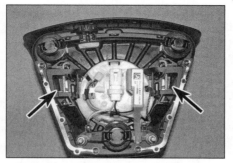

24.3b Note the location of the retaining springs (arrowed)

24.5 Disconnect the wiring plugs

operated by gas cartridges in the belt inertia reel assembly. The pyrotechnical units are also triggered by the crash sensor, in conjunction with the airbags, to tighten the seat belts and provide additional collision protection.

All models also incorporate a side impact protection system (SIPS) as standard equipment. In its basic form, the SIPS system is essentially an integral part of the vehicle structure in which strengthening agents are used to distribute side impacts through the bodywork. This is done by reinforcing the lower areas of the doors and door pillars, and providing strengthening bars in the seats and centre console. In this way, side impacts are absorbed by the body structure as a whole, giving exceptional impact strength.

⚠️ *Warning: The safe handling of the SRS components requires the use of Volvo special equipment. Any attempt to dismantle the airbag module, SIPS bag, crash sensors, contact reel, seat belt tensioners or any associated wiring or components without this equipment, and the specialist knowledge needed to use it correctly, could result in severe personal injury and/or malfunction of the system.*

• *Before carrying out any work on the SRS components, disconnect the battery and wait for at least 10 minutes for any residual electrical energy to dissipate before proceeding.*

• *Handle the airbag unit with extreme care as a precaution against personal injury, and always hold it with the cover facing away from the body. If in doubt concerning any proposed work involving the airbag unit or its control circuitry, consult a Volvo dealer.*

• *Note that the airbag(s) must not be subjected to temperatures in excess of 90°C. When the airbag is removed, ensure that it is stored with the pad up to prevent possible inflation.*

• *Do not allow any solvents or cleaning agents to contact the airbag assemblies. They must be cleaned using only a damp cloth.*

• *The airbag(s) and control unit are both sensitive to impact. If either is dropped or damaged they should be renewed.*

• *Disconnect the airbag control unit wiring plug prior to using arc-welding equipment on the vehicle.*

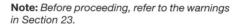

24 Airbag system components – removal and refitting 🔧

Note: *Before proceeding, refer to the warnings in Section 23.*

Driver's airbag

1 Lower the drivers side window and then disconnect the battery negative lead (see Chapter 5). Wait 10 minutes before proceeding.
2 Remove the upper and lower steering column shrouds as described In Chapter 10.
3 Insert a flat-bladed screwdriver (with a tip 7mm wide and approximately 225mm in length) in through the holes in the rear of the steering wheel, lift up the screwdriver handle and release the spring clip each side **(see illustrations)**. Turn the steering wheel 90° in each direction to gain access to the holes. Note that the clips can be tricky to reach and this task requires patience.
4 Return the wheel to the straight-ahead position.
5 Lift the airbag module off the steering wheel, disconnect the wiring connectors from the rear of the unit **(see illustration)** and remove it from the vehicle.

⚠️ *Warning: Position the airbag unit in a safe place, with the pad facing upwards as a precaution against accidental operation. Do not attempt to open or repair the airbag unit, or apply any electrical current to it. Do not use any airbag which is visibly damaged or which has been tampered with.*

6 Refitting is a reversal of removal.
7 Make sure that no-one is inside the car. Reach in through the open drivers window and turn the ignition on. On XC60 models it is essential that the key slot in the facia is accessed from behind the steering wheel, via the passenger side of the vehicle. Switch the ignition off, then on again, and check that the SRS warning light comes on, then goes out within 7 seconds. On XC90 models turn the key to position two and then reconnect the battery negative lead.

Driver's airbag contact reel (clockspring)

8 Remove the airbag, as described above, and the steering wheel as described in Chapter 10.
9 Take care not to rotate the contact unit. A peg should be present (clipped to the steering wheel) to enable the clockspring to be locked into position. If necessary use masking tape to lock the 2 sections of the clockspring together **(see illustrations)**. Undo the 4 retaining screws and remove the clockspring from the steering column switch assembly. Disconnect the wiring plug.
10 If a new clockspring is being fitted, cut the cable-tie which is fitted to prevent the unit accidentally rotating.
11 A new reel should be supplied in the centralised position – if not, or if there is a chance the unit is not centralised, proceed as follows. Turn the reel gently anti-clockwise as far as it will go, then turn it back clockwise two complete revolutions. Continue turning until a yellow mark is visible in the contact unit window – at the one o'clock position.

24.9a Insert the contact reel locking screw (arrowed) on XC60 models...

24.9b ...and on XC90 models (arrowed)

24.16 Remove the support bracket mounting bolts (arrowed)

24.21 XC90 passenger airbag mounting bolts (arrowed)

12 Fit the unit to the steering column switch assembly and securely tighten its retaining screws.

13 Refit the steering wheel as described in Chapter 10, and the airbag unit as described above.

Passenger's airbag

14 Disconnect the battery negative lead (see Chapter 5), and wait 10 minutes before proceeding.

15 Remove the glovebox as described in Chapter 11.

XC60

16 Undo the bolts securing the plate below the unit **(see illustration)** and then disconnect the wiring plug.

17 Remove the 6 bolts and lower the airbag from the facia.

18 Refitting is a reversal of removal.

19 Reconnect the battery negative lead and then reach through the drivers window and (from the rear of the steering wheel) insert the key into the key slot on the facia. Switch the ignition off, then on again, and check that the SRS warning light comes on, then goes out within 7 seconds.

XC90

20 Remove the facia end panel to access the facia mounting bolts. Remove the bolts and then remove the facia central mounting bolts - as described in Chapter 11. In theory this action will allow the facia to be moved out enough to allow the airbag to be

removed, however we found this impossible and resorted to removing the complete facia (with the passenger airbag) as described in Chapter 11, Section 27.

21 Disconnect the wiring plug, undo the 6 retaining nuts, and remove the airbag from its mounting **(see illustration)**.

22 Refitting is a reversal of removal.

23 Turn the key to position two and then reconnect the battery negative lead. Reach through the drivers window, switch the ignition on, then off and on again. Check that the SRS warning light comes on, then goes out within 7 seconds.

Airbag control unit

24 Disconnect the battery negative lead as described in Chapter 5. Wait at least 10 minutes before proceeding, to allow and residual electrical energy to dissipate.

25 Remove the centre console and dismantle the lower section as described in Chapter 11.

26 Release the locking catch and disconnect the sensor wiring plug.

27 Note its fitted location, undo the 3 or 4 screws and remove the module **(see illustrations)**.

28 Refitting is a reversal of removal, ensuring the module is fitted with the arrow on its top surface facing forwards.

29 On completion, make sure that no-one is inside the car. On XC60 models reconnect the battery negative lead. On XC90 models turn the key to position two and then reconnect the battery. Switch the ignition off, then on

again, and check that the SRS warning light comes on, then goes out within 7 seconds. **Note:** *If a new control unit has been fitted, suitable software will need to be downloaded and installed from Volvo. Entrust this task to a Volvo dealer or suitably-equipped specialist.*

Side airbags

30 The side airbag units are built into the front seats, and their removal requires that the seat fabric be removed. This is not considered to be a DIY operation, and should be referred to a Volvo dealer or upholstery specialist.

Side crash sensors

31 The side crash sensors are fitted to the B-pillar (between the driver's and passenger's doors), and at the base of the C-pillar. The battery should be disconnected, as described in Chapter 5, before any work is undertaken on the sensors.

32 To remove the sensor on the B-pillar, remove the pillar trim as described in Chapter 11. Release the clips and disconnect the wiring plug from the sensor **(see illustration)**. Undo the retaining screw and remove the sensor.

33 To remove the sensor at the base of the C-pillar, remove the rear seat side pad as described in Chapter 11. Undo the retaining screw and remove the sensor.

34 Refit the sensor(s) to the pillar(s) and tighten the retaining screws to the specified torque. Reconnect the wiring plug.

35 The remainder of refitting is a reversal of removal.

Front crash sensors – XC90 only

36 The front crash sensors are located behind each headlamp. Disconnect the battery, as described in Chapter 5, before removing the sensors.

37 Remove the headlamp as described in Section 10. Disconnect the wiring plug from the sensor, undo the retaining screw and remove the sensor.

38 Refitting is a reversal of removal.

Side curtain airbag

38 In order to remove the side curtain airbag(s), the headlining must be removed.

24.27a Removing the XC60 airbag control unit

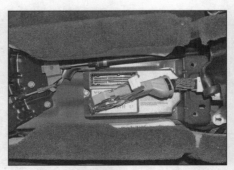

24.27b XC90 airbag control unit

24.32 B-pillar crash sensor

24.41 The passenger airbag disabling switch (arrowed)

25.4a Remove the trim clips...

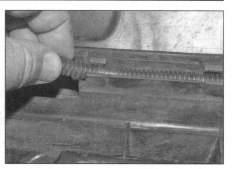

25.4b ...release the wiring loom...

This is not considered a DIY operation, and should be entrusted to a Volvo dealer or upholstery specialist.

Airbag deactivation switch

39 Where fitted, the switch to deactivate the front passenger airbag is located in the trim panel at the end of the facia on the passenger side.

40 To remove the switch, first disconnect the battery negative terminal as described in Chapter 5.

41 Carefully prise off the trim panel, pull forward slightly, and disconnect the wiring plug (see illustration).

42 On the rear of the panel, release the securing clips and remove the switch.

43 Refitting is a reversal of removal.

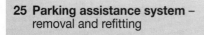

25 Parking assistance system – removal and refitting

Control module

1 On XC60 models the parking assistance module (PAM) is located behind the load area right-hand side trim panel. On XC90 models the PAM is located behind the left-hand load area trim panel. Remove the appropriate panel as described in Chapter 11.

2 Release the retaining clips, remove the module and disconnect the wiring plugs.

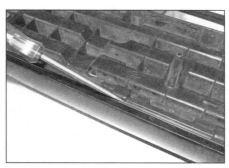

25.4c ...and prise free the bumper reinforcement panel

3 Refitting is a reversal of removal. A new unit may require recalibration and this should be entrusted to a Volvo dealer or suitably-equipped specialist.

Sensors

4 The sensors are set into the rear bumper and on some models into the front bumper. Remove the appropriate bumper as described in Chapter 11. On the rear bumper (XC90 models only) separate the reinforcing panel from the bumper cover (see illustrations).

5 Disconnect the wiring plug from each sensor (see illustration).

6 Spread the retaining clips and pull the sensor from the inside of the bumper (see illustrations).

7 Refitting is a reversal of removal.

25.5 Disconnect the wiring plug from the sensor

26 Fuel filler flap locking motor – removal and refitting

Removal

1 With reference to Chapter 11, remove the right-hand side luggage compartment side trim panel.

2 Disconnect the wiring plug, pull on the emergency release tab to withdraw the plunger, and gently push the top of the motor towards the right-hand side to release it from the bracket. The motor can now be withdrawn (see illustration).

Refitting

3 Refitting is a reversal of removal.

25.6a Spread the retaining clips and...

25.6b ...remove the sensor from the rear of the bumper

26.2 The fuel filler cap locking motor (XC60)

Volvo XC60 wiring diagrams   Diagram 1

 WARNING: This vehicle is fitted with a supplemental restraint system (SRS) consisting of a combination of driver (and passenger) airbag(s), side impact protection airbags and seatbelt pre-tensioners. The use of electrical test equipment on any SRS wiring systems may cause the seatbelt pre-tensioners to abruptly retract and airbags to explosively deploy, resulting in potentially severe personal injury. Extreme care should be taken to correctly identify any circuits to be tested to avoid choosing any of the SRS wiring in error.

For further information see airbag system precautions in body electrical systems chapter.

Note: The SRS wiring harness can normally be identified by yellow and/or orange harness or harness connectors.

Key to symbols

Bulb	⊗	Wire splice, soldered joint, or unspecified connector		Solenoid actuator	
Switch		Connecting wires		Earth point and location	E7
Fuse/Fusible link	F26	Diode		Dashed outline denotes part of a larger item, containing in this case an electronic or solid state device (pins 1 and 2 of a single connector designated c5).	c5/1 c5/2 K
Resistor		Light-emitting diode			
Variable resistor		Item number	12		
Variable resistor		Motor/pump	M	Wire colour (red with black tracer)	Rd/Bk
		Heating element			

Engine fusebox ⑤

Lower fusebox

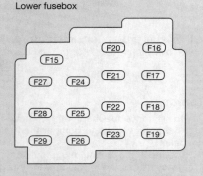

Upper fusebox

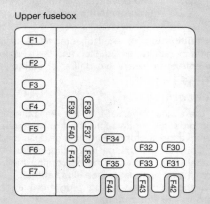

Front fusebox

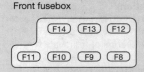

Fuse	Rating	Circuit		Fuse	Rating	Circuit
F1	50A	Main fuse for central electronics control unit		F23	5A	Lighting control unit
F2	50A	Main fuse for central electronics control unit		F24	-	Spare
F3	60A	Main fuse for luggage compartment fusebox		F25	-	Spare
F4	60A	Main fuse for central electronics control unit		F26	-	Spare
F5	60A	Main fuse for central electronics control unit		F27	5A	Headlight washer, horn, ignition relay
F6	-	Spare		F28	20A	Auxiliary lights
F7	100A	Air preheater		F29	15A	Horn
F8	20A	Headlight washers		F30	10A	Engine management
F9	30A	Windscreen wipers		F31	15A	Transmission control unit
F10	25A	Combustion preheater		F32	15A	Air conditioning, coolant pump
F11	40A	Heater blower motor		F33	5A	Climate control
F12	-	Spare		F34	30A	Starter motor
F13	40A	ABS pump		F35	10A	Glow plugs
F14	20A	ABS valves		F36	15A	Engine management
F15	-	Spare		F37	15A	Engine management
F16	10A	Healight levelling, xenon headlights		F38	10A	Engine management
F17	20A	Main fuse for central electronics control unit		F39	10A	Engine management
F18	5A	ABS		F40	20A	Engine management
F19	5A	Power steering		F41	10A	Crankcase ventilation heater
F20	10A	Engine management control unit, transmission control unit		F42	70A	Glow plugs
F21	10A	Heated washer nozzles		F43	80A	Engine cooling fan
F22	5A	Vacuum pump relay		F44	100A	Power steering

H47622

Volvo XC60 wiring diagrams

Diagram 2

Central electronics control unit ⑨
(models up to 2010)

Fuse	Rating	Circuit
F1	5A	Rain sensor
F2	10A	SRS
F3	5A	ABS, electric handbrake
F4	7.5A	Accelerator pedal, heated seats
F5	-	Spare
F6	15A	Display, CD & radio
F7	7.5A	Steering wheel control unit
F8	-	Spare
F9	15A	Main beam headlights
F10	20A	Panoramic roof
F11	7.5A	Reversing lights
F12	-	Spare
F13	15A	Front fog light
F14	15A	Windscreen washers
F15	10A	Adaptive cruise control
F16	-	Spare

Fuse	Rating	Circuit
F17	7.5A	Courtesy lighting, driver's door control panel
F18	5A	Information display
F19	5A	Driver's powered seat
F20	15A	Tailgate wiper
F21	5A	Remote receiver, alarm sensors
F22	20A	Fuel pump
F23	20A	Electric steering column lock
F24	-	Spare
F25	10A	Tailgate lock, fuel filler lock
F26	5A	Alarm siren
F27	5A	Stop/start button
F28	5A	Stop light switch

Note: models from approximately 2010 use an additional
separate passenger fusebox.

Central electronics control unit ⑨
(models from 2010)

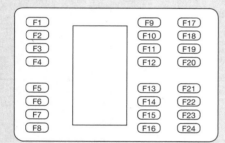

Fuse	Rating	Circuit
F1	15A	Rear wiper
F2	-	Spare
F3	7.5A	Interior lighting, driver's door control unit, electric windows, electric seats
F4	5A	Information display
F5	10A	Adaptive cruise control, collision warning system
F6	7.5A	Interior lighting, rain sensor
F7	7.5A	Steering wheel control unit
F8	10A	Central locking
F9	15A	Rear window washer
F10	15A	Windscreen washers
F11	10A	Tailgate release
F12	-	Spare
F13	20A	Fuel pump
F14	5A	Alarm, climate control panel
F15	15A	Steering lock
F16	5A	Alarm, diagnostic connector
F17	-	Spare
F18	10A	Airbags
F19	5A	Collision warning system
F20	7.5A	Rear heated seats, interior rear view mirror
F21	-	Spare
F22	5A	Stop lights
F23	20A	Sunroof
F24	5A	Immobiliser

Passenger fusebox ⑱
(models from 2010)

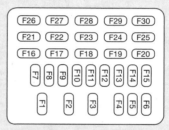

Fuse	Rating	Circuit
F1	40A	Audio control unit, supply to fuses 16-20
F2	-	Spare
F3	-	Spare
F4	-	Spare
F5	-	Spare
F6	-	Spare
F7	15A	Luggage compartment accessory socket
F8	20A	Driver's door control unit
F9	20A	Passenger's door control unit
F10	20A	RH rear door control unit
F11	20A	LH rear door control unit
F12	20A	Keyless entry
F13	20A	Driver's electric seat
F14	20A	Passenger's electric seat
F15	15A	Folding head restraint
F16	5A	Infotainment control unit
F17	10A	Audio system control unit
F18	15A	Audio system
F19	5A	Telematics, bluetooth
F20	10A	Engine management control unit, transmission control unit
F21	7.5A	Rear seat entertainment system
F22	15A	Front & rear accessory sockets
F23	15A	RH rear seat heater
F24	15A	LH rear seat heater
F25	-	Spare
F26	15A	Passenger's seat heater
F27	15A	Driver's seat heater
F28	5A	Parking assistant, trailer control unit
F29	10A	4 wheel drive control unit
F30	10A	Active chassis Four-C

H47623

Volvo XC60 wiring diagrams

Diagram 3

Luggage compartment fusebox 74

Fuse	Rating	Circuit
F1	30A	LH parking brake
F2	30A	RH parking brake
F3	30A	Heated rear window
F4	15A	Trailer socket
F5	20A	Electric tailgate
F6	-	Spare
F7	-	Spare
F8	-	Spare
F9	-	Spare
F10	-	Spare
F11	40A	Trailer control unit
F12	-	Spare

Key to circuits

Diagram 1	Information for wiring diagrams
Diagram 2	Information for wiring diagrams
Diagram 3	Information for wiring diagrams
Diagram 4	Starting & charging, horn, engine cooling fan & accessory sockets
Diagram 5	Stop & reversing lights, running/parking lights, number plate & tail lights, headlights & fog lights
Diagram 6	Direction indicators & hazard warning lights, auxiliary lights & interior lighting
Diagram 7	Headlight levelling, driver information, wash/wipe, headlight washers & heated washer jets
Diagram 8	Power steering, electric sunroof, heated rear window & electric handbrake
Diagram 9	Audio system & climate control
Diagram 10	Central locking
Diagram 11	Electric windows & electric mirrors

Earth locations

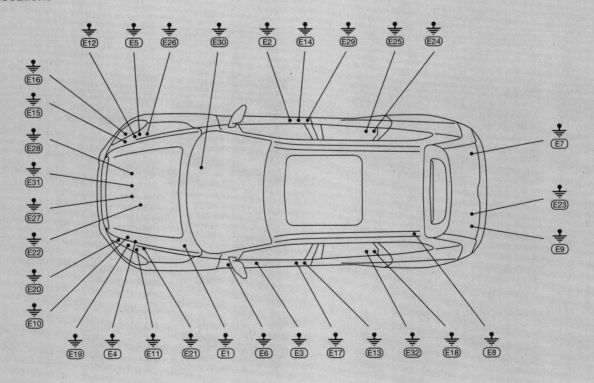

H47624

Wire colours

Bk	Black	**Og**	Orange
Ye	Yellow	**Bu**	Blue
Bn	Brown	**Wh**	White
Gy	Grey	**LGn**	Light Green
Vt	Violet	**Nl**	Natural
Rd	Red	**Gn**	Green
Pk	Pink		

Key to items

1 Battery
2 Battery sensor
3 Alternator
4 Starter motor
5 Engine fusebox
  a = starter relay
  b = ignition relay
  c = horn relay
6 Diesel engine man. control unit

7 Clutch pedal switch
8 Ignition switch
9 Central electronics control unit
10 Steering column lock unit
11 Engine cooling fan
12 Coolant temperature sensor
13 Air conditioning pressure sensor
14 Horn
15 Horn switch

16 Steering wheel clock spring
17 Steering wheel control unit
18 Passenger fusebox
  a = comfort function relay
19 Front accessory socket
20 Rear accessory socket
21 Luggage compartment accessory socket

Diagram 4

H47625

Starting & charging

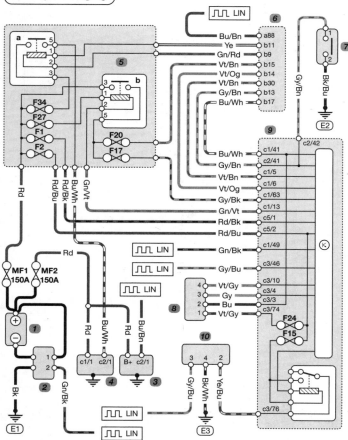

Horn

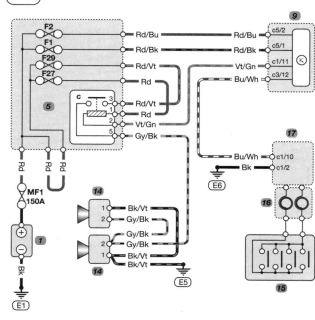

Engine cooling fan

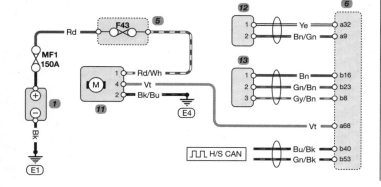

Accessory sockets

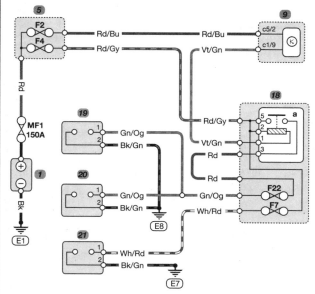

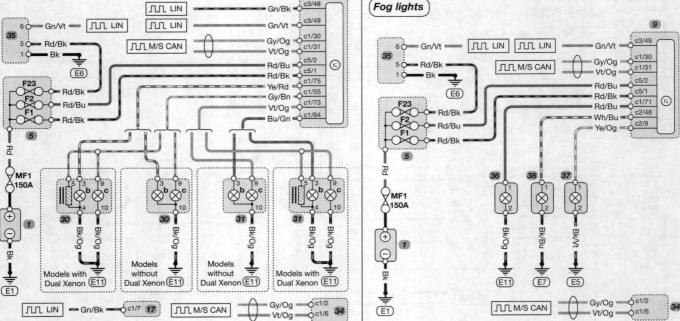

Wire colours

Bk	Black	Og	Orange
Ye	Yellow	Bu	Blue
Bn	Brown	Wh	White
Gy	Grey	LGn	Light Green
Vt	Violet	Nl	Natural
Rd	Red	Gn	Green
Pk	Pink		

Key to items

1 Battery
5 Engine fusebox
9 Central electronics control unit
17 Steering wheel control unit
25 Stop light switch
26 Reversing light switch
27 LH rear light unit
   a = stop light
   b = reversing light
   c = tail light

28 RH rear light unit
   (a to c as above)
29 High level stop light
30 LH front headlight unit
   a = running/parking light
   b = dip beam
   c = main beam
31 RH front headlight unit
   (a to c as above)
32 LH front running/parking light

33 RH front running/parking light
34 Driver information control unit
35 Light switch control unit
36 LH front fog light
37 RH front fog light
38 RH rear fog light
39 Number plate lights/tailgate switch

Diagram 5

H47626

Stop & reversing lights

Running/parking, number plate & tail lights

Headlights

Fog lights

Wire colours

Bk	Black	**Og**	Orange
Ye	Yellow	**Bu**	Blue
Bn	Brown	**Wh**	White
Gy	Grey	**LGn**	Light Green
Vt	Violet	**NI**	Natural
Rd	Red	**Gn**	Green
Pk	Pink		

Key to items

1 Battery
5 Engine fusebox
9 Central electronics control unit
17 Steering wheel control unit
18 Passenger fusebox
   a = comfort function relay
27 LH rear light unit
   d = direction indicator
28 RH rear light unit
   d = direction indicator
30 LH front headlight unit
   d = direction indicator
31 RH front headlight unit
   d = direction indicator

34 Driver's information control unit
42 Hazard warning light switch
43 Driver's door control unit
44 Passenger's door control unit
45 Passenger's mirror assembly
   (direction indicator)
46 Driver's mirror assembly
   (direction indicator)
47 Auxiliary light switch
48 Climate control unit
49 Auxiliary light realy
50 LH auxiliary light
51 RH auxiliary light
52 Electric handbrake switch

53 Front ashtray illumination
54 Rear headphone socket illumination
55 LH front courtesy light
56 RH front courtesy light
57 Glovebox light
58 LH vanity mirror illumination
59 RH vanity mirror illumination
60 Front interior light
   a = interior light
   b = map light
61 Rear reading light
62 Alarm indicator & solar/twilight sensor
63 Luggage compartment light
64 Tailgate lock motor

Diagram 6

H47627

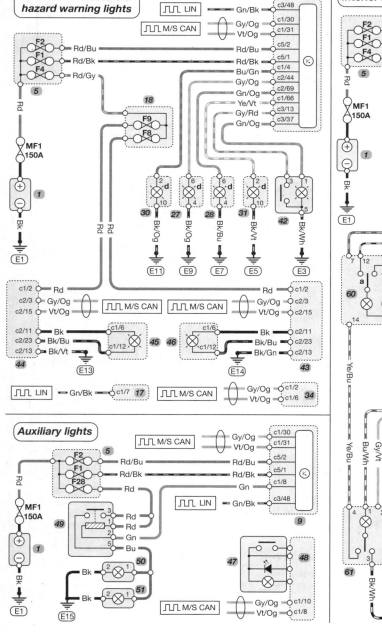

Direction indicators & hazard warning lights

Auxiliary lights

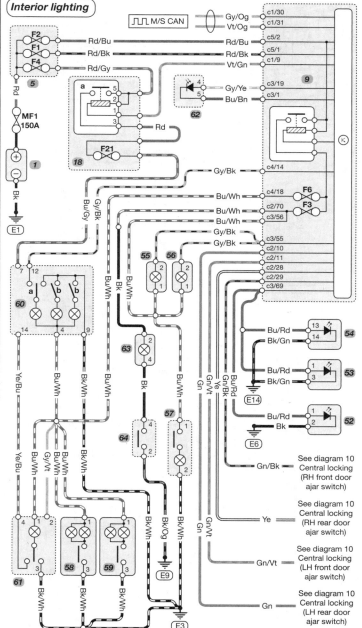

Interior lighting

See diagram 10
Central locking
(RH front door
ajar switch)

See diagram 10
Central locking
(RH rear door
ajar switch)

See diagram 10
Central locking
(LH front door
ajar switch)

See diagram 10
Central locking
(LH rear door
ajar switch)

Wire colours

Bk Black Og Orange
Ye Yellow Bu Blue
Bn Brown Wh White
Gy Grey LGn Light Green
Vt Violet Nl Natural
Rd Red Gn Green
Pk Pink

Key to items

1 Battery
5 Engine fusebox
 b = ignition relay
 d = headlight washer relay
9 Central electronics control unit
17 Steering wheel control unit
30 LH front headlight unit
 e = headlight levelling actuator
31 RH front headlight unit
 e = headlight levelling actuator

34 Driver's information control unit
35 Light switch control unit
67 Headlight washer pump
68 LH heated washer jet
69 RH heated washer jet
70 Front wiper motor
71 Washer pump
72 Rear wiper motor
73 Rain sensor

74 Luggage compartment fusebox
 a = rear wiper relay
75 Electric handbrake control unit
76 Coolant level sensor
77 Washer fluid level sensor
78 Brake fluid level sensor
79 Fuel level sensor/fuel pump

Diagram 7

H47628

Headlight levelling

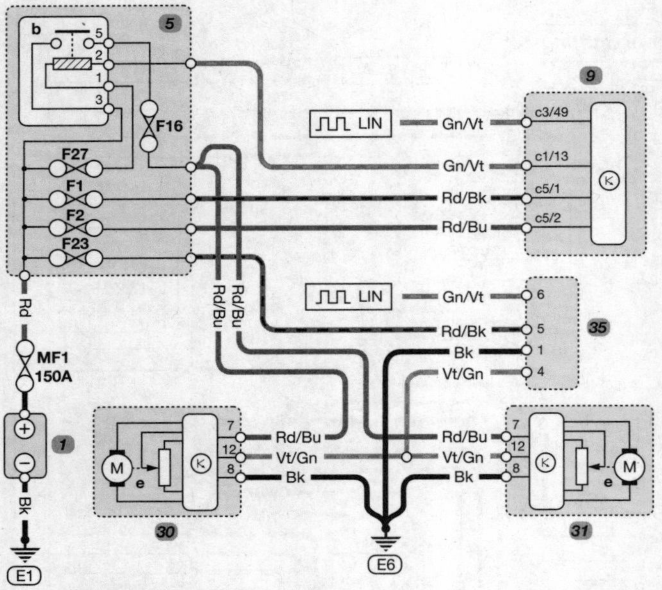

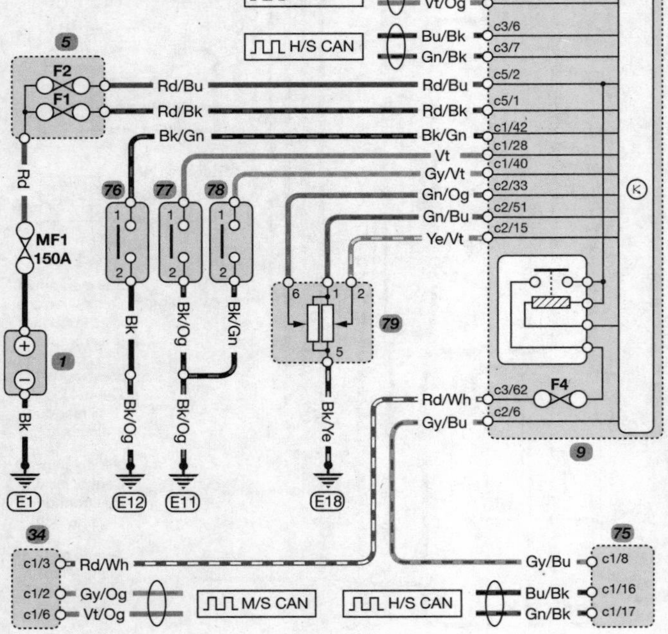

Wash/wipe, headlight washers & heated washer jets

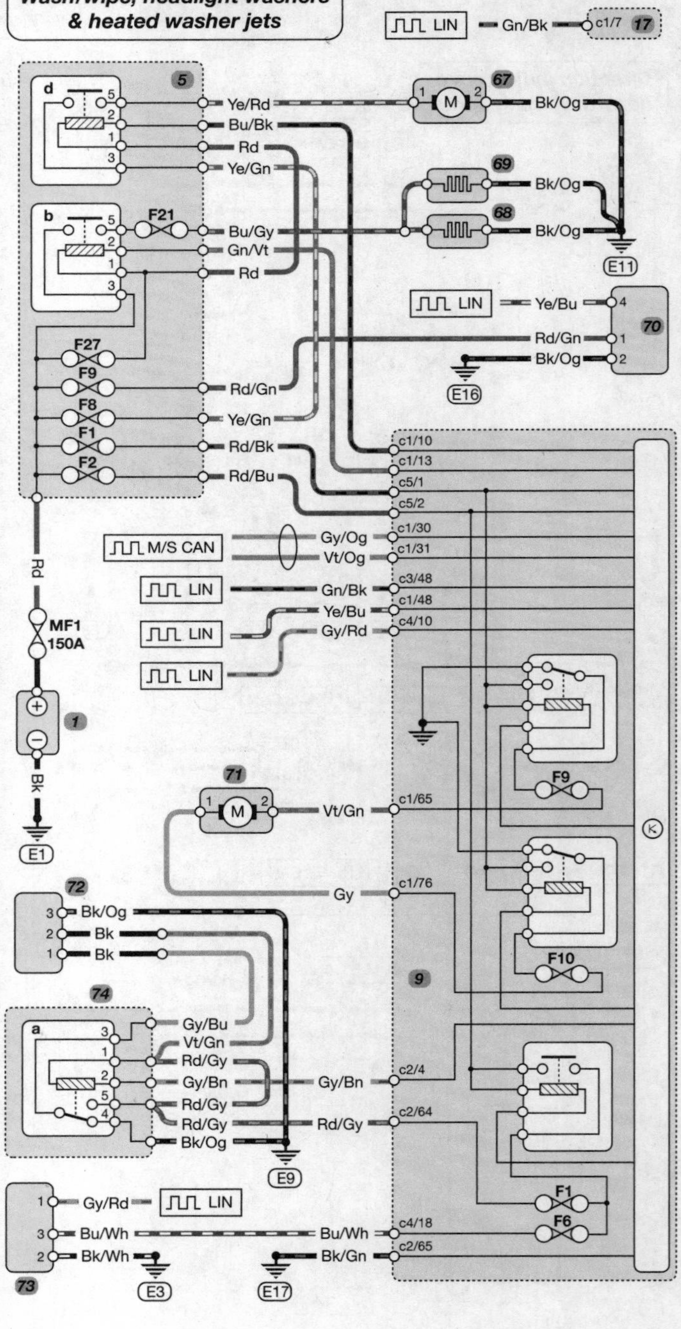

Driver information

Wire colours

Bk	Black	Og	Orange
Ye	Yellow	Bu	Blue
Bn	Brown	Wh	White
Gy	Grey	LGn	Light Green
Vt	Violet	Nl	Natural
Rd	Red	Gn	Green
Pk	Pink		

Key to items

1 Battery
5 Engine fusebox
  b = ignition relay
9 Central electronics control unit
18 Passenger fusebox
  a = comfort function relay
48 Climate control unit
52 Electric handbrake switch
74 Luggage compartment fusebox
  b = heated rear window relay

75 Electric handbrake control unit
83 Power steering motor
84 Power steering control unit
85 Power steering valve
86 LH rear disc lock motor
87 RH rear disc lock motor
88 Sunroof control unit
89 Sunroof control switch
90 Heated rear window/heater mirror switch
91 Heated rear window

Diagram 8

H47629

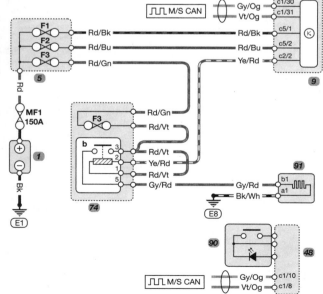

Wire colours

Bk	Black	**Og**	Orange
Ye	Yellow	**Bu**	Blue
Bn	Brown	**Wh**	White
Gy	Grey	**LGn**	Light Green
Vt	Violet	**Nl**	Natural
Rd	Red	**Gn**	Green
Pk	Pink		

Key to items

1   Battery
5   Engine fusebox
   e   = engine management relay
   f   = climate control relay
6   Diesel engine management control unit
9   Central electronics control unit
13   Air conditioning pressure sensor
17   Steering wheel control unit
18   Passenger fusebox
   a   = comfort function relay
45   LH mirror assembly
   (outside air temperature sensor)
48   Climate control unit

62   Alarm indicator & solar/twilight sensor
95   Infotainment control unit
96   USB port
97   Auxiliary input
98   Microphone
99   Window antenna amplifier
100   Rear spoiler antenna
101   RH rear window antenna
102   Audio unit
103   LH tweeter
104   RH tweeter
105   LH front door speaker
106   RH front door speaker

107   LH rear speaker
108   RH rear speaker
109   Compressor clutch
112   Heater blower motor
113   Heater blower motor control unit
114   RH temperature flap
115   LH temperature flap
116   Recirculation flap
117   Defroster flap
118   Floor/ventilation flap
119   Air quality sensor
120   Evaporator sensor

Diagram 9

H47630

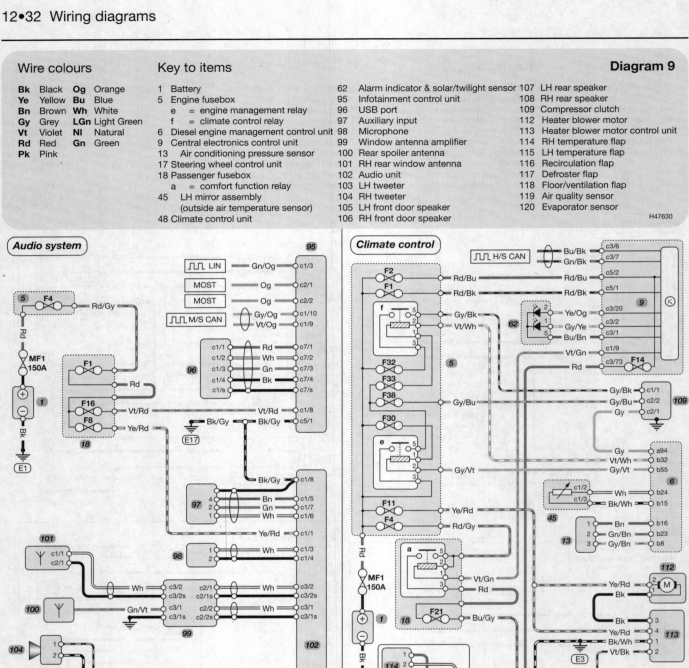

Audio system

Climate control

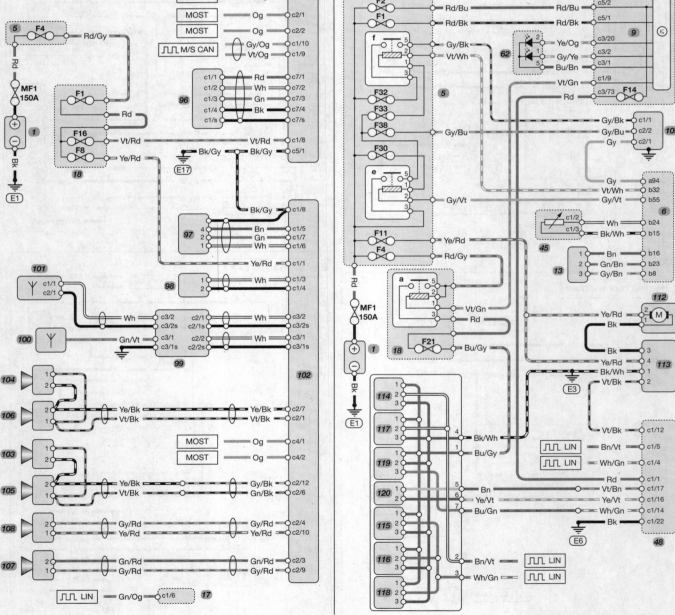

Wire colours

Bk	Black	**Og**	Orange
Ye	Yellow	**Bu**	Blue
Bn	Brown	**Wh**	White
Gy	Grey	**LGn**	Light Green
Vt	Violet	**Nl**	Natural
Rd	Red	**Gn**	Green
Pk	Pink		

Key to items

1	Battery
5	Engine fusebox
9	Central electronics control unit
18	Passenger fusebox
35	Light switch control unit
39	Number plate light/tailgate switch
43	Driver's door control unit
44	Passenger's door control unit
64	Tailgate lock motor
125	Fuel filler flap lock motor
126	Remote receiver unit
127	LH rear door control unit
128	RH rear door control unit
129	Driver's door lock motor assembly
130	Passenger's door lock motor assembly
131	LH rear door lock motor assembly
132	RH rear door lock motor assembly
133	Driver's door lock switch
134	Passenger's door lock switch

Diagram 10

H47631

Central locking

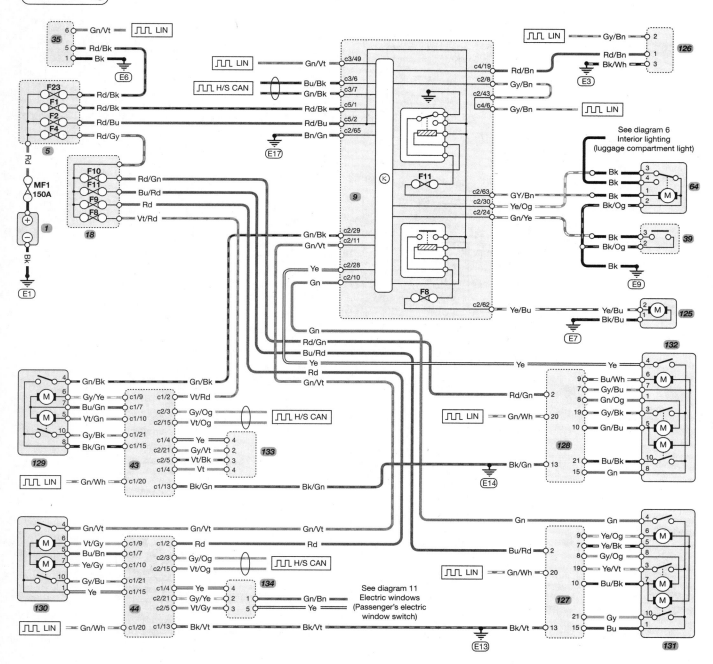

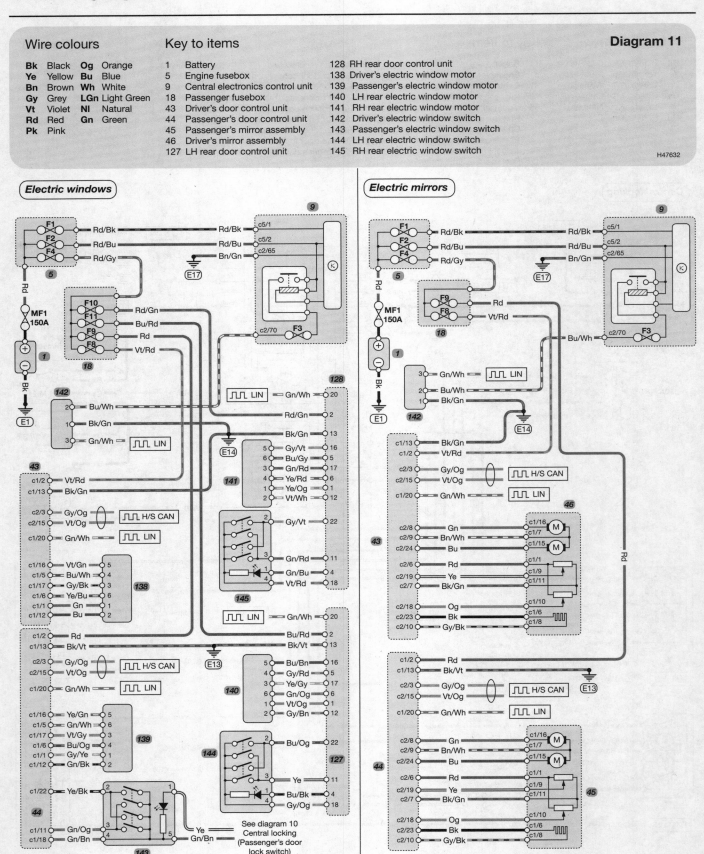

Wire colours

Bk	Black	**Og**	Orange
Ye	Yellow	**Bu**	Blue
Bn	Brown	**Wh**	White
Gy	Grey	**LGn**	Light Green
Vt	Violet	**Nl**	Natural
Rd	Red	**Gn**	Green
Pk	Pink		

Key to items

1	Battery
5	Engine fusebox
9	Central electronics control unit
18	Passenger fusebox
43	Driver's door control unit
44	Passenger's door control unit
45	Passenger's mirror assembly
46	Driver's mirror assembly
127	LH rear door control unit

128	RH rear door control unit
138	Driver's electric window motor
139	Passenger's electric window motor
140	LH rear electric window motor
141	RH rear electric window motor
142	Driver's electric window switch
143	Passenger's electric window switch
144	LH rear electric window switch
145	RH rear electric window switch

Diagram 11

H47632

Electric windows

Electric mirrors

See diagram 10
Central locking
(Passenger's door
lock switch)

Volvo XC90 wiring diagrams

Diagram 1

 WARNING: This vehicle is fitted with a supplemental restraint system (SRS) consisting of a combination of driver (and passenger) airbag(s), side impact protection airbags and seatbelt pre-tensioners. The use of electrical test equipment on any SRS wiring systems may cause the seatbelt pre-tensioners to abruptly retract and airbags to explosively deploy, resulting in potentially severe personal injury. Extreme care should be taken to correctly identify any circuits to be tested to avoid choosing any of the SRS wiring in error.
For further information see airbag system precautions in body electrical systems chapter.
Note: The SRS wiring harness can normally be identified by yellow and/or orange harness or harness connectors.

Key to symbols

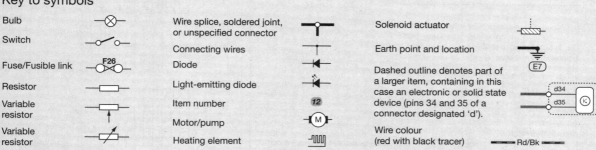

Bulb		Wire splice, soldered joint, or unspecified connector		Solenoid actuator	
Switch		Connecting wires		Earth point and location	
Fuse/Fusible link	F26	Diode		Dashed outline denotes part of a larger item, containing in this case an electronic or solid state device (pins 34 and 35 of a connector designated 'd').	
Resistor		Light-emitting diode			
Variable resistor		Item number	12		
Variable resistor		Motor/pump	M	Wire colour (red with black tracer)	Rd/Bk
		Heating element			

Engine fusebox 5

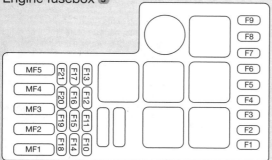

Fuse	Rating	Circuit
MF1	60A	Glow plugs
MF2	60A	Engine cooling fan
MF3	-	Spare
MF4	-	Spare
MF5	-	Spare
F1	30A	ABS
F2	30A	ABS
F3	35A	Headlight washers
F4	-	Spare
F5	35A	Auxiliary lights
F6	35A	Starter motor relay
F7	25A	Front wiper motor
F8	15A	Fuel pump
F9	15A	Transmission control unit
F10	20A	Ignition coils, engine management control unit
F11	10A	Throttle pedal sensor, A/C compressor
F12	15A	Engine management control unit, fuel injectors, air flow sensor
F13	10A	Intake manifold actuator
F14	20A	Oxygen sensor
F15	15A	Crankcase ventilation, A/C, engine management control unit
F16	20A	Driver's dip beam headlight
F17	20A	Passenger's dip beam headlight
F18	-	Spare
F19	5A	Engine management control unit, engine management relay
F20	15A	Parking lights
F21	20A	Vacuum pump

Passenger fusebox 13

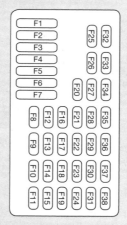

Fuse	Rating	Circuit
F1	30A	Heater blower motor
F2	30A	Audio amplifier
F3	25A	Powered driver's seat
F4	25A	Powered passenger seat
F5	25A	Driver's door control unit
F6	25A	Passenger's door control unit
F7	-	Spare
F8	15A	Audio system
F9	10A	Navigation system
F10	5A	On board diagnostics, lighting switch, steering wheel control unit and angle sensor
F11	7.5A	Ignition switch, SRS, engine management and transmission control unit, immobiliser
F12	10A	Interior light, upper electronics control unit
F13	15A	Sunroof
F14	5A	Bluetooth
F15/	-	Spare
F38	-	Spare

H47642

Volvo XC90 wiring diagrams

Diagram 2

Central electronics control unit ⑨

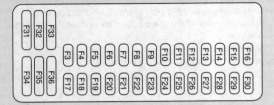

Fuse	Rating	Circuit
F1	15A	Heated passenger seat
F2	15A	Heated driver's seat
F3	15A	Horn
F4	-	Spare
F5	10A	Audio system
F6	-	Spare
F7	-	Spare
F8	5A	Alarm siren
F9	5A	Stop light switch
F10	10A	Instruments, climate cntrol, powered driver's seat, occupant weight sensor
F11	15A	Front and rear accessory sockets
F12	-	Spare
F13	-	Spare
F14	-	Spare
F15	5A	ABS, DSTC
F16	10A	Power steering, active headlights
F17	7.5A	Driver's side daytime running lights
F18	7.5A	Passener's side daytime running lights
F19	-	Spare
F20	-	Spare
F21	10A	Transmission control unit
F22	10A	Driver's main beam
F23	10A	Passenger's main beam
F24	-	Spare
F25	-	Spare
F26	-	Spare
F27	-	Spare
F28	5A	Powered passenger seat, rear seat entertainment system
F29	7.5A	Fuel pump
F30	5A	Blind spot information system
F31	-	Spare
F32	-	Spare
F33	20A	Vacuum pump
F34	15A	Front and rear washer pump
F35	-	Spare
F36	-	Spare

Rear electronics control unit ㉒

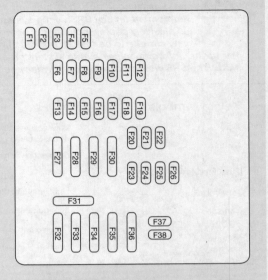

Fuse	Rating	Circuit
F1	10A	Reversing lights
F2	20A	Side lights, number plate lights, stop lights, rear fog lights, luggage compartment light
F3	15A	Accessories
F4	-	Spare
F5	10A	Rear electronic control unit
F6	-	Spare
F7	15A	Trailer wiring 30
F8	15A	Luggage compartment accessory socket
F9	20A	LH rear electric window
F10	20A	RH rear electric window
F11	-	Spare
F12	-	Spare
F13	-	Spare
F14	15A	Rear A/C
F15	-	Spare
F16	-	Spare
F17	5A	Accessory audio
F18	-	Spare
F19	15A	Rear wiper
F20	20A	Trailer wiring 15
F21	-	Spare
F22	-	Spare
F23	7.5A	AWD
F24	-	Spare
F25	-	Spare
F26	5A	Parking assist
F27	30A	Trailer wiring, parking assist, AWD
F28	15A	Central locking
F29	25A	Driver's side trailer lighting, side lights, direction indicators
F30	25A	Passenger's side trailer lighting, stop light, rear fog lights, direction indicator
F31	40A	Main fuse for F37 and F38
F32	-	Spare
F33	-	Spare
F34	-	Spare
F35	-	Spare
F36	-	Spare
F37	20A	Heated rear window
F38	20A	Heated rear window

Earth locations

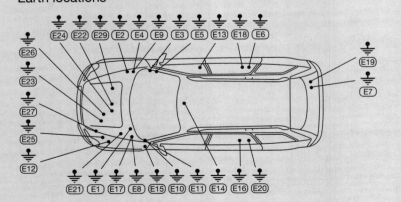

H47643

Wire colours

Bk	Black	**Og**	Orange
Ye	Yellow	**Bu**	Blue
Bn	Brown	**Wh**	White
Gy	Grey	**LGn**	Light Green
Vt	Violet	**Nl**	Natural
Rd	Red	**Gn**	Green
Pk	Pink		

Key to items

1 Battery
2 Battery charging terminal
3 Alternator
4 Starter motor
5 Engine fusebox
  a = starter relay
6 Diesel engine man. control unit
7 Clutch pedal switch
8 Ignition switch
9 Central electronics control unit
10 Transmission control unit
11 Impulse sensor
12 Battery fusebox
13 Passenger fusebox
14 Climate control pressure sensor
15 Coolant temperature sensor
16 Engine cooling fan control unit
17 Engine cooling fan motor
18 Steering wheel control unit
19 Steering wheel clock springs
20 Horn switch
21 Horn
22 Rear electronics control unit
23 Front accessory socket
24 Rear accessory socket
25 Luggage compartment accessory socket

Diagram 3

H47644

Starting & charging

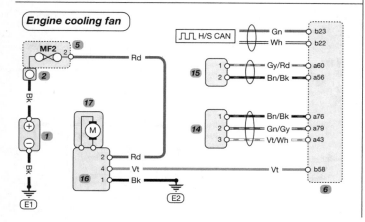

Engine cooling fan

Horn

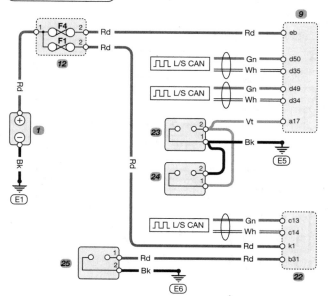

Accessory sockets

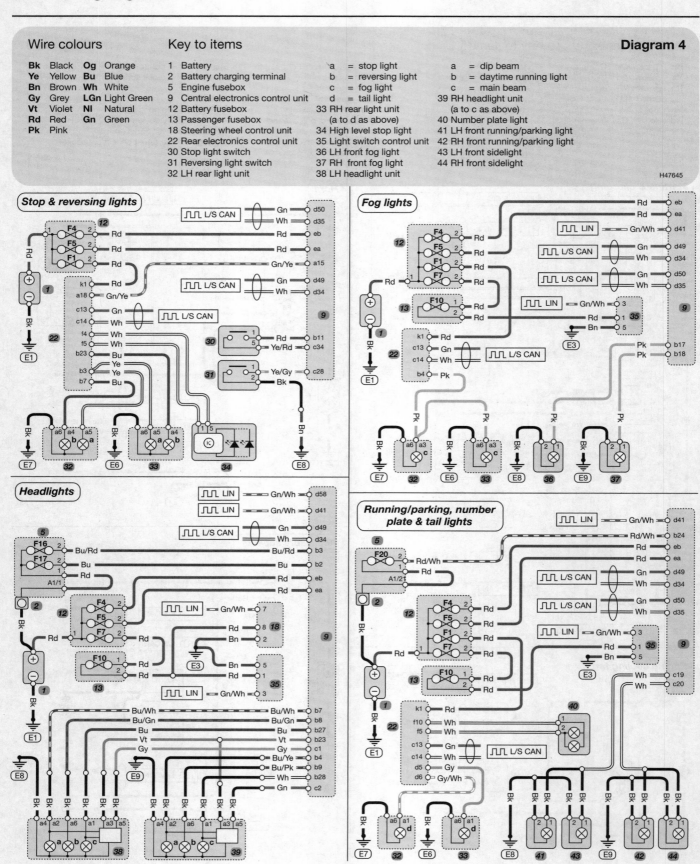

Wire colours

Bk Black **Og** Orange
Ye Yellow **Bu** Blue
Bn Brown **Wh** White
Gy Grey **LGn** Light Green
Vt Violet **Nl** Natural
Rd Red **Gn** Green
Pk Pink

Key to items

1 Battery
2 Battery charging terminal
5 Engine fusebox
9 Central electronics control unit
12 Battery fusebox
13 Passenger fusebox
18 Steering wheel control unit
22 Rear electronics control unit
30 Stop light switch
31 Reversing light switch
32 LH rear light unit

a = stop light
b = reversing light
c = fog light
d = tail light
33 RH rear light unit
(a to d as above)
34 High level stop light
35 Light switch control unit
36 LH front fog light
37 RH front fog light
38 LH headlight unit

a = dip beam
b = daytime running light
c = main beam
39 RH headlight unit
(a to c as above)
40 Number plate light
41 LH front running/parking light
42 RH front running/parking light
43 LH front sidelight
44 RH front sidelight

Diagram 4

H47645

Stop & reversing lights

Fog lights

Headlights

Running/parking, number plate & tail lights

Wire colours

Bk	Black	**Og**	Orange
Ye	Yellow	**Bu**	Blue
Bn	Brown	**Wh**	White
Gy	Grey	**LGn**	Light Green
Vt	Violet	**Nl**	Natural
Rd	Red	**Gn**	Green
Pk	Pink		

Key to items

1 Battery
2 Battery charging terminal
5 Engine fusebox
9 Central electronics control unit
12 Battery fusebox
13 Passenger fusebox
22 Rear electronics control unit
32 LH rear light unit
  e = direction indicator
33 RH rear light unit
  e = direction indicator

50 LH front direction indicator
51 RH front direction indicator
52 LH mirror assembly
  (indicator side repeater)
53 RH mirror assembly
  (indicator side repeater)
54 Hazard warning switch
55 LH auxiliary light
56 RH auxiliary light
57 Upper electronics control unit
58 Interior light

59 LH vanity mirror illumination
60 RH vanity mirror illumination
61 Rear reading light
62 Luggage compartment light
63 Tailgate lock assembly
64 LH front courtesy light
65 RH front courtesy light
66 Glovebox light/switch
67 Ignition switch illumination
68 Auxiliary light relay

Diagram 5

H47646

Direction indicators & hazard warning lights

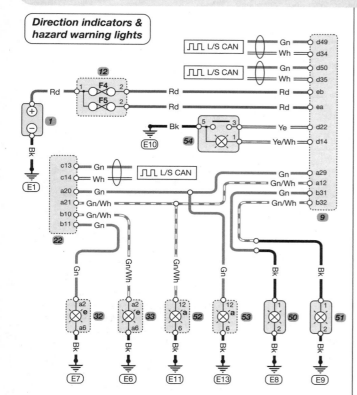

Auxiliary lights

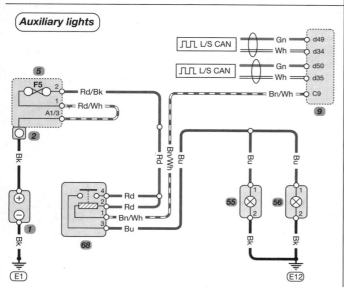

Interior lighting

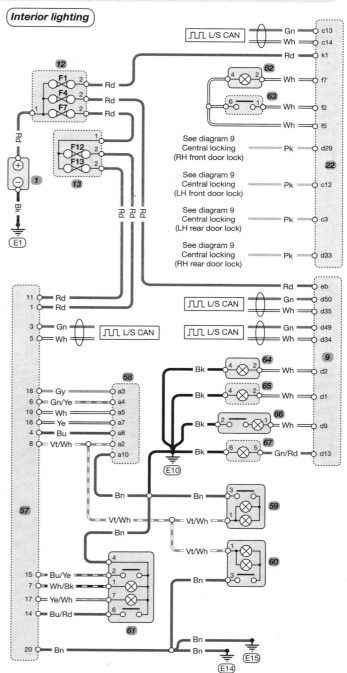

Wire colours

Bk	Black	**Og**	Orange
Ye	Yellow	**Bu**	Blue
Bn	Brown	**Wh**	White
Gy	Grey	**LGn**	Light Green
Vt	Violet	**Nl**	Natural
Rd	Red	**Gn**	Green
Pk	Pink		

Key to items

1 Battery
2 Battery charging terminal
5 Engine fusebox
6 Diesel engine man. control unit
9 Central electronics control unit
11 Impulse sensor
12 Battery fusebox
13 Passenger fusebox
15 Coolant temperature sensor
18 Steering wheel control unit
22 Rear electronics control unit
35 Light switch control unit

53 RH mirror assembly
   (outside air temperature sensor)
57 Upper electronics control unit
71 LH headlight levelling motor
72 RH headlight levelling motor
73 Fuel level sensor
74 Washer fluid level sensor
75 Handbrake switch
76 Low brake fluid sensor
77 Coolant level sensor
78 Oil level sensor
80 Passenger/driver door control unit

81 Driver's information control unit
82 Front wiper motor
83 Rear wiper motor
84 Headlight washer relay
85 Headlight washer pump
86 Windscreen washer pump
87 Intermittent wiper relay
88 Wiper low/high speed relay
89 Rain sensor

Diagram 6

H47647

Headlight levelling / Driver information

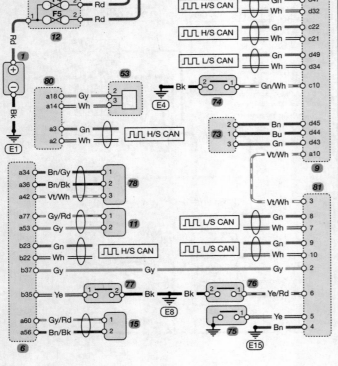

Wash/wipe & headlight washers

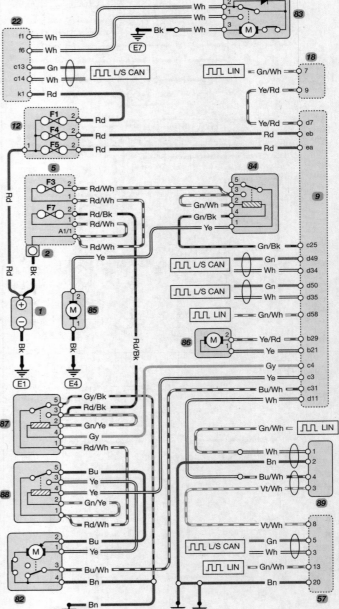

Wire colours

Bk	Black	Og	Orange
Ye	Yellow	Bu	Blue
Bn	Brown	Wh	White
Gy	Grey	LGn	Light Green
Vt	Violet	Nl	Natural
Rd	Red	Gn	Green
Pk	Pink		

Key to items

1 Battery
9 Central electronics control unit
12 Battery fusebox
13 Passenger fusebox
18 Steering wheel control unit
22 Rear electronics control unit
52 LH mirror assembly (mirror heating)
53 RH mirror assembly (mirror heating)
57 Upper electronics control unit
58 Interior light

80 Passenger/driver door control unit
93 Power steering control unit
94 Power steering valve
95 Sunroof motor
96 Sunroof control unit
97 Sunroof switch
98 Climate control unit
99 Heated rear window/mirror switch
100 Heated rear window
101 Driver's heated seat switch
102 Passenger's heated seat switch
103 Driver's heated seat control unit

104 Passenger's heated seat control unit
105 Driver's seat backrest heating pad
106 Driver's seat temperature sensor
107 Driver's seat heating pad
108 Passenger's seat backrest heating pad
109 Passenger's seat temperature sensor
110 Passenger's seat heating pad
111 Driver/passenger door control unit

Diagram 7

H47648

Power steering
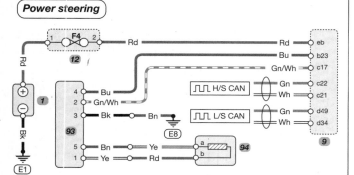

Heated rear window
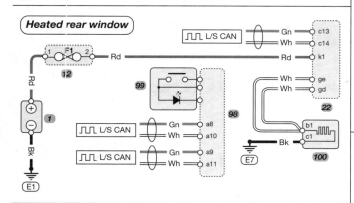

Heated mirrors
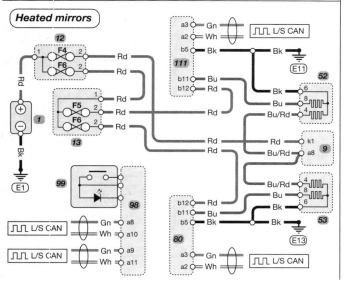

Electric sunroof
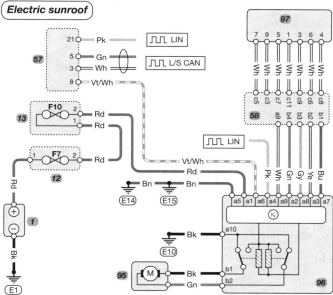

Heated seats
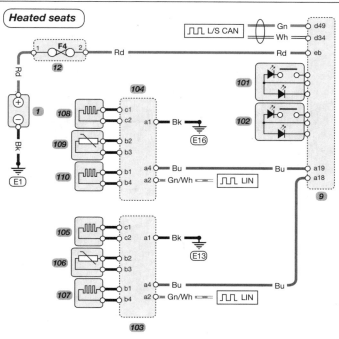

Diagram 8

Wire colours

Bk	Black	**Og**	Orange
Ye	Yellow	**Bu**	Blue
Bn	Brown	**Wh**	White
Gy	Grey	**LGn**	Light Green
Vt	Violet	**Nl**	Natural
Rd	Red	**Gn**	Green
Pk	Pink		

Key to items

1 Battery
2 Battery charging terminal
5 Engine fusebox
6 Diesel engine man. control unit
9 Central electronics control unit
12 Battery fusebox
13 Passenger fusebox
14 Climate control pressure sensor
15 Coolant temperature sensor
53 RH mirror assembly
  (outside air temperature sensor)
80 Passenger/driver door control unit
98 Climate control unit

115 Audio unit
116 USB port
117 External equipment aux input
118 LH window antenna amplifier
119 RH window antenna amplifier
120 LH front speaker
121 LH front tweeter
122 LH rear speaker
123 RH front speaker
124 RH front tweeter
125 RH rear speaker
126 Engine management relay
127 Heater blower control unit

128 Heater blower motor
129 Compressor clutch relay
130 Compressor clutch
131 Evaporator temperature sensor
132 LH side temperature flap motor
133 RH side temperature flap motor
134 Defrost flap motor
135 Recirculation flap motor
136 Floor/ventilation flap motor
137 Air quality sensor
138 Solar sensor

H47649

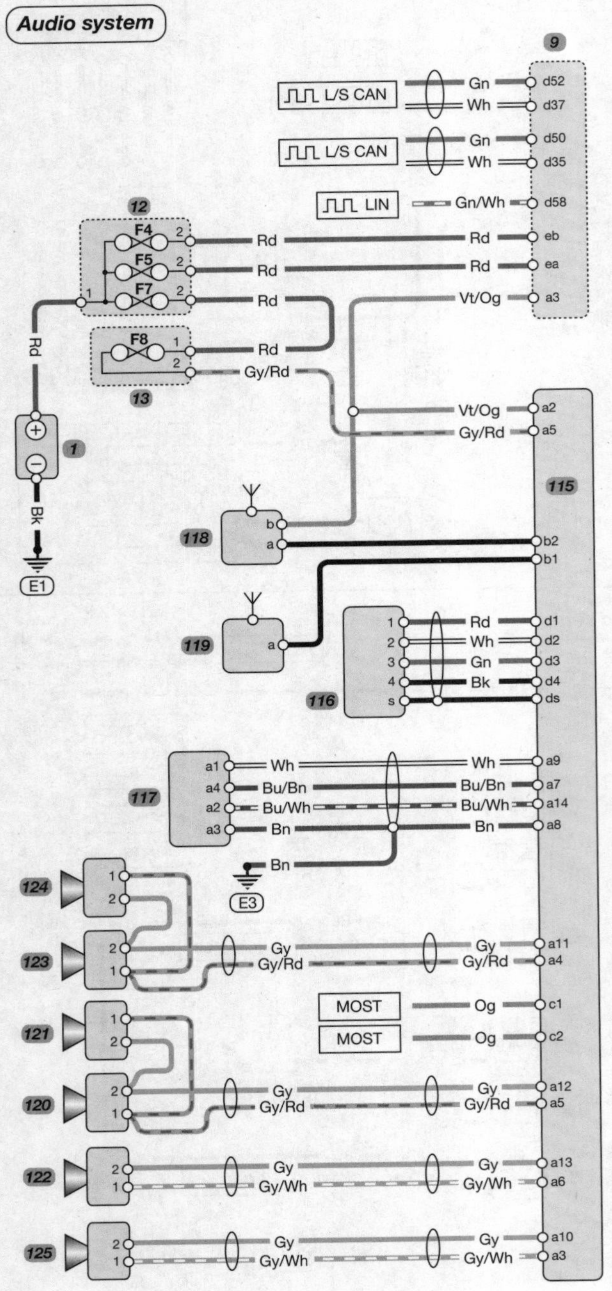

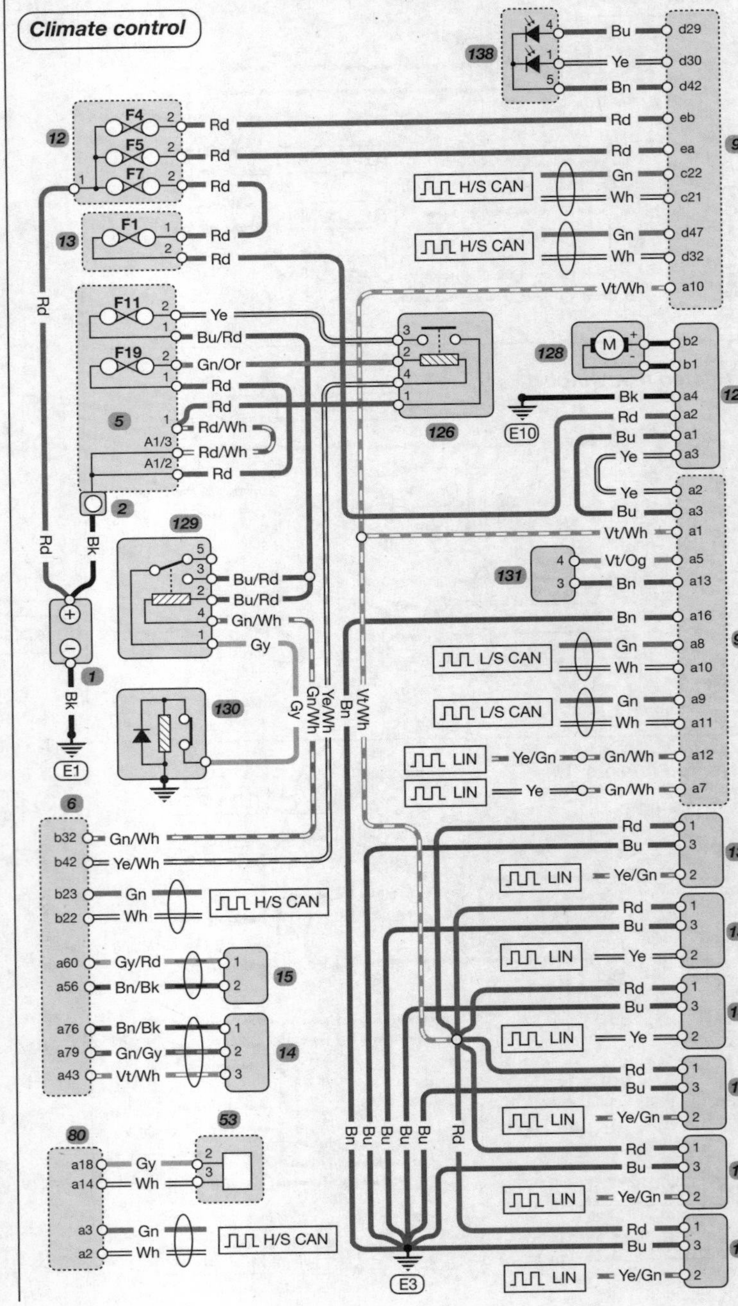

Audio system

Climate control

Wire colours

Bk	Black	Og	Orange
Ye	Yellow	Bu	Blue
Bn	Brown	Wh	White
Gy	Grey	LGn	Light Green
Vt	Violet	Nl	Natural
Rd	Red	Gn	Green
Pk	Pink		

Key to items

1 Battery
9 Central electronics control unit
12 Battery fusebox
13 Passenger fusebox
22 Rear electronics control unit
57 Upper electronics control unit
63 Tailgate lock assembly
80 Passenger/driver door control unit
98 Climate control unit
111 Driver/passenger door control unit
140 Master lock switch

141 Child safety lock switch
142 LH front door lock assembly
143 RH front door lock assembly
144 LH rear door lock assembly
145 RH rear door lock assembly
146 LH rear door deadlocking relay
147 RH rear door deadlocking relay
148 LH rear electric window switch
149 RH rear electric window switch
151 Fuel filler flap motor

Diagram 9

H47650

Central locking

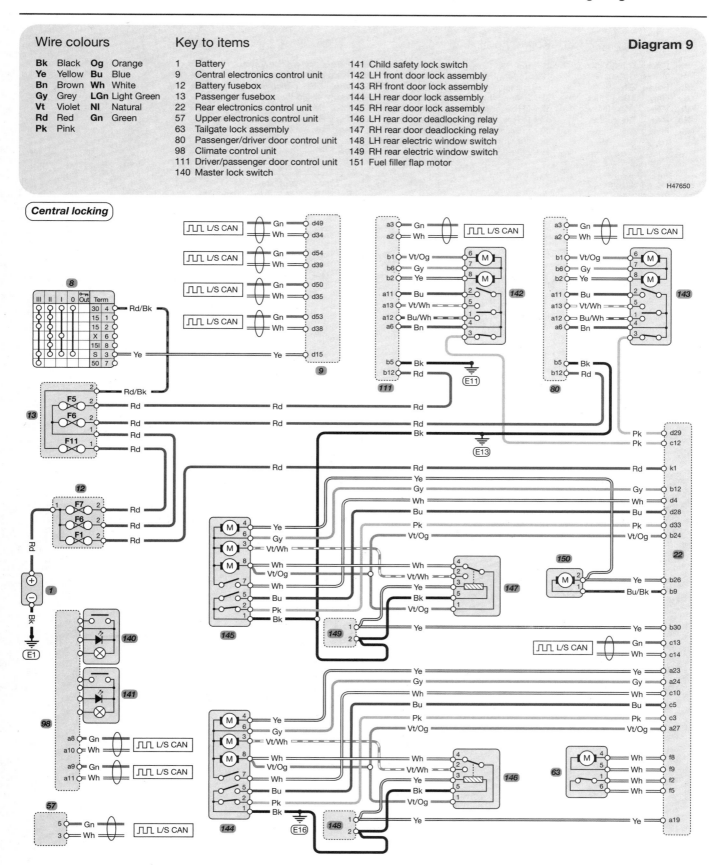

Wire colours

Bk Black **Og** Orange
Ye Yellow **Bu** Blue
Bn Brown **Wh** White
Gy Grey **LGn** Light Green
Vt Violet **Nl** Natural
Rd Red **Gn** Green
Pk Pink

Key to items

1 Battery
12 Battery fusebox
13 Passenger fusebox
22 Rear electronics control unit
52 LH mirror assembly
53 RH mirror assembly
80 Passenger/driver door control unit
98 Climate control unit
111 Driver/passenger door control unit

148 LH rear electric window switch
149 RH rear electric window switch
155 LH front electric window switch
156 RH front electric window switch
157 LH rear electric window motor
158 RH rear electric window motor
159 Retractable mirror switch

Diagram 10

H47651

Electric windows

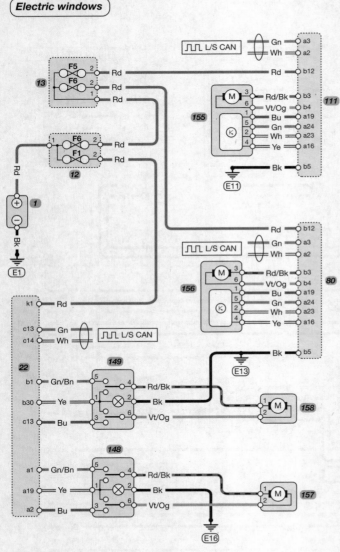

Electric mirrors

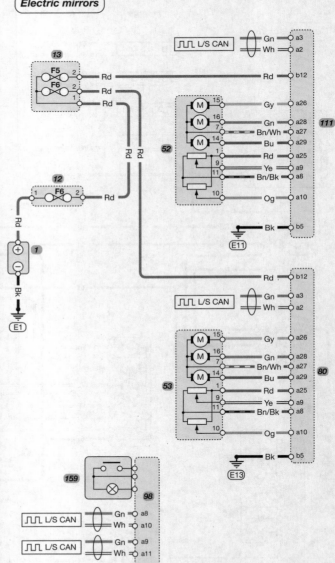

Dimensions and weights

Note: *All figures are approximate, and may vary according to model. Refer to manufacturer's data for exact figures.*

Dimensions

XC60 models

Overall length	4627 mm
Overall width (including door mirrors)	2120 mm
Overall height	1713 mm
Wheelbase	2774 mm

XC90 models

Overall length	4807 mm
Overall width (including door mirrors)	2112 mm
Overall height	1784 mm
Wheelbase	2857 mm

Weights

All models

Kerb weight	Refer to the vehicle identification plate on the right-hand B-pillar.
Maximum roof rack load	100 kg
Maximum trailer weight (braked)	Refer to the vehicle identification plate on the right-hand B-pillar.

Fuel economy

Although depreciation is still the biggest part of the cost of motoring for most car owners, the cost of fuel is more immediately noticeable. These pages give some tips on how to get the best fuel economy.

Working it out

Manufacturer's figures

Car manufacturers are required by law to provide fuel consumption information on all new vehicles sold. These 'official' figures are obtained by simulating various driving conditions on a rolling road or a test track. Real life conditions are different, so the fuel consumption actually achieved may not bear much resemblance to the quoted figures.

How to calculate it

Many cars now have trip computers which will

display fuel consumption, both instantaneous and average. Refer to the owner's handbook for details of how to use these.

To calculate consumption yourself (and maybe to check that the trip computer is accurate), proceed as follows.

1. Fill up with fuel and note the mileage, or zero the trip recorder.
2. Drive as usual until you need to fill up again.
3. Note the amount of fuel required to refill the tank, and the mileage covered since the previous fill-up.
4. Divide the mileage by the amount of fuel used to obtain the consumption figure.

For example:

    Mileage at first fill-up (a) = 27,903
    Mileage at second fill-up (b) = 28,346
    Mileage covered (b - a) = 443
    Fuel required at second fill-up = 48.6 litres

The half-completed changeover to metric units in the UK means that we buy our fuel

in litres, measure distances in miles and talk about fuel consumption in miles per gallon. There are two ways round this: the first is to convert the litres to gallons before doing the calculation (by dividing by 4.546, or see Table 1). So in the example:

    48.6 litres ÷ 4.546 = 10.69 gallons
    443 miles ÷ 10.69 gallons = 41.4 mpg

The second way is to calculate the consumption in miles per litre, then multiply that figure by 4.546 (or see Table 2).

So in the example, fuel consumption is:

    443 miles ÷ 48.6 litres = 9.1 mpl
    9.1 mpl x 4.546 = 41.4 mpg

The rest of Europe expresses fuel consumption in litres of fuel required to travel 100 km (l/100 km). For interest, the conversions are given in Table 3. In practice it doesn't matter what units you use, provided you know what your normal consumption is and can spot if it's getting better or worse.

Table 1: conversion of litres to Imperial gallons

litres	1	2	3	4	5	10	20	30	40	50	60	70
gallons	0.22	0.44	0.66	0.88	1.10	2.24	4.49	6.73	8.98	11.22	13.47	15.71

Table 2: conversion of miles per litre to miles per gallon

miles per litre	5	6	7	8	9	10	11	12	13	14
miles per gallon	23	27	32	36	41	46	50	55	59	64

Table 3: conversion of litres per 100 km to miles per gallon

litres per 100 km	4	4.5	5	5.5	6	6.5	7	8	9	10
miles per gallon	71	63	56	51	47	43	40	35	31	28

Maintenance

A well-maintained car uses less fuel and creates less pollution. In particular:

Filters

Change air and fuel filters at the specified intervals.

Oil

Use a good quality oil of the lowest viscosity specified by the vehicle manufacturer (see *Lubricants and fluids*). Check the level often and be careful not to overfill.

Spark plugs

When applicable, renew at the specified intervals.

Tyres

Check tyre pressures regularly. Under-inflated tyres have an increased rolling resistance. It is generally safe to use the higher pressures specified for full load conditions even when not fully laden, but keep an eye on the centre band of tread for signs of wear due to over-inflation.

When buying new tyres, consider the 'fuel saving' models which most manufacturers include in their ranges.

Driving style

Acceleration

Acceleration uses more fuel than driving at a steady speed. The best technique with modern cars is to accelerate reasonably briskly to the desired speed, changing up through the gears as soon as possible without making the engine labour.

Air conditioning

Air conditioning absorbs quite a bit of energy from the engine – typically 3 kW (4 hp) or so. The effect on fuel consumption is at its worst in slow traffic. Switch it off when not required.

Anticipation

Drive smoothly and try to read the traffic flow so as to avoid unnecessary acceleration and braking.

Automatic transmission

When accelerating in an automatic, avoid depressing the throttle so far as to make the transmission hold onto lower gears at higher speeds. Don't use the 'Sport' setting, if applicable.

When stationary with the engine running, select 'N' or 'P'. When moving, keep your left foot away from the brake.

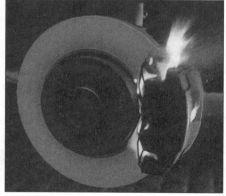

Braking

Braking converts the car's energy of motion into heat – essentially, it is wasted. Obviously some braking is always going to be necessary, but with good anticipation it is surprising how much can be avoided, especially on routes that you know well.

Carshare

Consider sharing lifts to work or to the shops. Even once a week will make a difference.

Electrical loads

Electricity is 'fuel' too; the alternator which charges the battery does so by converting some of the engine's energy of motion into electrical energy. The more electrical accessories are in use, the greater the load on the alternator. Switch off big consumers like the heated rear window when not required.

Freewheeling

Freewheeling (coasting) in neutral with the engine switched off is dangerous. The effort required to operate power-assisted brakes and steering increases when the engine is not running, with a potential lack of control in emergency situations.

In any case, modern fuel injection systems automatically cut off the engine's fuel supply on the overrun (moving and in gear, but with the accelerator pedal released).

Gadgets

Bolt-on devices claiming to save fuel have been around for nearly as long as the motor car itself. Those which worked were rapidly adopted as standard equipment by the vehicle manufacturers. Others worked only in certain situations, or saved fuel only at the expense of unacceptable effects on performance, driveability or the life of engine components.

The most effective fuel saving gadget is the driver's right foot.

Journey planning

Combine (eg) a trip to the supermarket with a visit to the recycling centre and the DIY store, rather than making separate journeys.

When possible choose a travelling time outside rush hours.

Load

The more heavily a car is laden, the greater the energy required to accelerate it to a given speed. Remove heavy items which you don't need to carry.

One load which is often overlooked is the contents of the fuel tank. A tankful of fuel (55 litres / 12 gallons) weighs 45 kg (100 lb) or so. Just half filling it may be worthwhile.

Lost?

At the risk of stating the obvious, if you're going somewhere new, have details of the route to hand. There's not much point in achieving record mpg if you also go miles out of your way.

Parking

If possible, carry out any reversing or turning manoeuvres when you arrive at a parking space so that you can drive straight out when you leave. Manoeuvering when the engine is cold uses a lot more fuel.

Driving around looking for free on-street parking may cost more in fuel than buying a car park ticket.

Premium fuel

Most major oil companies (and some supermarkets) have premium grades of fuel which are several pence a litre dearer than the standard grades. Reports vary, but the consensus seems to be that if these fuels improve economy at all, they do not do so by enough to justify their extra cost.

Roof rack

When loading a roof rack, try to produce a wedge shape with the narrow end at the front. Any cover should be securely fastened – if it flaps it's creating turbulence and absorbing energy.

Remove roof racks and boxes when not in use – they increase air resistance and can create a surprising amount of noise.

Short journeys

The engine is at its least efficient, and wear is highest, during the first few miles after a cold start. Consider walking, cycling or using public transport.

Speed

The engine is at its most efficient when running at a steady speed and load at the rpm where it develops maximum torque. (You can find this figure in the car's handbook.) For most cars this corresponds to between 55 and 65 mph in top gear.

Above the optimum cruising speed, fuel consumption starts to rise quite sharply. A car travelling at 80 mph will typically be using 30% more fuel than at 60 mph.

Supermarket fuel

It may be cheap but is it any good? In the UK all supermarket fuel must meet the relevant British Standard. The major oil companies will say that their branded fuels have better additive packages which may stop carbon and other deposits building up. A reasonable compromise might be to use one tank of branded fuel to three or four from the supermarket.

Switch off when stationary

Switch off the engine if you look like being stationary for more than 30 seconds or so. This is good for the environment as well as for your pocket. Be aware though that frequent restarts are hard on the battery and the starter motor.

Windows

Driving with the windows open increases air turbulence around the vehicle. Closing the windows promotes smooth airflow and

reduced resistance. The faster you go, the more significant this is.

And finally . . .

Driving techniques associated with good fuel economy tend to involve moderate acceleration and low top speeds. Be considerate to the needs of other road users who may need to make brisker progress; even if you do not agree with them this is not an excuse to be obstructive.

Safety must always take precedence over economy, whether it is a question of accelerating hard to complete an overtaking manoeuvre, killing your speed when confronted with a potential hazard or switching the lights on when it starts to get dark.

Conversion factors

Length (distance)

Inches (in)	x 25.4	=	Millimetres (mm)	x 0.0394	= Inches (in)
Feet (ft)	x 0.305	=	Metres (m)	x 3.281	= Feet (ft)
Miles	x 1.609	=	Kilometres (km)	x 0.621	= Miles

Volume (capacity)

Cubic inches (cu in; in^3)	x 16.387	=	Cubic centimetres (cc; cm^3)	x 0.061	= Cubic inches (cu in; in^3)
Imperial pints (Imp pt)	x 0.568	=	Litres (l)	x 1.76	= Imperial pints (Imp pt)
Imperial quarts (Imp qt)	x 1.137	=	Litres (l)	x 0.88	= Imperial quarts (Imp qt)
Imperial quarts (Imp qt)	x 1.201	=	US quarts (US qt)	x 0.833	= Imperial quarts (Imp qt)
US quarts (US qt)	x 0.946	=	Litres (l)	x 1.057	= US quarts (US qt)
Imperial gallons (Imp gal)	x 4.546	=	Litres (l)	x 0.22	= Imperial gallons (Imp gal)
Imperial gallons (Imp gal)	x 1.201	=	US gallons (US gal)	x 0.833	= Imperial gallons (Imp gal)
US gallons (US gal)	x 3.785	=	Litres (l)	x 0.264	= US gallons (US gal)

Mass (weight)

Ounces (oz)	x 28.35	=	Grams (g)	x 0.035	= Ounces (oz)
Pounds (lb)	x 0.454	=	Kilograms (kg)	x 2.205	= Pounds (lb)

Force

Ounces-force (ozf; oz)	x 0.278	=	Newtons (N)	x 3.6	= Ounces-force (ozf; oz)
Pounds-force (lbf; lb)	x 4.448	=	Newtons (N)	x 0.225	= Pounds-force (lbf; lb)
Newtons (N)	x 0.1	=	Kilograms-force (kgf; kg)	x 9.81	= Newtons (N)

Pressure

Pounds-force per square inch (psi; lbf/in^2; lb/in^2)	x 0.070	=	Kilograms-force per square centimetre (kgf/cm^2; kg/cm^2)	x 14.223	= Pounds-force per square inch (psi; lbf/in^2; lb/in^2)
Pounds-force per square inch (psi; lbf/in^2; lb/in^2)	x 0.068	=	Atmospheres (atm)	x 14.696	= Pounds-force per square inch (psi; lbf/in^2; lb/in^2)
Pounds-force per square inch (psi; lbf/in^2; lb/in^2)	x 0.069	=	Bars	x 14.5	= Pounds-force per square inch (psi; lbf/in^2; lb/in^2)
Pounds-force per square inch (psi; lbf/in^2; lb/in^2)	x 6.895	=	Kilopascals (kPa)	x 0.145	= Pounds-force per square inch (psi; lbf/in^2; lb/in^2)
Kilopascals (kPa)	x 0.01	=	Kilograms-force per square centimetre (kgf/cm^2; kg/cm^2)	x 98.1	= Kilopascals (kPa)
Millibar (mbar)	x 100	=	Pascals (Pa)	x 0.01	= Millibar (mbar)
Millibar (mbar)	x 0.0145	=	Pounds-force per square inch (psi; lbf/in^2; lb/in^2)	x 68.947	= Millibar (mbar)
Millibar (mbar)	x 0.75	=	Millimetres of mercury (mmHg)	x 1.333	= Millibar (mbar)
Millibar (mbar)	x 0.401	=	Inches of water (inH$_2$O)	x 2.491	= Millibar (mbar)
Millimetres of mercury (mmHg)	x 0.535	=	Inches of water (inH$_2$O)	x 1.868	= Millimetres of mercury (mmHg)
Inches of water (inH$_2$O)	x 0.036	=	Pounds-force per square inch (psi; lbf/in^2; lb/in^2)	x 27.68	= Inches of water (inH$_2$O)

Torque (moment of force)

Pounds-force inches (lbf in; lb in)	x 1.152	=	Kilograms-force centimetre (kgf cm; kg cm)	x 0.868	= Pounds-force inches (lbf in; lb in)
Pounds-force inches (lbf in; lb in)	x 0.113	=	Newton metres (Nm)	x 8.85	= Pounds-force inches (lbf in; lb in)
Pounds-force inches (lbf in; lb in)	x 0.083	=	Pounds-force feet (lbf ft; lb ft)	x 12	= Pounds-force inches (lbf in; lb in)
Pounds-force feet (lbf ft; lb ft)	x 0.138	=	Kilograms-force metres (kgf m; kg m)	x 7.233	= Pounds-force feet (lbf ft; lb ft)
Pounds-force feet (lbf ft; lb ft)	x 1.356	=	Newton metres (Nm)	x 0.738	= Pounds-force feet (lbf ft; lb ft)
Newton metres (Nm)	x 0.102	=	Kilograms-force metres (kgf m; kg m)	x 9.804	= Newton metres (Nm)

Power

Horsepower (hp)	x 745.7	=	Watts (W)	x 0.0013	= Horsepower (hp)

Velocity (speed)

Miles per hour (miles/hr; mph)	x 1.609	=	Kilometres per hour (km/hr; kph)	x 0.621	= Miles per hour (miles/hr; mph)

Fuel consumption*

Miles per gallon, Imperial (mpg)	x 0.354	=	Kilometres per litre (km/l)	x 2.825	= Miles per gallon, Imperial (mpg)
Miles per gallon, US (mpg)	x 0.425	=	Kilometres per litre (km/l)	x 2.352	= Miles per gallon, US (mpg)

Temperature

Degrees Fahrenheit = (°C x 1.8) + 32   Degrees Celsius (Degrees Centigrade; °C) = (°F - 32) x 0.56

It is common practice to convert from miles per gallon (mpg) to litres/100 kilometres (l/100km), where mpg x l/100 km = 282

Spare parts are available from many sources, including maker's appointed garages, accessory shops, and motor factors. To be sure of obtaining the correct parts, it will sometimes be necessary to quote the vehicle identification number. If possible, it can also be useful to take the old parts along for positive identification. Items such as starter motors and alternators may be available under a service exchange scheme – any parts returned should be clean.

Our advice regarding spare parts is as follows.

Officially appointed garages

This is the best source of parts which are peculiar to your car, and which are not otherwise generally available (eg, badges, interior trim, certain body panels, etc). It is also the only place at which you should buy parts if the car is still under warranty.

Accessory shops

These are very good places to buy materials and components needed for the maintenance of your car (oil, air and fuel filters, light bulbs, drivebelts, greases, brake pads, touch-up paint, etc). Components of this nature

sold by a reputable shop are usually of the same standard as those used by the car manufacturer.

Besides components, these shops also sell tools and general accessories, usually have convenient opening hours, charge lower prices, and can often be found close to home. Some accessory shops have parts counters where components needed for almost any repair job can be purchased or ordered.

Motor factors

Good factors will stock all the more important components which wear out comparatively quickly, and can sometimes supply individual components needed for the overhaul of a larger assembly (eg, brake seals and hydraulic parts, bearing shells, pistons, valves). They may also handle work such as cylinder block reboring, crankshaft regrinding, etc.

Engine reconditioners

These specialise in engine overhaul and can also supply components. It is recommended that the establishment is a member of the Federation of Engine Re-Manufacturers, or a similar society.

Tyre and exhaust specialists

These outlets may be independent, or members of a local or national chain. They frequently offer competitive prices when compared with a main dealer or local garage, but it will pay to obtain several quotes before making a decision. When researching prices, also ask what extras may be added – for instance fitting a new valve, balancing the wheel and tyre disposal all both commonly charged on top of the price of a new tyre.

Other sources

Beware of parts or materials obtained from market stalls, car boot sales, on-line auctions or similar outlets. Such items are not invariably sub-standard, but there is little chance of compensation if they do prove unsatisfactory. In the case of safety-critical components such as brake pads, there is the risk not only of financial loss, but also of an accident causing injury or death.

Second-hand components or assemblies obtained from a car breaker can be a good buy in some circumstances, but this sort of purchase is best made by the experienced DIY mechanic.

Vehicle identification numbers

Modifications are a continuing and unpublicised process in vehicle manufacture, quite apart from major model changes. Spare parts manuals and lists are compiled upon a numerical basis, the individual vehicle identification numbers being essential to correct identification of the component concerned.

When ordering spare parts always give as much information as possible. Quote the vehicle type and year, vehicle identification number (VIN), and engine number, as appropriate.

The vehicle identification number (VIN) appears in a number of locations, including on a plastic tag attached to the passenger side of the facia panel, visible through the windscreen

and on the right-hand side door pillar (see illustrations).

The engine number is stamped on the right-hand end of the cylinder block.

The transmission identification numbers are located on a plate attached to the top of the transmission casing, or cast into the casing itself.

Chassis (VIN) number at the base of the windscreen

Chassis (VIN) number on the right-hand B-pillar

Whenever servicing, repair or overhaul work is carried out on the car or its components, observe the following procedures and instructions. This will assist in carrying out the operation efficiently and to a professional standard of workmanship.

Joint mating faces and gaskets

When separating components at their mating faces, never insert screwdrivers or similar implements into the joint between the faces in order to prise them apart. This can cause severe damage which results in oil leaks, coolant leaks, etc upon reassembly. Separation is usually achieved by tapping along the joint with a soft-faced hammer in order to break the seal. However, note that this method may not be suitable where dowels are used for component location.

Where a gasket is used between the mating faces of two components, a new one must be fitted on reassembly; fit it dry unless otherwise stated in the repair procedure. Make sure that the mating faces are clean and dry, with all traces of old gasket removed. When cleaning a joint face, use a tool which is unlikely to score or damage the face, and remove any burrs or nicks with an oilstone or fine file.

Make sure that tapped holes are cleaned with a pipe cleaner, and keep them free of jointing compound, if this is being used, unless specifically instructed otherwise.

Ensure that all orifices, channels or pipes are clear, and blow through them, preferably using compressed air.

Oil seals

Oil seals can be removed by levering them out with a wide flat-bladed screwdriver or similar implement. Alternatively, a number of self-tapping screws may be screwed into the seal, and these used as a purchase for pliers or some similar device in order to pull the seal free.

Whenever an oil seal is removed from its working location, either individually or as part of an assembly, it should be renewed.

The very fine sealing lip of the seal is easily damaged, and will not seal if the surface it contacts is not completely clean and free from scratches, nicks or grooves. If the original sealing surface of the component cannot be restored, and the manufacturer has not made provision for slight relocation of the seal relative to the sealing surface, the component should be renewed.

Protect the lips of the seal from any surface which may damage them in the course of fitting. Use tape or a conical sleeve where possible. Where indicated, lubricate the seal lips with oil before fitting and, on dual-lipped seals, fill the space between the lips with grease.

Unless otherwise stated, oil seals must be fitted with their sealing lips toward the lubricant to be sealed.

Use a tubular drift or block of wood of the appropriate size to install the seal and, if the seal housing is shouldered, drive the seal down to the shoulder. If the seal housing is unshouldered, the seal should be fitted with its face flush with the housing top face (unless otherwise instructed).

Screw threads and fastenings

Seized nuts, bolts and screws are quite a common occurrence where corrosion has set in, and the use of penetrating oil or releasing fluid will often overcome this problem if the offending item is soaked for a while before attempting to release it. The use of an impact driver may also provide a means of releasing such stubborn fastening devices, when used in conjunction with the appropriate screwdriver bit or socket. If none of these methods works, it may be necessary to resort to the careful application of heat, or the use of a hacksaw or nut splitter device. Before resorting to extreme methods, check that you are not dealing with a left-hand thread!

Studs are usually removed by locking two nuts together on the threaded part, and then using a spanner on the lower nut to unscrew the stud. Studs or bolts which have broken off below the surface of the component in which they are mounted can sometimes be removed using a stud extractor.

Always ensure that a blind tapped hole is completely free from oil, grease, water or other fluid before installing the bolt or stud. Failure to do this could cause the housing to crack due to the hydraulic action of the bolt or stud as it is screwed in.

For some screw fastenings, notably cylinder head bolts or nuts, torque wrench settings are no longer specified for the latter stages of tightening, "angle-tightening" being called up instead. Typically, a fairly low torque wrench setting will be applied to the bolts/nuts in the correct sequence, followed by one or more stages of tightening through specified angles.

When checking or retightening a nut or bolt to a specified torque setting, slacken the nut or bolt by a quarter of a turn, and then retighten to the specified setting. However, this should not be attempted where angular tightening has been used.

Locknuts, locktabs and washers

Any fastening which will rotate against a component or housing during tightening should always have a washer between it and the relevant component or housing.

Spring or split washers should always be renewed when they are used to lock a critical component such as a big-end bearing retaining bolt or nut. Locktabs which are folded over to retain a nut or bolt should always be renewed.

Self-locking nuts can be re-used in non-critical areas, providing resistance can be felt when the locking portion passes over the bolt or stud thread. However, it should be noted that self-locking stiffnuts tend to lose their effectiveness after long periods of use, and should then be renewed as a matter of course.

Split pins must always be replaced with new ones of the correct size for the hole.

When thread-locking compound is found on the threads of a fastener which is to be re-used, it should be cleaned off with a wire brush and solvent, and fresh compound applied on reassembly.

Special tools

Some repair procedures in this manual entail the use of special tools such as a press, two or three-legged pullers, spring compressors, etc. Wherever possible, suitable readily-available alternatives to the manufacturer's special tools are described, and are shown in use. In some instances, where no alternative is possible, it has been necessary to resort to the use of a manufacturer's tool, and this has been done for reasons of safety as well as the efficient completion of the repair operation. Unless you are highly-skilled and have a thorough understanding of the procedures described, never attempt to bypass the use of any special tool when the procedure described specifies its use. Not only is there a very great risk of personal injury, but expensive damage could be caused to the components involved.

Environmental considerations

When disposing of used engine oil, brake fluid, antifreeze, etc, give due consideration to any detrimental environmental effects. Do not, for instance, pour any of the above liquids down drains into the general sewage system, or onto the ground to soak away. Many local council refuse tips provide a facility for waste oil disposal, as do some garages. You can find your nearest disposal point by calling the Environment Agency on 08708 506 506 or by visiting www.oilbankline.org.uk.

Note: It is illegal and anti-social to dump oil down the drain. To find the location of your local oil recycling bank, call 08708 506 506 or visit www.oilbankline.org.uk.

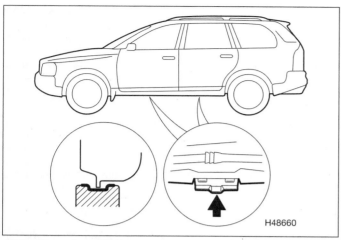

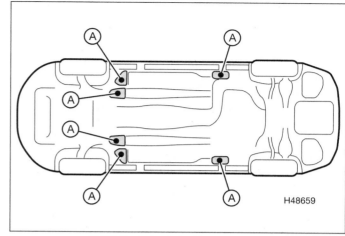

Sill jacking points. XC90 model shown, but XC60 models are similar

XC60 Underbody jacking points (A)

The jack supplied with the vehicle tool kit should **only** be used for changing the roadwheels in an emergency – see *Wheel changing* at the front of this book. When carrying out any other kind of work, raise the vehicle using a heavy-duty hydraulic (or 'trolley') jack, and always supplement the jack with axle stands positioned under the vehicle jacking points. If the roadwheels do not have to be removed, consider using wheel ramps – if wished, these can be placed under the wheels once the vehicle has been raised using a hydraulic jack, and the vehicle lowered onto the ramps so that it is resting on its wheels.

Only ever jack the vehicle up on a solid, level surface. If there is even a slight slope, take great care that the vehicle cannot move as the wheels are lifted off the ground. Jacking up on an uneven or gravelled surface is not recommended, as the weight of the vehicle will not be evenly distributed, and the jack may slip as the vehicle is raised.

As far as possible, do not leave the vehicle unattended once it has been raised, particularly if children are playing nearby.

Before jacking up the front of the car, ensure that the handbrake is firmly applied. When jacking up the rear of the car, place wooden chocks in front of the front wheels, and engage first gear (or P).

The jack supplied with the vehicle locates in the sill flanges, at the points marked on each side of the car **(see illustration)**. Ensure that the jack head is correctly engaged before attempting to raise the vehicle.

When using a hydraulic jack or axle stands, the jack head or axle stand head may be placed under one of the four jacking points inboard of the door sills **(see illustrations)**. When jacking or supporting the vehicle at these points, always use a block of wood between the jack head or axle stand, and the vehicle body. It is also considered good practice to use a large block of wood when supporting under other areas, to spread the load over a wider area, and reduce the risk of damage to the underside of the car (it also

helps to prevent the underbody coating from being damaged by the jack or axle stand). **Do not** jack the vehicle under any other part of the sill, engine sump, floor pan, subframe, or directly under any of the steering or suspension components.

Never work under, around, or near a raised vehicle, unless it is adequately supported on stands. Do not rely on a jack alone, as even a hydraulic jack could fail under load. Makeshift methods should not be used to lift and support the car during servicing work.

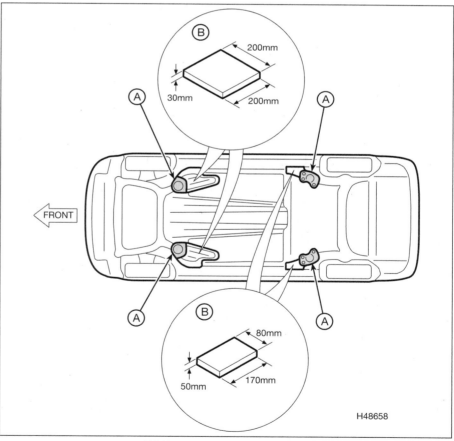

XC90 underbody jacking points.

Support the vehicle on the subframe bracket (A) or just behind the subframe (B). If using position 'B' at the front of the vehicle a block of wood approximately 200mm X 200mm X 30mm should be used to spread the load. If using position 'B' at the rear of the vehicle a block of wood approximately 170mm X 80mm X 50mm should be used to spread the load

Introduction

A selection of good tools is a fundamental requirement for anyone contemplating the maintenance and repair of a motor vehicle. For the owner who does not possess any, their purchase will prove a considerable expense, offsetting some of the savings made by doing-it-yourself. However, provided that the tools purchased meet the relevant national safety standards and are of good quality, they will last for many years and prove an extremely worthwhile investment.

To help the average owner to decide which tools are needed to carry out the various tasks detailed in this manual, we have compiled three lists of tools under the following headings: *Maintenance and minor repair*, *Repair and overhaul*, and *Special*. Newcomers to practical mechanics should start off with the *Maintenance and minor repair* tool kit, and confine themselves to the simpler jobs around the vehicle. Then, as confidence and experience grow, more difficult tasks can be undertaken, with extra tools being purchased as, and when, they are needed. In this way, a *Maintenance and minor repair* tool kit can be built up into a *Repair and overhaul* tool kit over a considerable period of time, without any major cash outlays. The experienced do-it-yourselfer will have a tool kit good enough for most repair and overhaul procedures, and will add tools from the *Special* category when it is felt that the expense is justified by the amount of use to which these tools will be put.

Maintenance and minor repair tool kit

The tools given in this list should be considered as a minimum requirement if routine maintenance, servicing and minor repair operations are to be undertaken. We recommend the purchase of combination spanners (ring one end, open-ended the other); although more expensive than open-ended ones, they do give the advantages of both types of spanner.

☐ *Combination spanners:*
  Metric - 8 to 19 mm inclusive
☐ *Adjustable spanner - 35 mm jaw (approx.)*
☐ *Spark plug spanner (with rubber insert) - petrol models*
☐ *Spark plug gap adjustment tool - petrol models*
☐ *Set of feeler gauges*
☐ *Brake bleed nipple spanner*
☐ *Screwdrivers:*
  Flat blade - 100 mm long x 6 mm dia
  Cross blade - 100 mm long x 6 mm dia
  Torx - various sizes (not all vehicles)
☐ *Combination pliers*
☐ *Hacksaw (junior)*
☐ *Tyre pump*
☐ *Tyre pressure gauge*
☐ *Oil can*
☐ *Oil filter removal tool (if applicable)*
☐ *Fine emery cloth*
☐ *Wire brush (small)*
☐ *Funnel (medium size)*
☐ *Sump drain plug key (not all vehicles)*

Repair and overhaul tool kit

These tools are virtually essential for anyone undertaking any major repairs to a motor vehicle, and are additional to those given in the *Maintenance and minor repair* list. Included in this list is a comprehensive set of sockets. Although these are expensive, they will be found invaluable as they are so versatile - particularly if various drives are included in the set. We recommend the half-inch square-drive type, as this can be used with most proprietary torque wrenches.

The tools in this list will sometimes need to be supplemented by tools from the *Special* list:

☐ *Sockets to cover range in previous list (including Torx sockets)*
☐ *Reversible ratchet drive (for use with sockets)*
☐ *Extension piece, 250 mm (for use with sockets)*
☐ *Universal joint (for use with sockets)*
☐ *Flexible handle or sliding T "breaker bar" (for use with sockets)*
☐ *Torque wrench (for use with sockets)*
☐ *Self-locking grips*
☐ *Ball pein hammer*
☐ *Soft-faced mallet (plastic or rubber)*
☐ *Screwdrivers:*
  Flat blade - long & sturdy, short (chubby), and narrow (electrician's) types
  Cross blade – long & sturdy, and short (chubby) types
☐ *Pliers:*
  Long-nosed
  Side cutters (electrician's)
  Circlip (internal and external)
☐ *Cold chisel - 25 mm*
☐ *Scriber*
☐ *Scraper*
☐ *Centre-punch*
☐ *Pin punch*
☐ *Hacksaw*
☐ *Brake hose clamp*
☐ *Brake/clutch bleeding kit*
☐ *Selection of twist drills*
☐ *Steel rule/straight-edge*
☐ *Allen keys (inc. splined/Torx type)*
☐ *Selection of files*
☐ *Wire brush*
☐ *Axle stands*
☐ *Jack (strong trolley or hydraulic type)*
☐ *Light with extension lead*
☐ *Universal electrical multi-meter*

Sockets and reversible ratchet drive

Brake bleeding kit

Torx key, socket and bit

Hose clamp

Angular-tightening gauge

Special tools

The tools in this list are those which are not used regularly, are expensive to buy, or which need to be used in accordance with their manufacturers' instructions. Unless relatively difficult mechanical jobs are undertaken frequently, it will not be economic to buy many of these tools. Where this is the case, you could consider clubbing together with friends (or joining a motorists' club) to make a joint purchase, or borrowing the tools against a deposit from a local garage or tool hire specialist.

The following list contains only those tools and instruments freely available to the public, and not those special tools produced by the vehicle manufacturer specifically for its dealer network. You will find occasional references to these manufacturers' special tools in the text of this manual. Generally, an alternative method of doing the job without the vehicle manufacturers' special tool is given. However, sometimes there is no alternative to using them. Where this is the case and the relevant tool cannot be bought or borrowed, you will have to entrust the work to a dealer.

☐ Angular-tightening gauge
☐ Valve spring compressor
☐ Valve grinding tool
☐ Piston ring compressor
☐ Piston ring removal/installation tool
☐ Cylinder bore hone
☐ Balljoint separator
☐ Coil spring compressors (where applicable)
☐ Two/three-legged hub and bearing puller
☐ Impact screwdriver
☐ Micrometer and/or vernier calipers
☐ Dial gauge
☐ Tachometer
☐ Fault code reader
☐ Cylinder compression gauge
☐ Hand-operated vacuum pump and gauge
☐ Clutch plate alignment set
☐ Brake shoe steady spring cup removal tool
☐ Bush and bearing removal/installation set
☐ Stud extractors
☐ Tap and die set
☐ Lifting tackle

Buying tools

Reputable motor accessory shops and superstores often offer excellent quality tools at discount prices, so it pays to shop around.

Remember, you don't have to buy the most expensive items on the shelf, but it is always advisable to steer clear of the very cheap tools. Beware of 'bargains' offered on market stalls, on-line or at car boot sales. There are plenty of good tools around at reasonable prices, but always aim to purchase items which meet the relevant national safety standards. If in doubt, ask the proprietor or manager of the shop for advice before making a purchase.

Care and maintenance of tools

Having purchased a reasonable tool kit, it is necessary to keep the tools in a clean and serviceable condition. After use, always wipe off any dirt, grease and metal particles using a clean, dry cloth, before putting the tools away. Never leave them lying around after they have been used. A simple tool rack on the garage or workshop wall for items such as screwdrivers and pliers is a good idea. Store all normal spanners and sockets in a metal box. Any measuring instruments, gauges, meters, etc, must be carefully stored where they cannot be damaged or become rusty.

Take a little care when tools are used. Hammer heads inevitably become marked, and screwdrivers lose the keen edge on their blades from time to time. A little timely attention with emery cloth or a file will soon restore items like this to a good finish.

Working facilities

Not to be forgotten when discussing tools is the workshop itself. If anything more than routine maintenance is to be carried out, a suitable working area becomes essential.

It is appreciated that many an owner-mechanic is forced by circumstances to remove an engine or similar item without the benefit of a garage or workshop. Having done this, any repairs should always be done under the cover of a roof.

Wherever possible, any dismantling should be done on a clean, flat workbench or table at a suitable working height.

Any workbench needs a vice; one with a jaw opening of 100 mm is suitable for most jobs. As mentioned previously, some clean dry storage space is also required for tools, as well as for any lubricants, cleaning fluids, touch-up paints etc, which become necessary.

Another item which may be required, and which has a much more general usage, is an electric drill with a chuck capacity of at least 8 mm. This, together with a good range of twist drills, is virtually essential for fitting accessories.

Last, but not least, always keep a supply of old newspapers and clean, lint-free rags available, and try to keep any working area as clean as possible.

Micrometers

Dial test indicator ("dial gauge")

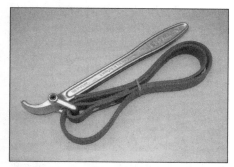
Oil filter removal tool (strap wrench type)

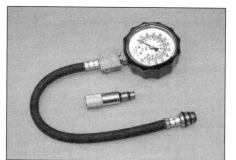
Compression tester

Bearing puller

This is a guide to getting your vehicle through the MOT test. Obviously it will not be possible to examine the vehicle to the same standard as the professional MOT tester. However, working through the following checks will enable you to identify any problem areas before submitting the vehicle for the test.

It has only been possible to summarise the test requirements here, based on the regulations in force at the time of printing. Test standards are becoming increasingly stringent, although there are some exemptions for older vehicles.

An assistant will be needed to help carry out some of these checks.

The checks have been sub-divided into four categories, as follows:

1 Checks carried out **FROM THE DRIVER'S SEAT**

2 Checks carried out **WITH THE VEHICLE ON THE GROUND**

3 Checks carried out **WITH THE VEHICLE RAISED AND THE WHEELS FREE TO TURN**

4 Checks carried out on **YOUR VEHICLE'S EXHAUST EMISSION SYSTEM**

---

1 Checks carried out **FROM THE DRIVER'S SEAT**

Handbrake (parking brake)

☐ Test the operation of the handbrake. Excessive travel (too many clicks) indicates incorrect brake or cable adjustment.
☐ Check that the handbrake cannot be released by tapping the lever sideways. Check the security of the lever mountings.

☐ If the parking brake is foot-operated, check that the pedal is secure and without excessive travel, and that the release mechanism operates correctly.
☐ Where applicable, test the operation of the electronic handbrake. The brake should engage and disengage without excessive delay. If the warning light does not extinguish when the brake is disengaged, this could indicate a fault which will need further investigation.

Footbrake

☐ Depress the brake pedal and check that it does not creep down to the floor, indicating a master cylinder fault. Release the pedal, wait a few seconds, then depress it again. If the pedal travels nearly to the floor before firm resistance is felt, brake adjustment or repair is necessary. If the pedal feels spongy, there is air in the hydraulic system which must be removed by bleeding.

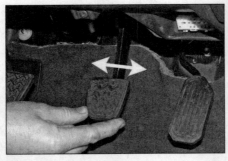

☐ Check that the brake pedal is secure and in good condition. Check also for signs of fluid leaks on the pedal, floor or carpets, which would indicate failed seals in the brake master cylinder.
☐ Check the servo unit (when applicable) by operating the brake pedal several times, then keeping the pedal depressed and starting the engine. As the engine starts, the pedal will move down slightly. If not, the vacuum hose or the servo itself may be faulty.

Steering wheel and column

☐ Examine the steering wheel for fractures or looseness of the hub, spokes or rim.
☐ Move the steering wheel from side to side and then up and down. Check that the steering wheel is not loose on the column, indicating wear or a loose retaining nut. Continue moving the steering wheel as before, but also turn it slightly from left to right.

☐ Check that the steering wheel is not loose on the column, and that there is no abnormal movement of the steering wheel, indicating wear in the column support bearings or couplings.
☐ Check that the ignition lock (where fitted) engages and disengages correctly.
☐ Steering column adjustment mechanisms (where fitted) must be able to lock the column securely in place with no play evident.

Windscreen, mirrors and sunvisor

☐ The windscreen must be free of cracks or other significant damage within the driver's field of view. (Small stone chips are acceptable.) Rear view mirrors must be secure, intact, and capable of being adjusted.

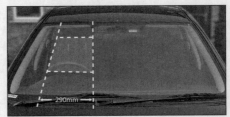

☐ The driver's sunvisor must be capable of being stored in the "up" position.

Seat belts and seats

Note: *The following checks are applicable to all seat belts, front and rear.*

☐ Examine the webbing of all the belts (including rear belts if fitted) for cuts, serious fraying or deterioration. Fasten and unfasten each belt to check the buckles. If applicable, check the retracting mechanism. Check the security of all seat belt mountings accessible from inside the vehicle, ensuring any height adjustable mountings lock securely in place.

☐ Seat belts with pre-tensioners, once activated, have a "flag" or similar showing on the seat belt stalk. This, in itself, is not a reason for test failure.

☐ The front seats themselves must be securely attached and the backrests must lock in the upright position.

Doors

☐ Both front doors must be able to be opened and closed from outside and inside, and must latch securely when closed.

Bonnet and boot/tailgate

☐ The bonnet and boot/tailgate must latch securely when closed.

2 Checks carried out WITH THE VEHICLE ON THE GROUND

Vehicle identification

☐ Number plates must be in good condition, secure and legible, with letters and numbers correctly spaced – spacing at (A) should be 33 mm and at (B) 11 mm. At the front, digits must be black on a white background and at the rear black on a yellow background. Other background designs (such as honeycomb) are not permitted.

☐ The VIN plate and/or homologation plate must be permanently displayed and legible.

Electrical equipment

☐ Switch on the ignition and check the operation of the horn.

☐ Check the windscreen washers and wipers, examining the wiper blades; renew damaged or perished blades. Also check the operation of the stop-lights.

☐ Check the operation of the sidelights and number plate lights. The lenses and reflectors must be secure, clean and undamaged.

☐ Check the operation and alignment of the headlights. The headlight reflectors must not be tarnished and the lenses must be undamaged.

☐ Switch on the ignition and check the operation of the direction indicators (including the instrument panel tell-tale) and the hazard warning lights. Operation of the sidelights and stop-lights must not affect the indicators - if it does, the cause is usually a bad earth at the rear light cluster. Indicators should flash at a rate of between 60 and 120 times per minute – faster or slower than this could indicate a fault with the flasher unit or a bad earth at one of the light units.

☐ Check the operation of the rear foglight(s), including the warning light on the instrument panel or in the switch.

☐ The warning lights must illuminate in accordance with the manufacturer's design. For most vehicles, the ABS and other warning lights should illuminate when the ignition is switched on, and (if the system is operating properly) extinguish after a few seconds. Refer to the owner's handbook.

Footbrake

☐ Examine the master cylinder, brake pipes and servo unit for leaks, loose mountings, corrosion or other damage. If ABS is fitted, this unit should also be examined for signs of leaks or corrosion.

☐ The fluid reservoir must be secure and the fluid level must be between the upper (**A**) and lower (**B**) markings.

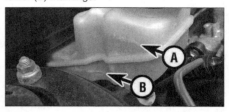

☐ Inspect both front brake flexible hoses for cracks or deterioration of the rubber. Turn the steering from lock to lock, and ensure that the hoses do not contact the wheel, tyre, or any part of the steering or suspension mechanism. With the brake pedal firmly depressed, check the hoses for bulges or leaks under pressure.

Steering and suspension

☐ Have your assistant turn the steering wheel from side to side slightly, up to the point where the steering gear just begins to transmit this movement to the roadwheels. Check for excessive free play between the steering wheel and the steering gear, indicating wear or insecurity of the steering column joints, the column-to-steering gear coupling, or the steering gear itself.

☐ Have your assistant turn the steering wheel more vigorously in each direction, so that the roadwheels just begin to turn. As this is done, examine all the steering joints, linkages, fittings and attachments. Renew any component that shows signs of wear or damage. On vehicles with power steering, check the security and condition of the steering pump, drivebelt and hoses.

☐ Check that the vehicle is standing level, and at approximately the correct ride height.

Shock absorbers

☐ Depress each corner of the vehicle in turn, then release it. The vehicle should rise and then settle in its normal position. If the vehicle continues to rise and fall, the shock absorber is defective. A shock absorber which has seized will also cause the vehicle to fail.

Exhaust system

☐ Start the engine. With your assistant holding a rag over the tailpipe, check the entire system for leaks. Repair or renew leaking sections.

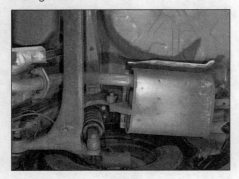

3 Checks carried out **WITH THE VEHICLE RAISED AND THE WHEELS FREE TO TURN**

Jack up the front and rear of the vehicle, and securely support it on axle stands. Position the stands clear of the suspension assemblies. Ensure that the wheels are clear of the ground and that the steering can be turned from lock to lock.

Steering mechanism

☐ Have your assistant turn the steering from lock to lock. Check that the steering turns smoothly, and that no part of the steering mechanism, including a wheel or tyre, fouls any brake hose or pipe or any part of the body structure.

☐ Examine the steering rack rubber gaiters for damage or insecurity of the retaining clips. If power steering is fitted, check for signs of damage or leakage of the fluid hoses, pipes or connections. Also check for excessive stiffness or binding of the steering, a missing split pin or locking device, or severe corrosion of the body structure within 30 cm of any steering component attachment point.

Front and rear suspension and wheel bearings

☐ Starting at the front right-hand side, grasp the roadwheel at the 3 o'clock and 9 o'clock positions and rock gently but firmly. Check for free play or insecurity at the wheel bearings, suspension balljoints, or suspension mount-ings, pivots and attachments.

☐ Now grasp the wheel at the 12 o'clock and 6 o'clock positions and repeat the previous inspection. Spin the wheel, and check for roughness or tightness of the front wheel bearing.

☐ If excess free play is suspected at a component pivot point, this can be confirmed by using a large screwdriver or similar tool and levering between the mounting and the component attachment. This will confirm whether the wear is in the pivot bush, its retaining bolt, or in the mounting itself (the bolt holes can often become elongated).

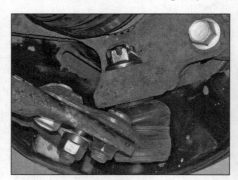

☐ Carry out all the above checks at the other front wheel, and then at both rear wheels.

Springs and shock absorbers

☐ Examine the suspension struts (when applicable) for serious fluid leakage, corrosion, or damage to the casing. Also check the security of the mounting points.

☐ If coil springs are fitted, check that the spring ends locate in their seats, and that the spring is not corroded, cracked or broken.

☐ If leaf springs are fitted, check that all leaves are intact, that the axle is securely attached to each spring, and that there is no deterioration of the spring eye mountings, bushes, and shackles.

☐ The same general checks apply to vehicles fitted with other suspension types, such as torsion bars, hydraulic displacer units, etc. Ensure that all mountings and attachments are secure, that there are no signs of excessive wear, corrosion or damage, and (on hydraulic types) that there are no fluid leaks or damaged pipes.

☐ Inspect the shock absorbers for signs of serious fluid leakage. Check for wear of the mounting bushes or attachments, or damage to the body of the unit.

Driveshafts (fwd vehicles only)

☐ Rotate each front wheel in turn and inspect the constant velocity joint gaiters for splits or damage. Also check that each driveshaft is straight and undamaged.

Braking system

☐ If possible without dismantling, check brake pad wear and disc condition. Ensure that the friction lining material has not worn excessively, (A) and that the discs are not fractured, pitted, scored or badly worn (B).

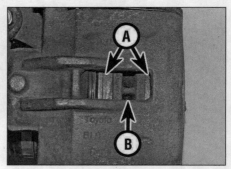

☐ Examine all the rigid brake pipes underneath the vehicle, and the flexible hose(s) at the rear. Look for corrosion, chafing or insecurity of the pipes, and for signs of bulging under pressure, chafing, splits or deterioration of the flexible hoses.

☐ Look for signs of fluid leaks at the brake calipers or on the brake backplates. Repair or renew leaking components.

☐ Slowly spin each wheel, while your assistant depresses and releases the footbrake. Ensure that each brake is operating and does not bind when the pedal is released.

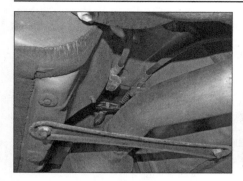

□ Examine the handbrake mechanism, checking for frayed or broken cables, excessive corrosion, or wear or insecurity of the linkage. Check that the mechanism works on each relevant wheel, and releases fully, without binding.

□ It is not possible to test brake efficiency without special equipment, but a road test can be carried out later to check that the vehicle pulls up in a straight line.

Fuel and exhaust systems

□ Inspect the fuel tank (including the filler cap), fuel pipes, hoses and unions. All components must be secure and free from leaks. Locking fuel caps must lock securely and the key must be provided for the MOT test.

□ Examine the exhaust system over its entire length, checking for any damaged, broken or missing mountings, security of the retaining clamps and rust or corrosion.

Wheels and tyres

□ Examine the sidewalls and tread area of each tyre in turn. Check for cuts, tears, lumps, bulges, separation of the tread, and exposure of the ply or cord due to wear or damage. Check that the tyre bead is correctly seated on the wheel rim, that the valve is sound and properly seated, and that the wheel is not distorted or damaged.

□ Check that the tyres are of the correct size for the vehicle, that they are of the same size and type on each axle, and that the pressures are correct.

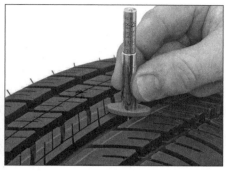

□ Check the tyre tread depth. The legal minimum at the time of writing is 1.6 mm over the central three-quarters of the tread width. Abnormal tread wear may indicate incorrect front wheel alignment or wear in steering or suspension components.

□ If the spare wheel is fitted externally or in a separate carrier beneath the vehicle, check that mountings are secure and free of excessive corrosion.

Body corrosion

□ Check the condition of the entire vehicle structure for signs of corrosion in load-bearing areas. (These include chassis box sections, side sills, cross-members, pillars, and all suspension, steering, braking system and seat belt mountings and anchorages.) Any corrosion which has seriously reduced the thickness of a load-bearing area (or is within 30 cm of safety-related components such as steering or suspension) is likely to cause the vehicle to fail. In this case professional repairs are likely to be needed.

□ Damage or corrosion which causes sharp or otherwise dangerous edges to be exposed will also cause the vehicle to fail.

Towbars

□ Check the condition of mounting points (both beneath the vehicle and within boot/hatchback areas) for signs of corrosion, ensuring that all fixings are secure and not worn or damaged. There must be no excessive play in detachable tow ball arms or quick-release mechanisms.

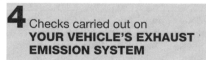

4 Checks carried out on
YOUR VEHICLE'S EXHAUST EMISSION SYSTEM

Petrol models

□ The engine should be warmed up, and running well (ignition system in good order, air filter element clean, etc).

□ Before testing, run the engine at around 2500 rpm for 20 seconds. Let the engine drop to idle, and watch for smoke from the exhaust. If the idle speed is too high, or if dense blue or black smoke emerges for more than 5 seconds, the vehicle will fail. Typically, blue smoke signifies oil burning (engine wear);

black smoke means unburnt fuel (dirty air cleaner element, or other fuel system fault).

□ An exhaust gas analyser for measuring carbon monoxide (CO) and hydrocarbons (HC) is now needed. If one cannot be hired or borrowed, have a local garage perform the check.

CO emissions (mixture)

□ The MOT tester has access to the CO limits for all vehicles. The CO level is measured at idle speed, and at 'fast idle' (2500 to 3000 rpm). The following limits are given as a general guide:

At idle speed – Less than 0.5% CO
At 'fast idle' – Less than 0.3% CO
Lambda reading – 0.97 to 1.03

□ If the CO level is too high, this may point to poor maintenance, a fuel injection system problem, faulty lambda (oxygen) sensor or catalytic converter. Try an injector cleaning treatment, and check the vehicle's ECU for fault codes.

HC emissions

□ The MOT tester has access to HC limits for all vehicles. The HC level is measured at 'fast idle' (2500 to 3000 rpm). The following limits are given as a general guide:

At 'fast idle' – Less then 200 ppm

□ Excessive HC emissions are typically caused by oil being burnt (worn engine), or by a blocked crankcase ventilation system ('breather'). If the engine oil is old and thin, an oil change may help. If the engine is running badly, check the vehicle's ECU for fault codes.

Diesel models

□ The only emission test for diesel engines is measuring exhaust smoke density, using a calibrated smoke meter. The test involves accelerating the engine at least 3 times to its maximum unloaded speed.

Note: *On engines with a timing belt, it is VITAL that the belt is in good condition before the test is carried out.*

□ With the engine warmed up, it is first purged by running at around 2500 rpm for 20 seconds. A governor check is then carried out, by slowly accelerating the engine to its maximum speed. After this, the smoke meter is connected, and the engine is accelerated quickly to maximum speed three times. If the smoke density is less than the limits given below, the vehicle will pass:

Non-turbo vehicles: 2.5m-1
Turbocharged vehicles: 3.0m-1

□ If excess smoke is produced, try fitting a new air cleaner element, or using an injector cleaning treatment. If the engine is running badly, where applicable, check the vehicle's ECU for fault codes. Also check the vehicle's EGR system, where applicable. At high mileages, the injectors may require professional attention.

Engine

- ☐ Engine fails to rotate when attempting to start
- ☐ Engine rotates, but will not start
- ☐ Engine difficult to start when cold
- ☐ Engine difficult to start when hot
- ☐ Starter motor noisy or excessively-rough in engagement
- ☐ Engine starts, but stops immediately
- ☐ Engine idles erratically
- ☐ Engine misfires at idle speed
- ☐ Engine misfires throughout the driving speed range
- ☐ Engine hesitates on acceleration
- ☐ Engine stalls
- ☐ Engine lacks power
- ☐ Engine backfires
- ☐ Oil pressure warning light illuminated with engine running
- ☐ Engine runs-on after switching off
- ☐ Engine noises

Cooling system

- ☐ Overheating
- ☐ Overcooling
- ☐ External coolant leakage
- ☐ Internal coolant leakage
- ☐ Corrosion

Fuel and exhaust systems

- ☐ Excessive fuel consumption
- ☐ Fuel leakage and/or fuel odour
- ☐ Excessive noise or fumes from exhaust system

Clutch

- ☐ Pedal travels to floor – no pressure or very little resistance
- ☐ Clutch fails to disengage (unable to select gears)
- ☐ Clutch slips (engine speed increases, with no increase in vehicle speed)
- ☐ Judder as clutch is engaged
- ☐ Noise when depressing or releasing clutch pedal

Manual transmission

- ☐ Noisy in neutral with engine running
- ☐ Noisy in one particular gear
- ☐ Difficulty engaging gears
- ☐ Jumps out of gear
- ☐ Vibration
- ☐ Lubricant leaks

Automatic transmission

- ☐ Fluid leakage
- ☐ Transmission fluid brown, or has burned smell
- ☐ General gear selection problems
- ☐ Transmission will not downshift (kickdown) with accelerator pedal fully depressed
- ☐ Engine will not start in any gear, or starts in gears other than Park or Neutral
- ☐ Transmission slips, shifts roughly, is noisy, or has no drive in forward or reverse gears

Driveshafts

- ☐ Vibration when accelerating or decelerating
- ☐ Clicking or knocking noise on turns (at slow speed on full-lock)

Braking system

- ☐ Vehicle pulls to one side under braking
- ☐ Noise (grinding or high-pitched squeal) when brakes applied
- ☐ Excessive brake pedal travel
- ☐ Brake pedal feels spongy when depressed
- ☐ Excessive brake pedal effort required to stop vehicle
- ☐ Judder felt through brake pedal or steering wheel when braking
- ☐ Brakes binding
- ☐ Rear wheels locking under normal braking

Suspension and steering

- ☐ Vehicle pulls to one side
- ☐ Wheel wobble and vibration
- ☐ Excessive pitching and/or rolling around corners, or during braking
- ☐ Wandering or general instability
- ☐ Excessively-stiff steering
- ☐ Excessive play in steering
- ☐ Lack of power assistance
- ☐ Tyre wear excessive

Electrical system

- ☐ Battery will not hold a charge for more than a few days
- ☐ Ignition/no-charge warning light remains illuminated with engine running
- ☐ Ignition/no-charge warning light fails to come on
- ☐ Lights inoperative
- ☐ Instrument readings inaccurate or erratic
- ☐ Horn inoperative, or unsatisfactory in operation
- ☐ Windscreen wipers inoperative, or unsatisfactory in operation
- ☐ Windscreen washers inoperative, or unsatisfactory in operation
- ☐ Electric windows inoperative, or unsatisfactory in operation
- ☐ Central locking system inoperative, or unsatisfactory in operation

Introduction

The vehicle owner who does his or her own maintenance according to the recommended service schedules should not have to use this section of the manual very often. Modern component reliability is such that, provided those items subject to wear or deterioration are inspected or renewed at the specified intervals, sudden failure is comparatively rare. Faults do not usually just happen as a result of sudden failure, but develop over a period of time. Major mechanical failures in particular are usually preceded by characteristic symptoms over hundreds or even thousands of miles. Those components which do occasionally fail without warning are often small and easily carried in the vehicle.

With any fault finding, the first step is to decide where to begin investigations. Sometimes this is obvious, but on other occasions, a little detective work will be necessary. The owner who makes half a dozen haphazard adjustments or replacements may be successful in curing a fault (or its symptoms), but will be none the wiser if the fault recurs, and ultimately may have spent more time and money than was necessary. A calm and logical approach will be found to be more satisfactory in the long run. Always take into account any warning signs or abnormalities that may have been noticed in the period preceding the fault – power loss, high or low gauge readings, unusual smells,

etc – and remember that failure of components such as fuses or spark plugs may only be pointers to some underlying fault.

The pages which follow provide an easy-reference guide to the more common problems which may occur during the operation of the vehicle. These problems and their possible causes are grouped under headings denoting various components or systems, such as Engine, Cooling system, etc. The general Chapter which deals with the problem is also shown in brackets; refer to the relevant part of that Chapter for system-specific information. Whatever the fault, certain basic principles apply. These are as follows:

Verify the fault. This is simply a matter of

being sure that you know what the symptoms are before starting work. This is particularly important if you are investigating a fault for someone else, who may not have described it very accurately.

Don't overlook the obvious. For example, if the vehicle won't start, is there fuel in the tank? (Don't take anyone else's word on this particular point, and don't trust the fuel gauge either). If an electrical fault is indicated, look for loose or broken wires before digging out the test gear.

Cure the disease, not the symptom. Substituting a flat battery with a fully-charged one will get you off the hard shoulder, but if the underlying cause is not attended to, the new battery will go the same way. Similarly, changing oil-fouled spark plugs for a new set will get you moving again, but remember that the reason for the fouling (if it wasn't simply an incorrect grade of plug) will have to be established and corrected.

Don't take anything for granted. Particularly, don't forget that a 'new' component may itself be defective (especially if it's been rattling around in the boot for months), and don't leave

components out of a fault diagnosis sequence just because they are new or recently-fitted. When you do finally diagnose a difficult fault, you'll probably realise that all the evidence was there from the start.

Consider what work, if any, has recently been carried out. Many faults arise through careless or hurried work. For instance, if any work has been performed under the bonnet, could some of the wiring have been dislodged or incorrectly routed, or a hose trapped? Have all the fasteners been properly tightened? Were new, genuine parts and new gaskets used? There is often a certain amount of detective work to be done in this case, as an apparently-unrelated task can have far-reaching consequences.

Diesel engine fault diagnosis

The majority of starting problems on small diesel engines are electrical in origin. The mechanic who is familiar with petrol engines but less so with diesel may be inclined to view the diesel's injectors and pump in the same light as the spark plugs and distributor, but this is generally a mistake.

When investigating complaints of difficult starting for someone else, make sure that the correct starting procedure is understood and is being followed. Some drivers are unaware of the significance of the preheating warning light – many modern engines are sufficiently forgiving for this not to matter in mild weather, but with the onset of winter, problems begin. Glow plugs in particular are often neglected – just one faulty plug will make cold-weather starting very difficult.

As a rule of thumb, if the engine is difficult to start but runs well when it has finally got going, the problem is electrical (battery, starter motor or preheating system). If poor performance is combined with difficult starting, the problem is likely to be in the fuel system. The low-pressure (supply) side of the fuel system should be checked before suspecting the injectors and high-pressure pump. The most common fuel supply problem is air getting into the system, and any pipe from the fuel tank forwards must be scrutinised if air leakage is suspected.

Engine

Engine fails to rotate when attempting to start

- [ ] Battery terminal connections loose or corroded (see *Weekly checks*)
- [ ] Battery discharged or faulty (Chapter 5)
- [ ] Broken, loose or disconnected wiring in the starting circuit (Chapter 5)
- [ ] Defective starter solenoid or ignition switch (Chapter 5 or 12)
- [ ] Defective starter motor (Chapter 5)
- [ ] Starter pinion or flywheel ring gear teeth loose or broken (Chapter 2A, 2B or 5)
- [ ] Engine earth strap broken or disconnected (Chapter 5)
- [ ] Engine suffering 'hydraulic lock' (eg, from water ingested after traversing flooded roads, or from a serious internal coolant leak) – consult a Volvo dealer or specialist for advice
- [ ] Automatic transmission not in position P or N (Chapter 7B)

Engine rotates, but will not start

- [ ] Fuel tank empty
- [ ] Battery discharged (engine rotates slowly) (Chapter 5)
- [ ] Battery terminal connections loose or corroded (see *Weekly checks*)
- [ ] Immobiliser fault, or 'uncoded' remote unit being used (Chapter 12 or Roadside repairs)
- [ ] Crankshaft sensor fault (Chapter 4A)
- [ ] Preheating system faulty (Chapter 5)
- [ ] Fuel injection system fault (Chapter 4A)
- [ ] Air in fuel system (Chapter 4B)
- [ ] Major mechanical failure (eg, timing belt snapped) (Chapter 2A or 2B)

Engine difficult to start when cold

- [ ] Battery discharged (Chapter 5)
- [ ] Battery terminal connections loose or corroded (see Weekly checks)
- [ ] Preheating system faulty (Chapter 5)
- [ ] Fuel injection system fault (Chapter 4A)
- [ ] Wrong grade of engine oil used (Weekly checks, Chapter 1)
- [ ] Low cylinder compression (Chapter 2A or 2B)

Engine difficult to start when hot

- [ ] Air filter element dirty or clogged (Chapter 1)
- [ ] Fuel injection system fault (Chapter 4A)
- [ ] Low cylinder compression (Chapter 2A or 2B)

Starter motor noisy or excessively-rough in engagement

- [ ] Starter pinion or flywheel ring gear teeth loose or broken (Chapter 2A, 2B or 5)
- [ ] Starter motor mounting bolts loose or missing (Chapter 5)
- [ ] Starter motor internal components worn or damaged (Chapter 5)

Engine starts, but stops immediately

- [ ] Vacuum leak at the throttle body or inlet manifold (Chapter 4A)
- [ ] Blocked injectors/fuel injection system fault (Chapter 4A)
- [ ] Air in fuel, possibly due to loose fuel line connection (Chapter 4A)

Engine idles erratically

- [ ] Air filter element clogged (Chapter 1)
- [ ] Vacuum leak at the throttle body, inlet manifold or associated hoses (Chapter 4A)
- [ ] Uneven or low cylinder compression (Chapter 2A or 2B)
- [ ] Camshaft lobes worn (Chapter 2A or 2B)
- [ ] Timing belt incorrectly fitted (Chapter 2A or 2B)
- [ ] Blocked injectors/fuel injection system fault (Chapter 4A)
- [ ] Air in fuel, possibly due to loose fuel line connection (Chapter 4A)

Engine misfires at idle speed

- [ ] Vacuum leak at the throttle body, inlet manifold or associated hoses (Chapter 4A)
- [ ] Blocked injectors/fuel injection system fault (Chapter 4A)
- [ ] Faulty injector(s) (Chapter 4A)
- [ ] Uneven or low cylinder compression (Chapter 2A or 2B)
- [ ] Disconnected, leaking, or perished crankcase ventilation hoses (Chapter 4B)

Engine (continued)

Engine misfires throughout the driving speed range

- ☐ Fuel filter choked (Chapter 1)
- ☐ Fuel pump faulty, or delivery pressure low (Chapter 4A)
- ☐ Fuel tank vent blocked, or fuel pipes restricted (Chapter 4A)
- ☐ Vacuum leak at the throttle body, inlet manifold or associated hoses (Chapter 4A)
- ☐ Faulty injector(s) (Chapter 4A)
- ☐ Uneven or low cylinder compression (Chapter 2A or 2B)
- ☐ Blocked injector/fuel injection system fault (Chapter 4A)
- ☐ Blocked catalytic converter (Chapter 4B)
- ☐ Engine overheating (Chapter 3)
- ☐ Fuel tank level low (Chapter 4A)

Engine hesitates on acceleration

- ☐ Vacuum leak at the throttle body, inlet manifold or associated hoses (Chapter 4A)
- ☐ Blocked injectors/fuel injection system fault (Chapter 4A)
- ☐ Faulty injector(s) (Chapter 4A)
- ☐ Faulty clutch pedal switch (Chapter 6)

Engine stalls

- ☐ Vacuum leak at the throttle body, inlet manifold or associated hoses (Chapter 4A)
- ☐ Fuel filter choked (Chapter 1)
- ☐ Fuel pump faulty, or delivery pressure low (Chapter 4A)
- ☐ Fuel tank vent blocked, or fuel pipes restricted (Chapter 4A)
- ☐ Blocked injectors/fuel injection system fault (Chapter 4A)
- ☐ Faulty injector(s) (Chapter 4A)

Engine lacks power

- ☐ Air filter element blocked (Chapter 1)
- ☐ Fuel filter choked (Chapter 1)
- ☐ Fuel pipes blocked or restricted (Chapter 4A)
- ☐ Engine overheating (Chapter 3)
- ☐ Fuel tank level low (Chapter 4A)
- ☐ Accelerator position sensor faulty (Chapter 4A)
- ☐ Vacuum leak at the throttle body, inlet manifold or associated hoses (Chapter 4A)
- ☐ Blocked injectors/fuel injection system fault (Chapter 4A)
- ☐ Faulty injector(s) (Chapter 4A)
- ☐ Timing belt incorrectly fitted (Chapter 2A or 2B)
- ☐ Fuel pump faulty, or delivery pressure low (Chapter 4A)
- ☐ Uneven or low cylinder compression (Chapter 2A or 2B)
- ☐ Blocked catalytic converter (Chapter 4B)
- ☐ Brakes binding (Chapter 9)
- ☐ Clutch slipping (Chapter 6)

Engine backfires

- ☐ Timing belt incorrectly fitted (Chapter 2A or 2B)
- ☐ Vacuum leak at the throttle body, inlet manifold or associated hoses (Chapter 4A)
- ☐ Blocked injectors/fuel injection system fault (Chapter 4A)
- ☐ Blocked catalytic converter (Chapter 4B)

Oil pressure warning light illuminated with engine running

- ☐ Low oil level, or incorrect oil grade (see *Weekly checks*)
- ☐ Faulty oil pressure sensor, or wiring damaged (Chapter 12)
- ☐ Worn engine bearings and/or oil pump (Chapter 2A or 2B)
- ☐ High engine operating temperature (Chapter 3)
- ☐ Oil pump pressure relief valve defective (Chapter 2A or 2B)
- ☐ Oil pump pick-up strainer clogged (Chapter 2A or 2B)

Engine runs-on after switching off

- ☐ Excessive carbon build-up in engine (Chapter 2A or 2B)
- ☐ High engine operating temperature (Chapter 3)
- ☐ Fuel injection system fault (Chapter 4A)

Engine noises

Pre-ignition (pinking) or knocking during acceleration or under load

- ☐ Vacuum leak at the throttle body, inlet manifold or associated hoses (Chapter 4A)
- ☐ Excessive carbon build-up in engine (Chapter 2A or 2B)
- ☐ Blocked injector/fuel injection system fault (Chapter 4A)
- ☐ Faulty injector(s) (Chapter 4B)

Whistling or wheezing noises

- ☐ Leaking inlet manifold or throttle body gasket (Chapter 4A)
- ☐ Leaking exhaust manifold gasket or pipe-to-manifold joint (Chapter 4A or 4B)
- ☐ Leaking vacuum hose (Chapter 4A or 9)
- ☐ Blowing cylinder head gasket (Chapter 2A or 2B)
- ☐ Partially blocked or leaking crankcase ventilation system (Chapter 4B)

Tapping or rattling noises

- ☐ Worn valve gear or camshaft (Chapter 2A or 2B)
- ☐ Ancillary component fault (coolant pump, alternator, etc) (Chapter 3, 5, etc)

Knocking or thumping noises

- ☐ Worn big-end bearings (regular heavy knocking, perhaps less under load) (Chapter 2D)
- ☐ Worn main bearings (rumbling and knocking, perhaps worsening under load) (Chapter 2D)
- ☐ Piston slap – most noticeable when cold, caused by piston/bore wear (Chapter 2D)
- ☐ Ancillary component fault (coolant pump, alternator, etc) (Chapter 3, 5, etc)
- ☐ Engine mountings worn or defective (Chapter 2C)
- ☐ Front suspension or steering components worn (Chapter 10)

Cooling system

Overheating

- ☐ Insufficient coolant in system (see *Weekly checks*)
- ☐ Thermostat faulty (Chapter 3)
- ☐ Radiator core blocked, or grille restricted (Chapter 3)
- ☐ Cooling fan faulty, or control module fault (Chapter 3)
- ☐ Inaccurate coolant temperature sender (Chapter 3)
- ☐ Airlock in cooling system (Chapter 3)
- ☐ Expansion tank pressure cap faulty (Chapter 3)
- ☐ Engine management system fault (Chapter 4A)

Overcooling

- ☐ Thermostat faulty (Chapter 3)
- ☐ Inaccurate coolant temperature sender (Chapter 3)
- ☐ Cooling fan faulty (Chapter 3)
- ☐ Engine management system fault (Chapter 4A)

External coolant leakage

- ☐ Deteriorated or damaged hoses or hose clips (Chapter 1)
- ☐ Radiator core or heater matrix leaking (Chapter 3)
- ☐ Expansion tank pressure cap faulty (Chapter 1)
- ☐ Coolant pump internal seal leaking (Chapter 3)
- ☐ Coolant pump gasket leaking (Chapter 3)
- ☐ Boiling due to overheating (Chapter 3)
- ☐ Cylinder block core plug leaking (Chapter 2B)

Internal coolant leakage

- ☐ Leaking cylinder head gasket (Chapter 2A)
- ☐ Cracked cylinder head or cylinder block (Chapter 2A or 2B)

Corrosion

- ☐ Infrequent draining and flushing (Chapter 1)
- ☐ Incorrect coolant mixture or inappropriate coolant type (see *Weekly checks*)

Fuel and exhaust systems

Excessive fuel consumption

- ☐ Air filter element dirty or clogged (Chapter 1)
- ☐ Fuel injection system fault (Chapter 4A)
- ☐ Engine management system fault (Chapter 4A)
- ☐ Crankcase ventilation system blocked (Chapter 4B)
- ☐ Tyres under-inflated (see *Weekly checks*)
- ☐ Brakes binding (Chapter 9)
- ☐ Fuel leak, causing apparent high consumption (Chapter 1 or 4A)

Fuel leakage and/or fuel odour

- ☐ Damaged or corroded fuel tank, pipes or connections (Chapter 4A)

Excessive noise or fumes from exhaust system

- ☐ Leaking exhaust system or manifold joints (Chapter 4A or 4B)
- ☐ Leaking, corroded or damaged silencers or pipe (Chapter 4A or 4B)
- ☐ Broken mountings causing body or suspension contact (Chapter 1, 4A or 4B)

Clutch

Pedal travels to floor – no pressure or very little resistance

- ☐ Air in hydraulic system/faulty master or slave cylinder (Chapter 6)
- ☐ Faulty hydraulic release system (Chapter 6)
- ☐ Clutch pedal return spring detached or broken (Chapter 6)
- ☐ Broken clutch release bearing or fork (Chapter 6)
- ☐ Broken diaphragm spring in clutch pressure plate (Chapter 6)

Clutch fails to disengage (unable to select gears)

- ☐ Air in hydraulic system/faulty master or slave cylinder (Chapter 6)
- ☐ Faulty hydraulic release system (Chapter 6)
- ☐ Clutch disc sticking on transmission input shaft splines (Chapter 6)
- ☐ Clutch disc sticking to flywheel or pressure plate (Chapter 6)
- ☐ Faulty pressure plate assembly (Chapter 6)
- ☐ Clutch release mechanism worn or incorrectly assembled (Chapter 6)

Clutch slips (engine speed increases, with no increase in vehicle speed)

- ☐ Faulty hydraulic release system (Chapter 6)
- ☐ Clutch disc linings excessively worn (Chapter 6)
- ☐ Clutch disc linings contaminated with oil or grease (Chapter 6)
- ☐ Faulty pressure plate or weak diaphragm spring (Chapter 6)

Judder as clutch is engaged

- ☐ Clutch disc linings contaminated with oil or grease (Chapter 6)
- ☐ Clutch disc linings excessively worn (Chapter 6)
- ☐ Faulty or distorted pressure plate or diaphragm spring (Chapter 6).
- ☐ Worn or loose engine or transmission mountings (Chapter 2C)
- ☐ Clutch disc hub or transmission input shaft splines worn (Chapter 6)

Noise when depressing or releasing clutch pedal

- ☐ Worn clutch release bearing (Chapter 6)
- ☐ Worn or dry clutch pedal bushes (Chapter 6)
- ☐ Worn or dry clutch master cylinder piston (Chapter 6)
- ☐ Faulty pressure plate assembly (Chapter 6)
- ☐ Pressure plate diaphragm spring broken (Chapter 6)
- ☐ Broken clutch disc cushioning springs (Chapter 6)

Manual transmission

Noisy in neutral with engine running

- ☐ Lack of oil (Chapter 1)
- ☐ Input shaft bearings worn (noise apparent with clutch pedal released, but not when depressed) (Chapter 7A)*
- ☐ Clutch release bearing worn (noise apparent with clutch pedal depressed, possibly less when released) (Chapter 6)

Noisy in one particular gear

- ☐ Worn, damaged or chipped gear teeth (Chapter 7A)*

Difficulty engaging gears

- ☐ Clutch fault (Chapter 6)
- ☐ Worn or damaged gearchange cables (Chapter 7A)
- ☐ Lack of oil (Chapter 7A)
- ☐ Worn synchroniser units (Chapter 7A)*

Jumps out of gear

- ☐ Worn or damaged gearchange cables (Chapter 7A)
- ☐ Worn synchroniser units (Chapter 7A)*
- ☐ Worn selector forks (Chapter 7A)*

Vibration

- ☐ Lack of oil (Chapter 7A)
- ☐ Worn bearings (Chapter 7A)*

Lubricant leaks

- ☐ Leaking driveshaft or selector shaft oil seal (Chapter 7A)
- ☐ Leaking housing joint (Chapter 7A)*
- ☐ Leaking input shaft oil seal (Chapter 7A)*

Although the corrective action necessary to remedy the symptoms described is beyond the scope of the home mechanic, the above information should be helpful in isolating the cause of the condition, so that the owner can communicate clearly with a professional mechanic.

Automatic transmission

Note: *Due to the complexity of the automatic transmission, it is difficult for the home mechanic to properly diagnose and service this unit. For problems other than the following, the vehicle should be taken to a dealer service department or automatic transmission specialist. Do not be too hasty in removing the transmission if a fault is suspected, as most of the testing is carried out with the unit still fitted. Remember that, besides the sensors specific to the transmission, many of the engine management system sensors described in Chapter 4A are essential to the correct operation of the transmission.*

Fluid leakage

- ☐ Automatic transmission fluid is usually dark red in colour. Fluid leaks should not be confused with engine oil, which can easily be blown onto the transmission by airflow.
- ☐ To determine the source of a leak, first remove all built-up dirt and grime from the transmission housing and surrounding areas using a degreasing agent, or by steam-cleaning. Drive the vehicle at low speed, so airflow will not blow the leak far from its source. Raise and support the vehicle, and determine where the leak is coming from. The following are common areas of leakage:
  - a) *Fluid pan*
  - b) *Dipstick tube*
  - c) *Transmission-to-fluid cooler unions (Chapter 7B)*

Transmission fluid brown, or has burned smell

- ☐ Transmission fluid level low (Chapter 1)

General gear selection problems

- ☐ Chapter 7B deals with checking the selector cable on automatic transmissions. The following are common problems which may be caused by a faulty cable or sensor:

a) *Engine starting in gears other than Park or Neutral.*
b) *Indicator panel indicating a gear other than the one actually being used.*
c) *Vehicle moves when in Park or Neutral.*
d) *Poor gear shift quality or erratic gear changes.*

Transmission will not downshift (kickdown) with accelerator pedal fully depressed

- ☐ Low transmission fluid level (Chapter 1)
- ☐ Engine management system fault (Chapter 4A)
- ☐ Faulty transmission sensor or wiring (Chapter 7B)
- ☐ Faulty selector cable (Chapter 7B)

Engine will not start in any gear, or starts in gears other than Park or Neutral

- ☐ Faulty transmission sensor or wiring (Chapter 7B)
- ☐ Engine management system fault (Chapter 4A)
- ☐ Faulty selector cable (Chapter 7B)

Transmission slips, shifts roughly, is noisy, or has no drive in forward or reverse gears

- ☐ Transmission fluid level low (Chapter 1)
- ☐ Faulty transmission sensor or wiring (Chapter 7B)
- ☐ Engine management system fault (Chapter 4A)

Note: *There are many probable causes for the above problems, but diagnosing and correcting them is considered beyond the scope of this manual. Having checked the fluid level and all the wiring as far as possible, a dealer or transmission specialist should be consulted if the problem persists.*

Propeller shaft

Knock or clunk when taking up drive
- [ ] Worn universal joint (Chapter 8B)
- [ ] Worn Haldex or bevel gear pinion splines (Chapter 8B)
- [ ] Loose drive flange bolts (Chapter 8B)
- [ ] Excessive backlash in axle gears (Chapter 8B)

Metallic grating sound consistent with vehicle speed
- [ ] Severe wear in universal/constant velocity joint bearings (Chapter 8B)

Vibration
- [ ] Wear in sliding sleeve splines (Chapter 8B)
- [ ] Worn universal joint bearings (Chapter 8B)
- [ ] Worn constant velocity joints (Chapter 8B)
- [ ] Propeller shaft out of balance (Chapter 8B)

Final drive

Noise on drive and overrun
- [ ] Wear in crownwheel and pinion gears (Chapter 8B)
- [ ] Worn differential bearings (Chapter 8B)
- [ ] Main transmission or transfer box fault (Chapter 7A, 7B or 8B)

Noise consistent with road speed
- [ ] Worn hub bearings (Chapter 9)
- [ ] Worn differential bearings (Chapter 8B)
- [ ] Main transmission or transfer box fault (Chapter 7A, 7B or 8B)

Knock or clunk when taking up drive
- [ ] Excessive crownwheel and pinion backlash (Chapter 8B)
- [ ] Worn differential bearings (Chapter 8B)
- [ ] Worn driveshaft joints (Chapter 8A)
- [ ] Driveshaft nut or roadwheel nuts loose (Chapter 9)
- [ ] Broken, damaged or worn suspension components (Chapter 9)
- [ ] Main transmission or transfer box fault (Chapter 7A, 7B or 8B)

Oil leakage
- [ ] Faulty differential pinion or halfshaft oil seals (Chapter 8B)
- [ ] Damaged driveshaft oil seal (Chapter 8A)

Driveshafts

Vibration when accelerating or decelerating
- [ ] Worn inner constant velocity joint (Chapter 8)
- [ ] Bent or distorted driveshaft (Chapter 8)
- [ ] Worn intermediate bearing (Chapter 8)

Clicking or knocking noise on turns (at slow speed on full-lock)
- [ ] Worn outer constant velocity joint (Chapter 8)
- [ ] Lack of constant velocity joint lubricant, possibly due to damaged gaiter (Chapter 8)
- [ ] Worn intermediate bearing (Chapter 8)

Braking system

Note: *Before assuming that a brake problem exists, make sure that the tyres are in good condition and correctly inflated, that the front wheel alignment is correct, and that the vehicle is not loaded with weight in an unequal manner. Apart from checking the condition of all pipe and hose connections, any faults occurring on the anti-lock braking system should be referred to a Volvo dealer or specialist for diagnosis.*

Vehicle pulls to one side under braking

- [ ] Worn, defective, damaged or contaminated brake pads on one side (Chapter 9)
- [ ] Seized or partially-seized brake caliper piston (Chapter 9)
- [ ] A mixture of brake pad lining materials fitted between sides (Chapter 9)
- [ ] Brake caliper mounting bolts loose (Chapter 9)
- [ ] Worn or damaged steering or suspension components (Chapter 1 or 10)

Noise (grinding or high-pitched squeal) when brakes applied

- [ ] Brake pad friction lining material worn down to metal backing (Chapter 9)
- [ ] Excessive corrosion of brake disc (may be apparent after the vehicle has been standing for some time (Chapter 9)
- [ ] Foreign object (stone chipping, etc) trapped between brake disc and shield (Chapter 9)

Excessive brake pedal travel

- [ ] Faulty master cylinder (Chapter 9)
- [ ] Air in hydraulic system (Chapter 6 or 9)
- [ ] Faulty vacuum servo unit (Chapter 9)

Brake pedal feels spongy when depressed

- [ ] Air in hydraulic system (Chapter 6 or 9)
- [ ] Deteriorated flexible rubber brake hoses (Chapter 1 or 9)
- [ ] Master cylinder mounting nuts loose (Chapter 9)
- [ ] Faulty master cylinder (Chapter 9)

Excessive brake pedal effort required to stop vehicle

- [ ] Faulty vacuum servo unit (Chapter 9)
- [ ] Faulty vacuum pump – diesel models (Chapter 9)
- [ ] Disconnected, damaged or insecure brake servo vacuum hose (Chapter 9)
- [ ] Primary or secondary hydraulic circuit failure (Chapter 9)
- [ ] Seized brake caliper piston (Chapter 9)
- [ ] Brake pads incorrectly fitted (Chapter 9)
- [ ] Incorrect grade of brake pads fitted (Chapter 9)
- [ ] Brake pad linings contaminated (Chapter 9)

Judder felt through brake pedal or steering wheel when braking

Note: *Under heavy braking on models equipped with ABS, vibration may be felt through the brake pedal. This is a normal feature of ABS operation, and does not constitute a fault*

- [ ] Excessive run-out or distortion of discs (Chapter 9)
- [ ] Brake pad linings worn (Chapter 1 or 9)
- [ ] Brake caliper mounting bolts loose (Chapter 9)
- [ ] Wear in suspension or steering components or mountings (Chapter 1 or 10)
- [ ] Front wheels out of balance (see Weekly checks)

Brakes binding

- [ ] Seized brake caliper piston (Chapter 9)
- [ ] Faulty handbrake mechanism (Chapter 9)
- [ ] Faulty master cylinder (Chapter 9)

Rear wheels locking under normal braking

- [ ] Rear brake pad linings contaminated or damaged (Chapter 9)
- [ ] Rear brake discs warped (Chapter 9)

Suspension and steering

Note: *Before diagnosing suspension or steering faults, be sure that the trouble is not due to incorrect tyre pressures, mixtures of tyre types, or binding brakes.*

Vehicle pulls to one side

- ☐ Defective tyre (see *Weekly checks*)
- ☐ Excessive wear in suspension or steering components (Chapter 1or 10)
- ☐ Incorrect front wheel alignment (Chapter 10)
- ☐ Accident damage to steering or suspension components

Wheel wobble and vibration

- ☐ Front wheels out of balance (vibration felt mainly through the steering wheel) (see *Weekly checks*)
- ☐ Rear wheels out of balance (vibration felt throughout the vehicle) (see *Weekly checks*)
- ☐ Roadwheels damaged or distorted (see *Weekly checks*)
- ☐ Faulty or damaged tyre (see *Weekly checks*)
- ☐ Worn steering or suspension joints, bushes or components (Chapter 1 or 10)
- ☐ Wheel bolts loose (Chapter 1)

Excessive pitching and/or rolling around corners, or during braking

- ☐ Defective shock absorbers (Chapter 10)
- ☐ Broken or weak spring and/or suspension component (Chapter 10)
- ☐ Worn or damaged anti-roll bar or mountings (Chapter 10)

Wandering or general instability

- ☐ Incorrect front wheel alignment (Chapter 10)
- ☐ Worn steering or suspension joints, bushes or components (Chapter 1or 10)
- ☐ Roadwheels out of balance (see *Weekly checks*)
- ☐ Faulty or damaged tyre (see *Weekly checks*)
- ☐ Wheel bolts loose (Chapter 1)
- ☐ Defective shock absorbers (Chapter 10)

Excessively-stiff steering

- ☐ Seized steering linkage balljoint or suspension balljoint (Chapter 1or 10)
- ☐ Broken or incorrectly-adjusted auxiliary drivebelt (Chapter 1)
- ☐ Incorrect front wheel alignment (Chapter 10)
- ☐ Steering rack damaged (Chapter 10)

Excessive play in steering

- ☐ Worn steering column/intermediate shaft joints (Chapter 10)
- ☐ Worn track rod balljoints (Chapter 1 or 10)
- ☐ Worn steering rack (Chapter 10)
- ☐ Worn steering or suspension joints, bushes or components (Chapter 1or 10)

Lack of power assistance

- ☐ Broken or incorrectly-adjusted auxiliary drivebelt (Chapter 1)
- ☐ Incorrect power steering fluid level (see *Weekly checks*)
- ☐ Restriction in power steering fluid hoses (Chapter 1)
- ☐ Faulty power steering pump (Chapter 10)
- ☐ Faulty steering rack (Chapter 10)

Tyre wear excessive

Tyres worn on inside or outside edges

- ☐ Tyres under-inflated (wear on both edges) (see *Weekly checks*)
- ☐ Incorrect camber or castor angles (wear on one edge only) (Chapter 10)
- ☐ Worn steering or suspension joints, bushes or components (Chapter 1 or 10)
- ☐ Excessively-hard cornering or braking
- ☐ Accident damage

Tyre treads exhibit feathered edges

- ☐ Incorrect toe-setting (Chapter 10)

Tyres worn in centre of tread

- ☐ Tyres over-inflated (see *Weekly checks*)

Tyres worn on inside and outside edges

- ☐ Tyres under-inflated (see *Weekly checks*)

Tyres worn unevenly

- ☐ Tyres/wheels out of balance (see *Weekly checks*)
- ☐ Excessive wheel or tyre run-out
- ☐ Worn shock absorbers (Chapter 10)
- ☐ Faulty tyre (see *Weekly checks*)

Electrical system

Note: *For problems associated with the starting system, refer to the faults listed under 'Engine' earlier in this Section.*

Battery will not hold a charge for more than a few days

- ☐ Battery defective internally (Chapter 5)
- ☐ Battery terminal connections loose or corroded (see *Weekly checks*)
- ☐ Auxiliary drivebelt worn or incorrectly adjusted (Chapter 1)
- ☐ Alternator not charging at correct output (Chapter 5)
- ☐ Alternator or voltage regulator faulty (Chapter 5)
- ☐ Short-circuit causing continual battery drain (Chapter 5 or 12)

Ignition/no-charge warning light remains illuminated with engine running

- ☐ Auxiliary drivebelt broken, worn, or incorrectly adjusted (Chapter 1)
- ☐ Internal fault in alternator or voltage regulator (Chapter 5)
- ☐ Broken, disconnected, or loose wiring in charging circuit (Chapter 5 or 12)

Ignition/no-charge warning light fails to come on

- ☐ Warning light bulb blown (Chapter 12)
- ☐ Broken, disconnected, or loose wiring in warning light circuit (Chapter 5 or 12)
- ☐ Alternator faulty (Chapter 5)

Lights inoperative

- ☐ Bulb blown (Chapter 12)
- ☐ Corrosion of bulb or bulbholder contacts (Chapter 12)
- ☐ Blown fuse (Chapter 12)
- ☐ Faulty relay (Chapter 12)
- ☐ Broken, loose, or disconnected wiring (Chapter 12)
- ☐ Faulty switch (Chapter 12)

Instrument readings inaccurate or erratic

Fuel or temperature gauges give no reading

- ☐ Faulty gauge sender unit (Chapter 3 or 4A)
- ☐ Wiring open-circuit (Chapter 12)
- ☐ Faulty instrument cluster (Chapter 12)

Fuel or temperature gauges give continuous maximum reading

- ☐ Faulty gauge sender unit (Chapter 3 or 4A)
- ☐ Wiring short-circuit (Chapter 12)
- ☐ Faulty instrument cluster (Chapter 12)

Horn inoperative, or unsatisfactory in operation

Horn operates all the time

- ☐ Horn push either earthed or stuck down (Chapter 12)
- ☐ Horn cable-to-horn push earthed (Chapter 12)

Horn fails to operate

- ☐ Blown fuse (Chapter 12)
- ☐ Cable or connections loose, broken or disconnected (Chapter 12)
- ☐ Faulty horn (Chapter 12)

Horn emits intermittent or unsatisfactory sound

- ☐ Cable connections loose (Chapter 12)
- ☐ Horn mountings loose (Chapter 12)
- ☐ Faulty horn (Chapter 12)

Windscreen wipers inoperative, or unsatisfactory in operation

Wipers fail to operate, or operate very slowly

- ☐ Wiper blades stuck to screen, or linkage seized or binding (Chapter 12)
- ☐ Blown fuse (Chapter 12)
- ☐ Battery discharged (Chapter 5)
- ☐ Cable or connections loose, broken or disconnected (Chapter 12)
- ☐ Faulty wiper motor (Chapter 12)

Wiper blades sweep over too large or too small an area of the glass

- ☐ Wiper blades incorrectly fitted, or wrong size used (see *Weekly checks*)
- ☐ Wiper arms incorrectly positioned on spindles (Chapter 12)
- ☐ Excessive wear of wiper linkage (Chapter 12)
- ☐ Wiper motor or linkage mountings loose or insecure (Chapter 12)

Wiper blades fail to clean the glass effectively

- ☐ Wiper blade rubbers dirty, worn or perished (see *Weekly checks*)
- ☐ Wiper blades incorrectly fitted, or wrong size used (see *Weekly checks*)
- ☐ Wiper arm tension springs broken, or arm pivots seized (Chapter 12)
- ☐ Insufficient windscreen washer additive to adequately remove road film (see *Weekly checks*)

Windscreen washers inoperative, or unsatisfactory in operation

One or more washer jets inoperative

- ☐ Blocked washer jet
- ☐ Disconnected, kinked or restricted fluid hose (Chapter 12)
- ☐ Insufficient fluid in washer reservoir (see *Weekly checks*)

Washer pump fails to operate

- ☐ Broken or disconnected wiring or connections (Chapter 12)
- ☐ Blown fuse (Chapter 12)
- ☐ Faulty washer switch (Chapter 12)
- ☐ Faulty washer pump (Chapter 12)

Washer pump runs for some time before fluid is emitted from jets

- ☐ Faulty one-way valve in fluid supply hose (Chapter 12)

Electric windows inoperative, or unsatisfactory in operation

Window glass will only move in one direction

- ☐ Faulty switch (Chapter 12)

Window glass slow to move

- ☐ Battery discharged (Chapter 5)
- ☐ Regulator seized or damaged, or in need of lubrication (Chapter 11)
- ☐ Door internal components or trim fouling regulator (Chapter 11)
- ☐ Faulty motor (Chapter 11)

Window glass fails to move

- ☐ Blown fuse (Chapter 12)
- ☐ Faulty relay (Chapter 12)
- ☐ Broken or disconnected wiring or connections (Chapter 12)
- ☐ Faulty motor (Chapter 11)
- ☐ Faulty control module (Chapter 11)

Electrical system (continued)

Central locking system inoperative, or unsatisfactory in operation

Complete system failure

- [ ] Remote handset battery discharged, where applicable
- [ ] Blown fuse (Chapter 12)
- [ ] Defective control module (Chapter 12)
- [ ] Broken or disconnected wiring or connections (Chapter 12)
- [ ] Faulty motor (Chapter 11)

Latch locks but will not unlock, or unlocks but will not lock

- [ ] Remote handset battery discharged, where applicable
- [ ] Faulty master switch (Chapter 12)
- [ ] Broken or disconnected latch operating rods or levers (Chapter 11)
- [ ] Faulty control module (Chapter 12)
- [ ] Faulty motor (Chapter 11)

One solenoid/motor fails to operate

- [ ] Broken or disconnected wiring or connections (Chapter 12)
- [ ] Faulty operating assembly (Chapter 11)
- [ ] Broken, binding or disconnected latch operating rods or levers (Chapter 11)
- [ ] Fault in door latch (Chapter 11)

A

ABS (Anti-lock brake system) A system, usually electronically controlled, that senses incipient wheel lockup during braking and relieves hydraulic pressure at wheels that are about to skid.

Air bag An inflatable bag hidden in the steering wheel (driver's side) or the dash or glovebox (passenger side). In a head-on collision, the bags inflate, preventing the driver and front passenger from being thrown forward into the steering wheel or windscreen.

Air cleaner A metal or plastic housing, containing a filter element, which removes dust and dirt from the air being drawn into the engine.

Air filter element The actual filter in an air cleaner system, usually manufactured from pleated paper and requiring renewal at regular intervals.

Air filter

Allen key A hexagonal wrench which fits into a recessed hexagonal hole.

Alligator clip A long-nosed spring-loaded metal clip with meshing teeth. Used to make temporary electrical connections.

Alternator A component in the electrical system which converts mechanical energy from a drivebelt into electrical energy to charge the battery and to operate the starting system, ignition system and electrical accessories.

Ampere (amp) A unit of measurement for the flow of electric current. One amp is the amount of current produced by one volt acting through a resistance of one ohm.

Anaerobic sealer A substance used to prevent bolts and screws from loosening. Anaerobic means that it does not require oxygen for activation. The Loctite brand is widely used.

Antifreeze A substance (usually ethylene glycol) mixed with water, and added to a vehicle's cooling system, to prevent freezing of the coolant in winter. Antifreeze also contains chemicals to inhibit corrosion and the formation of rust and other deposits that would tend to clog the radiator and coolant passages and reduce cooling efficiency.

Anti-seize compound A coating that reduces the risk of seizing on fasteners that are subjected to high temperatures, such as exhaust manifold bolts and nuts.

Asbestos A natural fibrous mineral with great heat resistance, commonly used in the composition of brake friction materials.

Asbestos is a health hazard and the dust created by brake systems should never be inhaled or ingested.

Axle A shaft on which a wheel revolves, or which revolves with a wheel. Also, a solid beam that connects the two wheels at one end of the vehicle. An axle which also transmits power to the wheels is known as a live axle.

Axleshaft A single rotating shaft, on either side of the differential, which delivers power from the final drive assembly to the drive wheels. Also called a driveshaft or a halfshaft.

B

Ball bearing An anti-friction bearing consisting of a hardened inner and outer race with hardened steel balls between two races.

Bearing The curved surface on a shaft or in a bore, or the part assembled into either, that permits relative motion between them with minimum wear and friction.

Bearing

Big-end bearing The bearing in the end of the connecting rod that's attached to the crankshaft.

Bleed nipple A valve on a brake wheel cylinder, caliper or other hydraulic component that is opened to purge the hydraulic system of air. Also called a bleed screw.

Brake bleeding Procedure for removing air from lines of a hydraulic brake system.

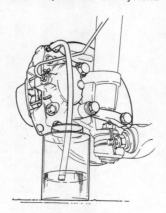
Brake bleeding

Brake disc The component of a disc brake that rotates with the wheels.

Brake drum The component of a drum brake that rotates with the wheels.

Brake linings The friction material which contacts the brake disc or drum to retard the vehicle's speed. The linings are bonded or riveted to the brake pads or shoes.

Brake pads The replaceable friction pads that pinch the brake disc when the brakes are applied. Brake pads consist of a friction material bonded or riveted to a rigid backing plate.

Brake shoe The crescent-shaped carrier to which the brake linings are mounted and which forces the lining against the rotating drum during braking.

Braking systems For more information on braking systems, consult the *Haynes Automotive Brake Manual.*

Breaker bar A long socket wrench handle providing greater leverage.

Bulkhead The insulated partition between the engine and the passenger compartment.

C

Caliper The non-rotating part of a disc-brake assembly that straddles the disc and carries the brake pads. The caliper also contains the hydraulic components that cause the pads to pinch the disc when the brakes are applied. A caliper is also a measuring tool that can be set to measure inside or outside dimensions of an object.

Camshaft A rotating shaft on which a series of cam lobes operate the valve mechanisms. The camshaft may be driven by gears, by sprockets and chain or by sprockets and a belt.

Canister A container in an evaporative emission control system; contains activated charcoal granules to trap vapours from the fuel system.

Canister

Carburettor A device which mixes fuel with air in the proper proportions to provide a desired power output from a spark ignition internal combustion engine.

Castellated Resembling the parapets along the top of a castle wall. For example, a castellated balljoint stud nut.

Castor In wheel alignment, the backward or forward tilt of the steering axis. Castor is positive when the steering axis is inclined rearward at the top.

Catalytic converter A silencer-like device in the exhaust system which converts certain pollutants in the exhaust gases into less harmful substances.

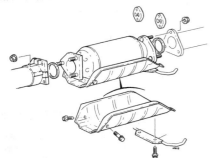

Catalytic converter

Circlip A ring-shaped clip used to prevent endwise movement of cylindrical parts and shafts. An internal circlip is installed in a groove in a housing; an external circlip fits into a groove on the outside of a cylindrical piece such as a shaft.

Clearance The amount of space between two parts. For example, between a piston and a cylinder, between a bearing and a journal, etc.

Coil spring A spiral of elastic steel found in various sizes throughout a vehicle, for example as a springing medium in the suspension and in the valve train.

Compression Reduction in volume, and increase in pressure and temperature, of a gas, caused by squeezing it into a smaller space.

Compression ratio The relationship between cylinder volume when the piston is at top dead centre and cylinder volume when the piston is at bottom dead centre.

Constant velocity (CV) joint A type of universal joint that cancels out vibrations caused by driving power being transmitted through an angle.

Core plug A disc or cup-shaped metal device inserted in a hole in a casting through which core was removed when the casting was formed. Also known as a freeze plug or expansion plug.

Crankcase The lower part of the engine block in which the crankshaft rotates.

Crankshaft The main rotating member, or shaft, running the length of the crankcase, with offset "throws" to which the connecting rods are attached.

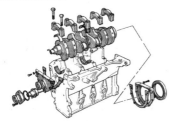

Crankshaft assembly

Crocodile clip See Alligator clip

D

Diagnostic code Code numbers obtained by accessing the diagnostic mode of an engine management computer. This code can be used to determine the area in the system where a malfunction may be located.

Disc brake A brake design incorporating a rotating disc onto which brake pads are squeezed. The resulting friction converts the energy of a moving vehicle into heat.

Double-overhead cam (DOHC) An engine that uses two overhead camshafts, usually one for the intake valves and one for the exhaust valves.

Drivebelt(s) The belt(s) used to drive accessories such as the alternator, water pump, power steering pump, air conditioning compressor, etc. off the crankshaft pulley.

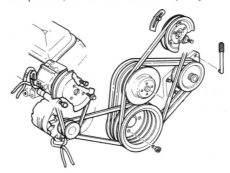

Accessory drivebelts

Driveshaft Any shaft used to transmit motion. Commonly used when referring to the axleshafts on a front wheel drive vehicle.

Drum brake A type of brake using a drum-shaped metal cylinder attached to the inner surface of the wheel. When the brake pedal is pressed, curved brake shoes with friction linings press against the inside of the drum to slow or stop the vehicle.

E

EGR valve A valve used to introduce exhaust gases into the intake air stream.

Electronic control unit (ECU) A computer which controls (for instance) ignition and fuel injection systems, or an anti-lock braking system. For more information refer to the *Haynes Automotive Electrical and Electronic Systems Manual*.

Electronic Fuel Injection (EFI) A computer controlled fuel system that distributes fuel through an injector located in each intake port of the engine.

Emergency brake A braking system, independent of the main hydraulic system, that can be used to slow or stop the vehicle if the primary brakes fail, or to hold the vehicle stationary even though the brake pedal isn't depressed. It usually consists of a hand lever that actuates either front or rear brakes mechanically through a series of cables and linkages. Also known as a handbrake or parking brake.

Endfloat The amount of lengthwise movement between two parts. As applied to a crankshaft, the distance that the crankshaft can move forward and back in the cylinder block.

Engine management system (EMS) A computer controlled system which manages the fuel injection and the ignition systems in an integrated fashion.

Exhaust manifold A part with several passages through which exhaust gases leave the engine combustion chambers and enter the exhaust pipe.

F

Fan clutch A viscous (fluid) drive coupling device which permits variable engine fan speeds in relation to engine speeds.

Feeler blade A thin strip or blade of hardened steel, ground to an exact thickness, used to check or measure clearances between parts.

Feeler blade

Firing order The order in which the engine cylinders fire, or deliver their power strokes, beginning with the number one cylinder.

Flywheel A heavy spinning wheel in which energy is absorbed and stored by means of momentum. On cars, the flywheel is attached to the crankshaft to smooth out firing impulses.

Free play The amount of travel before any action takes place. The "looseness" in a linkage, or an assembly of parts, between the initial application of force and actual movement. For example, the distance the brake pedal moves before the pistons in the master cylinder are actuated.

Fuse An electrical device which protects a circuit against accidental overload. The typical fuse contains a soft piece of metal which is calibrated to melt at a predetermined current flow (expressed as amps) and break the circuit.

Fusible link A circuit protection device consisting of a conductor surrounded by heat-resistant insulation. The conductor is smaller than the wire it protects, so it acts as the weakest link in the circuit. Unlike a blown fuse, a failed fusible link must frequently be cut from the wire for replacement.

G

Gap The distance the spark must travel in jumping from the centre electrode to the side electrode in a spark plug. Also refers to the spacing between the points in a contact breaker assembly in a conventional points-type ignition, or to the distance between the reluctor or rotor and the pickup coil in an electronic ignition.

Adjusting spark plug gap

Gasket Any thin, soft material - usually cork, cardboard, asbestos or soft metal - installed between two metal surfaces to ensure a good seal. For instance, the cylinder head gasket seals the joint between the block and the cylinder head.

Gasket

Gauge An instrument panel display used to monitor engine conditions. A gauge with a movable pointer on a dial or a fixed scale is an analogue gauge. A gauge with a numerical readout is called a digital gauge.

H

Halfshaft A rotating shaft that transmits power from the final drive unit to a drive wheel, usually when referring to a live rear axle.
Harmonic balancer A device designed to reduce torsion or twisting vibration in the crankshaft. May be incorporated in the crankshaft pulley. Also known as a vibration damper.
Hone An abrasive tool for correcting small irregularities or differences in diameter in an engine cylinder, brake cylinder, etc.
Hydraulic tappet A tappet that utilises hydraulic pressure from the engine's lubrication system to maintain zero clearance (constant contact with both camshaft and valve stem). Automatically adjusts to variation in valve stem length. Hydraulic tappets also reduce valve noise.

I

Ignition timing The moment at which the spark plug fires, usually expressed in the number of crankshaft degrees before the piston reaches the top of its stroke.
Inlet manifold A tube or housing with passages through which flows the air-fuel mixture (carburettor vehicles and vehicles with throttle body injection) or air only (port fuel-injected vehicles) to the port openings in the cylinder head.

J

Jump start Starting the engine of a vehicle with a discharged or weak battery by attaching jump leads from the weak battery to a charged or helper battery.

L

Load Sensing Proportioning Valve (LSPV) A brake hydraulic system control valve that works like a proportioning valve, but also takes into consideration the amount of weight carried by the rear axle.
Locknut A nut used to lock an adjustment nut, or other threaded component, in place. For example, a locknut is employed to keep the adjusting nut on the rocker arm in position.
Lockwasher A form of washer designed to prevent an attaching nut from working loose.

M

MacPherson strut A type of front suspension system devised by Earle MacPherson at Ford of England. In its original form, a simple lateral link with the anti-roll bar creates the lower control arm. A long strut - an integral coil spring and shock absorber - is mounted between the body and the steering knuckle. Many modern so-called MacPherson strut systems use a conventional lower A-arm and don't rely on the anti-roll bar for location.
Multimeter An electrical test instrument with the capability to measure voltage, current and resistance.

N

NOx Oxides of Nitrogen. A common toxic pollutant emitted by petrol and diesel engines at higher temperatures.

O

Ohm The unit of electrical resistance. One volt applied to a resistance of one ohm will produce a current of one amp.
Ohmmeter An instrument for measuring electrical resistance.
O-ring A type of sealing ring made of a special rubber-like material; in use, the O-ring is compressed into a groove to provide the sealing action.
Overhead cam (ohc) engine An engine with the camshaft(s) located on top of the cylinder head(s).

Overhead valve (ohv) engine An engine with the valves located in the cylinder head, but with the camshaft located in the engine block.
Oxygen sensor A device installed in the engine exhaust manifold, which senses the oxygen content in the exhaust and converts this information into an electric current. Also called a Lambda sensor.

P

Phillips screw A type of screw head having a cross instead of a slot for a corresponding type of screwdriver.
Plastigage A thin strip of plastic thread, available in different sizes, used for measuring clearances. For example, a strip of Plastigage is laid across a bearing journal. The parts are assembled and dismantled; the width of the crushed strip indicates the clearance between journal and bearing.

Plastigage

Propeller shaft The long hollow tube with universal joints at both ends that carries power from the transmission to the differential on front-engined rear wheel drive vehicles.
Proportioning valve A hydraulic control valve which limits the amount of pressure to the rear brakes during panic stops to prevent wheel lock-up.

R

Rack-and-pinion steering A steering system with a pinion gear on the end of the steering shaft that mates with a rack (think of a geared wheel opened up and laid flat). When the steering wheel is turned, the pinion turns, moving the rack to the left or right. This movement is transmitted through the track rods to the steering arms at the wheels.
Radiator A liquid-to-air heat transfer device designed to reduce the temperature of the coolant in an internal combustion engine cooling system.
Refrigerant Any substance used as a heat transfer agent in an air-conditioning system. R-12 has been the principle refrigerant for many years; recently, however, manufacturers have begun using R-134a, a non-CFC substance that is considered less harmful to the ozone in the upper atmosphere.
Rocker arm A lever arm that rocks on a shaft or pivots on a stud. In an overhead valve engine, the rocker arm converts the upward movement of the pushrod into a downward movement to open a valve.

Rotor In a distributor, the rotating device inside the cap that connects the centre electrode and the outer terminals as it turns, distributing the high voltage from the coil secondary winding to the proper spark plug. Also, that part of an alternator which rotates inside the stator. Also, the rotating assembly of a turbocharger, including the compressor wheel, shaft and turbine wheel.

Runout The amount of wobble (in-and-out movement) of a gear or wheel as it's rotated. The amount a shaft rotates "out-of-true." The out-of-round condition of a rotating part.

S

Sealant A liquid or paste used to prevent leakage at a joint. Sometimes used in conjunction with a gasket.

Sealed beam lamp An older headlight design which integrates the reflector, lens and filaments into a hermetically-sealed one-piece unit. When a filament burns out or the lens cracks, the entire unit is simply replaced.

Serpentine drivebelt A single, long, wide accessory drivebelt that's used on some newer vehicles to drive all the accessories, instead of a series of smaller, shorter belts. Serpentine drivebelts are usually tensioned by an automatic tensioner.

Serpentine drivebelt

Shim Thin spacer, commonly used to adjust the clearance or relative positions between two parts. For example, shims inserted into or under bucket tappets control valve clearances. Clearance is adjusted by changing the thickness of the shim.

Slide hammer A special puller that screws into or hooks onto a component such as a shaft or bearing; a heavy sliding handle on the shaft bottoms against the end of the shaft to knock the component free.

Sprocket A tooth or projection on the periphery of a wheel, shaped to engage with a chain or drivebelt. Commonly used to refer to the sprocket wheel itself.

Starter inhibitor switch On vehicles with an automatic transmission, a switch that prevents starting if the vehicle is not in Neutral or Park.

Strut See MacPherson strut.

T

Tappet A cylindrical component which transmits motion from the cam to the valve stem, either directly or via a pushrod and rocker arm. Also called a cam follower.

Thermostat A heat-controlled valve that regulates the flow of coolant between the cylinder block and the radiator, so maintaining optimum engine operating temperature. A thermostat is also used in some air cleaners in which the temperature is regulated.

Thrust bearing The bearing in the clutch assembly that is moved in to the release levers by clutch pedal action to disengage the clutch. Also referred to as a release bearing.

Timing belt A toothed belt which drives the camshaft. Serious engine damage may result if it breaks in service.

Timing chain A chain which drives the camshaft.

Toe-in The amount the front wheels are closer together at the front than at the rear. On rear wheel drive vehicles, a slight amount of toe-in is usually specified to keep the front wheels running parallel on the road by offsetting other forces that tend to spread the wheels apart.

Toe-out The amount the front wheels are closer together at the rear than at the front. On front wheel drive vehicles, a slight amount of toe-out is usually specified.

Tools For full information on choosing and using tools, refer to the *Haynes Automotive Tools Manual*.

Tracer A stripe of a second colour applied to a wire insulator to distinguish that wire from another one with the same colour insulator.

Tune-up A process of accurate and careful adjustments and parts replacement to obtain the best possible engine performance.

Turbocharger A centrifugal device, driven by exhaust gases, that pressurises the intake air. Normally used to increase the power output from a given engine displacement, but can also be used primarily to reduce exhaust emissions (as on VW's "Umwelt" Diesel engine).

U

Universal joint or U-joint A double-pivoted connection for transmitting power from a driving to a driven shaft through an angle. A U-joint consists of two Y-shaped yokes and a cross-shaped member called the spider.

V

Valve A device through which the flow of liquid, gas, vacuum, or loose material in bulk may be started, stopped, or regulated by a movable part that opens, shuts, or partially obstructs one or more ports or passageways. A valve is also the movable part of such a device.

Valve clearance The clearance between the valve tip (the end of the valve stem) and the rocker arm or tappet. The valve clearance is measured when the valve is closed.

Vernier caliper A precision measuring instrument that measures inside and outside dimensions. Not quite as accurate as a micrometer, but more convenient.

Viscosity The thickness of a liquid or its resistance to flow.

Volt A unit for expressing electrical "pressure" in a circuit. One volt that will produce a current of one ampere through a resistance of one ohm.

W

Welding Various processes used to join metal items by heating the areas to be joined to a molten state and fusing them together. For more information refer to the *Haynes Automotive Welding Manual*.

Wiring diagram A drawing portraying the components and wires in a vehicle's electrical system, using standardised symbols. For more information refer to the *Haynes Automotive Electrical and Electronic Systems Manual*.

Note: *References throughout this index are in the form "**Chapter number**" • "**Page number**". So, for example, 2C•15 refers to page 15 of Chapter 2C.*

Note: *References throughout this index are in the form* "**Chapter number**" • "**Page number**". *So, for example, 2C•15 refers to page 15 of Chapter 2C.*